Illusion and Disillusion

John Fulling Crosby

University of Kentucky

Fourth Edition

Illusion and Disillusion

The Self in Love and Marriage

Wadsworth Publishing Company
Belmont, California
A Division of Wadsworth, Inc.

Sociology Editor: Serina Beauparlant
Senior Editorial Assistant: Marla Nowick
Production Editor: Karen Garrison
Designer: Paula Goldstein
Managing Designer: Stephen Rapley
Print Buyer: Karen Hunt
Copy Editor: Melissa Andrews
Compositor: Better Graphics
Cover: Paula Goldstein
Signing Representative: Harry M. Campbell

Printed in the United States of America

1 2 3 4 5 6 7 8 9 10—95 94 93 92 91

Library of Congress Cataloging in Publication Data

Crosby, John F.
     Illusion and disillusion : the self in love and marriage / John
Fulling Crosby. — 4th ed.
         p.   cm.
     Includes bibliographical references and index.
     ISBN 0-534-14316-4
     1. Marriage. 2. Marriage—Psychological aspects. I. Title.
HQ734.C895   1991
306.81′019—dc20   90-38543
                                                   CIP

---

to those who came before:
FULLING/CROSBY and WELLS/EASTWICK
and to those who came after:
RICK-ANDY-SCOTT
and way after:
VICKI

Contents

Chapter 3 Beyond the Grand Illusion: *Redefinitions and Integration of Love and Sex Within Marriage*   77

Chapter 4 Love Imperatives, Binds, and Double Binds: *Breaking the Pattern*   105

Chapter 5   Love and Anger:
Dynamics of Intimacy   *145*

Chapter 6   Sexuality, Value, and Meaning:
Owning Ourselves   *187*

Chapter 7   Getting In and Getting Out: *Preliminary Marriage, Divorce, and Remarriage*   219

Chapter 8   Making It Together: *Love Is Not Enough*   253

Foreword

by B. Kay Pasley, Ed.D.

Illusion and Disillusion: The Self in Love and Marriage represents one of a few books so well received that it merits yet a new fourth edition. Here readers are offered revised and new conceptualizations which add clarity to the complex nature of intimate relationships in a rapidly changing world. I am honored to write this foreword and do so with appreciation for what I believe is a volume which makes an important and unique contribution to the literature on marital relationships.

I have a long history with *Illusion* and its author. Early on I was a graduate student of Dr. Crosby while he was on the faculty at Indiana University. There we spent hours discussing and debating the ideas he chose to write about and include in the very first edition. At the same time, I was fortunate to be exposed to his superb skill as a teacher and observed him presenting many of the concepts presented here to undergraduate students. Even then I was impressed with his openness to those who ventured to challenge his beliefs and, in turn, have their own beliefs challenged. Too, his energy and passion for teaching were apparent in the classroom; this same energy and passion were evident throughout the pages of the first edition of *Illusion*.

As my own career in academia began and progressed, I had the opportunity to provide input into later editions, as I served as a reviewer for them. I provided criticism and feedback to his effort to refine his ideas and to identify and explain key issues and processes involved in fostering productive marital relationships. His eager response to feedback has continued and is a sign of his belief that learning is in fact an ongoing process. His desire to communicate complex theories and concepts clearly and dynamically is evident in this new edition as well. Thus, I am not an unbiased evaluator of Dr. Crosby's work. My involvement with *Illusion* over the years has resulted in a deep appreciation of this new edition and those which came before it, particularly when compared with the content of typical texts dealing with marriage.

Illusion most definitely is in a genre of its own. It is a unique book in that Crosby's commitment has always been to explain theories, concepts, and the important and vital processes that help individuals understand their own contribution to relationship survival and the resulting joy which is possible. His experience as a therapist and his competence as a teacher are again evident here. Unlike many authors, Dr. Crosby places less emphasis on the facts and figures surrounding marriage or divorce. While such information is interesting, it is rarely applicable to one's own life. Yet, students often are held responsible for such information; they memorize the facts, regurgitate them on tests, and promptly forget them. The ideas presented in *Illusion* are grounded in what is known both empirically and clinically, yet they are less forgettable. Here we are consistently offered explanations of theory, concepts, and processes which synthesize succinctly what's of real importance to marriage. Students who demonstrate true understanding of the theories, concepts, and processes offered here have meaningful information for use in their personal lives. This is the true value of *Illusion; Illusion* provides insight to building and maintaining intimate relationships over time based on what is known from both empirical and clinical sources.

This new edition has maintained some of the "meat" from earlier editions which is timeless and useful now some 17 + years later. For me this suggests that Crosby was and is able to capture ideas which are key to relationships. I particularly appreciate his clear identification and explanation of the "roots of disillusionment" as he calls it. Too, his distinguishing between happiness/ unhappiness as a personal trait and joy/sorrow as a relationship trait continues to have meaning for our understanding of self as the basis for developing productive and healthy relationships. His discussion of legitimate and illegitimate needs still offers readers a workable paradigm for understanding their conscious or unconscious motivations for certain patterns of interaction.

Yet, this edition also provides new insight into marriage and marriage-like relationships. Here Dr. Crosby emphasizes the influence of one's family of origin on later behavior patterns. His Appendix A, for example, makes a strong contribution to understanding that marriage includes all of one's past, including the role models presented by a parent or parents, interaction with siblings and friends, and for some even the first marriage experience. This is the baggage one brings to any marriage. Also, the new chapter dealing with divorce and remarriage is a valuable addition. With inclusion of this topic, however, Crosby does not bemoan the failure of marriage, but acknowledges the realities of today's marital institution. He continues to articulate the ways relationships are crippled by expectations which served us well historically but which unfairly inhibit the creativity necessary to enhance relationships and make them personally meaningful over time. What Crosby offers here is a look at divorce and remarriage from the standpoint of one who values reinvestment in a current relationship rather than the capricious termination of a marriage because of one's inability to anticipate how a relationship might change to better meet the changing needs of the individuals.

What continues to be unique to *Illusion* is its focus on self as the basis and foundation for caring relationships within marriage. Other books typically focus on simply the relationship or some unique aspects of it such as sex-role issues. Crosby again has the courage to explore the individual within the relationship. He has the foresight to identify the self as the foundation and integrative thread for relationships. As a dear friend, Dr. Kathryn Hatch, once said, "Perception is everything; reality is nothing." Her comment suggests that it is the individual's perception of himself/herself and experience that becomes his/her reality. It may or may not have much to do with the perceptions of the spouse regarding the same situation, but nonetheless this perception or the lack of a shared perception certainly can raise havoc in the relationship. In *Illusion* Crosby explores an individual's perception, its source, and the interpretations one makes about such perceptions to help the reader understand that relationships do not occur in a vacuum but are part of a dynamic, ever-changing process.

Perhaps that is what *Illusion* offers best: a focus on the processes which can enhance an individual's response to his or her own change, as well as to change which may occur within the relationship. For it is to change that we, if we elect to be part of intimate relationships over time, must adapt. Crosby does not ask us to give up our dreams regarding marriage; he only cautions us to understand their source so we can adjust them to fit our experiences. He asks us to know and understand the self as the basis for developing healthful and meaningful relationships. He does not suggest the path to intimacy is easy, nor that it is arduous, but that what it does require is self-knowledge, constant attention, and energy and commitment to the welfare of both the self and the other.

In these pages are gifts that represent forethought and concern for the well-being of spouses and the marriages they create. Crosby suggests that each individual shares in the responsibility for nurturing the relationship. It is this sharing that is our hope for defining and building marriages which can grow and change with the growth and change of the individual. Only in this way can the needs of both the individual and the relationship be met.

B. Kay Pasley
Professor of Human Development and Family Studies
Colorado State University

Preface

Those who love the truth
Must seek love in marriage,
Love without illusions.

Albert Camus, *A Writer's Notebook*

I began writing *Illusion and Disillusion* in 1970, and now, two decades later, I am still writing it and rewriting it. In this sense this fourth edition is like a fourth marriage to the same partner. I keep redefining it, reinventing it, and re-creating it! It is never finished. I keep growing. I keep changing. Life keeps changing.

Readers may disagree with many of my ideas; to this I can only reply that if the disagreement is based on sound insight and widely observed phenomena rather than on the strength of custom, tradition, and romanticized folklore, I welcome it! I wish to challenge the reader to think of marriage as an opportunity for the enrichment of life, as a relationship between two self-aware people open to change and growth and thus not bound to traditional societal role definitions and expectations. With Sidney Jourard I believe marriage is for LIFE, not for DEATH.

If these pages serve to raise the reader's anxiety level and make him or her feel uncomfortable, then I am glad, because I fail to see how any change will take place in our marital system until people begin to question seriously the premises and assumptions underlying it. When serious challenges are made on our traditional belief system there is bound to be some degree of internal agony and pain, restlessness and uncertainty, doubt and insecurity.

I hope that what I have to say will speak equally to the single, the married, the divorced, and the remarried in more than an academic or intellectual way! My goal is to avoid platitudinous advice while yet pointing to significant research findings, experiential truth, and clinical insights. At heart, *Illusion and Disillusion* is a study of self and marriage set within a family systems framework. My viewpoint is based on the premise that individual dynamics cannot be understood apart from the lifelong interactions both within one's family of origin and within one's present relationships. Buttressing and supplementing the systemic superstructure are the frameworks of object relations, exchange, resource, and symbolic interaction. I believe each of these frameworks plays a part in our understanding of the issues, problems, and challenges of marriage.

Throughout these pages is an implicit emphasis on both mate selection and the growth of the self. Some people hold that the chief problem with marriage is the choice of mate! If only we had chosen our mate with more care we would not be feeling such frustration or misery! Often the self deludes itself into thinking that the problem of marriage is entirely in the choice of the right mate. This is but another way of saying that the problem is always and entirely with one's mate rather than with oneself. This is denial! This is stupid! Hundreds of thousands of divorced persons simply end one marriage only to take their same unchanged self and self-dynamics, replete with their sexual prejudices and stereotypes, into another marriage.

Although there may be many things wrong with the institution of marriage and also with one's mate, the primary theme is *the self in love and marriage.* The self is a system in its own right. It is also a subsystem within marriage and within the family. As such, we can never separate the self from the immediate environment and the immediate intimate relationship. We are what we are not only in relationship to ourselves but also in relationship to our mate and a widening circle of others who are most significant and important to us. Further, even though we may no longer live in the domicile of our family of origin, we are certainly the products of it. We deceive ourselves if we think that the dynamics of our family of origin do not continue to play through us in our dyadic relationships as well as in our future parental relations with our offspring.

The reader will note, however, that *Illusion and Disillusion* does not deal with *macro* issues such as changing work patterns, dual-employment pressures, technology, the economy, inflation, the cost of housing, environmental pollution, international relations, the greenhouse effect, or the future of our children and grandchildren on planet earth. Although each of these has a profound direct or indirect effect on every individual, on every marriage, and on every family, I have chosen to concentrate almost exclusively on the intraself and the intrafamily *micro* dynamics. I have done this in the interest of keeping this book singular in scope and as short and concise as possible. The intramarital and the intrafamilial patterns and forces are a part of our intimate environment, and as such we can exert immediate, direct, and ongoing pressure for change and redesign, redefinition, and re-creation.

I continue to be deeply appreciative to a host of people for their seen and unseen contributions to this latest edition of *'Lusion,* as I have come to call it.

The most unseen is Marjorie, my wife, who continues to be my best friend, second only to myself. When I wrote the first edition, Steve Rutter was a sales representative for Wadsworth Publishing Company. Now Steve is Editor-in-Chief, and I still appreciate his attention to the folks in the rank and file. I want to express my sincere thanks to Serina Beauparlant, Sociology Editor at Wadsworth, and to her assistant, Marla Nowick, for their support and assistance. I am indebted to the reviewers, James J. Berry, Western State College; Martha Bristor, Michigan State University; Richard Campbell, California State University, Northridge; and Scott Fuller, Santa Rosa Junior College. I remain indebted to Kay Pasley, who wrote the Foreword for this fourth edition. As the line from *The King and I* says, "When you become a teacher by your pupils you'll be taught." Kay was one of my first students, and now she is also my teacher and my friendly critic. I would also like to express my thanks to Ms. Mary Ortwein, who served as my permissions editor, and to Melissa Andrews, copy editor.

Last, but by no means least, I would like to thank my students and my clients without whom I would be nothing more than a desk-chair quarterback, devoid of the experience of the firing line and the trenches. I wish to thank those who wrote personal statements and all those others whose personal struggles formed the content of the "fabricated" case studies. Of course, I take total responsibility for the content of the book and for the interpretations I have placed on the thought of others.

John F. Crosby
University of Kentucky

Chapter 1

What's Wrong with Marriage?
The Roots of Disillusionment

Marriage is going to help us feel better about ourselves; it is going to make life easier and more secure. And behold, usually it does—for a while.

AUGUSTUS Y. NAPIER AND CARL A. WHITAKER,
THE FAMILY CRUCIBLE

HAD IT

"I'VE HAD IT! That's all. I've taken all I can take. The whole thing stinks! Marriage—ha! All that talk about love and caring and giving and taking. I'll tell you, I gave and gave and what did he give? You tell me. He wanted to own me—possess me. I was supposed to be grateful—grateful for being his wife and the mother of his kids. Be beautiful—be sexy—be a good mother, a good housekeeper, a good entertainer, passionate lover, adoring wife, taxi driver. I tell you . . . it's no use . . . all we do is fight. I should have known better . . . I thought we would be different—that our marriage would be something beautiful—that fighting and bickering, bitching and criticizing—well, that's the way it was for others but it wouldn't be that way for us. That's what I told myself. I'm sick of it—do you hear?—sick of it and the whole sorry mess. Marriage is hell. For me—no way—ever again."

BITTER

"I ADMIT I'M BITTER. You would be too if you worked your ass off for your family and all you got was a turnoff from your wife. You'd think I was some sort of sex pervert if you listen to her. Look, all I want is some loving—some affection, some peace and quiet instead of all this nagging and picking about all the things I'm doing wrong. She expects me to be some sort of a model husband—dedicated to making her happy—praising her—making over her, but never—and this is the worst part of it—never having any needs of my own. She should have married a guy who was handsome, athletic, handy with tools, good with kids, who inherited his daddy's business and was completely sexless. When I'm out of this thing you can bet I'm not going to tie myself down again—ever!"

SUZANNE AND SCOTT

Married 8 years. Two children: daughter, Karen, age 7, and son, Kevin, age 5. Both parents are gainfully employed, Suzanne at a fabric store as an assistant manager and Scott as an electrician for a large company. Both sets of parents are living. His parents live in a city 80 miles away. Her parents live about 3 miles

4

from Suzanne and Scott. Suzanne and Scott are seeing a marriage and family therapist on the advice of the family physician. Suzanne had been complaining of headaches and low energy. The physician found nothing unusual other than higher than desirable blood pressure. Scott balked at the idea of marital therapy, stating that the problem was entirely the result of Suzanne's "not knowing how to manage her time and not being able to handle stress very well." The couple's genogram is pictured in Figure 1-1.

In therapy Scott told the following story. He felt he could not please Suzanne no matter how hard he tried, so he quit trying. He "shut down." He complained about Suzanne's housekeeping and her inability to manage the kids. He mentioned that when he did try to help out with the housework she found fault with what he had done. Scott admitted that he drank a few beers every night but said that it was not to excess. He assured the therapist that he could control his drinking and that he could quit any time he wanted. Scott further complained about Suzanne's parents, who, he alleged, kept too close contact with Suzanne. Scott said he wants his in-laws to enjoy their grandchildren, but that there is too much interference and too much advice giving.

Suzanne denied that she ever criticized Scott for doing inferior or sloppy housework. She further complained that Scott drank "way too much" and that he was a "couch potato" who came home from work and did nothing but drink and feed his face while watching TV. Suzanne said she needed her parents

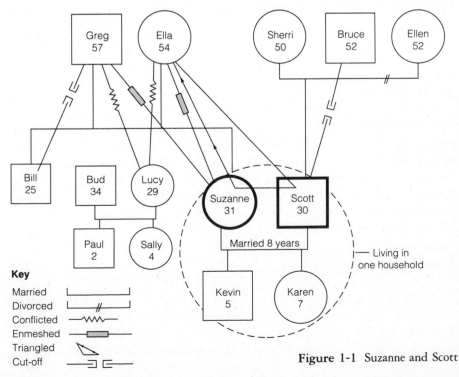

Figure 1-1 Suzanne and Scott

because Scott was a lousy companion and that her mother was a great comfort to her. Further, Suzanne complained that all her hopes and dreams of a "good" marriage were now dashed to pieces because Scott obviously "does not love me anymore. If he loved me he would talk with me and be supportive of me. He would know what I need and at least attempt to meet my needs. All we do is fight."

Ways of Looking at Suzanne and Scott

Suzanne and Scott can be studied and understood from many points of view. They can be viewed through a "Freudian" or "classical" model. They can be studied in a behavioristic mode, in a rational emotive framework, or by using a transactional analysis approach. We will be looking at Suzanne and Scott primarily from a systems or systemic mode with an emphasis on the entire extended family, including brothers, sisters, parents, and even grandparents. In Chapter 2 we will also be looking at other couples from the vantage point of object relations theory, which emphasizes internalized objects, especially the early internalized mother and father. Further, we will be looking at Suzanne and Scott's marriage from the point of view of their expectations of each other and of marriage in general. These expectations cannot be separated from societal norms and attitudes about marriage and the roles of men and women in marriage. Finally, we will be looking at Suzanne and Scott from the perspective of communication and interaction skills, such as their ability to communicate clearly and without contamination, metacommunication, and double messages. The ability to resolve conflict constructively (to fight fairly) without resorting to destructive maneuvers and games is also a part of the communication process.

Before we proceed any further with Suzanne and Scott, let us address the following questions: What is wrong with marriage today? Why is there so much anger, bitterness, and disillusionment? Why do so many marriages end in divorce? Why are there apparently so many unbroken unhappy marriages wherein the couple stays together even when love appears to be dead? Why is there so much pseudomutuality wherein the couple appear to be close, caring, and affectionate, yet in reality this is only a facade or a pretense?

Disillusionment

Disillusionment is the state we reach when our hopes and dreams are either in the process of being destroyed or in fact are destroyed. When we are disillusioned we feel let down, betrayed, and sometimes empty inside. Disillusionment is coming to terms with the fact that something in which we invested our emotions and our energy is not measuring up to our expectations. Disillusionment is a continuous variable. This means that there are progressive degrees of disillusionment, ranging from slightly or mildly disillusioned to extremely or totally disillusioned. The two people who spoke at the beginning of this chapter, *Had It* and *Bitter*, appear to be totally disillusioned. They are at the extreme end of the disillusionment scale. Their statements reflect bitterness and anger. Each partner felt that she/he had been hurt and had suffered pain at the hands of her/his mate. In despair, both were giving vent to deep-seated feelings of anger, resentment, and futility. We can assume that both partners had entered the marriage with high hopes and lofty dreams, but in all likelihood they had never shared their expectations about marriage with their mate. Even more likely, each wanted the personality and behavior of the other to conform to his/her own image of how the other should be and act. Although no one ever admits it, we often want our mate to be "just like me" rather than a separate and independent human being. The message we give is "Be what I want you to be. Do what I want you to do. Don't be you. Be only for me."

Both *Had It* and *Bitter* protested the terrible deal they had received. Both swore they would not marry again. Both will probably remarry! Both will carry new or renewed bundles of fantastic expectations into their new relationships, and both will make some of the same mistakes again. It is safe to assume that prior to their second marriage they will not share their expectations or attempt to negotiate their different expectations in creative or productive ways. Instead they will swear their undying and unwavering love for each other, and they will steadfastly tell themselves and each other that as long as they truly love each other there is no obstacle too great or too small that cannot be overcome.

We live in a romantic society. We are bombarded with stimuli that tell us love is the only acceptable criterion for marriage. At the same time we are given a definition of love that precludes any notion of working at love or of creating love. Consequently we believe that love is something that happens to us. We learn that love, romance, sex, and marriage are instinctual and natural and that therefore there is really nothing we need to learn. After all, what is there to learn about marriage? What is there to learn about sex? What is there to learn about love, anger, conflict, and hurt? And certainly there is no need to learn how to fight fairly (resolve conflict constructively). Although we nod knowingly that good communication is important, we scoff at any attempt to teach us the fundamentals of open communication and constructive resolution of conflict.

Educational and governmental institutions in the United States spend billions of dollars annually on almost every conceivable type of education except education that deals with self and with primary relationships. With few exceptions our public school system teaches us little about human development, interpersonal relationship theory and skills, family theory and dynamics, and human sexuality. The average person will learn math, grammar, science, geography, history, and social studies for at least 8 to 10 years of a 12-year public school education. Yet we fail to prepare young people for intimacy and the maintenance of intimate relationships. This is a national shame and disgrace. One reason we fail to do this is because we have not redressed the philosophy of the ultraconservative far political right. Yet a more important reason is that we as a society simply *do not believe in the importance of this kind of personal and interpersonal education.*

As a society, we tend to believe that issues of love, sex, and marriage will somehow assimilate themselves into the feelings and thoughts of our young people and that given the right opportunity, these things will "just come naturally." And of course they do come naturally, as reflected by one of the highest, if not the highest, teenage pregnancy rates in the developed countries of the world and a divorce rate that predicts the failure of just less than one out of every two marriages.[1,2] Will today's star-struck lover become tomorrow's love addict? Will today's romantic hero become tomorrow's embittered and disillusioned cynic? How can we avoid this culturally embedded disillusionment? What can we do as individuals to color our future with a realistic hope for a better outcome? This disillusionment exacts a terrible toll on the participants and ultimately on society. This toll includes financial, ethical, and behavioral outcomes that affect the entire fabric of our society.

In our quest to escape the misery of disillusionment we need to ask, What is an illusion?

Illusion

Dictionary definitions of *illusion* include references to misperception of reality, distortion of reality, the state or condition of being deceived, and deception caused by false impressions. Illusion, as used here, refers to beliefs that are rooted in the folklore and folkways of the culture but that are either inaccurate or only partially accurate. Thus, illusions lead to expectations based on unexamined assumptions. Marriage, family, interpersonal relations, sex, intimacy, and conflict are areas of deep personal importance, but these areas often are obscured by illusions. An *illusion* is different from a *myth*. An illusion is a deception or misapprehension of what is considered to be reality, whereas a myth is a belief that is accepted as true without any critical questioning concerning its truth or veracity. (In Chapter 3 we will consider some of the most common myths related to love, marriage, and sex.)

Illusion indicates a personal investment in belief. Each person creates illusions according to his or her personal investment of self in the object of belief. Illusion is a form of self-deception that enables us to perceive what we wish to perceive and prevents us from perceiving the reality of a situation. Freud claimed that an illusion is not the same thing as an error. Illusions, according to Freud, are derived from human wishes. "Thus we call a belief an illusion when a wish-fulfillment is a prominent factor in its motivation, and in doing so we disregard its relation to reality."[3] For example, if one believes that the expression of anger is bad, then one lives his or her daily routine under the illusion that a good marriage has very little anger. The illusion is based on the belief and on the wish to have the belief be true.

Disillusion

Disillusion may be a noun or a verb. As a verb *disillusion* refers to the process of ridding ourselves of our illusions. "I am disillusioning myself." Hence, "I am seeking to get rid of my illusory beliefs." When used as a noun, *disillusion* refers to a state of being that is identical in meaning with the word *disillusionment*. To be in a state of disillusion means we are overcome with many illusions (disillusioned, disillusionment).

Dis-illusion, the process of ridding ourselves of our illusions, cannot be dealt with by wiping the slate clean, much as we would erase a blackboard. Rather, it is taking a series of actions designed to show the unreasonableness or fallacy of our belief. Dis-illusion is the process of dealing with our illusions so that they no longer have power over us, either to control us or to influence us unduly. We deal with myths by demythologizing, by showing the error or the fallacy of the myth. We deal with illusion by dis-illusioning ourselves, by confronting and challenging the assumptions that are the bases of our illusions. Disillusionment is based on the illusory beliefs that people hold regarding love, sex, marriage, and how one's partner ought to act. In order to remove disillusion and the state of disillusionment we need to actively challenge our belief systems. This is necessary in order to avoid the despair and bitterness that result from feelings of being let down, hurt, or betrayed. The greater and more outlandish our expectations the greater the probability of being disillusioned and overcome with cynicism and despair.

To rid ourselves of illusions, we must have both an intellectual commitment and an emotional commitment. The intellectual process requires an open-mindedness as we investigate the various beliefs, myths, customs, and traditions that surround love, romance, sex, and marriage. Although these customs and traditions have become a part of our common culture and have been transmitted from generation to generation, they are not necessarily meaningful or appropriate to us. The questioning of traditional attitudes and belief systems may cause some anxiety and emotional discomfort, but these are inevitable if we are to eradicate the illusions that have become deeply ingrained in our emotions.

Sometimes it is much easier to see through a destructive belief on the intellectual level than on the emotional level. For example, we may know and honestly understand that conflict within a relationship is both normal and necessary. Nevertheless, when we are involved in conflict we may wish we weren't. Conflict causes us to feel ill at ease and uncomfortable. Conflict produces anxiety. Because of these unwelcome feelings we wish there were no conflict. We wish it would just go away. And if it won't go away we can at least attempt to avoid it or sidestep it. Perhaps we deny it. Often we push the conflict down within us, suppressing it, telling ourselves that our marriage is good because we get along so well and therefore it is all right not to deal with whatever is troubling us. On a purely intellectual level we may know that healthy intimate relationships require that we face and deal with conflict constructively. However, on an emotional level we often defend against conflict in order to protect our illusion that our relationship is void of conflict. Therefore we protect ourselves against the disquieting feelings that come with the facing of conflict. In short, we often resist ridding ourselves of our illusions, and then later, when past practices and patterns have caught up with us, we wonder why we have become disillusioned.

Scapegoating

Critics of marriage and family sometimes blame particular ideas and practices for all the difficulties associated with marriage and the family. Such critics frequently offer the following explanations for the breakdown of marriage.

Young people today have no morals. Free sex and the idea of instant gratification are ruining our country.

No one under 30 understands the meaning of duty, commitment, and responsibility.

People divorce because they are selfish.

Marriage no longer has a strong religious foundation.

People lack commitment. They take the easy way out.

Long-term marriage is a dying institution. People today believe in discarding and replacing old relationships with new ones.

Marriage is in trouble today because of women's liberation.

Working mothers are the cause of our problems.

Marriage is in bad shape because men are doing women's things and women are doing men's things. Roles today are all mixed up.

Scapegoating always picks on a single, all-encompassing answer. The answer is usually very simple. If only there were more trust, or more commitment, or more love, or less selfishness, then marriage would be like it should be or like it was in the "good old days." By definition, a **scapegoat*** is a person, object, or belief (value, attitude, or ideal) that bears the brunt of the blame. A scapegoat is therefore an alleged offender, falsely accused. The causes listed previously focus attention on easy and simplistic explanations that may contain some degree of truth and validity regarding the breakdown of marriage, but when marriage is scapegoated, each of these items is made to bear the total amount of blame, and we are led to believe that if it weren't for this or that, all would be well.

In any discussion of marriage and family the entire list of scapegoats is eventually brought into the conversation either directly or by implication. There are at least two types of scapegoating in discussions of marriage. The first blames the institution of marriage, and the second singles out moralistic (not necessarily moral or ethical) reasons for marital decay. Institutional scapegoating is likely to be practiced by those who are disillusioned, embittered, or feeling trapped. They probably blame marriage for their loss of freedom. The moralistic scapegoaters bemoan the lack of responsibility, commitment, love, and similar values. Generally speaking, most people who have experienced an unpleasant marriage tend to blame either the institution of marriage or the partner, or both, whereas the observers of society (the barber, the beautician, the clergy, the politicians and other elected officials) tend to be moralistic scapegoaters.

Those who blame the institution of marriage cite divorce statistics as proof that the institutions of marriage and the family are decaying.[4] Their solution is to retreat to the past and to glory in nostalgia. They would have us believe that the American family, from the arrival of the Mayflower until the end of World War II, was a happy unit composed of three generations who lived harmoniously under one roof and had few divorces, little serious maladjustment, and even less sexual activity. William Goode's famous phrase, "The classical family of Western nostalgia," is pertinent here.[5] As Goode says, "It is a pretty picture of life down on grandma's farm. There are lots of happy children, and many kinfolk live together in a large rambling house. Everyone works hard. . . . All boys and girls marry, and marry young. Young people, especially the girls, are likely to be virginal at marriage and faithful afterward. . . . After marriage, the couple lives harmoniously, either near the boy's parents or with them, for the couple is slated to inherit the farm. No one divorces." As a retort to this nostalgic description Goode concludes, "Like most stereotypes, that of the

---

* Boldface terms appear in the Glossary at the end of the book.

classical family of Western nostalgia leads us astray. When we penetrate the confusing mists of recent history we find few examples of this 'classical' family. Grandma's farm was not economically self-sufficient. Few families stayed together as large aggregations of kinfolk. Most houses were small, not large. We now see more large old houses than small ones; they survived longer because they were likely to have been better constructed. The one-room cabins rotted away. True enough, divorce was rare, but we have no evidence that families were generally happy. Indeed, we find, as in so many other pictures of the glowing past, that in each past generation people write of a period *still* more remote, *their* grandparents' generation, when things really were much better."[6]

So much for scapegoating! The causes of disillusionment are complex and varied. There are no simple and easy one-shot answers or cure-alls. In fact, modern society repeatedly extols the value of strong marital and familial structure, and yet this same societal interface of institutions constantly impinges on the functioning of the family. There is not a marriage or family today that is not affected by political ideology, defense policy, economics, the wage-price index, inflation, agricultural policy, minimum wage laws, and laws dealing with income taxes, including exclusions, deductions for dependents, and the relative tax assessed singles versus marrieds. Our analysis of the factors that contribute to marital disillusionment are divided into four basic areas: (1) the institution, (2) expectations, (3) the socialization process, and (4) personal development.

The First Root of Disillusionment: The Institution

THE LEGAL-ECCLESIASTICAL TRADITION

An institution is "an organization or establishment devoted to the promotion of a particular object, especially one of a public, educational, or charitable character . . . a well-established and structured pattern of behavior or of relationships that is accepted as a fundamental part of a culture, as marriage."[7] Marriage in the United States is an institution. It has legal definition, is protected by the courts, and requires a license to enter it. Marriage is a contract breakable only by action of a court of law or by death.

The **legal-ecclesiastical** tradition refers to the totality of laws, customs, and traditions that have evolved from the Judeo-Christian tradition, that have been officially codified in the Anglo-Saxon and American bodies of law, and that have been transmitted via judicial and legislative guidelines. Marriage as a legal-ecclesiastical institution encompasses the full range of ecclesiastical tradition that guided the lives of many of the English colonists. The tradition has been transmitted to us by Saint Paul, Saint Augustine, the early Church

Fathers, the Protestant Reformation, the Council of Trent (the Roman Catholic reply to the Protestant Reformation), the Puritans, the American frontier, and the Victorians.

The early colonists at Jamestown and at Plymouth did not get together and say, "Boys (women were excluded from the legal and religious bodies), we have a new colony on our hands. We need to design new rules for marriage, sex, and family. What kind of laws should we propose relating to conditions for marriage, divorce, annulment, adultery, and fornication (sex before either partner is married)?" The reason the early colonists did not bother to write new laws is that for the most part the laws, the customs, the mores, and the traditions from the old country were simply transferred to the new country. The new legal systems simply "piggy-backed" the old religious and ecclesiastical traditions to such an extent that it was difficult to tell the new colonies from the old country. After all, the colonies were English colonies and as such would reflect English parliamentary law and English ecclesiastical traditions, except that there would be no established (state-authorized) church.

Many scholars believe that Christianity is antisexual, largely as a result of the bias of Saint Paul and Saint Augustine. It is more accurate to say, however, that the Christian *tradition* has become rigidly antisexual, even though Jesus gave little indication of being antisexual. Saint Paul counseled chastity because of his commitment to the belief that people should be totally free of earthly ties if they were to be ready for the imminent end of the world. Marriage, of course, would weaken this commitment. Paul also disapproved of sexual relations outside the marital state; his acceptance of sex within marriage came out most clearly in his advice that it was better to marry than to be aflame with passion.[8]

According to tradition, we think of the Puritans as a very antisexual people. Today it is common to hear people talk about puritanical sexual ethics. Actually this image of the Puritans is based exclusively on the sermons of the divines such as Cotton Mather. Church marriage records, baptismal records, and court records reveal that the Puritans were not antisexual. There is little question that the multitude of Puritan "blue laws" were enacted because this was the only way the town magistrates could control the young people. There is ample evidence that the favorite sin of the Puritans was fornication.[9] All in all, the Puritans were a very sensuous people, and a minority of them were strongly tempted to imbibe alcohol excessively. The attire of the Puritan male likewise did not point to prudishness inasmuch as there was criticism of the dressing habits of the Puritan "dandies." Unfortunately the Puritans have been confused with the Victorians.

The Victorian era, more than any other era in American history, is responsible for modern attitudes of prudishness and antisexual beliefs and practices. Victorianism was a style of living popularized during the reign of Queen Victoria of England (1837–1901); it was characterized by stuffy, hypocritical, or prudish manners and morals. Victorianism had the effect of removing the genitals from the self. People were desexualized. Our sexual natures were thought to be inferior to our spiritual natures and embarrassing to our more noble selves. Victorianism has had a significant effect on marital standards and expectations in the late 19th and early 20th centuries in the United States. Only in post-World War II times, especially beginning in the early 1960s, did the influence of Victorianism wane to a significant degree.

THE BELIEF IN THE INDISSOLUBILITY OF MARRIAGE

A major tenet in the legal-ecclesiastical tradition has been the permanence of marriage. Marriage is supposed to be indissoluble; that is, it cannot or should not be dissolved. Even though there has been provision for divorce under Anglo-Saxon rule since the break of England from the authority of the Pope, there still remains the belief that marriage is a contract that should be binding "until death do us part" or "for as long as we both shall live." The belief in the indissolubility of marriage is not a matter of tradition alone (as are attitudes toward sexuality). Jesus appears to have permitted divorce only on the grounds of unchastity or adultery. [10] The Old Testament is not clear about this matter, despite the commandment regarding adultery. Before Moses, there was an acceptance of divorce, and after Moses, there was concubinage (the practice of keeping a concubine: a woman who shares sexual intimacies with a man or, in some societies, a secondary wife who enjoys protection and support but who lacks the status of a primary wife). After Moses, sexual relations with non-Hebrew females continued. The ancient Jews during Moses' time classified adultery as the taking of a Jewish woman (married or not). However, if a married Jewish man had sexual intercourse with a non-Jewish woman, it was not considered adultery. The Jewish female could have sexual intercourse only with her husband because the purity of the "seed of Israel" had to be preserved because the Messiah must come from pure Hebrew stock. Hence no devout Jewish woman would dare to have sex with anyone other than her husband, and no Jewish man would have sex with any Jewish woman except his wife. The ancient Jews believed adultery was wrong because it involved taking what rightfully belonged to another person. Thus the sin of adultery was offensive, not because of the sexual conduct involved but because of the violation of the property rights of other Hebrews and the necessity to preserve the bloodline.

The Judeo-Christian tradition influenced the course of marriage and family relationships in Western societies more than any other tradition or doctrine. The legal tradition in both Anglo-Saxon and American cultures has reflected the Judeo-Christian beliefs in the indissolubility of marriage, the evils of fornication and adultery, the rights of the husband over the wife, and the legally reinforced roles prescribed by religion, culture, and society for husbands and wives, men and women. The ancient Hebrews, even more strongly than the ancient Greeks and Romans, considered the female to be inferior to her husband, and a wife was considered to be the husband's legal chattel or property. What we will later refer to as comparative resource theory is the act of the society or culture bestowing on the male or female certain rights or privileges simply on the basis of gender. In the Judeo-Christian tradition the bestowing has favored the male and the husband over the female and the wife. This fact helps explain 2000 years of male dominance in Western cultures.

Most sociologists, anthropologists, and historians agree that society has a vested interest in the mate selection process and in the establishment of a societal definition of legal marriage. This interest is not based on any genuine concern for the happiness or well-being of the marital couple. It is based instead on a concern for the socialization of the younger generation. There is no known society that has not created an established procedure by which children are to be legally protected and safeguarded, as well as indoctrinated and socialized into the customs, traditions, and mores of the culture. This responsibility is usually assigned to the legal parents. Hence, a society's concern with mate selection is its prime method for ensuring its own survival.

A legal definition of marriage and a societal dependence on some form of family structure have been indispensible in all known societies. In America, all of the states have traditionally upheld the indissolubility of marriage. As has been pointed out, this is not a cross-cultural phenomenon but rather is a result of our cultural heritage. People who deviate from the norm of indissolubility still face societal labels and are often treated with a subtle form of prejudice. They are often told that they are failures and therefore must be made to feel guilt and shame. Formal sanctions against Roman Catholics who divorce and wish to remarry are enforced by the church's insistence that annulment (a declaration that no valid marriage ever really existed) must precede remarriage.

NO-FAULT DIVORCE

Until the 1970s the legal system in the United States reflected the tradition of indissolubility in its full judicial process for divorce. This process included a plaintiff, a defendant, a judge, and separate attorneys representing the plaintiff and the defendant. Underlying this practice was the assumption that there was an innocent party and a guilty party: One member of the marital dyad alleged that she or he had been wronged or harmed by the other. Collusion or any secret agreement or understanding between the couple was illegal. In other words, if the couple pretended to present the judge with a scenario of alleged infidelity even though there never was any infidelity or if the couple pretended that the woman was suffering mental cruelty when she really was not, this was called collusion and was illegal. A married couple could not simply ask the judge for a divorce without presenting authentic and valid legal grounds for divorce.

This system, called the client-defender system, was in force in the United

States since the earliest times in Plymouth colony until the early 1970s. There was much antipathy toward the system. Treatment of such issues as alimony, child support, division of property, and visitation rights continued to make the entire system a farce. Lying and perjury were encouraged by the system. Legal grounds for divorce such as adultery and mental cruelty became catchalls and hence meaningless. The postdivorce testimony of many is that they intended to part on friendly terms but ended up embittered, vengeful, and hateful of one another. Why? Because their attorneys transformed the proceedings into a contest for money, child custody, and property. When a person felt that his/her mate had injured him/her, the all too common retort was, "I'll make him/her pay for what he/she did to me. I'll take him/her for all he/she is worth." (The man punished the woman by suing for custody of the children and in extreme cases denial of visitation. The woman punished the man by suing not only for the children but also for alimony and child support and perhaps denial of visitation privilege.) All in all, the legal system became part of the problem, embittering the former mates to an intolerable degree and creating an atmosphere detrimental to the best interests of the children.

By the last decade of the 20th century some form of no-fault divorce was common in almost all of the 50 states. No-fault divorce means that where one previously had to prove the partner's guilt according to at least one of several grounds of divorce (adultery, mental cruelty, desertion, nonsupport, and so on), now a couple or only one partner may claim irreconcilable breakdown (or its functional equivalent) and the divorce will be granted. Now a couple knows even as they are going into the divorce procedure that they in fact will be granted a divorce. Whereas in the past it took two to marry and usually two to divorce, now it takes two to marry and only one to secure the divorce.

It now takes only one to divorce *unless* the couple can't agree on child custody and division of property. When this happens we are no better off with no-fault divorce than we were with the client-defender system. This is because once again there is a contest, and each party in the contest must protect himself or herself by securing an attorney who will do everything in his or her power to get the best possible deal for his or her client. Now we have all the bitterness, the anger, the revenge, and the punishment that we had before. Although no-fault divorce legislation has been much needed and long overdue as a means to humanize the divorce process, it has in some cases only moved the line of battle from the question of divorce to the question of settlement. Practically speaking, no-fault divorce is very workable as long as the partners agree on terms of settlement. When partners disagree on terms of settlement one of two things may happen.

The first thing that may happen when the partners disagree has already been mentioned. They hire attorneys and let the attorneys take over the entire process. This usually increases the degree of disillusionment and bitterness. The second thing that can happen when the partners disagree is called divorce mediation. Divorce mediation assumes that the couple is at least on civil speaking terms and can handle their anger in a constructive manner. Given this assumption, a mediator is engaged who will mediate the dispute and attempt to work out a settlement that is fair for both parties. Details of the settlement will usually include child custody, clarity of primary versus secondary child caretaking, division of property, child support, financing of higher or other post-high school education, life insurance policies on the breadwinners, health insurance policies, and division of accrued pension benefits if applicable. When the mediator has effected an agreement between the divorcing couple, the mediator will retain the services of an attorney who will put the entire agreement into a legal terminology that is acceptable to the presiding judge. Usually this ends the matter and the divorce and its legal conditions become a matter of court record. Most mediators are marriage and family therapists who have special training in mediation. However, some mediators are attorneys who have special training in mediation.

The obvious and desirable feature of divorce mediation is in bypassing the formal plaintiff-defendant system wherein each partner hires an attorney. By using a mediator and the mediator's attorney there is a much greater possibility for cooperation and compromise without the negative side effects of a legal contest. Of even greater importance is the fact that a cooperative climate is created whereby future communication between the parents (who are now ex-mates and perhaps remarried) is greatly enhanced. This will help the children as they learn to live with parents who are no longer married to one another.

The first root of marital disillusionment, the institutional root, enables us to see why thousands upon thousands of people attack, criticize, and in other ways attempt to discredit the institution of marriage. Feelings are not so much the result of our intellect as of our personal experiences. When our experience of marriage is colored and tainted by the legal-ecclesiastical system, which is based on the Judeo-Christian tradition of male superiority and restrictively stereotyped sex roles, it is predictable that there will be great disillusionment. Is it any wonder that women and men who have gone through the devastation of marital dissolution place a good deal of the blame on the institution of marriage? Perhaps as the practice and popularity of divorce mediation grows there will be less reason to become embittered and/or disillusioned.

The Second Root of Disillusionment: Expectations

There is little likelihood that any society ever expected as much as does ours in regard to the union of one woman with one man in the estate of marriage. Expectations come from every corner: the church, the synagogue, the state, the community, the immediate or nuclear family, the extended family, and most powerful of all, our own internalized expectations of what marital happiness is all about. The contention is that our society is dominated by historical romanticism. Society in general exacerbates disillusionment by fostering unrealistic and sometimes fantastic and impossible expectations. Our society has inherited the courtly-romantic tradition as well as the Victorian and Judeo-Christian traditions. These traditions are essentially antisexual and emphasize purity of motive and spiritual oneness between lovers. If we look to opera, literature, drama, movies, television, magazines, newspapers, and commercial advertisements we may begin to appreciate how deeply the concept of **romantic love** has influenced our heritage. This heritage is transmitted by our courts, our religious institutions, our educational institutions, and our families.

HISTORICAL ROMANTICISM

If we define romantic love as a feeling of caring and sharing, of moonlight, roses, and music, then there probably would be no serious problem with romance. However, historical romanticism is not just moonlight, roses, and music combined with a feeling of sharing and caring. Historical romanticism is, in short, a philosophy of love that idolizes love itself and idealizes the lover to such an extent that it is impossible to combine this type of highly charged electrical and chemical experience with the day-in and day-out reality of marital love, sometimes referred to as conjugal love.

A reading of Andreas Capellanus's *The Art of Courtly Love*, a 13th-century statement on the nature of love, provides a glimpse of the forerunner of the movement known as romanticism.

> Now let us see what ways love may be decreased. Too many opportunities for exchanging solaces, too many opportunities of seeing the loved one, too much chance to talk to each other all decrease love, and so does an uncultured appearance or manner of walking on the part of the lover or the sudden loss of his property. Love decreases, too, if the woman finds that her lover is foolish and indiscreet, or if he seems to go beyond reasonable bounds in his demands for love, or if she sees that he has no regard for her modesty and will not forgive her bashfulness. Love decreases, too, if the woman considers that her lover is cowardly in battle, or sees that he is unrestrained in his speech or spoiled by the vice of arrogance.[11]

The tradition of courtly love spread over much of Europe and was primarily an upper-class pastime. The nobility were often bored with marriage. A person married because this was how one carried forth the family name and the family tradition. Marriage among the aristocracy was never meant to bring happiness to the participants. Marital love was a duty and a responsibility. Mate selection was intended to solidify and expand, if possible, the family's holdings, power, and wealth. A person's *real* love, however, was *outside* of marriage.

In Europe, chiefly in southern France between the 11th and 13th centuries, troubadours wrote poems of love and set the lyrics to music. The theme of the troubadour's lyric was the extolling of the virtues of love, especially when this love is directed toward a specific lover or would-be lover.

A further development of this period was in the chivalry of the warrior in shining armor who would sally forth and dedicate his great deeds of battle to his lady. The lady, if duly impressed, would then knight the warrior. Aside from the dubbing ceremony, knight and lady may never meet face to face or alone, yet love is served, if only as a distant and unobtainable longing and desire. The legends of the Knights of the Round Table, especially the legend of Guinevere and Lancelot, are prototypes of courtly love.

Courtly love was essentially antisexual. This does not mean that love was never consummated with sexual union, but it does mean that sex was pushed into the background. Love was noble; sex was crude. Love was of the gods; sex was a perfunctory physical act. Love was exquisite; sex was crass or gross. Love emphasized purity of motive and spiritual oneness between lovers; sex for its own pleasure was debauchery.

The tradition of courtly love undergirds our modern idolization and idealization of love. As a forerunner to the historical movement known as romanticism, courtly love provided a foundation wherein the principle of love for its own sake (love for the sake of love; in love with love) became one of the two cornerstones. The idolization and idealization of the lover or the beloved became the other cornerstone.

IMPOSSIBLE EXPECTATIONS

Historical romanticism combined with courtly love to create a tradition that emphasized certain principles, which in turn became the expectations surrounding love, sex, and marriage. Following is a list of some of the most obvious and prominent of these expectations.

People should marry primarily for love. Love is the sine qua non or indispensible condition for marriage. No matter what other factors are attractive, love is absolutely the prime requirement.

Sex is always an expression of love.

Lovers should forgo their individual identities and become *one* with each other in a state of fusion.

Falling in love is the expected emotional reaction to meeting the person of your dreams.

Love will flourish once you have really fallen in love.

True love will enable the couple to conquer all obstacles.

Love and anger are opposites because one cannot love if one is angry, nor can one have anger if one loves.

Conflict is a bad sign, is always destructive, and should be avoided at all costs.

Unity implies uniformity.

Men should always be dominant; women should always be submissive.

Good women are for marriage; bad women are for fun and sex.

Men enjoy sex; women tolerate it.

Men use the language of love in order to get sex; women participate in sex in order to reveal their love and to feel loved.

Children strengthen marriage; marriage without children is abnormal.

Marriage should fulfill all or nearly all of one's needs for love, affection, romance, sex, companionship, and friendship.

Marriage should satisfy all or nearly all of one's economic and status needs.

These expectations are the result of romanticism interacting with other cultural traditions within American society. When a people embraces the Judeo-Christian tradition with its emphasis on the woman as chattel or property of the man; a courtly-romantic view of love; a Victorian view of sex; a traditionally restrictive attitude toward sex roles and sex-role division of labor; a sentimental, idealistic view of children; an almost religious veneration of the American founding fathers; and an idolatry of motherhood, the flag, and God, it is not surprising that our societal expectations for love, marriage, and sex are so incredibly naive and impossible to realize.

Our second root of marital disillusionment, expectations, probably accounts for a far greater share of misery, disappointment, and disillusionment than does the institutional root discussed earlier. The expectation level of most Americans is utterly out of sync with any rational assessment of marriage. We may ask, Why is this? Basically we *want* these expectations to be true. We *wish* for these expectations to be true. We then *believe* they are true, and we *behave* as if they are true, thus creating the illusion of truth. Underneath these wants, wishes, beliefs, and behaviors is an infrastructure that serves to socialize us and propel us in this direction. This process is the third root of disillusionment.

The Third Root of Disillusionment: The Socialization Process

Socialization cannot be separated from expectations. These expectations determine the customs, mores, beliefs, attitudes, and life-style into which the child is indoctrinated. We will examine the process of **socialization** as carried out by the institutions of family, education, religion, the peer group, and the political establishment.

THE FAMILY

Parents and the family are the primary socializing agents in society. Each partner brings to marriage his or her life orientation, life-style, value structure, religious and philosophical viewpoints, and personality. When children are born, they are socialized by the combined orientation of their parents. The cycle begins again. Not only is the family the primary socializing agent of society, it is the most powerful as well. **Family systems theory** holds that our development as human beings is a function of familial interaction and communication patterns and that much of what we are and do in life is either in conformity to these patterns, principles, and beliefs or in reaction against parental patterns, principles, and beliefs (Appendix A). The internalized parents and the internalized family remains with us until we die. The quest for maturity and differentiation is a lifelong endeavor. It is hoped that the bulk of the process of breaking away and becoming one's own person will be accomplished in the late teen years and throughout the early and mid twenties. Some people remain enmeshed with their parents all their lives, whereas others have completely disengaged from their family of origin yet remain enmeshed because they never really worked through any of the issues. Instead, all they did was separate themselves by running away or physically distancing themselves by not phoning or writing or by maintaining only perfunctory and/or ritualistic contact.

The family is the first transmitter of the values, expectations, and mores of the society. As a result of role modeling, children begin to learn the traditional sexual and marital roles while they are still in diapers. Role modeling is a process whereby children copy, imitate, and mimic their models. At the same time the child is imitating the roles of its parents and elders, he or she also is receiving messages that contain a multitude of "shoulds," "oughts," "musts," and "you'd better not" or "you'd better." These messages are usually repetitive and tend to accumulate.

The result of role modeling combined with the repetitive instructional messages is what we refer to as *internalization*. The child internalizes what she/he hears, sees, and experiences. As the word suggests, when we **internalize** something we take it inside ourselves, and it becomes a part of us without our being aware of it or thinking about it.

One of the things we internalize is the type of behavior that is permissible and whether or not it is permissible for girls as well as for boys and vice versa. Traditional patterns of socialization insisted that girls wear dresses, play with dolls, and learn how to do domestic things such as cooking and keeping house, "just like Mommy." Boys were to wear pants; play with toy guns, trucks, cars, footballs, softballs, baseballs, soccer balls, and basketballs; and do all the exciting things that Daddy does. Girls were taught to look pretty, petite, passive, and submissive. Boys were taught to be active, assertive, competitive, and to show leadership, even aggressiveness. Carol Gilligan's research has shown that the socialization process for girls is remarkably different than for boys and that because of this the female identity may result from a set of expectations and experiences that lead to a greater capacity for intimacy and openness, whereas the identity of boys is more the result of experiences of industriousness, competitiveness, and aggressiveness, which tend to lessen the male's capacity for intimacy and openness.[12]

The women's liberation movement has advocated that men and women restructure much of their sex-role stereotyping. In this view, women should work outside as well as inside the home, and men should assume equal responsibility for child care and household chores. Parents who agree with these views are attempting to break down rigid stereotyping of sex roles in the socialization of their children. They hope that this approach will allow children to develop their individual potential more fully and assume a greater variety of roles in adult life.

EARLY ATTITUDES TOWARD SEX

Children likewise develop their attitudes toward sexuality by imitating the attitudes of their parents and other significant adults. These attitudes are learned early on an emotional level, and they become a deeply believed and accepted part of the self. If children are taught that going to the toilet is a function that is dirty and therefore not to be talked about, then this attitude will likely become internalized. If a little boy is caught scratching his penis and then is scolded with a message of shame, naughtiness, dirtiness, and "nice people don't do that," it is very likely that the internalized message will eventually become one of guilt whenever the boy touches himself or explores his genitals or fondles himself.

Erik Erikson has shown us that shame and doubt develop quite early in a child's life, as do guilt and feelings of inferiority.[13] Erikson's developmental schema is referred to as psychosocial because it is based on the psychology of social development. Erikson held that basic mistrust led to feelings of self-doubt and shame, which then became the foundation for guilt, inferiority, and an unclear or confused identity. This resulted in a sense of insecurity and a lack of self-confidence and self-acceptance. Erikson's theoretical schema, although widely used and greatly respected, has not been empirically validated in a rigorous and thorough manner. We cannot be certain that it applies equally to all ethnic groups and to both genders. There is a question concerning whether or not the psychosocial development of females is identical in all respects to the psychosocial development of males. Nevertheless, it is fairly well accepted that there is a definite developmental sequence that includes physiological, psycho-logical, and sociological dimensions. Further, these developmental phases take place within the intimate context of the family replete with its rules, regulations, rituals, prohibitions, conflict resolution/denial, and patterns of interaction.

LOVE AND CONFLICT

Because children begin to learn attitudes toward sex and marriage early in childhood, parents must provide realistic models for their children to emulate. Two especially crucial areas for the socialization of the child are the sharing of affection between parents and the sharing of disagreement and conflict. If we accept the fact that there is early internalization, then why not let the child experience the warmth of emotional bonds between Mom and Dad? It is important that parents share some intimacies with one another in the presence of the children. Kissing, hugging, holding, handholding, and sofa snuggling are activities that children should see and be witness to inasmuch as they contribute to the child's sense of safety, security, and well-being. Likewise, it is of vital importance that parents express differences of opinion and disagreements with one another in the presence of the children in order that the children may experience the honesty of disagreement and the steps necessary for positive conflict resolution. Some parents consider it a virtue *not* to fight (or constructively seek to resolve the conflict) in the presence of the children. When these children grow up they may be under the illusion that their parents never had any important areas of conflict. Worse, the young adult finds himself/herself without any viable and constructive model in the handling of intimate conflict. By refusing to share at least some of the milder forms of affection and conflict, parents deprive their children of meaningful models of mature adult living. [14]

Sometimes the people who avoid conflict in adult life are those who lacked models in facing conflict directly, fairly, and creatively. How many times do marriage therapists and psychotherapists hear their clients say, "My parents never fought and never argued"? Such a remark would indicate one of several possible situations: (1) one of the partners usually gave in on all issues; (2) both partners suppressed their feelings, attitudes, and beliefs; (3) they let it all out when no one was around or when they were behind closed doors. In Chapter 5, we will discuss the entire range of issues in conflict resolution and rules for fair fighting.

PEER SOCIALIZATION

Although the family is the primary agent of socialization it by no means is the only significant agent. In the past the community was a significant agent in that neighbors, townspeople, and community folk all made it their business to watch out for other people's children and teenagers. Except in small-town America, this type of caretaking and socializing is a relic of the past. In suburbia and urban America, the prevailing social milieu is characterized by anonymity. In this vacuum of adult caretaking and overseeing, the peer group has evolved into a powerful determinant of the mores, habits, beliefs, myths, and illusions of both children and adolescents.

If the group says it is good, it is good. If the group endorses something, it is endorsed. If the circle of friends dresses a certain way, with a certain label on their jeans or their sunglasses, then would-be adherents to this group are sure to emulate. In short, the peer group has become a powerful source of authority. This authority extends into attitudes about what music is acceptable, which teen idols will make it, and which would-be aspirants will fall short or fade into the abyss of has-beens. The teen culture makes its own rules about sex, tobacco, alcohol, and drugs, and the pressure to conform is extremely powerful.

The lure of *acceptance* endows the peer group with authority and power. Young people are willing to pay almost any price in order to be accepted, to be considered a member of the in-group, or even to be on the fringe of the in-group. Junior high or middle school cliques give way to high school cliques, and the cliques are unofficially rank ordered from the most prestigious to the least prestigious. Peer acceptance is such an established reality that the manufacturing of clothing, music, magazines, and videos has become a multi-billion-dollar industry.

What does all of this have to do with disillusionment in marriage? The third root of disillusionment, the socialization process, is indeed responsible for a large share of disillusionment inasmuch as the ideology of the peer group personifies, promotes, and perpetuates the romanticization of love. This romanticization is not very different from the courtly love of the 13th century and the historical romanticism to which courtly love gave birth. Love is extolled as the supreme value in the relationship between the sexes. Sex is its servant. Love justifies sex. Love is all that is necessary to ensure the functioning of a relationship. Love conquers all. Love is the alpha and the omega. When love wanes or begins to erode the only decent remedy is to give it a decent burial.

Sex education is dispensed by the peer group in a very straightforward manner. Material thus transmitted is often erroneous at worst and misleading at best. In the absence of solid and accurate information that could come from parents, school, or religious institutions, the knowledge gained via peer education is a study in futility. It is a "folk wisdom" of the streets, the locker rooms, the rest rooms, and the back (and front) seats of cars. We may rest assured that children and young people will engage delightedly in the mutual swapping of mistruth, misinformation, and sexual myth if there is no intervening source of positive and correct information. Because there is little or nothing in terms of positive instruction in sex education, it is only logical that children and young people turn to the streets, the TV, and the boombox for answers.

Folklore transmitted by the media, especially through popular songs, love ballads, magazines, and pornographic material, increases the expectation level by reinforcing societal norms, especially those that convey the belief that love is the answer to lovelessness, loneliness, unhappiness, and lack of identity or purpose in life. Peer group influence is probably the most powerful motivator toward the romanticized picture of love, sex, and marriage.

The Fourth Root of Disillusionment: Personal Development

INTRAPSYCHIC AND INTERPSYCHIC CAUSATION

The fourth root of marital disillusionment is both **intrapsychic (intrapersonal)** and **interpsychic (interpersonal)** in nature. Intrapsychic indicates the inner feelings, thoughts, and psychological processes that, however formed, operate from *within* the individual and make up our internal viewpoint and perspective on life and the world around us. Interpsychic indicates the relationships *with* and *between* two or more people.

Traditionally, people have believed that the intrapersonal causes or creates the interpersonal. This is not a valid assumption. Our interpersonal relationships are extremely important in forming our intrapersonal makeup. The question of which comes first, intra or inter, can be answered only by taking a circular view of causation rather than a linear or straight line view. This is a situation similar to the question of which came first, the chicken or the egg. There is no single first cause. Rather, there are many causes, and they are circular in that each cause is also an effect and each effect becomes a cause. This means that interpersonal dynamics contribute to our intrapersonal makeup, *and* our intrapersonal dynamics contribute to our interpersonal makeup. The circularity exists because there is a constant interaction between the two, neither being the exclusive cause of the other.

In the discussion that follows I will use the word *theory* in a very loose and nontechnical manner. I refer to family systems theory as a theory much in the manner that I refer to psychoanalytic (Freudian) theory. Neither of these is true theory inasmuch as theory depends on rigorous empirical validation via use of the scientific method. Technically speaking, family systems, object relations, and psychoanalytic derivatives are conceptual frameworks. A conceptual framework is a way of looking at or viewing a subject or a phenomenon. Within the conceptual framework there are numerous hypotheses that remain hypotheses until they are established through empirical verification.

TRADITIONAL INTRAPSYCHIC VIEWS
OF PERSONALITY STRUCTURE AND DEVELOPMENT

Psychoanalytic theories of psychotherapy and of personality structure posit the development of the individual as being a struggle between the ego, the libido (including the id, the basic sex drive), and the superego. The ego seeks to resolve conflicts between the id and the superego. This is essentially a struggle between the forces of pleasure and the forces of rules and cultural moral norms. Psychoanalytic theory posits the **psychosexual** developmental sequence of the individual through the **oral, anal,** phallic, latent, and genital stages. Although Freud did refer to the child's family, it was only as a backdrop for the child's internal Oedipal struggle, that is, the male child's fear that if his father discovered the son's love-sexual attraction to his mother, the father would castrate him. Likewise for the female child, the Electra complex posits a similar rivalry between the daughter and her mother. Instead of a fear of castration, the daughter fears that her mother will simply deprive her of her father or take her away from her father. Freud's theory has taken deep root in the United States, especially in the 1940s and 1950s, and to a lesser extent in the 1960s. Today it is still a powerful influence on the way people think about the cause of dysfunctional behavior, emotional distress, and mental illness.

Object relations theorists such as Margaret Mahler, Melanie Klein, W. R. D. Fairbairn, D. W. Winnicott, Otto Kernberg, and ego psychologist Heinz Kohut are basically intrapsychic in perspective, although most of these have broken away from orthodox Freudian theory by placing much more emphasis on the process of mothering and parenting.[15] The theorists are basically intrapsychic in orientation in that they focus on the fact that something within the individual has gone haywire or has failed to develop normally. The remedy is to "fix" whatever it is that has gone wrong within the individual or to rectify the "mal" or bad development. An intrapsychic orientation always sees the individual as the problem. In intrapsychic theory the individual is always the central player in the drama because the problem is believed to be "inside" the individual.

Developmental theories, as opposed to psychoanalytic theories and their derivatives, are based on the works of such researchers as Erik Erikson, E. O. Wilson, B. F. Skinner, Albert Bandura, J. Piaget, and L. Kohlberg.[16] Generally speaking, developmental theories are based on empirical evidence. Developmentalists employ direct observation of subjects' behavior as well as sampling techniques and various testing measures. Developmental theories are intrapsychic inasmuch as they focus almost exclusively on the development of the individual. Although a significant portion of human development concerns the ability to interact and interrelate with one's peers and intimates, the focus remains on the individual and is thus considered to be intrapsychic.

THE INTERPSYCHIC ORIENTATION OF FAMILY SYSTEMS

Increasingly we are realizing that our intrapsychic orientation (that is, how we view ourselves and feel about ourselves, including our security mechanisms, defense mechanisms, and other ego-protective devices) is the result of our interpsychic environment. In this view the individual is seen as a subsystem within a larger system known as the family. The family system molds and shapes much of our personality, including our manner of relating to others; our feelings about ourselves, including our self-esteem; and our manner of coping with life and its exigencies.

Within the family system there are several subsystems. There is the *marital* subsystem, the husband and the wife. The husband and the wife, in turn, are the products of their own family of origin in which they were part of the *sibling* subsystem. In addition to the sibling and marital subsystems is the *parental* subsystem of mother and father, the *children* subsystem, and perhaps the *grandparent* subsystem. In systems theory, each of us is a system in our own right, and within ourselves we have a series of subsystems such as the respiratory, vascular, digestive, and nervous subsystems. Family systems theory includes all subsystems, and it relates to other systems such as the educational, the social, the economic, and the political. General systems theory posits that all of these various systems are interrelated and mutually causative. Each of these systems acts on and is acted on by all other systems, and it is folly to think that any given entity is able to function apart from the immediate and greater environment.

Family systems theory does not approach the self from the internal perspective of the self. Rather, the self is viewed as being an integral part of the immediate family system replete with its style of communication, rule setting, behavioral sequences, and all manner of interactive patterning. An underlying premise of family systems theory is that "an individual's symptoms, presenting problems, or complaints are an expression of a family's dysfunction, and appear in one member in an effort to maintain homeostasis, to hide, obscure, or distract the family from that dysfunction."[17] What this means in practical terms is that little Billy's problem with reading may become a means whereby the attention of mother and father are focused increasingly on Billy, thus preventing mother and father from dealing with their own problem. Or Billy's reading problem may serve to preserve the family's appearance of unity, when in truth there is a great deal of quarreling. As long as people focus on Billy, the quarreling is minimal. Or perhaps Dad is a problem drinker and his problem is obscured by his and everybody else's preoccupation with Billy. The principle of **homeostasis** states that the system will always attempt to preserve itself, even if the basic state, the homeostasis, is an unhealthy state.

TWO WAYS OF LOOKING AT A PROBLEM: LINEAL AND CIRCULAR INTERACTIVE

THE SITUATION

Roger and Tamara are having marital difficulties. Roger is verbally abusive of Tamara and behaves in a hostile manner toward the children, Jerry, age 4, and Glenda, age 6. Both Tamara and Roger complain of the incessant fighting and aggressiveness between the children. Roger has begun to threaten divorce, saying he can't exist in such an uncooperative home atmosphere where no one appreciates him or lends a hand toward doing their share of the work. Roger displays an increasingly explosive temper. Tamara increasingly protects Roger from the unpleasant fighting between the children.

Roger is an industrial engineer. He had worked for a small company with offices in seven states, which he visited regularly. Recently Roger's company was bought out by a huge engineering firm with international offices. Although Roger was not demoted he now has a narrowed focus of responsibility. Roger feels hurt, anger, and loss. He no longer enjoys his work and talks of quitting. He feels he is powerless to make any other changes. He feels "trapped" because he feels he cannot earn as much elsewhere and it's too late to go into a new career.

Tamara was gainfully employed for several years until the birth of Glenda. Since then she has acceded to her husband's wishes to "be a wife and mother." Tamara and Roger both claim that the family has no other problems except those stemming from Roger's work.

A LINEAL AND INTRAPSYCHIC UNDERSTANDING OF THIS FAMILY'S SITUATION

A lineal and intrapsychic understanding of this family's situation would likely focus on the hurt, anger, and loss experienced by Roger in the aftermath of his company having been bought out by a much larger and more impersonal corporation. Roger brings home his pent-up frustrations and his diminished sense of self. Roger's anxiety, perhaps reflecting an inner struggle with himself, is at a very high level and seems to find expression in his hostility and aggression with his family.

In this view the causative dynamic is considered to be **lineal** in terms of cause and effect. In straight lineal cause and effect the blame and responsibility are placed on the company. "It's your fault" becomes "It's not your fault, Roger, it's the company's fault." The cause of the family's problem is the change in conditions of Roger's employment. If the conditions of employment were to change or if new, more desirable employment were secured, the problem would be resolved.

A CIRCULAR AND INTERPSYCHIC UNDERSTANDING OF THE FAMILY'S SITUATION

A circular and interpsychic understanding of this family's situation would consider many things other than the change in Roger's employment. Direct (lineal) causality is minimized in favor of multicausality, which seeks to understand the interactive and circular processes that affect each member of the family. In this view "blame" and "whose fault it is" are put aside so that the various members of the family system may see the interactive patterns that contribute to the present situation. What was going on between Roger and Tamara in the months and years preceding the work change? Because Roger mentioned divorce we would want to consider the history of the marital relationship, the closeness/distance of the couple, and their ability to deal directly with each other without triangling or scapegoating the children. We would want to consider what else may have been going on in Roger's family of origin and in Tamara's family of origin. We would want to know what role both Roger and Tamara played in their families of origin. We would want to know more about the covert and overt understandings between Tamara and Roger. Also, we would want to know more about how this family functions. What are the expectations, the rules, and the beliefs this family has regarding daily functioning and behavior? What function is filled by the increasing fighting between the two children? Why has this fighting escalated in recent months? What is the function of Tamara's protectiveness of Roger? What is the meaning of Tamara's "acceding" to Roger's wishes regarding Tamara not being gainfully employed?

A systemic, interpsychic approach to understanding Roger, Tamara, Glenda, and Jerry focuses on the assumptions and interactions arising out of family relationships. It is never a simple matter of pointing to one person or event and saying "It's your fault." Although Roger's conditions of employment have affected this family's functioning, other significant factors may have preceded the change in employment. These are factors relating to how the members protect and avoid one another, how intimacy is avoided, how closeness is pretended, how conflict is handled, and how coalitions between members serve to reduce the family's anxiety level.

SYSTEMS THEORY AND THE CONTEXTUAL FRAMEWORK

Family systems theory and family systems therapy will be discussed again in later chapters. For now our emphasis is on the importance of systems theory as it encompasses many, if not all, of our personality quirks, mannerisms, modus operandi, communication patterns, and styles of personal presentation, that is, how we present ourselves and how we relate to others. These characteristics stem from our positions and roles within both our families of origin and our families of procreation. Systems patterns reflect the maneuvers and protective mechanisms that families use in their efforts to avoid conflict and reduce anxiety. Beliefs, rules, and roles may serve the purpose of holding the family together in a dysfunctional manner, protecting against the threat of intimacy and closeness as well as distance and individuality.

Although we may be unaware of it, as children we learned a style or manner of acting to provide for our own security and safety. We learned that when we were ill we could get attention or divert attention away from our quarreling parents. We learned how to use helplessness in order to manipulate. We learned that pouting, sulking, throwing tantrums, or being depressed did something for us. Perhaps we learned that when we were assertive or aggressive we would be put down or shamed. Or perhaps just the opposite: We learned that being assertive or aggressive gave us a sense of power and security. Perhaps when we were compliant or pleasing, adapting ourselves to everybody else's wishes, we received more affection and praise, and this payoff felt so good that we wanted more. On the other hand, perhaps compliance didn't pay off, and we decided to take our chances regardless of the consequences, and as a result we were tagged as the "problem child" or the "black sheep" of the family.

A child often experiences pain when he or she feels that a brother or sister is a parent's favorite. For some it is excruciatingly painful to be left out, put down, or rejected. Also, it is entrapment to be smothered by a parent who needs the child to need the parent. In countless families the children become the battleground for the acting out of the problems of the husband and/or wife. Or the husband-wife (marital) subsystem dysfunction is diverted to the father-mother (parental) subsystem, which in turn triangles in one of the children. To triangle or to triangulate is to bring a third person or object into one's emotional field so that the energy that would ordinarily be invested in the dyadic or one-on-one relationship is now diverted and invested into a third person (or object). When this happens the third person or object is said to be triangulated. A triangulated child can become a scapegoated child whom everyone picks on, or he/she could become the emotional savior of one of the triangling parents, who then treats the child somewhat as an intimate confidant.

Differentiation is the process of separating and distinguishing one's inner cognitive system from one's emotional system. As this process proceeds and matures, the individual also becomes increasingly differentiated from the emotional orbit of one's family of origin. The emotional system does not mean merely the expression of sentiment and emotion. The emotional system is essentially a response system or a reactivity that leads us to behave in unexamined and unquestioned ways that we have learned (internalized) in our growing-up years within our family of origin. When a person is reasonably differentiated, he/she is able to function as a mature and autonomous adult, free of dependency and co-dependency and not burdened with excessive anxiety. The differentiated self is able to love his/her parents and to relate to them in an adult-adult manner without being burdened with the need to conform to their expectations or wishes. (Appendix A will give the reader a more complete treatment of family systems theory.)

The fourth root of disillusionment is, in fact, the sum total of our upbringing. We have internalized all that has happened to us since the very beginning. We have learned to cope. We are what we are because of the myriad of interactive processes and recurring patterns that characterized and dominated our family environment. Unless we can see clearly what it is we choose to change, we will bring these processes and patterns and styles of coping and being into our marriage and into every intimate relationship in which we become involved. Because of this, our total experience within our family of origin, from the time of our birth until we leave home, will have lasting profound ramifications for our own future and our future family. In fact, although the person may leave his/her family, the family will never leave the person. Thus when we marry the person of our dreams we are also marrying his/her family of origin. This is so, even if we deny it or minimize it or proclaim that our beloved "broke" from his/her family years ago and therefore is free of their influence.

Suzanne and Scott . . . Again!

Suzanne and Scott are almost at the point of indifference. Indifference is when we are no longer vulnerable to the charges, the barbs, the insults, and all the ravages that pain and hurt visit on us. Indifference means that we have succeeded in covering ourselves with an invisible plastic shield so that nothing gets through to hurt us anymore. Everything negative bounces off of us.

In the state of indifference there is no emotion. Even the pain of hurt, anger, and hatred is numbed or anesthetized. Scott had "shut down." He had quit trying to relate to Suzanne except in the most perfunctory ways. The problem, according to Scott, was very simple: Suzanne did not know how to manage her time or how to handle stress. If we take Scott at face value, he does not drink very much, and he is not part of the problem. The problem is Suzanne and perhaps the intrusiveness of Suzanne's parents.

In light of the four roots of disillusionment we can see several things:

Root 1. Even though Suzanne is gainfully employed it appears that she is in a dual role in that she is still responsible for performing the predominant housekeeping and child caretaking roles (her management of time and her handling of household functions). The marriage is still defined by the rules and standards of the institution, and the participants do not attempt to redefine or re-create these criteria and guidelines.

Root 2. Suzanne's hopes and dreams are now dashed to pieces because Scott "obviously does not love me anymore. If he loved me he would talk with me and be supportive of me. He would know what I need and at least attempt to meet my needs." Here Suzanne is echoing the societal expectation concerning the nature of romantic love: "If he loved me, really loved me, he would know what I need, and he would know what I am feeling and thinking." This, of course, is the myth of magical knowing.

Root 3. The socialization process has had its effect on both these young people. Scott has been socialized to believe that his salary and his job are more important than Suzanne's. Scott likely carries around within himself a bundle of stereotypes concerning how males are to act compared to females. Is it really his privilege to be a "couch potato"? Suzanne probably carries some notions that her parents imparted to her. Likely there is guilt for not being a better housewife, mother, and lover to her husband. Both Suzanne and Scott seem to be weak in self-esteem, otherwise they would not be so defensive and critical.

Root 4. Scott doubtless has never worked through a lot of the conflict he experienced with his parents, especially his father. Suzanne, socialized to be adaptive, obliging, and the one who is supposed to keep peace and provide stability, doesn't know how to ask for what she needs or wants, nor does she face the conflict directly with Scott. After all, Suzanne is likely still very attached to her parents, especially her mother. She is triangled by her mother, who confides in her and to this extent replaces her father as mother's confidant. This, of course, could serve the purpose of keeping her father and mother in a stable relationship because their anxiety is now invested in their daughter's relationship. As long as the parents overinvest in their daughter, they will not face or deal with the issues of their own relationship. In the eyes of Suzanne's parents, Scott will be labeled as the bad guy, the one who is at fault.

What docs all this mean? How can this process of disillusionment be reversed? How can Suzanne and Scott work through the dead trappings of the past that serve to disillusion and embitter them? Among the answers is honest self-assessment in terms of their mutual needs and their ability to resolve conflict constructively, which in turn involves the practice of fair fight procedures and negotiation skills. Seeing through the romantic myths is vital, as is learning how to dis-illusion oneself, that is, rid oneself of one's own illusions that are part of our romanticized image of marriage. Along with these measures is perhaps the biggest challenge—the challenge of working through the layers of unfinished business relating to the family of origin. The less we work through the unfinished business of our childhood and youth the greater the likelihood that the emotionality and patterns of early relationships will be transferred onto our mate. The goal is to minimize transference and to maximize autonomy, to minimize enmeshment and to maximize differentiation.

Summary

In this chapter I have attempted to set the stage for dealing with marital disillusionment. I discussed disillusionment, illusions, and the process of ridding ourselves of illusions. Four roots of disillusionment were discussed in detail. The first root is the *institutional* root, which grew out of the ecclesiastical and legal traditions, especially English law and the Judeo-Christian tradition. The second root is the *expectations* root, which covers the fantastic and unrealistic expectations connected with courtly love and historic romanticism. The third root is the *socialization* process, which effectively bombards us with messages about how to live and about the differences between good and bad, right and wrong. Most importantly, the socialization process provides the basis of the messages we internalize about ourselves, our sense of self-value, self-worth, and self-esteem. The fourth root is *personal* development. This points to the origin of why we are the way we are in terms of our manner and style of relating to the world around us.

There are many theories of individual development that relate primarily to ages and stages of growth. These ages and stages are best understood within the larger framework of family systems. The family systems framework was introduced as being the major frame of reference through which we may understand why we are the way we are. Family systems is a major conceptual framework because it accounts for the recurring patterns of interaction, reactivity, and the overt and covert rules that guide the family beliefs, values, and behavior. Family systems is a framework for the development of the self within the context of one's family, the first and primary socializing agency.

Reading Suggestions

Belenky, M. F., B. M. Clinchy, and J. M. Tarule. *Women's Ways of Knowing*. New York: Basic Books, 1986.

Bernard, Jessie. *The Future of Marriage*. New York: Bantam Books, 1972.

Dornbusch, S. M. and M. H. Strober, eds., *Feminism, Children and the New Families*. New York: Guilford Press, 1988.

Filsinger, Erik E. and Robert A. Lewis. *Assessing Marriage*. Beverly Hills, Calif.: Sage Publications, 1981.

Gilligan, Carol. *In a Different Voice*. Cambridge, Mass.: Harvard University Press, 1982.

Goode, William J. *The Family*. 2d ed. Englewood Cliffs, N.J.: Prentice-Hall, 1982.

Lasch, Christopher. *Haven in a Heartless World*. New York: Basic Books, 1977.

Rubin, Lillian B. *Worlds of Pain*. New York: Basic Books, 1976.

Rubin, Lillian B. *Intimate Strangers*. New York: Harper & Row, 1983.

Scarf, Maggie. *Intimate Partners*. New York: Random House, 1987.

St. Clair, Michael. *Object Relations and Self Psychology*. Monterey, Calif.: Brooks/Cole, 1986.

Stein, Joseph. *Fiddler on the Roof*. New York: Crown Publishers, 1965.

Notes

1. Elise F. Jones et al., "Teenage Pregnancy in Developed Countries: Determinants and Policy Implications." *Family Planning Perspectives* Vol. 17, no. 2 (Mar/Apr 1985), 53–63. "Although it is one of the most highly developed countries examined, the United States has a teenage fertility rate much higher than those observed in countries that are comparably modernized; and the U.S. rates are considerably higher than those found in a number of much less developed countries. . . . The U.S. teenage birthrates are much higher than those of each of the five countries at every age, by a considerable margin (England and Wales, France, Canada, Sweden, and the Netherlands). The contrast is particularly striking for younger teenagers. In fact the maximum relative difference in the birthrate between the United States and other countries occurs at ages under 15. With more than five births per 1,000 girls aged 14, the U.S. rate is around four times that of Canada, the only other country with as much as one birth per 1,000 girls of comparable age."

2. Helen J. Raschke, "Divorce," In *Handbook of Marriage and the Family*, Marvin B. Sussman and Suzanne K. Steinmetz, eds. (New York: Plenum Press, 1987), 598.

3. Sigmund Freud, *The Future of an Illusion* (Garden City, N.Y.: Doubleday, 1964), 49.

4. John F. Crosby, "A Critique of Divorce Statistics and Their Interpretation," *Family Relations* 29 (1980): 51–58.

5. William J. Goode, *The Family* (Englewood Cliffs, N.J.: Prentice-Hall, 1982), 193–195.

6. *Ibid.*

7. *The Random House Dictionary of the English Language, College Edition.*

8. I Cor. 7: 1–9

9. Morton Hunt, *The Natural History of Love* (New York: Alfred A. Knopf, 1959).

10. Matt. 5: 31–32.

11. Andreas Capellanus, *The Art of Courtly Love*, Abridged and edited by Frederick W. Locke (New York: Columbia University Press, 1941). Copyright 1941, Columbia University Press. Quotation reprinted by permission.

12. Carol Gilligan, *In a Different Voice* (Cambridge, Mass.: Harvard University Press, 1982), 159–166.

13. Erik Erikson, *Childhood and Society* (New York: W. W. Norton, 1950).

14. Carl Williams, "Conflict: Modeling or Taking Flight," In *Choice and Challenge*, Carl E. Williams and John F. Crosby, eds. (Dubuque, Iowa: William C. Brown, 1974).

15. Michael St. Clair, *Object Relations and Self Psychology* (Monterey, Calif.: Brooks/Cole, 1986).

16. Michael Green, *Theories of Human Development* (Englewood Cliffs, N.J.: Prentice-Hall, 1989).

17. Irene Goldenberg and Herb Goldenberg, *Family Therapy: An Overview* (Monterey, Calif.: Brooks/Cole, 1980), 165.

The Heart of the Matter:

Marital Expectations and Need Fulfillment

Immature love says: "I love you because I need you."
Mature love says: "I need you because I love you."

ERICH FROMM,
THE ART OF LOVING

JEAN AND CARL

Before Marriage

JEAN: Since you are asking what I expect of Carl and our marriage I want to say that I don't really think Carl and I have many expectations of each other. We believe that loving each other deeply enough is the most important thing.

THERAPIST: Yes, Jean, but what exactly does this mean to you? For example do you expect Carl ever to be angry at you?

JEAN: Oh, I suppose so, but he'd better have a good reason. I don't think people who love each other need to get angry. If you really love each other there won't be any problems that can't be worked out!

THERAPIST: What might those problems be?

JEAN: He expects the same things I do. He expects me to do my share and to be a good wife.

THERAPIST: Jean, I'm wondering how you will feel if Carl doesn't pay enough attention to you or behave the way you expect him to behave.

JEAN: Carl has never disappointed me! He has always been set on his career, and he'll be earning a good income. We've decided to go ahead now and buy a big house so we'll be ready when we have children.

THERAPIST: Children?

JEAN: Yes, we want at least three children. Carl will make such a fine father. I really want a close family. Children need to be close to their father, not just to their mother.

THERAPIST: How much time will Carl have for you and the children if he is concentrating on his professional responsibilities?

JEAN: Oh that's no problem. Carl will always find the time. He'd better! I need him.

THERAPIST: What about you Carl? What do you expect of Jean?

CARL: Well, not much really. I guess I expect her to be a good wife.

THERAPIST: What does that mean?

CARL: Well, you know, take care of me and the kids, keep house, be my strong right arm—that sort of thing!

38

THERAPIST: What if the kids demand so much of her time that there's little left for you?

CARL: That won't happen! You see, I love kids, and I'll support Jean and help her in any way I can.

THERAPIST: What do you expect of Jean sexually?

CARL: Well, I'm always turned on to her. That's no problem. I think she is too. I've always believed that good sex is the ticket to a good marriage.

THERAPIST: I'm wondering how you will react when Jean seems too tired and really fed up with the demands of the children and . . .

CARL: (interrupting) Oh that's no problem. I'll help her. She knows how I feel about helping each other out. We've agreed that we will always have time for each other.

Six Years Later

JEAN: Carl expects me to keep the house clean, do all the cooking, manage the money, and be a good mother who never yells at the kids. I'm supposed to have dinner ready on time and the kids bathed and in bed by 8:00. What does he do? He has friends at work. He pals around with them and makes passes at the secretaries. He's always flirting.

CARL: I need lots of people and lots of different experiences in order to be happy. Jean says I'm supposed to meet her social needs and her intimacy needs, and on top of that she says we're supposed to be each other's best friend! Hell, I can't do it! Look, I'm out there every day busting my butt trying to get ahead. I have to be friends with everybody. As a matter of fact I have lots of needs that Jean just doesn't take care of. I've been faithful to Jean even though our sex life is practically nonexistent.

Jean and Carl's situation reflects a number of factors: their premarital romanticized concept of love with its magical staying power; Jean's blindness regarding her expectations of Carl and marriage in general; the sex-role division of labor along traditional lines and Jean's feeling that she is getting the worst of the bargain; the implicit demands that each is supposed to fill all the needs of the other, without any other sources of input; Jean's implicit assumption that individual identity is unimportant, and that the only important thing is couple identity; and Carl's implicit threat about his being faithful in spite of his perception of their poor sex life.

Carl and Jean are fairly typical of couples who marry with such romanticized expectations that they are unable to deal with day-in and day-out functioning. These people have a way of denying their expectations of one another. They do this by coloring over such mundane expectations with global statements about how much they love each other. They believe that because they love each other the fulfillment of their own needs will just happen!

Most people expect their partner to meet their basic needs, but few people actually make a list of these needs and the resulting expectations that arise from the needs. Consequently there is frustration and disillusionment when these needs are not met by one's partner.

Needs and Expectations

People generally expect marriage to satisfy most of their basic needs. They expect their partners to meet their physical needs, emotional needs, romantic needs, communication needs, economic needs, social needs, and sexual needs. As noted earlier, few societies expect as much from the marriage relationship as our society does.

We are socialized in ways that create marital expectations that are not consistent with a realistic assessment of marriage. Our society places marriage on a pedestal. Yet we learn that divorce is something that happens only to other people! Our society idolizes sex and yet refuses to educate for human sexuality; our society glorifies romance and yet insists that romance is only acceptable for the young and immature.

We learn roles from the time we are infants. During the first years of our lives, we internalize the teachings and examples of our parents and other role models. We build up an **ego ideal**, an idealized image of ourselves that is indicative of the way we would like to be. With this fantasized ego ideal we also create a mate ideal; that is, we form expectations of our idealized future spouse. As we grow through late childhood and into early adolescence the peer group becomes increasingly powerful and influential in our identity formation, and we internalize the values of the group. With the mass media pouring millions into teen advertising and with the frenzied devotion to musical heroes and heroines, young persons absorb the messages of the teen culture. Unfortunately these teen messages increase the romanticization of love and decrease the likelihood of a rational approach to marital expectations.

The focus of this chapter is the dilemma in which we put ourselves when we fail to recognize and identify the expectations we have of our partners. Most people are aware of only a small proportion of their total expectations. The result is that we put our partners into a no-win situation by expecting them to meet needs that we are not aware of and have not openly discussed. Expectations usually arise out of what we perceive as our inner needs. We all have needs that must be met one way or another—by the self, by the mate, by others, or by various interests and pursuits.

Before we delve into a more thorough discussion of needs and expectations, let us examine the one thing that almost every human being seems to want more than anything else in life—happiness.

Happiness and Pleasure

Young people frequently maintain that their chief goal in marriage is happiness. Happiness is the great god of married life. The expectation and hope of happiness is the greatest and highest of all expectations.

Of course! Why not? Everybody wants to be happy. The advertising industry knows this quite well. Happiness is a trip to Hawaii. Happiness is a Caribbean cruise. Happiness is a bottle of this or a drink of that. Happiness may be a new car, a new snowmobile, a new garden tractor, a new husband, a new wife, or a new sex partner. Most Americans are restless most of the time. We all have a certain amount of free-floating anxiety that can seize on the attraction of the moment. "I would be happy if only I had that," we say to ourselves. On a more rational level, even though most of us know that new things or objects or people cannot make us happy, we still display vulnerability to the seductive advertising of Madison Avenue. The reason for this vulnerability is in our inner restlessness, which tells us there must be more to life than what we are presently experiencing.

Unfortunately, it is easy to define marital happiness as "your meeting my expectations." This tends to reduce the partner to the status of an automaton who exists for the sole purpose of meeting my expectations and thus making me happy. "Be what I want you to be. Do what I want you to do. Don't be you. Be only for me. Never mind your needs or your expectations. You exist to meet my needs and to fulfill my expectations. In short, *you will make me happy.*"

A PHILOSOPHICAL CAVEAT: HAPPINESS VERSUS PLEASURE

Aristotle identified happiness as a state of self-fulfillment. W. T. Jones, summarizing Aristotle's thoughts about happiness, wrote:

> Pleasure is the name we give to immediate satisfaction, which is all that is open to the animal. Happiness is the name for that longer range, more complete satisfaction which reason gives us the possibility of achieving. . . . [T]he possibility of more ignominious failure than any animal has experienced is the risk the rational soul must run for the possibility of a much greater fulfillment. . . . Happiness, then, is what we experience when we are virtuous, that is, when we are living at our best and fullest, when we are functioning in accordance with our nature, when our end is realizing itself without impediment, when our form is becoming actual. [1]

There is little doubt that happiness is a function of more than satisfaction of needs. Happiness is an inner state wherein we attempt to fulfill our potential as human beings. Happiness has to do with a realization or actualization of ourselves. **Self-actualization** requires emotional freedom and autonomy, which in turn provide breathing space for the human psyche. Without space and freedom to evolve, the psyche becomes stymied, constricted, blocked, and shut in on itself, depriving the individual of the basic ingredients of self-expression. Under this condition the human psyche easily becomes oppressed and/or depressed, and the resulting human feeling is one of pervasive unhappiness.

Pleasure is an entirely different experience than happiness, although few people are aware of the distinction between the two. There is a conceptual and theoretical difference between happiness and pleasure. Happiness is the end result of an inner state of being, wherein the psyche is free to pursue its own expression. Pleasure is a fleeting emotional feeling. Experiences that bring a sense of enjoyment are considered to be pleasurable. Such experiences include eating, dancing, spectator and participant sports, listening to and performing music, and sexual expression. A pleasurable experience, by its very definition, is relatively short-lived.

Let us ponder the difference between happiness and pleasure. Can a happy person experience tragedy and grief yet remain an essentially happy person? Can an unhappy person have pleasurable experiences yet remain an essentially unhappy person? The answer is yes, in both cases. Many happy people experience tragedy and sorrow, grief and pain, yet this does not change them into unhappy people. Happiness is an inner core state of being that has been in the formative process of creation over a period of many years. This is why an unhappy person can enjoy having a good time and become caught up in the fun-filled quest for pleasure and yet, at heart, remain essentially an unhappy person. Increased amounts of pleasure will not make an unhappy person into a happy person any more than grief, pain, sadness, and sorrow will transform a happy person into an unhappy person.

Figure 2-1 shows happiness-unhappiness on a horizontal continuum and pleasure-sorrow on a vertical continuum. On each continuum there is room for a wide range of possibilities between the two polarities. The happiness-unhappiness continuum represents a state of being that is more or less constant—an ongoing state subject to mild mood fluctuations yet relatively constant. The pleasure-sorrow line represents a different quality of feeling based on periodic or fleeting experiences. The very nature of a pleasurable or fun experience is that it waxes and wanes, comes and goes. Sorrow and sadness, even boredom, usually come and go. Pleasurable experiences are not usually thought of as permanent and ongoing emotional states.

Happiness is more directly related to personality and to our interpsychic and intrapsychic makeup than is pleasure. Our peer group and our culture are likely to assume that fun-filled people who are having a good time are happy

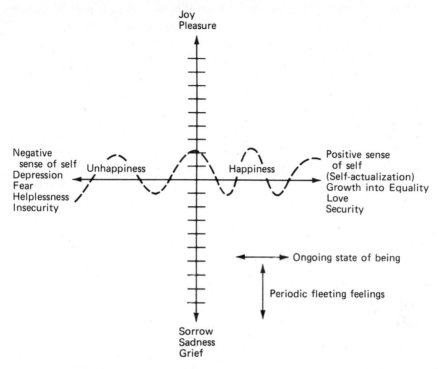

Figure 2-1 The Ongoing State of Happiness versus Periodic Fleeting Feelings

people. Likewise, people seem to assume that a happy person is one who is never sad or sorrowful.

TOM

Tom is an unhappy person. He seems to be in a perpetual state of "downness," and he appears to be restrained and constrained in his interpersonal relationships. Last weekend Tom had a wonderful time at a fraternity party. He drank quite a bit and became the center of attention as he told numerous jokes and stories. Everyone who knew Tom expressed delight that Tom seemed to be having such a good time and that he appeared to be so happy. Yet on Monday morning "good old Tom" was back to his old self again, looking bored and forlorn.

CONNIE

Connie is perceived to be a happy person. She seems to have a free spirit and to be autonomous, marching to her own tune and giving the appearance of "having things together." A few months ago Connie's younger brother was killed in an automobile accident, and since then Connie has been more subdued and withdrawn. Several people remarked that she seemed unhappy. Those who know her well say that she is going through a period of profound sorrow and grief. Connie herself speaks openly of her loss and her need to grieve. She says she feels she is coming along well and that before long she will be her old self again, although perhaps wiser and more insightful.

MARRIAGE WILL NOT TRANSFORM AN UNHAPPY PERSON INTO A HAPPY PERSON

The purpose of our philosophical caveat about the difference between happiness and pleasure was to drive home the point that no one can make an unhappy person happy. Further, marriage cannot make an unhappy person happy. Krich and Blum have said:

> Marriage will not make an unhappy person happy. Marriage is the relationship that most adults find conducive to attaining satisfaction from life, but marriage in itself does not create happiness. . . . Marriage can add to one's feeling of self-worth if one enters it feeling worth loving in the first place. But the love of a husband or wife cannot make up for the love one failed to get as a child. Countless people approach marriage counseling complaining of the inadequacy of their spouse's love, when actually no amount of love would be enough to make them feel good about themselves.[2]

By now the reader is probably protesting, "But shouldn't people be happy in marriage?" Our answer is an emphatic YES! It is one thing to expect to experience a shared state of happiness as two people travel the path of life together, loving each other and giving of themselves in the nurturance of this love. However, it is quite another thing to marry someone expecting him or her to "make me happy."

If a person is essentially happy, he or she will not seek a marital partner to make up for a love deficit. The needs that one partner expects the other partner to fulfill will be reasonable. They will be needs that are rational, stemming or arising from the present, not the past. Among these needs are sharing, communication, friendship, erotic love, and nonerotic love. The expectation that a mate will meet the major portion of each of these needs is legitimate because these are ongoing *being* needs—needs that arise in the present rather than out of deficits accumulated in the past.

Almost all needs are perceived as real or genuine. In this sense all needs are legitimate, even such needs as the need to be immature, pampered, or constantly reassured. Two things determine whether or not a need is legitimate or illegitimate. An illegitimate need (1) always arises from a developmental deficit and (2) thrusts the responsibility for meeting the need on someone else—a partner, parent, friend, lover, or child. If a person has never felt the security of being loved and does *not* attempt to shift the responsibility for meeting this need onto anyone else, then we would not call this an illegitimate need. However, if the responsibility for meeting this need is pressed on friend, parent, mate, lover, or child, then the need is illegitimate. People who ask for or demand constant reassurance that they are loved frequently are expressing a love deficit. The need itself may appear to be illegitimate, but it is the *expectation* that another person will fill this deficit that causes us to label the need as illegitimate. Throughout the remainder of this book a legitimate expectation of need fulfillment is a **legitimate ego need,** and an illegitimate expectation of need fulfillment is an **illegitimate ego need.** We should note here that it is legitimate to expect one's mate to meet our ongoing needs such as the need for love, reassurance, affection, and friendship. Needs that do not arise out of a developmental deficit cannot, by definition, be considered illegitimate. However, this does not mean that all nondeficit expectations are good or acceptable. As we have seen, many of our expectations are quite outlandish and ridiculous and virtually impossible to fulfill.

Deficit Need as a Framework for Looking at Expectations

Illegitimate ego needs arise primarily from a *perceived* love deficit. The deficit may be of three types: (1) a perceived or actual lack of love; (2) a parental smothering or overindulgence, including doting and pampering; and (3) a lack of ability to cope with the loss of authentic and mature parental love. All three types create a perceived love deficit and may lead to dependency and/or co-dependency.

PERCEIVED OR ACTUAL LACK OF LOVE

A deficit arising from a perceived or an actual lack of parental love leads to feelings of rejection and abandonment. A deficit arising from a perception that "I was not loved" leads to deep feelings of insecurity and rejection. Whether or not the deficit was actually real or only perceived as real makes little difference because of our tendency to base reality on what we perceive to be true or accurate.

PARENTAL SMOTHERING AND OVERINDULGENCE

A deficit arising from smothering, overindulgence, pampering, and doting is often extremely difficult to deal with. The child simply does not have the freedom to experience his or her own potency to cope with life's problems and exigencies. The child is deprived of the opportunity to fend for himself or herself. Without this opportunity the child is unable to build up a repertoire of positive experiences in dealing with everyday frustrations and problems. The child becomes a teenager or an adult lacking personal coping skills, chiefly the skill to accept oneself and to love oneself, which is critical in creating positive self-esteem, self-confidence, and self-reliance. The child was so dependent on the early parental overindulgence that he or she becomes ill equipped to grow into autonomy and self-sufficiency.

LACK OF ABILITY TO COPE WITH THE LOSS OF PARENTAL LOVE

Illegitimate ego needs may also arise after detachment from a source of love and reassurance. Accordingly, the child, teenager, or young adult fails to learn how to love himself or herself sufficiently. The child becomes emotionally dependent on the love and reassurance of the parents. It isn't that the child receives too much love but rather that the child is unable to break away from a dependence on the source of this love. Consequently, there is an attempt to replace parental love with partner love.[3]

No one can receive too much genuine and authentic love (as opposed to a suffocating and smothering superindulgence). Too much love, contrary to popular belief, does not create a spoiled child. Overindulgence and smothering lead to the spoiled syndrome.[4,5] The source of this third type of deficit love is the child's or teenager's inability to internalize the love and thereby learn to love himself or herself. Such a child simply is unable to deal with the loss arising from detachment from parents. Hence, although there is no real love deficit, there is a *perceived* love deficit, and this perception creates the feelings associated with insecurity.

Looking to One's Partner for Parenting

Illegitimate ego needs arise primarily from the insecurity of not feeling loved in early childhood, late childhood, and adolescence. The experience of being in love is often an emotional response to someone who is perceived as capable of meeting unmet or partially met needs that one has brought from earlier development to adulthood. When this happens, "I love you because I need you" accurately describes the condition of illegitimate need expectation.

What happens when a person loves out of need? For a while things may go well, but a spouse who is relatively stable and secure will eventually tire of being leaned on. One day the "needy" individual who loves because of need will perceive that he or she no longer loves the spouse and will wonder why. "I am falling out of love. My love has died." In reality, the stable, secure spouse has slowly tired of treating the dependent one as a child and of being leaned on. The secure one no longer chooses to play the parent substitute. Consequently, the needy one interprets the pulling away of the stable one as "he/she doesn't love me anymore, therefore I don't love him/her anymore either!"

When we become too dependent on the supportive love of parents we can easily fall into the pattern of expecting others to continue their supportive love. We then expect others to make us feel loved, important, and happy. We depend on people and things to make us happy, to give us love, and to make us feel good about ourselves. When this happens it is only a short step from expecting to demanding.

As one reviewer of an earlier edition of this book suggested, "We are truly a culture of dissatisfied consumers of each other." We learn to look to others to do for us what we have failed to do for ourselves. We often carry this type of consumerism into marriage. The quest for love, self-esteem, and happiness is my problem and my challenge, not yours. These are attainable only through my own growth and development. As long as I expect these from you, I will continue in my dependence on you. I will continue to need you to make me happy. And if you don't make me happy it obviously means that you don't love me anymore.

RON AND JUDY

Ron and Judy have been married for 7 years. Judy has had an increasing awareness that she is not happy, and she and Ron have an appointment with a marriage therapist.

JUDY: I feel sort of . . . well, sort of blah most of the time. It's to the point where I feel happy only when we go somewhere special, like to a party. Sometimes I go shopping just because it makes me feel better. Ron used to make me happy, but now he seems to be a drag. I love him, but we just don't seem to have any spark left in our marriage. He keeps telling me that I need to get out of myself more—and I'd like to but I don't know how. If only we had more money, then we could do more things together and enjoy life a little. I've thought of getting a job—and I might just as soon as Suzie reaches first grade. Then both children will be in school and I'll have more freedom. Maybe then I'll be happy. Ha! . . . (long pause) . . . I really feel it's Ron's fault. We both agreed when we got married that the most important thing we wanted was happiness. That's a laugh!

RON: I don't know what it is with her, but lately I feel totally frustrated. She seems depressed, low—and she's always expecting me to pull her up. We've spent money like crazy: buy this, buy that, go here, go there. Yet nothing seems to make her happy. We have sex about twice a week. I enjoy it and she says she does, but then she's still miserable. I suppose I should have been more encouraging when she mentioned she would like to get a job. I'm not against it, although I admit I'm not crazy about the idea.

It's starting to get me down. I've thought about divorce and of having relationships with other women. But I know that would only make things worse. I guess I'm worn down too! I keep feeling guilty because I can't make her happy. There are times I just have to push all my feelings into the back of my mind. I wonder if I even love her anymore.

Ron and Judy cannot be fully understood on the basis of such short statements, but for our purpose it is sufficient to point out the probability that Judy's unhappiness (restlessness, depression) is not the direct result of Ron's attitude or behavior. Judy's problem lies more within Judy and quite likely is the result of various patterns that kept being replayed in her growing-up years within her family of origin. Judy believes she would feel better if only Ron would make her happy, but it is not within Ron's power to make her happy. Nor is it within Ron's power to fulfill another person's lack of fulfillment. It is within Ron's power to become more supportive of Judy in general and in particular to encourage her to find a job outside the home. It is also within Ron's power to become as informed as possible about Judy's feelings and to be as supportive as possible of her efforts to work through her depression.

Judy may be a very gifted woman who is trying to find her fulfillment through her husband rather than through her own career efforts. If this is the case, Judy's lack of adjustment to the wife-mother pattern may, in fact, be a sign of emotional health. In other words, Judy's depressed feelings may be the result of interaction with Ron, especially if she perceives that Ron is against her working outside the home. When this is combined with messages that Judy received from her mother about "a woman's place is in the home," it is not difficult to see the logical development of Judy's depression. Nevertheless, Judy appears to me to be an emotionally dependent person who expects her husband to make her happy. This expectation is illegitimate! Somewhere along the line, whether it was due to the modeling of her mother who was very submissive to her father, to Judy's inability to differentiate adequately from her parents, or to a whole host of combinations of other logical reasons, the end result is that Judy has not learned how to depend on herself as her own major and primary source of happiness.

Dependency and Co-Dependency

If both partners enter a relationship with an "I love you because I need you" orientation, there is a symbiotic or mutual **dependency**. *Symbiosis* is a biological term referring to two organisms that are mutually dependent on each other in some way. Each needs the other in order to maintain itself. When two lovers and/or marital partners are unable to function independently in a truly self-fulfilling or mature manner, they may be said to be mutually dependent or symbiotic. Symbiosis and mutual dependency are not to be confused with interdependency. **Interdependency** is a positive mutuality wherein there is a hand-in-glove cooperation and complementarity between the couple. A symbiotic relationship is built around a mutual meeting of one another's illegitimate needs, whereas interdependence is based on the shared responsibility of meeting one another's legitimate needs.

Co-dependency is a term that has become widely used in recent years. A co-dependent person is one who is unable to define his or her own identity apart from a relationship with someone else. The term *co-dependency* was originally reserved for partners of alcoholics, partners of drug-addicted persons, partners of sexually addicted persons, and partners of any person who was the perpetrator of any kind of abusive behavior *when that partner went along with the patterns and modus operandi of the abuser*. The co-dependent person is usually an *enabler* who makes it possible for the perpetrator to continue in the familiar pattern of abuse, whether substance abuse or person abuse. Today the term *co-dependent* is used rather loosely, and its particular meaning has become similar to dependency, especially emotional dependency of any description.

Mutual dependency, symbiosis, and co-dependent marriage relationships frequently endure. If both partners experience enough satisfaction in meeting the illegitimate needs of the other and in turn receive gratification of their own illegitimate needs, they may have a basis for an enduring relationship, however immature and dependent it may be.[6] However, there is no such thing as a half symbiosis. If only one partner leans on the other or is emotionally dependent on the other, theirs is *not* a symbiotic relationship. If only one partner is emotionally dependent there is no symbiosis and no co-dependency. Under all three conditions—symbiosis, dependency, and co-dependency—the chances for survival of the marriage are slim. If the marriage endures it is extremely unlikely to be a happy union.

The Neurotic Need for Affection

Karen Horney has contributed to our understanding of legitimate and illegitimate ego needs by reviewing the characteristics and attributes of a legitimate need for affection and an illegitimate need for affection. (I use the word *illegitimate*, whereas Horney uses the word *neurotic*.)

> Although it is very difficult to say what is love, we can say definitely what is not love, or what elements are alien to it. One may be thoroughly fond of a person, and yet at times be angry with him, deny him certain wishes or want to be left alone. But there is a difference between such circumscribed reactions of wrath or withdrawal and the attitude of a neurotic, who is constantly on guard against others, feels that any interest they take in third persons is a neglect of himself, and interprets any demand as an imposition or any criticism as a humiliation. This is not love. . . . Of course we want something from the person we are fond of—We want gratification, loyalty, help; we may even want a sacrifice, if necessary. And it is in general an indication of mental health to be able to express such wishes or even fight for them. The difference between love and the neurotic need for affection lies in the fact that in love the feeling of affection is primary, whereas in the case of the neurotic the primary feeling is the need for reassurance, and the illusion of loving is only secondary. Of course there are all sorts of intermediate conditions.

> If a person needs another's affection for the sake of reassurance against anxiety, the issue will usually be completely blurred in his conscious mind . . . all that he feels is that here is a person whom he likes or trusts, or with whom he feels infatuated. But what he feels as spontaneous love may be nothing but a response of gratitude for some kindness shown him or a response of hope or affection aroused by some person or situation. The person who explicitly or implicitly arouses in him expectations of this kind will automatically be invested with importance, and *this feeling will manifest itself in the illusion of love*. . . . Such expectations . . . may be aroused by erotic or sexual advances, although these may have nothing to do with love.[7] (Italics added for emphasis.)

The truth is that most of us have a mixture of legitimate and illegitimate needs. Some of us have much more of one than of the other. It is a matter of degree. In general, the fewer illegitimate needs we have the greater the likelihood of maintaining a satisfactory and fulfilling marriage relationship. (See Figure 2-2 for representations of various mixtures.)

Deficiency Needs and Being Needs

Abraham Maslow offers us another way of looking at legitimate and illegitimate needs. His concept of deficiency needs, called "D needs," and being needs, called "B needs," is similar to the distinction between legitimate and illegitimate ego needs. Maslow outlines four deficiency needs that are prepotent in nature—that is, they are basic needs that must be met before a person seeks

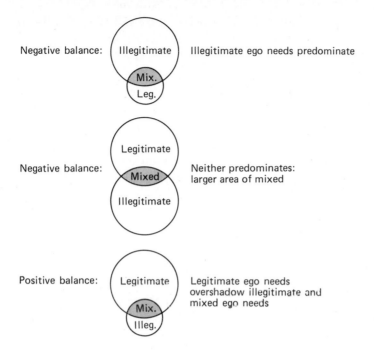

Negative balance: Illegitimate ego needs predominate

Negative balance: Neither predominates: larger area of mixed

Positive balance: Legitimate ego needs overshadow illegitimate and mixed ego needs

Figure 2-2 The Degree of Mixture of Legitimate and Illegitimate Ego Needs

fulfillment of less basic needs.[8] The higher or more elementary the need, the stronger its power, force, or influence in motivating the individual to action. According to Maslow, the hierarchy of D needs is (1) physical needs such as food, drink, sleep, warmth; (2) needs for psychological and physical safety; (3) the need to be loved or the need for love; and (4) the need for esteem, both self-esteem and the esteem of others. A person may be functioning fairly well in meeting all of these D needs, but if this person suddenly were to be cast adrift in a lifeboat in the Pacific ocean the person would quickly regress to prepotent physical and safety needs.

Each D need must receive some degree of satisfaction before a person can move up the ladder to the next need. Any level may collapse at any time because of specific circumstances and crises. Although all D needs arise from a deficit, in our terminology these D needs are illegitimate only if responsibility for their fulfillment is transferred or shifted to another person. Unfortunately the person to whom most of this responsibility is shifted is the spouse.

Deficiency Love and Being Love

Love can become confused with the partner's capacity to meet both legitimate and illegitimate ego needs. When an individual is able to unlearn illegitimate ego needs (a slow and sometimes painful process), he or she is free to express genuine love, which in its Maslow frame of reference we call B love or "being love." This same person is also better able to receive love from his or her mate. This love is interpreted as authentic B love rather than D love, which operates out of a deficit (that is, "Please love me because I never felt loved"). When we no longer function out of a love deficit or out of dependency, we discover that we do not need excessive amounts of authentic B love. It is only when we function out of the deficiency position that we fail to become sated and satisfied.

Illegitimate ego need fulfillment can give a person such a strong illusion of security, however temporary, that he or she mistakenly perceives the fulfillment of needs as genuine love. When this happens, the person is experiencing D love or "deficiency love," which is really a type of gratitude. The gratitude transforms into and is covered over by the feeling of love: "I am grateful that you fill my needs" is covered over by "I feel I am in love with you."

D love contributes to disillusionment in marriage because it is born of illegitimate expectations. The D lover lacks a strong sense of emotional security, and so his or her identity is excessively dependent on the partner's ability to provide constant support and reassurance of love. Emotional dependency masquerades under the guise of romantic love. Because it feels so good and so validating to be loved, one can very easily slip into the comforting and exciting feeling of "being in love." Or, because it can feel so good and so like being loved or indulged by mother or father, one can quickly develop the feeling of "being in love." This feeling continues as long as the partner keeps an abundance of love messages and communications flowing in sufficient amount to continue to make the person with a love deficit feel loved. However successful this is in the short run, the long-run prognosis is dismal because no human being can make up for the love one failed to get, or perceived that one failed to get, through the growing-up years.

When the partner who is attempting to fill the other's deficit begins to wear out and tire of the task, he or she will slowly realize the impossibility of making up the love deficit of the other person. He or she will come to realize that the partner is emotionally dependent and that the dependent partner will continue to expect and even demand the fulfillment of all the unmet sustenance and emotional gratification needs stemming from his or her childhood and youth. Slowly the giving person will begin to question his or her own love. The receiving person with the love deficit will become hurt and perhaps angry when the giver no longer delivers. Eventually, as this hurt becomes more painful and extends over a long period of time, it will turn into a deep and bitter anger. Finally, the inevitable conclusion is reached: "You don't love me anymore! You don't meet my needs. Therefore I no longer love you!"

The main point is that the love-deprived person very likely interpreted his or her response to the partner's original love stroking as reciprocal love, whereas a more accurate label for the experience of having one's D love needs met is gratitude, not love. As a general maxim we may say that whenever a person with a love deficit experiences what we generally label as "being in love," it is likely that in reality it is a closely allied emotional state of "being in gratitude." Karen Horney calls this the illusion of love.

William Glasser has pointed out that whenever we look to others to do for us what we ought to be doing for ourselves, we are, in effect, shifting responsibility for ourselves onto the other person.[9] The individual who can identify, label, and accept his or her own deficiency needs and becomes aware of the ploys, methods, and strategies he or she uses to get others to meet these illegitimate needs is now in a position to begin to break out of this destructive pattern. At this point there is no further reason to continue to play the game of shifting responsibility to others, a game that Eric Berne and Thomas Harris have described as "Look what you made me do" or "Look what you did to me."[10]

When an individual shifts responsibility from himself or herself to his or her partner, the partner is made to feel responsible for whatever it is that is happening or has happened to the individual. In essence, the individual is saying, "You are responsible for me." "You are responsible for my well-being, for my happiness, for my feelings of self-worth and self-esteem, and for my feelings of joy and pleasure." Basically it is a statement that "my life is your responsibility, and if you let me down it means that you do not love me."

Two related games or maneuvers that were mentioned earlier are "Be what I want you to be! Do what I want you to do!" These two games are the two most frequently used implicit demands made in marriage. They are implicit because they are not usually verbalized until there is conflict. Rather, they lurk behind the scenes waiting to be decoded from the conflict-laden dialogue.

HUSBAND: This house is a mess! (TRANSLATED: I expect you to keep the house neat and clean.)

WIFE: I'm too busy to clean and pick up everyday. I have my job all day and you expect me to do everything around here! (TRANSLATED: You're not being fair!)

HUSBAND: You know how I feel about your working! Nothing gets done around here anymore. (TRANSLATED: I expect you to do the wifely things: keep house, cook, do the laundry and marketing, and be a real mother to the kids.)

WIFE: All you care about is how comfortable your little world is. It doesn't matter to you about my feelings, my thoughts, my career! (TRANSLATED: You're selfish. The only thing you care about is you.)

HUSBAND: You should be contented and satisfied being a housewife and mother! (TRANSLATED: You should be what I want you to be—a wife and a mother, not some woman trying to compete in a man's world.)

WIFE: Who died and made you king? (TRANSLATED: Who do you think you are telling me how to live my life?)

HUSBAND: I thought I married a person who wanted to be my wife and the mother of my children. (TRANSLATED: You aren't being what I want you to be. You're not doing what I want you to do.)

This exchange will likely keep going for years. The underlying issues include the entire range of dual employment problems and challenges together with the husband's traditional view of the wife-mother role. There is much resentment on the part of both, since neither is living up to the expectations of the other. However, it is the husband who is playing the game of shifting responsibility and therefore blaming the wife for her failure to live up to his idea of what makes a good wife and mother.

The antidote to deficiency love and the shifting of responsibility onto one's mate for one's own well-being can be illustrated by picturing a glass that is about one-third full. The question is, Who in this world can fill your glass? The fact that your glass is only one-third full represents the perceived deficit. The deficit is a love deficit, an emotional security deficit, a self-esteem and self-confidence deficit. Your mate cannot fill it for you, or at least not for very long. Your parents have not filled it for you. Your children will not fill it for you. Your friends will get tired of trying to fill it for you. Who is left to make up your deficit? Who is left to fill your glass? The answer is obvious and perhaps painful! *You are the only person in this whole world who can fill your own glass and make up for your own deficit.*

Dependence—Independence—Interdependence

Marriages and other intimate relationships based on D love usually involve excessive dependency or symbiosis. This is referred to as an A-frame relationship (Figure 2-3). Each partner has a weakened self-identity; the relationship has a strong couple identity. Removal of either partner (by divorce, death, or prolonged absence) deprives the other partner of support. When this happens the remaining partner often feels totally unable to face life alone. Sometimes the remaining partner chooses to resign from life, either by crawling into a protected environment or by attempting to check out for good by killing himself or herself.

Many people express a strong desire for H-frame relationships (Figure 2-3). Each partner has a strong self-identity, and each partner disclaims any deep need for the other. The H-frame couple want mutuality but not depen-

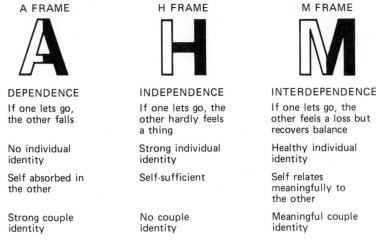

Figure 2-3 Dependence—Independence—Interdependence

dence. They want total individual autonomy with no claims on oneself by the other. There is no wish for couple identity.

A third type of relationship, the M-frame relationship, is a modification of the A-frame and H-frame relationships (Figure 2-3). The emphasis is on a strong individual identity for each of the partners as in the H-frame. There is also an equally strong emphasis on couple identity as in the A-frame. (Individual identity is not sacrificed at the cost of couple identity, and couple identity is not sacrificed at the cost of individual identity.) There is a strong commitment to the individual identity of each partner (autonomy) and also a strong commitment to the identity of the partners as a dyad or couple. Similarly, a meaningful intimate dyadic relationship requires a commitment to the other in addition to the self. The M-frame combines the best qualities of both the A-frame and the H-frame into a relationship characterized by individual identity and a meaningful measure of couple identity. The M-frame does not foster so much couple dependence that one partner would collapse if the other were to leave the relationship or die. In the M-frame the partners are committed to making an honest effort to meet the ongoing legitimate (being) needs but not the deficit-based illegitimate (deficiency) needs of the mate.

Under the M-frame model there is adequate room for closeness and distance, approach and withdrawal, intimacy and autonomy, togetherness and separateness, dependence and independence. This truly is the meaning of *interdependence*.

The primary theme of this chapter has been marital expectations. A deficit model of need fulfillment has been presented with an emphasis on legitimate and illegitimate ego needs. In addition to the deficit framework there are four additional frameworks that help explain why our expectations play such a pivotal role in determining our degree of relationship satisfaction and marital happiness. These frameworks are (1) exchange, (2) symbolic-interaction, (3) object relations, and (4) systems. Our purpose is to review the highlights of these frameworks and to attempt to show how each relates and contributes to a person's perception of relationship satisfaction and marital happiness.

Exchange as a Framework for Looking at Expectations

Exchange theory is based on obtaining the most goods or services for the least amount of output, cost, or effort. In terms of marriage it is based on the quid pro quo, something for something.

Romanticists generally do not like the idea of exchange because it smacks of being too commercial and too matter-of-fact and businesslike. After all, we are told that in marriage one is not to give and take on a 50–50 basis, but rather one is to give 100%. We are told that if everybody gave 100% there would be no problems in marriage.

Whether or not relationships form in the first place, regardless of how long they last, is a function of exchange in that potential rewards and costs are immediately estimated. Choices will almost always be made based on one's own estimate of one's ability to draw a good or fair bargain. If the cost outweighs the perceived reward, the endeavor will likely be abandoned. If the rewards are perceived to outweigh the perceived costs, the endeavor will likely be pursued. In this regard the principles of exchange are a factor in mate selection theory.

Once a couple is married, the exchange may take on a different appearance than it had during dating and courtship. During dating and engagement the partners may be overly nice and perhaps too eager to please each other. This leads both of them to gain an unrealistic and idyllic picture of what life together is going to be like. It is only after the couple has settled into an everyday routine that some of the dimensions of the exchange begin to appear and premarital expectations are compared to the realities of everyday married life. The truth is that most human beings have a healthy concept of fairness and equity. People simply are not going to keep giving and giving if they do not perceive that they are getting a fair measure in return. Historically the woman seems to be willing to settle for a lesser exchange than the man. For example, if a man feels that he is getting less than a fair deal, say 45% versus his perception of giving in the amount of 55%, then he may decide that the deal is not worthwhile and opt out of the marriage. On the other hand, many women might be very pleased to receive 45% while giving 55%.

Much of the value of the exchange depends not on actual value but on perceived value. In fact, a case can be made that the actual value *is* the perceived value. This is beacause our reality is what we perceive it to be. For us this is the only reality that we know.

Exchange theory is sometimes referred to as choice and exchange or as social exchange theory. Its roots are quite ancient in that many cultures and primitive civilizations depended on principles of reciprocity both in the realm of interpersonal relations and in the area of business relations such as trade and bartering. Exchange theory is also related to resource theory in that we bargain with our available or potential resources. Resources include physical appearance, mental acuity, academic and communication skills, emotional supportiveness, personality, family status, economic status, social status, one's gender, and one's degree of power and the ability to control others. Because people attempt to maximize their rewards and minimize their costs, it is important to have a realistic grasp of what resources one possesses in order that one may further enhance one's position in the bargaining-exchange process.

Nye defines the most general proposition of exchange theory in these terms: "Humans avoid costly behavior and seek rewarding statuses, relationships, interaction, and feeling states to the end that their profits are maximized. Of course, in seeking rewards they voluntarily accept some costs; likewise in avoiding costs, some rewards are forgone, but the person, group, or organization will choose the best outcome available, based on his/her/its perception of rewards and costs."[11] A key element in exchange theory is the comparison level. A comparison level is "a standard by which the person evaluates the rewards and costs of a given relationship in terms of what he feels he deserves."[12] For example, a husband may think he deserves to have a greater control over a larger portion of the family spending. He believes this is fair and right because he has confided in a number of other husbands with whom he works (his comparison level), and they all have more say over spending matters than he does.

Exchange theory may be applied to mate selection, his or her employment, parenting, sexual relations, budgeting, stepparenting, divorce, communication, and all manner of substantive areas wherein there is some exchange between partners. For our immediate purpose, we will focus on expectations the partners have regarding each other's behavior. Exchange theory postulates that where the greatest number of expectations are fulfilled for both partners there will be the highest degree of satisfaction with the relationship. This simple proposition relates back to our discussion of romantic expectations and the unrealistic nature of many of these expectations. Indeed, an abundance of expectations that have not been discussed and mutually arrived at is bound to create friction and disillusionment. Each of the partners begins to think that the costs (that is, what he or she pays to remain in the relationship) far exceed or outweigh the rewards. Many persons have had the experience of sitting down and listing the benefits of staying in the marriage versus the benefits of getting out of the marriage, as well as the costs of staying in versus the cost of getting out. In this vein we see that exchange theory is a pragmatic and practical way of determining the future course of one's actions. Likewise, most divorced persons who intend to remarry will do so expecting a better exchange than the one they experienced in their previous marriage. Everybody feels "I deserve better." In exchange theory it is axiomatic that we will always attempt to strike the best exchange possible.

Some marriage therapy is nothing more and nothing less than partners attempting to determine for themselves what a fair comparison level is. When a therapist is asked, "Is this normal?" the person asking the question is often attempting to establish a fair norm or standard. A wife may say to a therapist: "My husband wants sex three times a day. Is this normal?" Her expectation of sexual frequency was less, and she is now attempting to determine if her expectation is in line with some norm or comparison level or if it is out of line. A husband may say to the therapist: "I know guys that get it five times a day, so don't be telling me that I'm expecting too much." He is not attempting to find a normative comparison level because he already has one and he feels he is getting gypped in comparison to his alleged friends.

CINDY AND MICHAEL

CINDY: I feel that I have given and given and given! And what do I get? I get pain, loneliness, and feelings of guilt and inadequacy. I get the silent treatment from Michael for days at a time. When I ask him something, all he can do is either grunt or sigh in disgust or make some demeaning remark.

MICHAEL: Why should I bother to do things for her? For a long time I did everything a person could do. I worked all day, came home and listened to her talk about her day, helped her with her housework, and then did all the routine outside stuff, you know, cars, lawn, repairs around the house! And what did I ever get? You'd think I was a hired hand. Then I get blamed for not talking a lot and for not being romantic. I'll tell you, it's just not worth the hassle.

CINDY: Oh come on now! I'm the one who gives! I do all the housework, laundry, and grocery shopping, not to mention the kids, the band, Little League, scouts, and car pooling. God knows what else you expect me to do! I've had it. And the only thanks I get is your complaining that I'm not hot stuff in bed. You can take this marriage and stuff it because I'm not taking your crud anymore.

In exchange terms, neither Cindy nor Michael perceives she or he is getting a fair shake. Neither lives up to the expectations of the other. Both of them believe they give a lot more than they get. Both of them indicate that their marriage is a raw deal and isn't worth the hassle. Both of them probably feel that the other has more power and is more controlling.

Symbolic Interaction as a Framework for Looking at Expectations

The **symbolic interaction** framework is based on "face to face encounters and relationships of individuals who act in awareness of one another."[13] The symbolic part is the result of our human differences in assessing the meaning and value we place on words, behavior, and the expression of emotions. Symbolic interaction is, therefore, the perception of meaning that is attributed to the behavior and communication of those with whom we relate, especially within an intimate environment. Because the meaning we attribute to another's behavior and communication is often a function of the position or role that person plays, symbolic interaction is inseparable from role theory.

Burr et al. state, "The most fundamental part of a definition of *roles* is that they are more or less *integrated sets* of social norms that are distinguishable from other sets of norms that constitute other roles. *Social norms* are beliefs or expectations that people ought or ought not to behave in certain ways."[14] Burr et al. suggest that we use the terms *role enactment, role performance,* or *role behavior* when we are referring to how people take on and carry out specific roles. Burr et al. prefer the term *role enactment.*[15] Therefore we may say that a role is an integrated set of social norms and that role enactment refers to how we enact or carry out the role.

A symbolic interaction theory of satisfaction is directly related to the central theme of this chapter, marital expectations and need fulfillment. Burr et al. state as a formal proposition: "The more important a role expectation is to a person, the greater the effect that the quality of role enactment has on that person's satisfaction." Burr et al. then comment on this proposition by saying "the idea is that people's evaluation of how satisfied they are with something is partly a function of how they view their situation relative to reference groups, comparison points, or significant others."[16] This last statement illustrates how closely a proposition of symbolic interactionism may resemble the comparison level of exchange theory.

Burr et al. also state, "The amount of consensus on relevant role expectations in a relationship influences the satisfaction with the relationship, and this is a positive relationship."[17] Here again the dominant theme is the degree of consensus or agreement on what the partners expect of each other as a married couple. Perhaps the greatest error or mistake related to marriage today is that premarital couples do not make the effort to communicate their expectations. It is easy to make the assumption that people automatically know what it means to be a husband or a wife. Our culture, our society, our church or religious fellowship, and most of all our family of origin have taught us what we are to expect. In truth, even though there often is a consensus about what a given role entails, there remains a vast difference in individual interpretation of a role and expectations related to its enactment. Again, in our failure to identify, discuss, and negotiate our differences, we set ourselves up for misunderstanding, disagreement, disappointment, hurt, anger, and pain. The end result is disillusionment.

Sometimes we read meanings into our partner's behavior that were never intended, or we may fail to read meanings that were intended. We attach importance and value to certain things such as birthdays, Christmas, special religious days, and anniversaries. When our mate places a different value on these same days or occasions we become upset, perhaps angry. In one partner's family, birthdays were a huge event, whereas in the other partner's family, birthdays were played down. In one partner's family, Mother's Day was highly celebrated, whereas in the other partner's family, it was ignored. In one partner's family, graduations were considered to be meaningless rituals, whereas in the other partner's family, a graduation, any graduation, was considered to be a big occasion. In these different attributions of meaning there is much potential for strife and conflict.

I may place great meaning on my occasional confession, "I love you." You may remind me and the children daily that you love us by constant usage of the phrase "I love you." My intention and meaning may be one thing. Yours may be another. I may believe that your use of "I love you" is so perfunctory as to be almost meaningless, whereas you may wish that I said these words to you more often.

The different meanings we may attach to family rituals, personal rituals, friendships, daily events, and gifts may be quite different. A young husband, Alan, attaches a very negative meaning to communications that purport to correct him or tell him what to do or how to behave. Hence, when Alan's wife, Kay, tells him that he needs a haircut, Alan reacts with annoyance and impatience. Yet Kay would be pleased if Alan pointed out to her that her scarf clashed with her skirt. But Alan would never do that because he attaches negative meaning to corrective statements, even if they are made with much love and care. Kay attaches positive meaning to such statements. They tell her that her husband cares about her and is interested in her appearance.

One of the most common complaints marriage therapists hear is "He will not pick up his dirty socks and underwear," or "He is sloppy and doesn't take care of his clothes." The wife may protest that if she just leaves them where he has thrown them they will just pile higher and deeper until *she* does something about it. Likewise, both partners are often heard to complain about the lack of promptness, saying she/he is always late. Some of us read meaning and purpose into punctuality, whereas others appear to attach little meaning to it. This last group, it is said, will be late to their own funeral.

Our daily life is filled with symbols, be they gestures, words, ideas, rituals, events, or specific behaviors. And with the symbol there is attached some degree of meaning, either positive, negative, neutral, or ambivalent. Children learn from adults what meanings are to be attached to certain behaviors such as mealtime and bedtime rituals and activities. Uniforms are symbols that give meaning, as are red fire engines and white and black police cruisers. Clothing is symbolic, and sometimes it is publicly and/or privately seductive, depending on the message that people receive. The message they receive is likely to be the message they were taught to receive by their parents and other early authority figures.

When these symbols are attached to the roles that people fill and the role enactment or performance that people carry out, it is easy to see that symbolic interaction is at the very heart of relations between intimates. It is virtually impossible not to invest behaviors, rituals, language, pauses, silence, gasps, and sighs with meaning. The meaning may change according to the context of the symbol. A sigh under some circumstances may mean that I am getting increasingly exasperated with you. A sigh under amorous circumstances may mean that I feel totally overcome by your presence and that I am surrendering to your advances.

For our purposes we want to emphasize that every love relationship contains both explicit and implicit sets of expectations about how the other person should or ought to behave. Each of these sets of expectations is invested with meaning. In intimate relationships much of the meaning will center on the sending and receiving of messages dealing with the impact we make on each other. Are we loved? Are we made to feel loved? Are we important? Are we made to feel important? How well the partner carries out his or her role enactment or role performance will determine to a great extent how satisfied we are with the relationship, whether we are married or not. This is especially true if we attach a significant degree of meaning to the way our partner performs his or her role.

Symbolic interaction is, at heart, a theory about the attribution of meaning. Betsy and Bruce have been going together for about 3 months. They are not dating each other exclusively, but Bruce would like the relationship to be exclusive. Bruce initiates the conversation by saying to Betsy, "I tried to phone you last night." Actually, this may be a metacommunication, a message within a message. The unspoken part of the message could be asking the question "Where were you?" Betsy may take immediate offense at Bruce's question. She may respond by saying, "Wouldn't you like to know?" Betsy was down the hall talking to her girlfriend, but she will not admit this to Bruce. Because Bruce spoke to her in a manner that Betsy interpreted as accusing and a little bit attacking, she would not give him the satisfaction of an answer. Betsy attached a specific meaning to Bruce's statement. Bruce may not have intended that meaning, but now it is no longer in Bruce's control. Betsy will place her own meaning on Bruce's question. When Betsy did not answer the phone Bruce was afraid that Betsy was out with another guy. This became a message of potential threat to Bruce. This threat is made even more powerful when Betsy replies, "Wouldn't you like to know?"

Everything we say and do is open to interpretation by someone else. When our focus is on the intimate environment of two people in love, we can begin to realize that we are constantly making some kind of commentary about the actions and behavior of the other and that the other is likewise making commentary about us. This commentary arises out of our own frame of reference, which includes our interpretation of the roles, the meaning and value we place on these roles, the expectations to which the roles give rise, and our assessment of how well the other person enacts or performs these roles and thus lives up to our expectations.

As we think back to the four roots of disillusionment, symbolic interaction is strongly related to all four: marriage as an institution with historically well-defined roles, expectations and need fulfillment, the socialization process, and personal development. Burr et al. have said, "One area where there is a substantial body of empirical research that could easily be viewed from an interactionist perspective is the broad area of socialization. Interactionism has already provided a number of theoretical ideas about the nature of the self and the processes through which the self develops."[18]

Object Relations as a Framework for Looking at Expectations

Object relations is a school of therapy that has grown out of psychoanalytic theory. Object relations have to do with interpersonal relationships, especially those early relationships with significant others such as mother and father, brother and sister. These are the objects in object relations. The relations need not be actual or real. They can be fantasized relations or wished-for relations. Contrary to Freudian theory, the object is not the "target of a libidinal drive."[19] Cashdan says that because the "objects" in object relations theory are human beings, "it probably would clarify matters if the term 'human' could be substituted for 'object' wherever it occurred. But catchwords, being what they are, catch on."[20]

A number of object relations theorists have written extensively on object relations theory, and they all appear to have different emphases and different interpretations and usages for Freud's personality structure of the id, the ego, and the superego. Further, the theorists differ widely in their interpretation and use of Freud's developmental theory with its emphasis on oral, anal, phallic, latent, and genital stages. Suffice it to say that a "liberated" object relations theory does *not* need the schema of oral, anal, phallic, latent, and genital stages, nor does "liberated" object relations need the concepts of id, ego, and superego. "Fairbairn radically departs from Freud's model of libidinal energy by conceptually doing away with the id and developing the concept of a unitary ego with its own energy. . . . According to Fairbairn, if the child's relationship with the parents is good, the child's ego is whole."[21]

What then is object relations? Nichols says, "Object relations theory says that the past is alive—in memory—and it runs people's lives more than we know.[22] Quite simply, it is the internalization of good and bad relationships, good and bad feelings associated with mother, father, brother, sister, and even grandmother and grandfather. It is the internalization of the objects of our desires, our affections, and our needs to be loved. It is our desire and need for security, warmth, unconditional acceptance, and belongingness. But our desires and our needs can be filled only by people (objects), and so what is internalized is the object that has the potential to provide us with our desired gratification of our deepest needs. According to Israelstam, "[I]ndividuals internalize 'beliefs' and 'scripts' early on in their relationships with significant others. . . . [I]ndividuals from birth, create an internal representation of the external system, particularly in relationship to their primary caregivers. Bowlby calls this 'internal representation.' The object relations theorists call this 'the loved object;' or 'internalized mother.'"[23] However, the internalized object can be *any significant person* from one's early years. According to Heard and Lake the internalized object can reflect any internalized relationship.[24] This includes the possibility of father, mother, grandparent, sibling, or peer.

If for some reason our early months as a neonate were filled with experiences of being left alone for long periods of time; of being hungry for significant periods of time; of being cold, wet, soiled; or of being attended to with little human warmth, then it is likely that we would have later difficulty in terms of feeling good about ourselves. Likewise, if these early experiences are filled with sternness, crossness, and an imputed sense of shame, guilt, ineptness, and inferiority it is likely that self-esteem will suffer severely. If this same kind of psychological coldness continues into early and middle childhood, then we become prime candidates for continued poor self-esteem arising from poor self-image.

Object relations is concerned with how well our early and deepest psycho-emotional needs are met in infancy, in childhood, and even in adolescence. Object relations is concerned not only with the needs themselves but also with our expectation that a loving caregiver will meet these needs for us. The person who has not had these basic needs met becomes the perfect candidate for an A-frame type marriage wherein he or she expects the other to "meet my needs, take care of me, love me, hold me up, make me feel good about being me, reassure me, and never stop doing for me what I never learned how to do for myself."

SPLITTING

Splitting and projective identification are central to understanding object relations. **Splitting** is a way in which we separate the good from the bad. It is the good mother who meets my needs, and it is the bad mother who I suppress or "push down" inside me. "The process begins with the infant's primitive division of the world into satisfying and unsatisfying sensations: fullness is good, emptiness is bad; warmth is good, cold bad; to be held is good, to be denied contact bad. Long before children are able to assign labels to what is good or bad, much less conceptualize it, a primitive sensory intelligence exists that enables the child to recognize that the world—or whatever it is that is out there—is divided into good and bad. . . . Before children are even aware that people exist, the foundations of their interpersonal worlds are being set down."[25]

What does the child do with the good and bad? The child splits them apart so that the good mother can always remain the good mother and the bad mother has nothing to do with the good mother. The bad mother has been split off from the good mother so that now the child can hate the bad mother without endangering the good feelings that come from the good mother. When the child is frustrated at mother's breast, the bad breast is split off from the good breast. "By behaving as if the bad parts of the mother do not exist, or by minimizing them, the child transforms the mother into a perfect, all-good human being."[26] This is a form of idealization, and it is easy to see how this same kind of idealization can be done with one's future mate.

The opposite of splitting is integration. A well-integrated personality is one wherein the self not only accepts all aspects of himself/herself but also is in constant communication with all parts of the self. In short, the whole person is an integrated person: The angry me is in touch with the nice me; the intellectual me is in touch with the emotional me; the good me is in touch with the bad me; and the likable me is in touch with the antisocial me. We probably all grow out of childhood having done some splitting because it is a protective mechanism that enables us to feel good about our intimate environment. Nevertheless, too much splitting may cause severe problems later on, especially when one part of our inner self is not in communication with another part of our inner self. The essence of splitting is to repress the bad and reify the good. The essence of integration is to accept the bad and allow it to be in communication with the good. Some people, however, are not able to do this.

PROJECTIVE IDENTIFICATION

Projective identification is concerned with that part of the self that has been split off and is now repressed or out of consciousness. An object or part object is selected or chosen with which the repressed part of the split self can identify. If we think back to deficit need theory and the concept of illegitimate ego needs, there is always a developmental deficit and a shift in responsibility so that someone else is selected or chosen to fill these unfulfilled needs. Object relations theory is closely allied with the concept of illegitimate needs except that the terminology is such that object relations builds on the idea of unconscious splitting and unconscious projections on an identified object, who then is induced to play the role of need filler. Israelstam defines *projective identification* as "a process whereby one individual disowns (splits off) unacceptable aspects of themselves . . . by 'getting rid' of them by projecting them 'into' the other. This aspect, then, becomes identified as belonging to the other."[27] Nichols uses the word *induce* to explain the process of projective identification. He says, "Not only does the past produce expectations and shape what we see, we actively create it. We shape our partners to fit our inner models, projecting onto them our repudiated feelings and then *inducing* the spouse to live them out."[28] (Italics added.) Projective identification "describes an enactment in which split-off aspects of the self are induced in the other. The processes involved in projective identification include: (1) projection of the split-off part and (2) introjection by the recipient."[29] This means that any part of the self that has been disowned or unconsciously rejected may be projected onto one's partner by inducing the partner to be what I reject in myself. If I reject my sexual attraction to persons other than my mate (because of a long-standing belief that such attraction is wrong) it is likely that I will project this trait onto my partner and induce him or her to do or become the trait I rejected in myself.

Cashdan states:

> A key dynamic in projective identification is the *induction* that underlies it. Individuals who rely on projective identification engage in subtle but nonetheless powerful manipulations to induce those about them to behave in prescribed ways. It is as if one individual forces another to play a role in the enactment of that person's internal drama—one involving early object relationships. The target of the manipulation is induced to engage in an *identification* with a disowned aspect of the person doing the *projection*—hence the term 'projective identification.'[30]

PART OBJECTS AND TRANSITIONAL OBJECTS

Object relations thinking also includes the concept of **part object**, which refers to a part of the wished-for object, such as mother's arms or mother's breast. In adulthood, part objects are usually replaced with relationships with whole objects, that is, whole persons. If this does not happen there may be an "excessive interest in parts of the body such as hair, breasts, and feet. Most of the time such 'interests' represent harmless residuals of an early stage of life when part-objects were associated with pleasure and gratification."[31]

A **transitional object** is any object that serves the purpose of helping us go through a transition such as adjusting to mother's absence. The child clings to his/her blanket or other type of warm cuddly that serves to remind the child of mother's warmth and closeness even though mother is no longer physically in the room. Most people can identify some type of transitional object in their own childhood, be it a teddy bear or a bunny rabbit, a swatch of a blanket, or a piece of clothing.

GOOD ENOUGH MOTHERING

Every child wishes for a primary source of gratification that is total, complete, and neverending. In reality this wished-for object can never exist, but the child does not know this. Cashdan terms this childhood dilemma "trouble in paradise." "The split is there and it is not going to go away."[32] Cashdan says that "even under the best of circumstances, the infant naturally comes to experience the world as split."[33] "When milk is flowing the breast is good; when it is not, it is bad. And even if it is good, it may not be good all the time. The nature of life is such that the most well-intentioned mother cannot always respond to the child's beck and call. She cannot drop everything at a moment's notice and run to the infant every time the child is hungry."[34] A mother who does her best to meet the needs of her child and does so in a consistent and ongoing manner (even if the child feels he/she is not getting sufficient amounts of love, affection, cuddling, milk, and breast) is referred to by Winnicott as the "good enough mother."[35] Because of the fact that no mother could possibly bring an infant to total satiation and need satisfaction there will always be some splitting. This is to be expected. Like many things in life, it is the extremes that give rise to later problems and difficulties. With increasing frustration and rejection there is increased possibility of splitting and hence of use of projective identifications later in life.

How does object relations apply to marriage and family? Let us look at Dale and Marie in the light of object relations and see how some of the principles of the framework play into their marriage.

DALE AND MARIE

Dale and Marie have been married for 21 years. It is the first marriage for both of them. Dale is now 41, and Marie is 40. There are three children: Howie, age 19; Beth, age 17; and Alan, age 14. Marie complains that Dale is possessive of her and jealous of her friends. Marie says that she can't do anything outside the house or with her friends without Dale becoming upset and angry. At the same time, says Marie, Dale is dependent on Marie and looks to her to take leadership in everything the family does. Marie has been considering divorce because she feels stifled and suffocated by Dale. She says she feels like an old inner tube stuffed into a tire with no room to breathe or to express herself in any way.

Dale complains that Marie does not devote enough time to him as a proper wife should. He also complains that Marie doesn't spend enough quality time with the three teenagers. Dale says that Marie spends too much time with her friends and not enough time doing housework and taking care of the family. When it was suggested to Dale that he sounded very angry with his wife, he became enraged at the suggestion. He claimed that he had never been angry with his wife and that she was the nearest thing to a perfect wife any man could have.

AN OBJECT RELATIONS INTERPRETATION
OF DALE AND MARIE

An object relations interpretation of Dale and Marie would focus on Dale's early relationship with his mother and father. As a young child Dale was not able to see his mother as anything other than perfect. He always tried to please her because when he did she praised him and told him how wonderful he was. However, this became a problem for Dale when he misbehaved or in some way failed to measure up to mother's expectations. When this happened he unconsciously split his good, praising, and loving mother from his disapproving, scolding, and rejecting mother. This early split enabled Dale to idolize his mother and cling to her for ever increasing amounts of love and affection, which provided him with a sense of security. Dale also experienced his mother as very powerful and controlling, always able to manage any difficult situation. At the same time, Dale was afraid of his father. He kept as much distance as he could from his father, who always seemed to disapprove of Dale.

As a grown man Dale has still not overcome the early split between good mother and bad mother. The bad mother is still lurking deep down in the cobwebs of his unconscious. Therefore the same dynamic is played out with his wife, Marie, whom he looks up to and idolizes as the almost perfect wife, and yet he is forced to deny his anger toward her when she appears not to measure up to his expectations. Dale is forced to bury his anger because it would spoil his image of Marie. At the same time, Dale has created Marie to be his projective identification. Marie has become what Dale is not! Marie has become what Dale expected of his mother. Marie has become the strong leader, the organizer, the competent leader who will see to it that everybody's needs are taken care of. Over the years Dale has successfully induced Marie to be what he was not and what his "good mother" was, that is, the strong leader, caretaker, and protector. Dale has never dared to be strong in his own right because he is still fearful of his father's reprimands and criticism and his mother's threatened withdrawal of love. Dale has repressed his "strong" self and projected this strength onto Marie. Of course Dale is very angry about this, but he must deny his anger for fear that Marie will withdraw her love and acceptance of him.

Marie's friends are a threat to Dale. Time spent outside the orbit of the family is a threat to Dale. There can be no failure on Marie's part! She must be what Dale is not! In this sense Marie has played her own part in the projective identification by permitting and allowing Dale to lean on her and project onto her the never-ceasing role of leadership. When Marie takes steps to spend more time on her own interests and with her friends it becomes very threatening to Dale.

For the situation to change Marie must assert herself in claiming her own personhood and her own identity. She must take steps to relinquish the role of caretaker, protector, and leader. This will undoubtedly create an even greater crisis for Dale. However, there is no other way because as long as Marie plays Dale's game things will never change. According to object relations thinking, Dale needs to reclaim his bad mother and allow this image of the past to *merge* with his image of his good mother. When the bad and the good can both be put on the table and seen and accepted for what they are, an integration is possible. When Dale is able to achieve this adult integration he will be able to accept Marie for the person she really is, that is, not a superwife or supermom but a loving and fallible human being. At this point Dale can deal with his projective identification of Marie, and he can let go of his insistence that she must be a certain kind of person who must do certain things in certain ways.

A modernized and liberated object relations would place as much emphasis on the father as an early object as the mother. In truth, many males grow up with a powerful fear of the "bad" father who gave the early impression of being strict and stern and unyielding in his demands for accomplishment and achievement. Likewise, a modernized and liberated object relations would emphasize the need for all of us to integrate within ourselves our early images of caretaking, love, protection, and discipline.

There are numerous implications of object relations in understanding what contributes to the decline of many marriages. Nichols states: "In marriage, unlike dating, the partners no longer put their best foot forward. Moreover, once you get to know someone you have idealized and discover that that someone isn't perfect, you tend to devalue that person."[36] Object relations has direct bearing on our expectations of each other. Object relations has direct influence on how we react when our mate does not fill the image we have of him or her. When our internal belief system comes into conflict with our partner's internal belief system, or if we feel that we lack confirmation from our partner, we tend to become angry and claim that we are married to a person who is incompatible. When we unconsciously project onto our mate those very things we have rejected or disliked in ourselves we unwittingly contribute to marital discord and dysfunction because we are manipulating our partner into being and doing what we need them to be and to do. When people (finally) realize how they have been used and/or manipulated in this manner they become resentful and angry. The result is often increased anxiety, dissillusionment, despair, and alienation from one's mate.

The inherent truth of object relations is in the fact that when we do not work through and come to some resolution of our past we are bound to transfer the unfinished business and impaired relations to significant others in our present. This tends to play havoc with love relationships and marriage.

Systems as a Framework for Looking at Expectations

Systems theory holds that an organism, when perturbed or disturbed, will attempt to return to its normative or homeostatic state, its home base or baseline equilibrium. Systems theory also holds that every change within a system will bring about reactive changes within the system. There are feedback loops wherein as one person within the family system moves away from the system (husband distances himself from his wife and children because he feels rejected by his wife) the others in the system may be making increased efforts and "moves" to bring the husband and father back into the system (homeostasis). The husband breaking away or distancing is the positive part of the loop because it increases distance from the norm or baseline. The attempt to bring the husband/father back into the family unit is the negative part of the feedback loop because it is an attempt to restore the situation to the way it used to be. The positive part of the loop is activity that increases or amplifies the distance from the normative state. The negative part of the loop is activity that decreases or reduces the distance away from the normative state. (Negative and positive indicate direction only. They do *not* indicate whether a behavior or activity is good or bad, right or wrong.)

Systems thinking relates to marital expectations and need fulfillment in terms of family members' reactions to whether or not they believe that their needs are being fulfilled. We have stated throughout this chapter that marital happiness and satisfaction is the function of feeling that one's legitimate needs are at least partially fulfilled. Additionally, we have stressed the illegitimacy of our needs if these needs arise from a developmental deficit and if we attempt to make someone else responsible for filling these needs for us. However, whether the needs are legitimate or illegitimate, if we perceive that our partner is not meeting these needs to a satisfactory degree we are going to have some kind of response or reaction. It is this response or reaction that ties in with systems thinking and system theory.

When we believe or perceive that our needs, legitimate or illegitimate, are not being met to a satisfactory degree we tend to react in some way. We may distance ourselves, withdrawing our self-investment so as to protect ourselves against the pain and hurt of rejection or a sense of failure. We may become increasingly hostile and belligerent, or we may become increasingly passive-aggressive (taking out our anger and frustration in safe, yet passive ways). We may become surly, or we may pout, sulk, or become depressed. Whatever our reaction is, it will have an impact on our mate and the rest of the family. Our mate and the rest of the family may react with anger and hostility, or they may make their own attempts to distance themselves from the antics of the husband/father. The children may have no idea of any contention between the father and the mother, but they may *feel* the increased strain and tension, leading them to ask the mother, "What's wrong with Dad?"

Unless the husband can cut through his hurt and anger and deal constructively with his feelings of disappointment regarding how his wife meets (fails to meet) his needs, there will develop a circular series of events and behaviors between the husband and the wife. Husband distances; wife reacts with resentment and anger; husband distances more, now saying (at least to himself) that his wife has become cross and cranky; wife now reacts more vehemently, saying to her children and perhaps a friend that her husband has become unbearable in his selfish antics. Eventually no one in the family can remember when or how this whole chain of events got started. All anyone really knows is that it's no fun living together anymore.

Marriages and families are well known to live for many years without any basic change in the pattern of anger-distance-more anger-more distance. The final result may be emotional divorce, estrangement, or even a type of emotional warfare wherein the rules of the game are that nobody will ever win, and the fate of the couple is to maintain the game until death do they part. A more unfortunate result is that frequently one or more of the children becomes triangulated by one of the parents. **Triangulation** is when one or both parents invest their emotional energy into their relationship with a child, or a lover, or even their work. The emotional energy thus invested is then taken away from the husband-wife relationship. Although triangulation tends to stabilize the husband-wife relationship, it usually harms the person who is triangled, especially a child (Appendix A). There are countless marriages that are intact and stable but at the price of a triangled child on whom the parental dissatisfaction and disillusionment has become projected.

Summary

In this chapter we have looked closely at marital expectations as being the primary reason for marital disillusionment. The differences between happiness and pleasure were considered. Pleasure is an emotional feeling that, however desirable and sought after, is by its very nature a fleeting experience. Happiness is an inner state of being wherein the individual achieves some degree of self-fulfillment and self-realization. Happiness is a state of psychic freedom compared to oppression. Happiness is a moving toward the fulfillment of one's human potential.

The subject of needs was considered, and the concept of deficit needs was developed. We all have legitimate and illegitimate ego needs. However, the more we are able to identify and label our illegitimate needs, seeing through them and learning to fill them ourselves instead of shifting this responsibility (expectation) onto our mate, the more likely we will be able to experience marital happiness rather than disillusionment.

Four other frameworks were considered as means by which we could further understand the importance of marital expectations. Figure 2-4 illustrates the interrelationship of the five ways of looking at marital expectations and need fulfillment. Each of the five frameworks adds to the cumulation of persuasive evidence pointing toward the experience of marital disillusionment. Unfulfilled expectations, unfair or unbalanced exchange, different meanings placed on roles, disappointment with role enactment, identification of mate with objects and part objects from childhood, and systemic reactions to unmet needs and unfulfilled expectations all serve to create marital unhappiness, misery, and disillusionment.

The primary purpose of this chapter has been to attempt to understand and explain why so many marriages end up in a state of disillusionment with accompanying feelings of the loss of romantic love and meaningful intimacy and closeness. The answer, spanning Chapters 1 and 2, has been to say that the heart of the matter is marital expectations and need fulfillment. We have idealistic and sometimes outlandish expectations of what marriage is and what our partner will be able to do for us. When the partner's role enactment fails to

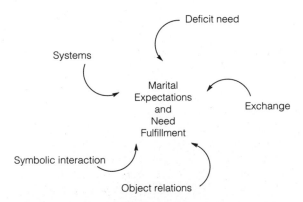

Figure 2-4 An Integration of Theoretical Perspectives

measure up to our unrealistic expectations we become hurt and usually very angry. If there is no resolution, we become disillusioned. We may or may not get divorced. Whether we do or not, it is frequently the children who suffer because they have become the ones on whom the parental despair has been projected, and children are the most vulnerable targets or objects of parental triangulation.

This is not to say that there are not other vitally important reasons for marital disillusionment, but I am saying that the heart of the matter is marital expectations and need fulfillment. In the ensuing chapters we will be considering the mythology of love, the necessity of learning fair-fight skills, and the constructive resolution of conflict. We will also be talking about commitment to one's mate and the importance of nurturing the bond of love.

Reading Suggestions

Becvar, Dorothy S. and Raphael J. Becvar. *Family Therapy: A Systemic Integration.* Boston: Allyn and Bacon, 1988.

Burr, Wesley, R.; Reben Hill; F. Ivan Nye; and Ira L. Reiss. *Contemporary Theories About the Family.* Vol. II. New York: The Free Press, 1979.

Fromm, Erich. *The Art of Loving.* New York: Harper & Row, 1956.

Kerr, Michael E. and Murray Bowen. *Family Evaluation.* New York: W. W. Norton, 1988.

Learner, Harriet Goldhor. *The Dance of Intimacy.* New York: Harper & Row, 1989.

Maslow, Abraham. *Toward A Psychology of Being.* 2d ed. Princeton, N.J.: D. Van Nostrand, 1962.

Nichols, Michael P. *The Self in the System.* New York: Brunner/Mazel, 1987.

O'Neill, Nena. *The Marriage Premise.* New York: M. Evans, 1977.

Peck, M. Scott. *The Road Less Traveled.* New York: Simon and Schuster (Touchstone), 1978.

Singer, Laura J., with Barbara Lang Stern. *Stages: The Crises That Shape Your Marriage.* New York: Grosset and Dunlap, 1980.

Skynner, Robin and John Cleese. *Families and How to Survive Them.* New York: Oxford University Press, 1983.

Notes

1. W. T. Jones, *A History of Western Philosophy* (New York: Harcourt Brace Jovanovich, 1952), 219, 233. Quotation reprinted by permission.
2. Aron Krich and Sam Blum, "Marriage and the Mystique of Romance," *Redbook,* Nov. 1970. Copyright 1970 McCall Corporation. Quotation reprinted by permission.

3. John Bowlby, *Attachment*. Vol. I (New York: Basic Books, 1969). *Separation and Loss*. Vol. II (New York: Basic Books, 1973). *Loss, Sadness, and Depression*. Vol. III (New York: Basic Books, 1980).

4. Burton L. White, *The First Three Years of Life* (Revised) (New York: Prentice-Hall, 1985), 11, 53, 64.

5. Bobbie Crew Nelms, "Attachment Versus Spoiling," *Pediatric Nursing*, Vol. 9, no. 1 (Jan/Feb 1983): 49–51.

6. Erich Fromm has treated the subject in Chapter 2 of *The Art of Loving* and in Chapter 5 of *Escape From Freedom* (New York: Holt, Rinehart and Winston, 1941).

7. Karen Horney, *The Neurotic Personality of Our Time*. Vol. I. *The Collected Works of Karen Horney* (New York: W. W. Norton, 1937), 107, 109–110. Quotation reprinted by permission.

8. Abraham Maslow, "A Theory of Human Motivation," *Psychological Review* 50 (1943): 370–396.

9. William Glasser, *Reality Therapy* (New York: Harper & Row, 1965).

10. Eric Berne, *Games People Play* (New York: Grove Press, 1964); and Thomas A. Harris, *I'm OK--You're OK: A Practical Guide to Transactional Analysis* (New York: Harper & Row, 1967).

11. F. Ivan Nye, "Choice, Exchange, and the Family," In *Contemporary Theories About the Family*. Vol. II. Wesley R. Burr, Reuben Hill, F. Ivan Nye, and Ira L. Reiss, eds. (New York: The Free Press, 1979), 1.

12. J. W. Thibaut and H. H. Kelley, *The Social Psychology of Groups* (New York: Wiley, 1959), 21.

13. Mary Ann Lamanna and Agnes Riedmann, *Marriages and Families*, 3rd ed. (Belmont, Calif.: Wadsworth, 1988), 282.

14. Wesley R. Burr, Geoffrey K. Leigh, Randall D. Day, and John Constantine, "Symbolic Interaction and the Family," In *Contemporary Theories About the Family*, Vol. II, Wesley R. Burr, Reben Hill, F. Ivan Nye, and Ira L. Reiss, eds. (New York: The Free Press, 1979), 54.

15. *Ibid.*, 54.

16. *Ibid.*, 71.

17. *Ibid.*, 73.

18. *Op. cit.*, Burr et al., 54.

19. Sheldon Cashdan, *Object Relations Therapy* (New York: W. W. Norton, 1988), 3.

20. *Ibid.*, 3.

21. *Ibid.*, 13–14.

22. Michael P. Nichols, *The Self in the System* (New York: Brunner/Mazel, 1987), 193.

23. Kenneth V. Israelstam, "Interacting Individual Belief Systems in Marital Relationships," *Journal of Marital and Family Therapy*, Vol. 15, no. 1 (1989): 53.

24. D. H. Heard and B. Lake, "The Attachment Dynamic in Adult Life," *British Journal of Psychiatry* 149 (1986): 430–438.

25. *Op. cit.*, Cashdan, 34.

26. *Op. cit.*, Cashdan, 38.

27. *Op. cit.*, Israelstam, 59.

28. *Op. cit.*, Nichols, 200.

29. *Op. cit.*, Nichols, 201.

30. *Op. cit.*, Cashdan, 56.

31. *Op. cit.*, Cashdan, 35.

32. *Op. cit.*, Cashdan, 36.

33. *Op. cit.*, Cashdan, 35.

34. *Op. cit.*, Cashdan, 35.

35. D. W. Winnicott, *Playing and Reality* (London: Tavistock Publications, 1971).

36. *Op. cit.*, Nichols, 199.

Beyond the Grand Illusion:

Redefinitions and Integration of Love and Sex Within Marriage

When two people are under the influence of the most violent, most insane, most delusive, and most transient of passions, they are required to swear that they will remain in that excited, abnormal, and exhausted condition continuously until death do them part.

GEORGE BERNARD SHAW

LOVE THEMES

Vintage 1174: Courtly Love

"We declare and affirm, by the tenor of these presents, that love cannot extend its rights over two married persons. For indeed lovers grant one another all things, mutually and freely, without being impelled by any motive of necessity, whereas husband and wife are held by their duty to submit their wills to each other and to refuse each other nothing. May this judgment, which we have delivered with extreme caution, and after consulting with a great number of other ladies, be for you a constant and unassailable truth."[1]

Vintage circa 1870: Victorian Advice to a Young Bride

"Women's alleged lack of passion was epitomized in the story of the English mother who was asked by her daughter before her marriage how she ought to behave on her wedding night. 'Lie still and think of the Empire,' the mother advised."[2]

Vintage 1886: Victorian Advice to Young Grooms

"At the outset of this important subject, we stop to correct a gross, but widely received popular error. Every woman, every physician, nearly every married man will support us in what we are going to say, and will thank us for saying it.

It is in reference to passion in woman. A vulgar opinion prevails that they are creatures of like passions with ourselves; that they experience desires as ardent, and often as ungovernable, as those which lead to so much evil in our sex. Vicious writers, brutal and ignorant men, and some shameless women combine to favor and extend this opinion.

Nothing is more utterly untrue. Only in very rare instances do women experience one tithe of the sexual feeling which is familiar to most men. Many of them are entirely frigid, and not even in marriage do they ever perceive any real desire. . . . The above considerations, which all married men will do well to ponder, should lead them to a very temperate enforcement of their conjugal rights. They should be always considerate, and not so yield themselves to their passions as to sacrifice their love to the woman they have married."[3]

The Grand Illusion

Although romantic love has been with us since the 12th century A.D., it has not always been a motivation to marry. Indeed, in the earliest stages of courtly love in the 12th century, no one would think of marrying the person with whom they were in love, nor would anyone look for love in one's relationship with one's mate. Love and marriage were mutually exclusive.

Morton Hunt has said that the Puritans "borrowed some of the ideals of romantic love, accepted the normality of sex and tried to fuse the two within marriage."[4]

In the 19th century, during the heyday of Victorianism, love was considered a divine gift, whereas sex was considered to be little more than a necessary evil.

At present, we embrace love and we affirm sex, but like the Puritans we hold that these two functions are to be united in the estate of marriage. Queen and Habenstein have said: "Romantic love as a basis for marriage is relatively new and is dominant mainly in the Western world, chiefly in the United States and Canada."[5]

In this chapter I will develop the idea of the Grand Illusion, which is the result of the attempt to fuse love and sex within the bonds of marriage. I will also discuss some of the most prevalent myths related to love, marriage, and sex. The Grand Illusion is the wished for and hoped for continuation within marriage of that supreme passion one felt for the beloved prior to sexual consummation and marriage.

> CLIENT: (first marriage; 32 years old; having an affair) I would come back to my wife if I could have the kind of passion I feel for my lover. I want passion in my marriage. I want excitement and great sex and wonderful feelings of closeness.
>
> THERAPIST: What will you do if you divorce your wife?
>
> CLIENT: I will marry ———
>
> THERAPIST: What will it be like with her?
>
> CLIENT: It will be passionate and full of love and caring and great sex. I know you don't believe me, but when I'm with her it's (pause) well it's just . . . you know (long pause). This marriage will be different. You'll see!

The Grand Illusion dies hard. There is something about our desire for deep erotic fusion and closeness that is addictive! When we discover that day-in and day-out marriage somehow changes the deep passion into a less romantic and more utilitarian and practical type of love we then conclude that something is terribly wrong. Some people handle this transition very well. Others stay married and yet become cynical. Others become disillusioned. Others seek out affairs. Others divorce and start over, still searching for the perfect partner with whom they can reexperience the passion. Why can't marriage sustain the great feelings the man and woman had for each other early on? Why does marriage seem to harden people, or at least change them so that they no longer feel the same way toward each other? Why can we not retain the original passion? The answer to these questions is in the nature of romanticism.

Romanticism

COURTLY LOVE

Hugo Beigel has delineated three periods of history in which the ideals of courtly love have surfaced in different ways. The ideals that originated in the 12th century were expressed in changing ways in the 18th and 19th centuries and are now present in modern American love, which Beigel sees as "a derivative, modified in concord with the conditions of our age and based more on ego demands than on ideal demands."[6] Thus, romanticism has changed as it has been adapted to the needs of a particular age. Beigel characterizes courtly love as follows:

> [Courtly love is] l'amour de lohh (distant love), or minne, and many
> documents, poems, and epics depict its form and the feelings
> involved. . . . Courtly love was the conventionalization of a new ideal that
> arose in the feudal class and institutionalized certain aspects of the male-
> female relationships outside marriage. In conformity with the Christian
> concept of and contempt for sex, the presupposition for minne was chastity.
> Being the spiritualization and sublimation of carnal desire, such love was
> deemed to be impossible between husband and wife. By application of the
> religious concept of abstract love to the "mistress," the married woman of the
> ruling class who had lost her economic function, was endowed with higher
> and more general values: gentleness and refinement. Unselfish service to the
> noble lady became a duty of the knight, explicitly sworn to the oath the
> young nobleman had to take at the dubbing ceremony.[7]

Denis de Rougemont claimed that courtly love was an arrangement contrived outside of legal marriage and was incompatible with marriage. "Now, passion and marriage are essentially irreconcilable. Their origins and their ends make them mutually exclusive."[8] De Rougemont points out, however, that not only are passion and marriage irreconcilable but passionate love itself must not be consummated via sexual intercourse. "As has been said, this loyalty [between a knight-lover and his lady] was incompatible with the fidelity of marriage. . . . This courtly love, however, displays one curious feature. It is opposed to the 'satisfaction' of love as much as to marriage."[9]

THE ROMANTIC PERIOD

In its formative stages romanticism was antisexual. Undoubtedly there were many exceptions to the rule of chastity, yet chastity was the norm. Chastity was the ideal. This, of course, contributed immensely to feelings of unrequited love and intensity of emotion. The beloved was sexually unattainable, and so the innocence of purity and chastity was somewhat ensured. As José Ortega y Gasset has said, "Desiring something is, without doubt, a move toward possession of that something (possession meaning that in some way or other the object should enter our orbit and become part of us). For this reason, desire automatically dies when it is fulfilled; it ends with satisfaction. Love, on the other hand, is eternally unsatisfied. Desire has a passive character; when I desire something, what I actually desire is that the object come to me. . . . Love . . . is the exact reverse of desire, for love is all activity."[10] Ortega y Gasset, in attempting to establish that desire automatically dies when it is fulfilled, is thereby suggesting that romantic love thrives on lack of fulfillment or, at least, on periodic or fleeting fulfillment.

Ernest van den Haag echoes this same theme when he says that "the only way to keep love is to try to keep up or re-establish the distance between lovers that was inevitably shortened by intimacy and possession, and thus, possibly, regain desire and longing."[11] The cure for desire and longing is to become one with one's lover. The trouble is that this very cure then becomes the problem because once the lovers have ongoing and predictable access to each other the desire and the longing dissipate. The solution becomes the problem. The solution to the problem of love becomes the problem of attempting to keep love alive when one has access to one's lover. In short, highly romanticized love cannot stand its own consummation. When it is consummated on a regular or predictable basis the feelings of passionate desire and longing begin to wane. When it is not consummated the longing and the desire tend to keep the emotions in such a state of excitement and frenzy that it is impossible to cease from thinking about one's beloved. "If one were to marry one's love, one would exchange the sweet torment of desire, the yearning, for that which fulfills it. Thus, the tension of hope would be replaced by the comfort of certainty. He who longs to long, who wants the tension of desire, surely should not marry."[12]

Slowly but surely through the ensuing centuries the chastity and antisexual nature of courtly love gave way to a compromise. Illicit love outside marriage with one's paramour would increasingly include sexual expression. The distance would still be sufficient to prevent the decay or loss of the feelings of yearning, desire, and longing. The 16th through the 19th centuries saw the increasing melding of romantic love with romantic sex outside of wedlock.

Beigel states:

> Under the increasing discomfort in a changing civilization, the aristocratic class had found a way to alleviate the defeats of a family-prescribed monogamous marriage by dividing duty and satisfaction; the woman reserved her loyalty for her husband and her love for her gallant. Continuing on the tracks laid by the concept of courtly love, the nobles of the seventeenth and eighteenth centuries . . . still adhered to the tenet that love and marriage were irreconcilable. [13]

This middle period between early courtly love and the modern period is characterized by the following:

Love is to be celebrated exclusively as a feeling.
Love and marriage are incompatible.
The beloved is idealized.
Love is idolized.
There always must exist distance between lovers.
Love cannot exist in an ongoing, day-in, day-out relationship.
Sex is always the servant of love. Love is never the servant of sex.
Time should stand still in the sense that feelings must never change in a
    negative direction. If they do the relationship is clearly on the way out.
Lovers must never take each other for granted and must never cease in their
    desire and endeavor to score points with the beloved.

THE MODERN PERIOD

The modern period has seen the cult of love spread, even if it be sparingly, around the globe. As has already been pointed out, the American colonists of the 17th century married for love, as well as for security, protection, economic survival, procreation, and the comforts of the flesh. Many married for love and the fulfillment of that longing and desire that sparks one person to pursue or to wish fervently to be pursued by another. "No longer was there to be a cleavage between the spirituality of love and the marital sex relation; but the latter was sanctified by the former."[14] This type of love became a hallmark of the literary and operatic works in the romantic tradition. As the new love and sex ethic spread downward to the middle classes and even to the lower classes there came an increasing expectation that passionate love and powerful sex could be forever united in marriage *and that the relationship would inevitably continue to be both loving and passionate.*

Hence, we see three stages: (1) *the courtly period:* love outside marriage with sex forbidden; (2) *the romantic period:* love outside marriage with sexual permissiveness; and (3) *the modern period:* romanticized love and passionate sex united within marriage. Such generalizations are, of course, oversimplified, and exceptions to the ideal in each period were legion. Nevertheless, there was a trend that drew sex and love into an adulterous union and then into a legal union. The hallmark of romanticism evolved into that of an idealized partner who is an object of veneration, adoration, and passionate desire with or without sexual consummation and within as well as without marriage.

DESIRE VERSUS LOVE

An indispensable aspect of romanticism is desire, the deep and passionate longing for that special person without whom we feel incomplete and alone. Desire and love are not the same, nor are they necessarily similar. Mature love may include a measure of desire, whereas romanticized love is frequently experienced as nothing but desire. The feeling of desire is one of yearning and even passionate burning. For some people this longing actually brings symptoms of abdominal pain. However, once the object of love is achieved, or once the desire is realized via sexual encounter, the desire subsides and wanes. It is precisely at this point that the romanticist is likely to experience a severe letdown or even a turnoff.

This abrupt change of feeling immediately after sexual consummation is usually a sign that what one was experiencing was desire rather than love. This is why romanticized love must make capital out of the lure of sex, or "the sex tease," as Albert Ellis calls it. The hope and promise of sexual consummation tends to obliterate the qualitative difference between desire and love so that one's ardent desire is experienced inwardly as being or falling in love. Being in the state of desire is experienced inwardly as being or falling in love. Being in the state of sexual desire is a hallmark of romanticism: It is not the same as being in love. Another way of saying the same thing is to say that sometimes we are "in lust," but this lust is disguised and experienced as being "in love." In terms of sexual desire it is not uncommon that once the object of desire is realized the feeling of love turns to scorn. The scorn is probably a form of self-anger that is then projected onto the partner.

American Romanticism

MARRIAGE AS THE IDEALIZED FULFILLMENT OF LOVE AND SEX

Today romanticism takes the form of a societal emphasis on certain aspects of the historical reality. The American version of romanticism is unique in that *it attempts to combine romanticized feelings with sexual expression within the institution of marriage* to a far greater degree than most other societies. Our society transmits the message that love is the ultimate justification for marriage; marriage alone justifies sex; sex and love are therefore the two basic hallmarks of the marital union and neither sex nor love is culturally acceptable outside of marriage.

> Romance is by its very nature incompatible with marriage even if the one has led to the other, for it is the very essence of romance to thrive on obstacles, delays, separations, and dreams, whereas it is the basic function of marriage daily to reduce and obliterate these obstacles. Marriage succeeds only in constant physical proximity to the monotonous present. Romance is . . . incapable of establishing a durable marriage, and it is not an act of courage but one of absurdity to marry someone forever because of a fever that endures for two months. [15]

THE DISTANCE FACTOR IN ROMANTICISM

The common expression "the honeymoon is over" is an interesting commentary on our dependence on the concept of traditional romantic love. Lovers that are deeply involved with one another have a distance between them that colors and heightens their interaction when they are together. Then, on marriage, the honeymoon places them together for a continuous period of time, during which they can simply enjoy each other. The experience may, however, prove to be a letdown. This is because the status quo has changed. Before the wedding, assuming they did not cohabit, they came together for a time and then separated. After the wedding they have ongoing access to one another. The change in status quo may not seem important, but in truth it will affect the relationship in many ways.

The distance factor nurtures and sustains the love quest. One might seriously question if there would be such a thing as romantic love if there were no distance between lovers. Ruth Underhill, writing about the Papago Indians of southern Arizona, states:

> Papago marriage had nothing to do with romance. In fact the couple, in their early teens, might never have seen each other until brought together on the nuptial night. Since romance depends largely on absence and the dreams of frustrated yearning, there was no opportunity for it. Almost before a boy or girl had begun to feel the sexual urge, he or she was provided with a mate. What then developed was companionship and loyalty rather than romantic love, for which the Papagos had no word. [16]

When conflict of any kind enters a romanticized relationship, there is a threatening, foreboding awareness that the union lacks perfection and that the man and woman are fallible human beings after all. The discovery, often disillusioning and upsetting, that the feverish, romantic, idealistic oneness and enchantment cannot be sustained on a daily basis gives birth to the common saying, "the honeymoon is over." Levy and Munroe had some commonsense thoughts about the change that takes place shortly after the honeymoon. Even though the following statement was written a long time ago, its truth has still not been fully absorbed.

> There are reasons for this almost universal feeling of disillusionment about marriage. One is that we are taught to expect too much from it. . . . But even if we have become profoundly cynical about marriage in general, we are apt to be disillusioned about our own, because most of us marry while we are in love. . . . The sexual excitement, the uncertainties and novelties of the new relationship, actually lift us out of ourselves for a time. With the best will in the world we cannot during the falling-in-love stage show ourselves to our beloved as we really are, nor see our beloved's everyday personality. We are quite genuinely not our everyday selves at this period. We are more intense, more vital than usual. Moreover we see ourselves through the eyes of our beloved. Unconsciously we match our feeling about ourselves with the glorified impression . . . formed of us.

> This excited state of mind cannot endure the protracted association of marriage. The thrilling sexual tension which normally keeps engaged couples in a state of fervid and delighted expectation abates with frequent, satisfying intercourse. The element of uncertainty is dissipated and there is no doubt that a goal we have not yet won is more intriguing than one which is wholly ours. . . . Sooner or later, when flamboyant anticipations of betrothal give way to the sober satisfactions of marriage, we lapse back into our ordinary selves. . . . We can run from a bear very fast indeed, but if we made that speed habitual we would soon collapse entirely. Walking is the most practicable gait for common use, and marriage too must be paced at the rate of our usual temperament. This inevitable change of pace is what we call disillusionment. Our disillusionment does not proceed wholly, or perhaps even primarily, from the unromantic facts we learn about our partner in the course of daily observation. It comes largely from our bored recognition of the same old self within our own breast. Our own newfound charm and prowess and glamour evaporate when we no longer read them in a worshipping gaze, when we are no longer stimulated by the desire for conquest. Woe unto him or her who cannot understand and accept this 'disillusionment' of marriage. [17]

HAL AND JAYNE

Hal and Jayne have been married 5 months. Jayne has felt increasing degrees of loneliness and discouragement.

JAYNE: I guess we aren't compatible. I just feel . . . well, like it's all over between us. Before we were married everything was great. We had fun together! Now . . . well . . . now we just seem to abide each other.

Honestly, I don't see how a person could change so quickly. Hal used to be fun! But now its work, work, work! Weekends are even a bore. At least we have a few friends. It's like we—would you believe it— like we don't have anything to say to each other anymore. He seems content to work all day and then sit and read the paper when he gets home. I thought marriage was going to be exciting and fun—Wow! He used to tease me and do things to turn me on—now I feel like all he really wants is sex. We had sex before marriage and it was great. I felt loved and . . . like I was really a part of him. We were one. Now we just seem to go through the motions.

HAL: I guess you could say things have changed. I love Jayne, but . . . (long pause) . . . it's just that I can't seem to do anything to make her happy or perk her up! Of course things aren't dashing and exciting anymore. Look, I enjoy doing the same things now that I did before we were married, only now instead of living apart we live together. I work all day and when I get home it's almost like I'm supposed to become a different person and court her all evening long. Sex is different too—I just can't spend an hour or so every time we have intercourse. I'm too tired. Look, I know I don't take the time to do lots of things with Jayne like we did before marriage, but Jayne doesn't seem to under- stand that things are different. I feel I must work hard at my job. My boss isn't known for his patience. All day long it's sell, sell, sell, and when I get home I want to be left alone. What gets me is that I never thought Jayne would be like this after we were married. She used to be . . . well, everything I did was okay with her. Now we're married. Big deal!

Of course the honeymoon is over. The assumption that a relationship will remain the same when its terms are changed so drastically can only be born of unrealistic expectations. Jayne and Hal probably have a great deal going for them, but they need to work through Jayne's feelings of loneliness and dis- couragement.

As a therapist I would want to explore the role expectations Hal and Jayne have of each other. If we knew more about their individual histories in each of their families of origin and their patterns of handling conflict, we would have a better understanding of how their problems developed. At a minimum we can see romanticized expectations that now cause the pain of loneliness. The mystique created by distance and time is now erased by a common living arrangement. The honeymoon *is* over.

The endeavor to combine passion-filled sex with a deep romantic feeling of unconditional devotion, commitment, and ecstatic abandon within the bonds of legal marriage is an impossible possibility! All young lovers hope that their love and desire and passion will endure. They protest that their love is different. They say they understand one another and that they will succeed where millions have failed. And who knows? Perhaps they will succeed . . . to a point! But again, the reason this is an impossible possibility is because of the hard cold facts relating to the breakdown of the distance factor. When the psycho-emotional and geographical distance is erased, that is, when the two lovers either move in together or legally marry, the partners have ongoing and almost constant access to one another, sexually, emotionally, intellectually, and behaviorally. Under these conditions the love must change. It cannot do otherwise because it is the very essence of romantic love to be separated. It is the separation and distance that gives birth to the desire, the yearning, and the passion-filled longing. Ongoing togetherness is a necessary and logical contradiction of romantic love.

LOVE AS FEELING

Love in America is celebrated almost exclusively as a feeling, with little honest recognition that the basis of the feeling may be unrealistic and superficial. Consequently, when a marriage is contracted with the expectation that the intense feeling (the chemistry; the electrifying, magnetic attraction) will continue unabated and unchanged, disappointment and disillusionment are inevitable. Marital love as distinct from romantic love celebrates love as both a feeling and a fact. By "fact" we mean that the underpinnings of the love feeling are a sense of trust and caring and commitment to the well-being of the mate.

Other Western cultures have attempted to combine romanticized love and sex within marriage, but it is unlikely that any culture has ever expected as much of the union of one woman with one man as we do in the United States. We are unique, if not in our insistence that we must combine passionate romance with great sex within marriage, then certainly in the naive and intense expectation that romance and sex are and will continue to be the most important ingredients in marriage and that little else is really necessary. The judgment of the house of the Countess of Champagne in 1174 (quoted in the beginning of this chapter) recognized the incompatibility of romantic love with marriage. Yet, more than eight centuries later, we still cling to this Grand Illusion.

ROMANCE AS A COVER FOR SEX

This acceptance of the belief regarding the compatibility of romantic love and sex within the bonds of marriage has given birth to a series of phenomena. A casual survey of television shows and commercials, movie and confession magazines, advertising of all description, and popular songs reveals that romantic love and sex are useful in marketing many commodities: Deodorants, hair sprays, shampoos, cosmetics, shaving lotions, perfumes, mouthwashes, swim and beach wear, lingerie, clothing in general, and even automobiles and motorcycles are advertised with a romantic-sexual motif. This advertising is aimed primarily at the unmarried. At least the allure appears to be to the single person who wants to be attractive to the opposite sex. Sexual attraction is portrayed as the ticket to romantic love, and romantic love is portrayed as the ticket to sexual encounter. In either case, sex and the allure of sex is a packaged commodity calculated to sell billions worth of merchandise. This is considered to be ethically acceptable because no one can accuse the advertising industry of selling blatant sex. Sex is always covered under the cloak of romance, and thus it is socially acceptable and permissible.

The romantic illusion is, in fact, the acceptable cultural cover for using sex to sell merchandise. The unspoken implication is that romanticism justifies sex. Romanticism redeems sex. Romanticism transforms sex and places it in the context of love, which makes it possible for the general public to accept the sexual connotations. Without the romantic motif, we would be face to face with sex for its own sake. Perhaps this would be more honest! However, as advertisers know quite well, such blatant honesty would meet with public uproar. Americans are not ready to view sex on its own terms but only as a romantic allure; sex is still viewed as ultimately justifiable only by wedlock.

Myths About Love, Marriage, and Sex

LOVE MYTHS

1. *Love conquers all.* This is one of the most popular and most dangerous of all myths. Essentially it says that love is everything, that skill in communication and conflict resolution are of no importance, nor is a rational matching of interests and values.
2. *Angerless love.* "If you love me you will not be angry with me. If you are angry with me it means you do not love me." Anger is an essential ingredient of healthy living and loving. Love and anger are not opposites: Indifference is the opposite of both love and anger.
3. *Love without conflict.* Conflict is neither right nor wrong. Conflict is unavoidable in human affairs, and it is unavoidable in love relations. The stark absence of conflict is a far greater sign of danger than is its presence.
4. *Magical knowing.* "If you love me you will know just what I am feeling, thinking, wanting, and needing." This is a pernicious myth that assumes that love somehow opens the inner doors of one's mind to the other person. It is usually an excuse for claiming that one is misunderstood and neglected.

5. *Love should lead to marriage.* This is one of the outgrowths of historic romanticism, and it is perhaps the biggest mistake of all. During a typical life span it is likely you will meet several people with whom you may "be in love," but you would be well advised not to marry. This too is an outgrowth of romanticism, which claims that love is the sole reason for marriage. In the modern version of romanticism such love *demands* marriage.

6. *Love means never having to say I'm sorry.* This myth gives one an excuse for being and doing whatever one wants regardless of its consequences on the other. It takes away all accountability.

7. *Love is dead, or at least dying, if we feel the slightest attraction to others.* You probably will be attracted to and attractive to many others. This means that you are alive and well. Mature love can accept such feelings *without acting* on them.

MARRIAGE MYTHS

1. *My partner will meet all my needs.* We have already covered this myth. No human being can or should meet all your needs. To expect your mate to meet all your needs is to lay a trip on your partner. It is an exercise in narcissism.

2. *All our love, affection, security, and sexual needs must be met.* No one must have all of their needs met in order to be whole and healthy. If you want to see where there is perfect security and no anxiety whatsoever, go to the nearest cemetery.

3. *Marriage will give me an identity.* If "who you are" depends on "to whom you are attached," then your identity is little more than an attachment identity. It is not based on one's own self-esteem and self-worth.

4. *Marriage will make me feel good about me.* If I enter marriage feeling good about me, then marriage will likely make me feel even better about me. However, if I enter marriage not feeling good about me, no amount of love from my mate will make me feel better about me.

5. *Marriage is the antidote for loneliness.* Just as loneliness is possible even if one is standing or sitting in the midst of a huge crowd, so also loneliness is very possible within marriage. Marriage no more cures loneliness than cancer cures smoking. Some people have experienced increased loneliness within marriage compared to singlehood. "Lonely people who marry each other to correct their situation usually discover that the most intense and excruciating loneliness is the loneliness that is shared with another."[18]

6. *Good marriges just "come naturally."* This is another pernicious belief arising out of romanticism. This myth does a good job of relieving one of all responsibility for working at the marriage.

7. *Right partner.* Although some people may be more "right" for you than others, the belief that there is somewhere a "right" partner out there just waiting for you is another tenet of romanticism and romanticized mate selection. Many fallouts from failed marriages claim "she/he wasn't the right person for me." This of course gives me an excuse for divorce by placing the responsibility on the other person who wasn't right for me. The problem is all and always with the other, never with me.

8. *Love never changes.* In effect, the essence of death is stagnation: The essence of life is growth. There can be no growth without change. All reasonably whole and healthy people change continually throughout their lives. Love will change. It may die or it may grow. Sometimes lovers grow apart. More often the partners kill their love and blame it on the partner changing.

9. *You don't marry the family.* The romanticist would have us believe that the individual is an isolated and unattached love object. On the contrary, both partners are the product of generations of socialization, rules, rituals, processes of interaction, and patterns of coping. Even if your partner claims "I have broken away from my family," he/she is still involved, if only in a reactive way. There is no escape from familial influence.

10. *Togetherness is the same as closeness and intimacy.* Not so! Genuine closeness and intimacy is not at all the same as "togetherness." Too much togetherness may be stultifying and smothering and may prevent the cultivation of one's own space and one's own interests.

11. *Children cement the marital bond of love.* The overwhelming evidence of research on marital satisfaction reveals that the single greatest negative influence on marital satisfaction is the birth of the first child. This is because the twosome becomes a threesome, and this changes the roles and the role enactment of the husband and wife, now become mother and father. Although the child may be much loved and much wanted, the child is a powerful influence on the relationship between the parents.[19]

SEX MYTHS

1. *Men are more sexual than women.* This myth is true only if orgasm, normal frequency, and reaction to specified stimuli is defined by the male. "Only if variety means uniformity, only if more diffuse physiological response is considered less powerful, and only if single episode multiorgasm capability is seen as less fulfilling, can we say that males are more sexual than females."[20]

2. *Love and sex are the same.* This myth points to the utter impoverishment of the English word *love.* There are those who would say that love is nothing more than sex, and there are those who would say that sex should be nothing

but love. There is sex without love, and there is love without sex. Sex may or may not be a part of love.

3. *Women want only love.* Since the waning of the influence of Victorianism and the important research by Masters and Johnson on the female's capacity for multi-orgasm, there is no basis for such a general statement. Some women want love without sex. Fewer women want sex without love. Probably the great majority of modern Western women want sex as an expression of love.

4. *Men want only sex.* Some men want sex without love some of the time. Some men want love without sex some of the time. To say that men want only sex is unfair to men.

5. *Persons divorcing must have been having poor sex.* On the contrary, many divorcing people have great sex but nothing else. Some divorcing people continue to have sexual relations with each other either because of the convenience or because sex is so good or because they want a safe sexual outlet without getting involved with other partners.

6. *Sex is unimportant in really good marriages.* An old adage states that if there is poor sex it counts about 90% against the relationship, but if there is good sex it counts about 10% in favor of the relationship. If this statement is taken for its symbolic rather than its literal meaning it illustrates how important sex is. It is so vital that if we do not have it the marriage is likely to be in trouble. On the other hand, even if we do have a good sexual adjustment it means that we are now free to pursue the other challenges and problems of married life.

7. *Simultaneous orgasm is the supreme sexual or lovemaking experience.* This is a belief related to middle and late Victorianism, and it was the cause of much sexual frustration. Although it is good to be committed to the satisfaction of one's mate, this becomes a most difficult and often self-defeating challenge because of the fact that one's mental concentration cannot be totally on both the mate and the self at the same time. Today the emphasis is on taking turns in petting and stimulation to **orgasm** so that both partners may be fully involved in both their own and their partner's orgastic experience. Taking turns allows for much more quality and concentration on the needs and wishes of the partner as well as providing both partners the enjoyment of bringing pleasure to the partner.

Redefinition and Integration of Love and Sex Within Marriage

THE CYCLE OF ROMANTIC LOVE

Myron Weiner posits five stages through which romantic love passes as it evolves into mature adult romantic love. "These stages, taken together, compose what may be called a love cycle. An intimate relationship that lasts over a significant period of time will go through many partial or full love cycles as the people change individually and as partners in the relationship."[21] Stage 1 is early courtship. This is the *pre-falling-in-love* stage in which partners "size up each other as sources of direct gratification." In this stage they find themselves "inexplicably drawn toward" each other with heightened desires.[22]

Stage 2 is the actual *falling in love*.

> The lover's ordinary interpersonal barriers . . . are lowered to allow the other 'in'. This leads to the feeling of emotional and physical fusion. It is at this stage that idealization of one's partner is at its height. . . . When one fails to meet the other's needs or expectations, a narcissistic injury occurs. . . . The result is the accusation that "you don't love me anymore."[23]

Stage 3 is the *unmasking* stage, which begins the process of transition from romantic love to a more subdued type of love often called companionate love. Unmasking involves seeing things that one's prior blindness prevented one from seeing. It involves making covert, unspoken, and unacknowledged expectations into overt, spoken, and acknowledged expectations. Stage 4 is the *enforcement* stage. "In stage four the disappointed lovers attempt to force their beloveds to become what they were thought to be or were expected to become." Weiner claims that compliance with a request for change is difficult because "their former idealness was not a true perception but an illusion or a wish."[24]

Weiner's Stage 5 is called *resolution*; each accepts the other as he or she really is. "Illusion is recognized as illusion. . . . [T]he ability to reach mutually satisfying resolutions sets the tone of the love relationship, whether it will be a series of stalemates, whether it will be a power struggle, or whether the legitimate needs of each will be recognized."[25]

Successful transition through the five stages operates best when both spouses have a healthy degree of personal maturity. If either of the partners suffers from a love deficit or carries an ultra-idealized internal representation of his or her parent of the opposite sex (see Chapter 2 for a discussion of object relations: projective identification), it will be difficult to traverse the next transitions required in Weiner's model. Weiner says quite forthrightly that love is not enough to sustain an intimate relationship.[26] Many couples never get beyond Stage 2. Immature lovers are trapped by their own need level and their own expectations and therefore have great difficulty working their way through the transitions, especially the transitions into the unmasking stage and the enforcement stage.

CLASSIFYING LOVE STYLES

There are many different frameworks or ways of looking at love. John Alan Lee has postulated the types of lovers and the kind of love in which these lovers participate.[27] Lee's research led him to develop a theory of three primary types of love and lovers. These are Eros, Ludus, and Storge. Lee likens the three primary types to the three primary colors: red, yellow, and blue. These are the pure colors from which all other hues are composed. The secondary types of love and lovers include Mania, Pragma, and Agape. There are also mixtures such as Ludus-Eros, Storge-Ludus, and Storge-Eros.

The **Eros**, or erotic, lover is sexually attracted to the partner. It is very much an attraction of the whole person: mental, emotional, and physical. The Ludus lover is playful. For Ludus, love is a game typically played with several partners at once, although it can be played with only one partner. This lover lacks the commitment of Eros and must defend against becoming overly involved emotionally.

Storge (pronounced stor-gay) is love without the motions of falling in love or the passions of the erotic lover. This love places a high value on sex but not as early in the relationship as Eros or Ludus. The Storge "lover is unaware of intense feeling. It simply doesn't occur . . . that a lover should be dewy-eyed and sentimental about a beloved."[28]

A major secondary type of love, Mania, is characterized by "agitation, sleeplessness, fever, loss of appetite, heartache. The Mania lover is consumed by thoughts of the beloved." Further, the Mania lover is prone to extreme mood swings, from ecstasy to despair, from joy to depression. The Mania lover wants to be possessed and is possessive. Jealousy erupts at the slightest threat of loss of love or love object.[29]

Pragma love is practical, utilitarian, and based on similarity in both sociological and psychological characteristics. Intense feelings may develop, but the characteristic tone is no-nonsense, with feet planted firmly on the ground. Arranged marriages are often of this type. Parents, matchmakers, or computerized matchmaking may select highly compatible personalities. Pragma love may deepen and grow over time.

Agape (a-gap-eh) is unconditional love based on the love of a deity for its creation. As such, it is a love that is both undeserved and unearned. It incorporates a selfless altruism. The only concern of Agape is not getting something in return but rather is a genuine and selfless concern for the well-being of the other.

The importance of Lee's work is in his attempt to distinguish different characteristics of various types of love and lovers. Mania comes closest to the experience of falling in love and to the romantic lover who thrives on the ecstasy of the romantic experience. Eros is far more capable than Mania of lasting commitment, spiritual affinity, and ongoing physical passion. Ludus appears to play at sex and love, and Mania appears to see sex only as the servant of love in true romantic fashion. Storge can be very deep, even if low key, while Pragma must value everything in the relationship according to utilitarian standards. Agape lovers may live so much for others that their own self-denial becomes oppressive and self-defeating.

THE COMPONENTS OF LOVE

The English language is truly impoverished when it comes to the usage and meaning of the word *love*. Love refers to anything, including football, movies, foods, cars, fashions, clothing, experiences, and, of course, feelings. We have all heard people say:

I love football.
I love sports.
I love to dance.
I love prime roast of beef.
I love to ski.
I love martinis and mint juleps.
I love to read.

Marital love, conjugal love, companionate love, infatuation, puppy love, sexual love, parental love, friendship love, patriotic love, and the love of a deity are all covered by the simple English word *love*.

The ancient Greeks used three words for love. **Philos** refers to friendship and to love between equals. Philos comes down to us in the word *Philadelphia*, the city of brotherly love (Philos = love; adelphos = brother). *Eros,* as used by the Greeks, describes the physical love between a man and a woman. Eros is the drive to create, to procreate, to communicate to another person in the most intimate of physical ways. *Agape* is the prototype of the unconditional and pure love that, in its theological form, represents the love of a deity for its creation. Agape is unearned, unmerited, unconditional, and undeserved. Agape says "I love you in spite of . . ." rather than "I love you because of. . . ." This is the kind of love parents have for their children, although in a less ideal state. "We love you in spite of the trouble you have gotten into" rather than "We love you because you are such a good girl or boy." On a deeper and perhaps more realistic note, agape is that deepest of all love that says I love you regardless of what you have done. Agape says I love you for you and not because of anything you have accomplished or done for me. In marriage, agape love implies an acceptance of one's mate as a fallible human being without implicit conditions or demands to change or to conform to the other's ideas of how you ought to be and what you ought to do.

In the West, since the impact of Freud, we have incorporated into our vocabulary another word that refers to the basic sexual drive of all human beings. The term for this basic sexual energy is **libido**. Rollo May refers to libido as sex love or as just plain sex. He points out that we have used sex to replace the combined physical and psychic intimacy of eros. May suggests that we have detached sexual love from erotic love and left little passion or creativity in sex.

My thesis . . . is that what underlies our emasculation of sex is the separation of sex from eros. Indeed, we have set sex over against eros, used sex precisely to avoid the anxiety-creating involvements of eros. . . . We are in a flight from eros and we use sex as the vehicle for the flight. Sex is the handiest drug to blot our awareness of the anxiety-creating aspects of eros. To accomplish this, we have had to define sex even more narrowly: the more we became preoccupied with sex, the more truncated and shrunken became the human experience to which is referred. We fly to the sensation of sex in order to avoid the passion of eros.[30]

Our culture has lost the true life-giving sense of eros. In fact, *eros* has become a dirty word, indicating lust, deviancy, and carnal degradation. This is extremely unfortunate because *eros* is the single greatest word for the nonromantic yet passionate love of a man and woman for each other. **Erotic** love is the best description of the passion, the love, the commitment, the caring, the affection, and the desire to fuse in the physical and mental warmth of sexual intercourse. If we must use a word for pornography, triple x-rated movies, and the loveless desires of the sex drive, let us henceforth use the proper word: The proper word is *libido*, that is, the sexual drive within us that is a part of our humanity. Pornographic movies are libidinous; uncensored and unbridled lust for sex is libidinous; carnal desire apart from any concern for the object of that desire is libidinous; prostitution and the commercial sale of sex is libidinous. *Libidinous sex is to be clearly distinguished from erotic sex in that eros is a good love, a healthy love; it indicates love that conveys both the commitment of love and the joy of passion and desire.*

Rollo May distinguishes libidinous sex from erotic sex:

Sex can be defined fairly adequately in physiological terms as consisting of the building up of bodily tensions and their release. Eros, in contrast, is the experiencing of the personal intentions and meaning of the act. Whereas sex is a rhythm of stimulus and response, eros is a state of being. . . . [E]ros seeks union with the other person in delight and passion, and the procreating of new dimensions of experience which broaden and deepen the being of both persons.[31]

Obviously, eros is what is missing in so much of the current emphasis on sex. The new sexual technology has its place, but it is reduced to ordinary libido when it loses the passion of eros. When the erotic element is lost we also lose the passion, the desire for union in aesthetic as well as physiological terms, the desire for creativity, expression, commitment, and spontaneity. Sex without the feelings, values, and emotions of eros may be caricatured by imagining two computers in bed programming orgasm. As Rollo May says, it is not physical nakedness that gives us pause, but spiritual, mental, and emotional nakedness. The "computers" may indeed be naked; yet there is a chastity belt drawn tight around the inner self of the person who avoids the passion and loving affection of eros. The chastity belt hides the heart, not the genitals.

Eros is a blended combination of sexual drive, sexual desire, affection, meaningful sharing, and depth communication. It is the unveiling and continued vulnerability of one's inner self to another. As such it must always contain the possibility of being hurt by the other and the possibility of experiencing the mental-emotional pain that is sometimes the inevitable concomitant of deep and abiding love. Eros is the deep inner urge to know the other, much as the ancient Hebrew word *yada* (to know) means to know in an intimate sexual sense. Yet, to know only sexually is not to know fully. Eros is the physical abandon of lovers who experience the reality of intimacy because they open themselves up to the passion of both emotional and physical love.

PAUL

Paul is 20 years old, is single, and considers himself to be sexually liberated from the binds of middle-class morality.

> I made this appointment because I'm having trouble! I've had all kinds of girls . . . pickups, townies, whores, and some real nice lays here on campus. As far as I'm concerned the townies put out the best.
>
> Well, everything seemed to be going along fine until about a month ago. For some time now I've been dating this girl who I really like. Maybe I love her—I don't know. I've had sex with her, but the last two times I had trouble getting an erection. Imagine that! This girl did something to me that I can't seem to get out of my mind. I even started to feel jealous when she told me she had sex with some other guy. The thing that really gets me now is that I'm having trouble making it with townies. I don't seem to get very excited . . . and after it's over I get this empty feeling like all it amounted to was a lot of nothing.

On a subsequent visit to the therapist Paul stated:

> I never would have believed it but I think I've discovered there is more to sex than just orgasm. Late last week I couldn't make it with a townie. Hell! I just couldn't get it on! Was I ever pissed with myself. What would people think? The guys? Wow! I had to tell them something because I always have. You know, bragging and stuff. So of course I told a pack of lies to the guys, but inside I was miserable. Remember that girl I told you about, the one who I got jealous about when I found out she had had sex with another guy? Well, we had the most fantastic weekend. We did everything. We ate together; went swimming; went to the movies; studied together; went horseback riding; we really . . . (pause) . . . we really opened up to each other . . . like it was great . . . I really emptied my guts to her and she to me. I never felt so close to another human being in my whole life. We had

sex a couple of times and it was the greatest I ever had. For the first time in my life I felt I really loved a girl. We were so close . . . its scary!

Paul's experience serves our purposes by showing that Paul had been experiencing libidinous love on almost a routine basis. He was using his sex partners with no regard for their dignity as persons. His thoughts about his recent weekend experience give testimony to the beginning development of the erotic type of love that Paul had never known before. We can begin to sense the blending of eros, libido, philos, and agape. Paul experienced a psychic intimacy with a female. That intimacy carried over into the passion-filled eros and included elements of philos and agape. Paul experienced a spiritual nakedness for the first time in his life.

Of course we may wish to raise some questions about Paul. Why is he so intent on sexual experiences? What does the variety of sex partners imply about his view of sex and of females in general? What kind of self-concept does Paul have? What does sexual conquest do for Paul's sense of self and his feelings of masculinity? What is the payoff for Paul when he boasts of his sexual prowess to his male friends? What might be the cause of Paul's failure to get an erection with his girlfriend and then later with the townie?

CONFIGURATION AND CONGRUENCY

If we are rejecting the romanticized definitions and explanations of love in favor of eros, libido, philos, and agape, then it is essential that we understand the love experience as a configuration, that is, a wholistic pattern that conveys a totality of meaning. A **configuration** is a patterned whole containing an arrangement of parts that blend together without conflict. **Congruency** is the absence of conflict: All the parts fit together in a mutually supportive manner. A configuration can be temporarily broken, and hence noncongruent, because of conflict between or among the parts that make up the whole. A configuration of eros, libido, philos, and agape represents a nonconflictual or congruent integration of values represented by the four kinds of love. Eros, libido, philos, and agape describe the various experiences most frequently associated with intimate relationships. Eros is a central concern here because it most accurately fulfills the passion and the dynamic impetus that most people associate with romantic love. Eros is a much deeper, fresher, and richer experience than the illusory and unrealistic concept of romanticism.

When marriage is based on a proportionate blending of eros, libido, philos, and agape, it is a marriage founded on a configuration of values capable of producing meaning and purpose (see Figure 3-1). If any one of the four kinds of love is missing, then the love configuration is broken. Furthermore, if either eros or libido love is lacking with one's mate (regardless of whether these are

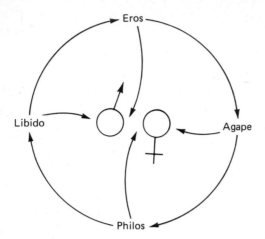

Figure 3-1 A Configuration in Which the Four Kinds of Love Are Congruent

being met in extramarital relations), there is no love configuration because the four-faceted configuration is broken.

If a marriage contains eros, libido, and philos but no agape, not only is the configuration broken but the entire relationship will very likely be conflict ridden. This is because there is a lack of basic acceptance of each other as persons. If there is no acceptance of one's partner as he/she is, it is likely that there will be ongoing friction between them. Each will try to remake the other, to change the other into an image of oneself projected largely on the other. Agape implies both total acceptance and forgiveness, both of which are necessary for emotional satisfaction in a shared climate of intimacy. Intimacy is the ability to be concerned about the partner and the self at the same time, a willingness to self-disclose, and a sharing of common interests and activities. Without agape, intimacy is impossible.

Likewise, if there is agape, eros, and libido but no philos, then again there is a broken configuration because there is no mental-emotional caring and sharing, the kind of friendship that is so important in a meaningful and dynamic marriage. Obviously, if there is libido but no eros, the whole relationship becomes one-sided and empty. And if there is eros but no libido or basic sex drive, then the eros will be of a spiritual nature only and will be lacking in physical intimacy and passion.

As Rollo May has said so well, it is the blending together in varying proportions of eros, libido, philos, and agape that constitutes the foundation for an enduring relationship.[32]

The love configuration is a central premise to which we will refer again in future sections of this book. For now let us be clear that the love configuration may not create ecstatic feelings such as being "on top of the world"; it may not be as romantic as "angel and lover, heaven and earth am I with you," or as dramatic as "I won't last a day without you," or as electrifying as "you light up my life," *but the love configuration does have the capability of producing a rich and satisfying marriage—something that romanticism has never been able to do.*

Synthesis

Romanticized love, sex, and marriage are an unlikely triad. Together they hold a contradiction because romanticized love is fed and nurtured by distance, obstacles, and illusory expectations. What then can we say about love, sex, and marriage? Is it possible to combine meaningful and passionate love with vibrant and playful sex in a long-term sexually exclusive dyadic relationship? My answer is yes, it is very possible.

First, I would agree that almost all lovers, even Pragma lovers, Storge lovers, and Agape lovers, would experience at least a small dose of the first two stages of the cycle of love as outlined by Myron Weiner. I would not quarrel with Weiner's stages. They may be more or less accurate and descriptive of most intimate relationships. In a general sense they seem to be logical and descriptive of a very large segment of the American population.

Second, Lee's attempt to identify various styles of loving and types of lovers makes a great deal of sense, even if the resulting style or type often is a hybrid with a blending of characteristics. The point is, however, that one type or style usually dominates the others, and this would indicate a person's primary manner of loving. Some people, perhaps legions of them, are primarily Mania lovers who very much want the best of both Eros and Ludus. Others are Pragma lovers, and they incorporate large portions of Storge and Agape, and usually less Ludus and Eros. The pure typology of Ludus is incompatible with a sexually exclusive marriage, but the idea of playfulness in sex is a very important ingredient that is too often painfully absent in far too many American marriages. In fact, if there were more Ludus (playful sex) in marriage there would also likely be an increase in Eros and possibly in Philos and Agape as well.

Third, the configuration of components—eros, libido, philos, and agape—has the distinct conceptual advantage of blending four entirely different definitions of love into a whole that is far greater than the sum of its parts. When we conceptualize love as a configuration of different experiences and components that may be expressed in one or several styles in the ongoing development of the relationship over time, we may begin to see why it is not an easy or simple task to build a mature, enduring, vital relationship.

Figure 3-2 presents a graphic representation of the components, styles, and cycle of love. At the center are the components of love: eros, libido, philos, and agape. I hold that these four components must always be blending with

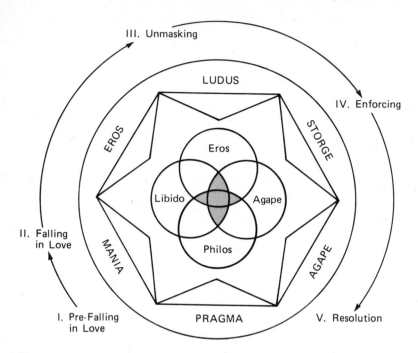

Figure 3-2 Love: Components—Styles—Cycle

each other in varying proportions in order for the relationship to have sufficient foundation. The proportion or amount of each of the four components may vary from day to day and even from hour to hour depending on mood, setting, situation, and stress. The styles of loving form the hexagon surrounding the four components. The four components may be expressed and enacted in any one of six basic styles or mixtures of styles.

Finally, certain stages will inevitably need to be negotiated to make the transition from Stage 1, pre-falling in love, to Stage 5, resolution. Every individual is different. Every couple is different. They will express the components in unique styles as they traverse the cycle of love development. Different styles of lovers will have different difficulties and problems as they grow together. The Agape lover will not experience the enforcing stage in the same way a Mania or Eros lover would experience it. The Mania lover will have the toughest struggle with Stage 3, unmasking, and Stage 4, enforcing. This is because the characteristics of Mania resemble historic romanticization more closely than do those of any other style. It is romanticism that so wants to enforce the other to remain idealized in the lover's mind, thus giving rise to the twin imperatives, "Be what I want you to be. Do what I want you to do."

When the component of eros and the style of Eros are combined, we come closest to a truly healthy view of what most people seem to mean when they talk about romantic love. By this I mean that when we discard the unrealistic and illusory aspects and trappings of romanticism with its style of Mania, we are able to embrace a more mature "romantic" orientation characterized by eros in balance with libido, philos, and agape on the component level. These blended components are then tempered by Ludus, Agape, and Pragma on the stylistic level.

Mania, working alone, gets many marriages into trouble. As we've seen, Mania is the emotional counterpart to historical romanticism. Unfortunately, many Americans equate Mania with "true love." Unbridled and untempered Mania leads us to the celebration of love exclusively as a feeling to be idolized rather than as an activity, an art, a commitment, and a fact.

Finally, what does all of this mean when a young man or woman is tempted to use the big "L" word and say "I love you"? Does it mean he/she should say "I Philos you" or "I Eros you" or "I Agape you"? Of course not! But there is a difference among being "in like," "in lust," or "in love." Probably the best solution is to continue to use the words *in love* but to be able to do two things: (1) know within oneself what one means when one uses these words, and (2) convey to one's partner a bit more precisely and clearly what is meant by these words.

Summary

The focus of this chapter has been on the American attempt to combine romanticized love with sexual expression within marriage. I have called this the Grand Illusion. The courtly and romantic traditions were outlined in order to set the stage for the American version of romanticism. The chief hypothesis of the chapter was that romanticism as a philosophy of sex and love is destructive of marital satisfaction because romanticism makes an idol of love and idealizes the beloved to such an extent that no one can live up to love's expectations.

Myths pertaining to love, marriage, and sex were presented. Most of these myths are related to romanticism in some form. A model was presented as a means of illustrating the integration of the components of love, the styles of loving, and the cycle of love. The redefinitions and the integration are based on the configuration of eros, libido, philos, and agape. When a dynamic eros is combined with the components of libido, philos, and agape, a broad foundation is established for the ongoing inclusion of love and sex within marriage. How this evolves into a mature relationship varies, depending on individual and couple styles and preferences.

Many will protest the substitution of the components for romanticized love. But the configuration of eros, libido, philos, and agape need not preclude moonlight, candlelight, roses, wine, and other romantic symbols and gestures.

Eros in particular involves tenderness and commitment, affection and mystique, as well as sexual desire. The couple that seeks to vitalize their relationship will use variety, spontaneity, and imagination. Instead of "falling in love" in a passive way as if something happened over which a person has no control, you are now an active agent in loving by creating different kinds of love with different meanings.

I am suggesting and encouraging the death of the movement known as historical romanticism. It is a philosophy that has outlived its usefulness because it is a philosophy of relationships between the sexes based on false hopes and idealistic and logically impossible expectations. Consequently it has created disillusionment, disenchantment, disappointment, resentment, and despair. In its place I am advocating an integration of different kinds and styles of love—a mature version of love that need not be unrealistic or illusory if it is based solidly on the daily blending of eros, libido, philos, and agape.

Reading Suggestions

Crosby, John F., ed. *Reply to Myth: Perspectives on Intimacy*. New York: Wiley, 1985.

de Rougemont, Denis. *Love in the Western World*. New York: Harcourt, Brace, and Company, 1940.

Ellis, Albert. *American Sexual Tragedy*. New York: Lyle Stewart, 1962.

Hunt, Morton M. *Tha Natural History of Love*. New York: Alfred A. Knopf, 1959.

Lederer, William J. and Don D. Jackson. *The Mirages of Marriage*. New York: W. W. Norton, 1968.

Lee, John Alan. "The Styles of Loving." *Psychology Today* (Oct 1974).

May, Rollo. *Love and Will*. New York: W. W. Norton, 1969.

Ortega y Gasset, José. *On Love: Aspects of a Single Theme*. New York: Meridian Books, 1957.

Pope, Kenneth, et al. *On Love and Loving*. San Francisco: Jossey-Bass, 1980.

Rubenstein, Carin. "The Modern Art of Courtly Love." *Psychology Today* (July 1983).

Notes

1. Denis de Rougemont, "A Judgment in the House of the Countess of Champagne. Delivered in this year 1174, on the third day before the Kalends of May, Proclamation VII." In *Love in the Western World* (New York: Harcourt Brace Jovanovich, 1940, Fawcett Premier Edition, Pantheon Books, 1956), 35. Quotation reprinted by permission of Pantheon Books, a division of Random House.

2. Carl Degler, "What Ought to Be and What Was: Women's Sexuality in the Nineteenth Century," *American Historical Review* 79 (Dec 1974): 1467–1490.

3. George Henry Napheys, *The Transmission of Life: Counsels on the Nature and Hygiene of the Masculine Functions* (Toronto, Canada: Rose Publishing, 1886), 164–165.

4. Morton M. Hunt, *The Natural History of Love* (New York: Alfred A. Knopf, 1959).

5. Stuart A. Queen and Robert W. Habenstein, *The Family in Various Cultures*. 3d ed. (New York: Harper & Row, 1974).
6. Hugo Beigel, "Romantic Love," *American Sociological Review* 14 (1951): 326–332.
7. *Ibid.*
8. *Op. cit.*, de Rougemont, 291.
9. *Op. cit.*, de Rougemont, 35.
10. José Ortega y Gasset, *On Love: Aspects of a Single Theme* (New York: Meridian Books, 1957), 12.
11. Ernest van den Haag, "Love or Marriage," *Harper's Magazine*, 224 (May 1962), 138–140.
12. *Ibid.*
13. *Op. cit.*, Beigel.
14. *Op. cit.*, Beigel.
15. Albert Ellis, *American Sexual Tragedy* (New York: Lyle Stewart, 1962), 97–121. All quotations reprinted by permission.
16. Ruth M. Underhill, "The Papago Family," In *Comparative Family Systems*, M. F. Nimkoff, ed. (Boston: Houghton Mifflin, 1965) 150–151.
17. John Levy and Ruth Munroe, *The Happy Family* (New York: Alfred A. Knopf, 1938), 66–67. Copyright 1938 and renewed 1966 by Ruth Munroe Levy. Reprinted by permission of Alfred A. Knopf, Inc.
18. William J. Lederer and Don D. Jackson, *The Mirages of Marriage* (New York: W. W. Norton, 1968), 75–78.
19. Gary W. Peterson and Boyd C. Rollins, "Parent-Child Socialization," In *Handbook of Marriage and the Family*, Marvin B. Sussman and Suzanne K. Steinmetz, eds. (New York: Plenum Press, 1987), 487–496.
20. John F. Crosby, ed., *Reply to Myth: Perspectives on Intimacy* (New York: Wiley, 1985), 292.
21. Myron F. Weiner, "Healthy and Pathological Love-Psychodynamic Views," In *On Love and Loving*. Kenneth Pope, ed. (San Francisco: Jossey-Bass, 1980), 121. All quotations reprinted by permission.
22. *Ibid.*
23. *Ibid.*
24. *Ibid*, 123.
25. *Ibid.*
26. *Ibid*, 126.
27. John Alan Lee, "The Styles of Loving," *Psychology Today* (Oct 1974).
28. *Ibid.*
29. *Ibid.*
30. Rollo May, *Love and Will* (New York: W. W. Norton, 1969), 65. All quotations reprinted by permission.
31. *Ibid*, 73–74.
32. *Ibid.*

Chapter 4

Love Imperatives, Binds, and Double Binds:

Breaking the Pattern

"All I want is for you to accept me as I am."
"Yes, and all I want is for you to accept my not accepting you."

HUGH PRATHER
NOTES TO MYSELF

The Use and Abuse of Love

LOVE AS JUSTIFICATION

In the name of love many things are justified and excused. Parents who physically abuse their children say they love their children. Husbands who beat their wives claim they love them. In the name of love people sometimes commit violent acts of passion. In the name of love we sometimes overprotect and overindulge our children, preventing them from experiencing necessary developmental changes to the fullest degree, and thereby impeding their growth and development. In the name of love husbands neglect their wives and wives their husbands, failing to take the time and effort to show signs of daily caring and loving acceptance.

THE LOVE TRIP

The *love trip* refers to the practice or the phenomenon of using the concept or idea of love to justify a multitude of human actions. More than this, however, we also use love as a means of attempting to exercise power *over* others. Love becomes a means of controlling or dominating those whom we say we love. Love seeks to impose its will on the beloved. By clever usage of the word *love* we attempt to manipulate and coerce the loved one to do our bidding. In short, *love* not only is an overworked word but also is frequently used as a weapon in the collection of devices and maneuvers of control, domination, and power. This leads to feelings of resentment, anger, doubt, and guilt for the person on the receiving end of such manipulations and coercions. In effect, the use of love as a coercive agent is akin to the "shaming" technique often used by parents on their children.

The shaming technique is a threatening of the child's or adolescent's sense of security. This is easily accomplished by threatening the withdrawal of love. This is usually done implicitly rather than explicitly. That is, the threatening message is seldom really spelled out all the way. "After all your mother and father have done for you, how can you even think of doing such a thing?" "To think that after all the sacrifices we've made for you, you would do such a

106

thing!" These messages are calculated to make the recipient feel bad, guilty, ashamed, and remorseful. They are also calculated to get the recipient to cease or commence a certain mode of behavior or belief. Love is made into a conditional commodity wherein the young person learns very quickly that one is loved only when pleasing the parent. Later in life there may be a transference from the parent to the mate, and the shamed person feels loved only as long as he or she is pleasing the mate. This causes the shamed person to become a person without an identity because he or she feels that he/she must always please or placate the other, thus slowly losing any semblance of his/her own individuality or identity. When love is placed in a wholly conditional framework, it is not love: It is merely a reward for compliant behavior.

Under these manipulative conditions we learn very quickly to bury or suppress our real feelings. We learn that it is risky at best and dangerous at worst to say, to verbalize, or otherwise to communicate what we are feeling and thinking. We learn to play the game of compliance at any price. Later on we may wonder why we are feeling so depressed! The answer is, of course, that we have allowed ourselves to be molded and shaped, dominated and controlled by a person who claims that if we love him or her, this is what we will let him or her do to us. The end result is, as has been suggested, that we become a nonperson or a person without an identity.

LOVE AS A MEANS OF CONTROL

This chapter contains examples and illustrations of how we frequently use love as a means of attempting to control or change the behavior of others. The theme is limited to marital and other intimate relationships between marital partners and lovers. That this "love trip," as I call it, usually leads to resentment and anger is an understatement. In truth, when love is used as a coercive technique it invariably tends to destroy the love the manipulated person once felt for the manipulator. As Paul Dell has pointed out, much misery is created by our attempts to change others. He says "I think that refusal to accept what is underlies all anger and leads inexorably to attempts to control things."[1]

Unfortunately we use the concept of love to destroy the relationship. The very weapon we employ to bring about compliance often destroys the marriage. And if the marriage as a legal entity is not destroyed, at least the relationship is severely wounded. Why? Because people do not like to be "had." They do not like to be manipulated, coerced, shamed, or made to feel guilty.

The root cause, of course, is the desire to change the partner in order to make one's own existence more pleasant, comfortable, and enjoyable. "Be what I want you to be. Do what I want you to do. Don't be for you. Be for me." In other words, never mind you living your life. All that matters is my life, and I want you to accommodate to me, bend to me, and *exist for me*. In thinking, feeling, and acting this way we rarely stop to consider what we are really doing. What we are doing, however, is no less than asking the other person to forfeit individuality, or selfhood, for us. In effect we are attempting to obliterate them as persons by making them into selfless automatons whose only purpose and function in life is to make us happy.

Confronting Irrational Beliefs

RATIONAL EMOTIVE THERAPY

Rational emotive therapy (RET) is a method of confronting one's beliefs. RET employs an ABC reasoning process wherein A refers to the activating agent; B refers to the belief, either rational or irrational; and C refers to the consequence or the result. Most people believe that A causes C, that an action causes a consequence. In truth, it is belief (B) about the activating agent (A) that causes the consequence (C).

You Should Have Reminded Them
(Mother of Teenagers to Husband)

Activating agent:	A	Mother: The kids didn't give me anything for Mother's Day.
Belief:	B	
Belief is *r*ational Br		
or Belief is *ir*rational Bi		
	Bi	Mother: Husbands should remind and contrive to have teenagers remember their mother on Mother's Day.
Consequence	C	Mother: (to father) I'm feeling depressed and I'm angry at you.

In this scenario, a mother feels depressed and angry at her husband at level C. The apparent cause is that the young people forgot to remember their mother on Mother's Day, level A. This act of forgetfulness or of negligence is not usually sufficient to cause depression and anger. The immediate cause of the depression and anger is the mother's *belief* that the husband *should* have reminded the young people about Mother's Day. If this belief is rational, that is, that fathers should remind teenagers and children, then the mother's depression and anger make sense. However, if the belief that fathers should remind their offspring is irrational, then the mother is making herself miserable because of a belief she holds that is irrational, illogical, false, or inaccurate. *The basis of RET is a judgment regarding whether a belief is rational or irrational.*

Much human misery and marital grief is the result of our irrational beliefs, attitudes, and assumptions. As long as the B item is irrational, illogical, or simply false, the person will experience level C, the consequence. According to Albert Ellis, the originator of RET, most people skip directly from level A to level C, blaming their feelings at level C on the activating agent of level A. Ellis claims that when we skip from level A to level C without stopping to challenge or question the belief at level B, we are really failing to see that our feelings or consequences at level C are the direct result of a faulty belief at level B, rather than the activity or activating agent at level A.[2]

You Should Know When I Am Depressed
(Wife Seems to Ignore or Is Not Aware of Husband's Slouching Around)

Activating agent: A   Husband: (to wife) You are insensitive to my needs. You don't care about me.

Belief: B

*r*ational Br or
*ir*rational Bi

Husband: (to wife) You should know when I am depressed and you should do something about it.

Consequence   C   Husband: (to wife) I am angry at you. I feel unwanted and unloved.

In this situation the husband blames his feeling of being unwanted and unloved on his mate. He is angry at his wife (level C) because of her insensitivity and uncaring (level A). In truth it is the husband's irrational belief that is causing the angry feelings (at level C). This husband believes that his wife *should* be able to read his moods correctly and take action to get him out of these moods. This is the myth of magical knowing with an imperative to make things right. "Magical knowing" is the irrational belief that because you love me you will know what I am thinking, feeling, and wanting.

According to Ellis a great deal of unhappiness and misery is due to our beliefs. "You should know when I am depressed." "You should do something about it." If I really believe that my partner should know what I am feeling and further, what to do about it, then I am going to be angry, or at least upset or irritated, if she fails to know what I am feeling.[3] Illogical or irrational level B statements almost always include or imply words that are imperatives. An imperative is a command. You *should,* you *ought,* you *must!* Throughout this chapter the reader is encouraged to identify, define, confront, and challenge the belief underlying the imperative, the bind, or the double bind. Once you identify the belief, the next crucial step is to make a judgment regarding the rationality or irrationality of the belief. The final goal of RET is to change ourselves by labeling our irrational beliefs as irrational, consequently altering the self-destructive consequences of level C. Karen Horney has written about the *Tyranny of the Should.*[4] Her point is that people who are constantly doing things because they should, or because they ought to, are often very unhappy people, always marching to the tune of an unseen drummer. Unless and until these beliefs are challenged and confronted as to their truth, their rationality, their legitimacy, and their veracity, the individual person or couple is enslaved by them. We insist that others perform as we believe they ought, must, or should. When they fail at measuring up to our irrational expectations, we become angry and often spiteful.

The following *love imperatives* are prime examples of how we attempt to control others by our own beliefs and the insistence that our partner do as we insist he or she ought or should do. As you read these imperatives please be searching for the belief at level B and determine if you think the belief is rational or irrational.

The Love Without Anger Imperative

INDIFFERENCE LEADS TO DEPRESSION

Within intimate relationships the opposite of love is not hate, anger, or resentment. It is indifference. Love and anger are two sides of the same coin. Within intimate relationships, love makes one vulnerable to deep feelings of pain and hurt, rejection, and misery. Because of the depth of feeling involved, the ordinary response is to transform the energy expended in the experience of pain and hurt into anger toward the person who is perceived to be causing these painful feelings. This response is usually engineered by the defenses of the ego. Often when we have exhausted ourselves in anger we become numb, dull, and lifeless. Although the anger appears to have subsided, it has simply become diffuse, invading our body and causing us to feel numb, dull, lethargic, fatigued, and lifeless. This is depression. This depression leads us to the cognitive and behavioral response known as indifference.

ANGER AND CONFLICT

This chain reaction of hurt and pain leading to anger, which in turn leads to depression and indifference, is often seen in marriage. As will be pointed out in greater detail in later chapters, we begin by questioning the popular belief that anger is somehow bad, wrong, or even sinful. Anger and conflict are neither right nor wrong. They are **amoral**. Amoral means to be without moral valence, weight, or direction. Something that is amoral is neither good nor bad in itself, neither right nor wrong in itself. To avoid anger or conflict by denial or by various accommodating or peacemaking maneuvers can be very damaging and harmful. It is akin to anesthetizing ourselves from physical pain without finding the source of pain. (The presence of bodily pain is, or course, a lifesaving phenomenon, alerting us to the fact that something within our bodies is wrong and needs attention.) Just as physical pain alerts us to the fact that something is wrong with our body, so also emotional and mental pain tell us that something is wrong with our relationship. To ignore or deny either kind of pain, physical or mental, may cause great harm to ourselves and our intimates.

THE BELIEF AND ITS IMPERATIVES

Thus, part of our problem in intimate relationships is our *belief* that anger is wrong. This belief and its imperative are often expressed by saying:

If you really love me, you would . . .

never be angry with me.
never fault me or criticize me.
always agree with me.
do things my way.
see things my way.
never hurt me.
not fight or quarrel with me or resist me.
not be so stubborn.
know I am right.

The old popular song says, "If you love me, really love me. . . ." The use of the phrase, "If you love me, you would . . ." is almost always an attempt to manipulate the partner into doing something that you want the partner to do. In order to get the partner to do something or to be a certain way, "love" is used as a coercive weapon. The implied message, rarely verbalized, is that if you don't do it my way (behave my way—think my way—see things my way), you really don't love me.

THE EFFECT ON THE RELATIONSHIP

When this manipulative ploy is used in connection with the myth of angerless love the results can be fatal to the relationship. "If you love me you will not be angry with me" is a way of saying that love cannot or must not include anger of any kind. It is saying that anger is proof of the absence of love. It is saying that true love is absolutely accommodating and accepting of everything I am and everything I do. The implicit demand is that you will yield to my every wish and request because this is what love is all about.

The recipient of this ploy will eventually become increasingly frustrated and angered, devastated and destroyed. The healthy individual will eventually push for confrontation of this destructive imperative. He or she will seek help, and if no breakthroughs or changes occur, divorce is a likely possibility. When both partners use the same ploy on each other the marriage will be threatened almost immediately. Myron Weiner calls this the "enforcement" stage of a relationship, wherein the partners attempt to thrust their own way of doing and being onto the partner.[5]

I am not suggesting that there is no room for compromise on these issues. There certainly is. Nor am I suggesting that people should not change or should not request the partners to change. I am suggesting that the implicit or explicit *demand* to change is self-defeating, egocentric, irrational, and illegitimate. I am attacking the manipulative ploy, together with the irrational beliefs that lend it credence. The basic irrational belief holds that the partner's love *should* be angerless and totally selfless.

Logically, my demand that my partner be self-sacrificing for me ought to imply that I would likewise be self-sacrificing for my partner. But somehow persons who use this ploy aren't concerned with logic or fairness.

The Magical Knowing Imperative

INTIMATE MIND READING

Perhaps one of the most outlandish claims made on behalf of love is the belief that if you really love me, you would know what I am thinking, feeling, needing, or wanting. And of course, if you know what I am thinking, feeling, needing, or wanting, you will know exactly what to do to fulfill my expectations. Those who believe that the partner should be adept at mind reading always have the unspoken expectation that the partner should respond appropriately to his/her feelings, wants, and needs. When this doesn't happen there is fertile soil for conflict and anger.

It is true that when two people live together as intimates over a period of time they become familiar with each other's moods, quirks, and idiosyncrasies. However, it does not necessarily follow that this familiarity is an accurate entrée into the other's thought or feeling process.

The myth of magical knowing is a way to describe the expectation that your partner *ought* to know you so well that he or she would "just know" what is on your mind and then would fill these needs and wants. In effect, the myth of magical knowing demands that we have extrasensory perception (ESP) or at least be mind readers.

THE BELIEF AND ITS IMPERATIVES

The imperative of magical knowing is not only irrational, it is presumptuous and outrageous. It is often expressed by saying:

If you really love me, you would . . .

know what I am thinking.
know what I am feeling.
know what I need.
know what I want.
know what's bothering me.
know why I am hurt.
know why I am angry.

First, the imperative of magical knowing claims that true love demands an ability to read the partner's mind. Second, it shifts the responsibility away from the self to the partner; that is, it makes the partner responsible for whatever is wrong. In short, the imperative of magical knowing shifts the responsibility away from the *offended* person (the complaining self) to the partner who is now labeled as the *offender*. Hence, in the name of love I have made my partner bear the responsibility for my unhappiness or my misery. This relieves me of the responsibility to know myself, to examine my motives, my maneuvers, and my games. It further relieves me of the responsibility to challenge my beliefs and my assumptions. In the absence of such self-scrutiny the consequences are your fault, not mine! Whatever happens to us is due to your failure, not mine.

The Sexual Imperative

THE BELIEF AND ITS IMPERATIVES

The imperative of "ought" and "should" carries over into the sexual arena. The partners assume not only that love will find a way but also that true love will lend a clairvoyance or magical clarity. There will be no need for informative communication or sharing of desires, wishes, or preferences. The sexual imperative states:

If you really love me, you would . . .

know how to turn me on.
know what I like and don't like.
like sex as much as I do.
want sex as often as I do.
never say no.
always want to please me.
not notice others.

not flirt with others.

trust me without question.

respect my wishes and wants.

In Chapter 6 we will consider human sexuality in greater detail. For now, we will demonstrate the abuse of love that occurs when one presses, in the name of love, for absolute cooperation, acquiescence, compliance, and blind submission.

The weapon employed is a coercive threat based on a fallacious definition of love. The recipient of such coercive love messages is immediately threatened because the failure to respond will be interpreted by the sender as confirmation that "you really don't love me." Therefore, the recipient is placed in a double-bind situation. Responding favorably to such a maneuver confirms and increases the power and control of the one using the love ploy. But refusing to comply confirms—as far as the one using the ploy perceives—a lack of love. And so the recipient is "damned if I do and damned if I don't."

In a double bind, whichever of the alternatives is chosen, the recipient is in the wrong. "If you refuse to have sex with me it means you don't love me, and if you do decide to have sex, it's only because you're trying to please me and your heart isn't really in it." No matter which alternative is chosen it is wrong. The placing of someone in a double-bind situation is a poor fight tactic. Not only does the constant use of double binds create resentment and destroy spontaneous feelings of love, it can cause serious emotional and mental disturbance because the recipient is bound to become increasingly frustrated and insecure, never knowing which way to turn or how to resolve the dilemma.

The double bind is tough to deal with. Often one doesn't realize one is in a double bind until it is too late. Later in this chapter we will consider methods for dealing with double binds. These include switching the turf, changing the tactics, naming or labeling the "game" the coercive partner is playing, and directly confronting the "player" and his or her implied threat.

LINES

The dating game and the entire range of lines contain limitless examples of this coercive use of love. Sol Gordon's book *You Would If You Loved Me* discusses sexual lines and is rich in its appeals to "love" as a coercive and manipulative technique. Of the many thousands of lines that Gordon has collected, by far the most widely used is *If you really love me. . . .* Gordon suggests countering this line with a similar imperative: *If you really love me, you won't put pressure on me.*[6]

Many males have learned that they can have ongoing and frequent sexual intercourse by employing the line, "You would if you loved me." Many very young and naive females are extremely susceptible to such an approach, since they fear losing the attention and affection of their boyfriends if they refuse their sexual advances. This is but one spin-off of the most famous (or infamous) **quid pro quo** (something for something) of the dating game, wherein the male feigns or pretends love in order to obtain sexual favors and the female feigns sexual ardor in order to gain the security of attention and ongoing affection (that is, to feel loved).

THE BARGAIN: SEX IN EXCHANGE FOR AFFECTION

The same game may be played in marriage with neither spouse challenging the other. The quid pro quo or trade-off is sensed, but neither partner chooses to do anything about it because of the fear of losing the other. The wife may reluctantly comply with her husband's imperative while he continues to make at least a pretense of affection. She is threatened with loss of the security of affection if she fails to comply with his demands for sex. He is threatened with loss of sexual access if he fails to comply with her demands for affection.

The sexual imperative, like most of the imperatives, leads to an *implied* ultimatum rather than a direct ultimatum. The sexual imperative, whether issued by the man or by the woman, is usually destructive to the relationship in the long run, if not also in the short run. People tend to lose their spontaneity and their feelings of affection and love when they are faced with endless imperatives and ultimatums.

The Togetherness Imperative

THE COUPLE FRONT

The social milieu bequeaths to us the hallowed image of the couple front.[7] The couple front is the belief that husband and wife should almost always appear together as a couple at social functions, leisure time functions, recreational functions, and so on.

Laura Singer has lamented the confusion of closeness with togetherness.[8] People lacking authentic closeness often appear to possess a strong togetherness. However, togetherness may be nothing but a cover for lack of closeness. Marriage therapists call this pseudomutuality. *Pseudomutuality* is a binding of the marital partners at the expense of separation and individuality.[9] As the term implies, the mutuality is a *false* or pretended mutuality. Marriage and family therapists also relate terms such as *togetherness* and *pseudomutuality* to the concept of **enmeshment.** Enmeshment is the failure to establish boundaries between family members, including marital partners, to such an extent that individuality is lost and the clarity and sharpness of individual identity and functioning is impaired or lost.[10]

Many couples enjoy a healthy sense of closeness without excessive togetherness and without pseudomutuality and enmeshment. Pseudomutuality is usually an *unspoken mutual pretense* that the couple is a smoothly operating partnership. Disagreements and conflict are explained away, downplayed, or denied. In short, there is self-deception on the part of each mate, whereby each tries to convince himself or herself "Yes, we are a really compatible couple."[11]

Pseudomutuality translates into a further expression of the couple front. It is important to note that the couple front is not just for the sake of others; it is also for the sake of the couple. The couple front becomes part of their own self-deception. The ideas of pseudomutuality and the couple front are quite antithetical to intimacy and emotional closeness because genuine intimacy and emotional closeness depend on self-disclosure and honest sharing where there is no pretense at playing games or attempts to manipulate each other. In short, when partners achieve authentic closeness, there is, by definition, no pseudomutuality and no need to carry out a charade of togetherness such as the couple front.

THE BELIEF AND ITS IMPERATIVES

The consideration of the couple front brings us to the togetherness imperative. The togetherness imperative is a command—a demand, almost an ultimatum—that the partner do things with me, not alone or individually or with others. This includes leisure time pursuits and recreation interests. It can even extend to a resentment of time and energy a partner may invest in a job, career, or hobby. The imperative states:

If you really love me, you would . . .

give up your friends for me.
take more time off.
not work evenings.
not spend so much time at the (office), (plant), or (shop).
come straight home from work.
want to be with me more (all the time).
want to go out (frequently) to dinner, dancing, movies, the theater.
be enthusiastic about doing things with me.
want to take short trips or go on long vacations.
play golf with me instead of with your friends.
go to the races with me.
want to play (bridge), (poker), or (tennis) with me.
never go fishing without me (even though I don't like to fish).
always go to church with me.
go to PTA with me.
participate in community activities with me.
not ever need or want to spend time with anyone else.

COERCION TO CHANGE THE PARTNER: THE FAILURE OF AGAPE LOVE

Again, the coercive power of love is employed in order to provoke change in the partner. The myth that if you really loved me you would be willing to do these things for me or with me compels the partner to take a defensive stance and often opens the door to a dirty or nonconstructive fight. The noncompliant partner may be justified in refusing the demands of love but may also feel low and uncomfortable at being placed in such a defensive or noncompliant stance. The person making the request or demand will now likely feel increased frustration. We assume that the requesting/demanding person was frustrated and perhaps very angry when making the imperative. Now when the imperative is resisted or scorned, the feelings of anger, hurt, frustration, and even despair have been redoubled.

Beneath the coercive attempt to change the partner is the lack or failure of agape love. As I explained earlier, agape is an unconditional love that accepts the partner "in spite of." It is not denial, and it is not condescension. Agape recognizes differences in temperament, personality, character, and other personal habits and preferences without any attempt to get the partner to change or to "be more like me." No enduring relationship of quality can survive without the blending of eros, libido, philos, and agape.

Unfortunately many people equate philos, or genuine friendship, with a strong similarity and togetherness in habits and personal preferences. In overdoing this mistaken definition of philos, they lose sight of agape. As one reader of an earlier edition of this book pointed out, "Agape is where it's at." Certainly agape is a significant part of "where it's at" because the attempt to change the partner can be a powerful indication of nonacceptance. Our refusal to accept "what is"—that is, to refuse to accept our mate as a totally independent person in his/her own right—becomes the basis for our anger, which then gives rise to our attempts to change and control others.

Binds and Double Binds

Binds and double binds may be illustrated by using the ideas of approach and avoidance. When we want to approach someone or something, we usually do, unless there is a stronger force within us that influences us to avoid the person or situation. Then we are in an approach-avoidance situation. The stronger force will win out at that moment. Sometimes we may have to choose between two attractive alternatives: This is called an approach-approach situation. When we are asked to choose between two undesirable alternatives, we are in an avoidance-avoidance situation.

A person who is caught between two alternatives is in a **bind**. The bind may be severe or very mild, such as choosing between chocolate or lemon-chiffon pie. Severe binds are said to occur when the stakes are higher, the issues more important, and the values in greater contradiction. The feeling of being caught in a bind refers to possible rewards and punishments that may result as a consequence of the choice. When the choice of either alternative will result in negative and undesirable consequences, we say that the person is in a **double bind:** He or she cannot possibly win. The situation has already determined that the person must lose.

The difference between a bind and a double bind is that the double bind leads us beyond a feeling of simple frustration, restriction, or restraint caused by the need to make a decision. In a double bind we usually experience a feeling of futility caused by the realization that no matter which alternative is chosen we are going to lose. We are damned if we do and damned if we don't. When we are in a simple bind we can choose to unbind ourselves. When we are in a double bind there is greatly reduced hope of finding a satisfactory solution. Technically a true double-bind situation places an individual in a predicament between two alternatives with the additional restriction that it is impossible for the double-bound person to leave the field or to escape the scene by simply walking away.[12] This is the predicament among children who are placed in double-bind situations and who cannot leave the field. For example, children involved in custodial wars between the parents are sometimes placed in a situation of having to state their preference concerning which parent they would prefer to live with. In this situation there is no escape for the child. The child cannot leave the field.

A well-known double bind pertaining to the area of sex between intimates is when one partner requests some change in the sexual behavior of the other. When the request is granted the requesting partner then says, "But you are doing this only because I asked you to, not because you want to." Thus the responding partner is in a double bind. He/she is damned if he/she does not go along with the original request, and on the other hand, if he/she does go along with the request he/she is accused of doing it only because he/she was requested to and not because he/she really wanted to.

I will come back to the subject of double binds after I discuss some of the more powerful single binds of intimate relationships.

The Identity in Marriage Bind

PAULA AND BRAD

BRAD: We married at 22. We took our time. We knew each other well. We didn't live together before the wedding. We weren't virgins, but neither of us had much sexual experience. What we had was unsatisfactory; at least it was for me. We both believed that marriage should not stunt our individual identities. We supported each other's need to grow and to become our own person. Yet we seem to be at each other constantly. We find it difficult to square our needs as independent human beings with the need to be together in marriage. It's as if when we are true to our own needs we end up hurting each other. If we focus on each other we begin to feel cheated. I know when I try to be there for Paula after awhile I begin to resent her. She says it's the same with her, that when she tries to be there for me it's okay for a time but then she starts to resent me. I feel I'm in a bind. If there is too much "us" there isn't enough "me." If there is too much "me" there isn't enough "us."

PAULA: I read Brad's statement and I agree with it. It makes me angry to think that we've done everything our parents and our society say that mature young people should do prior to getting married and we still have this terrible problem of our separate identities. I love Brad, but I really am beginning to doubt that either of us can get out of this predicament without losing either ourselves or each other.

THE INDIVIDUAL VERSUS THE MARRIAGE

Brad and Paula are in a bind. There is reasonable hope of satisfactory solution. At first the bind may appear to be a double bind, but it is not because of two things. First, either of them can leave the field. Although neither of them wants to do this, it is still a possibility. Second, the nature of Paula and Brad's bind is one of finding the proper mix between togetherness and separateness. It is not an either-or proposition. Let's consider the options open to Paula and Brad.

Brad and Paula could each come out of their situation as winners and losers. They could each win their own identity by divorcing. In this case they lose the marriage. Or they could salvage the relationship and lose their own identity. These two solutions are at the extreme either-or end of the scale. Assuming that Brad and Paula would survive the breakup of their marriage and further assuming that the marriage would survive a deemphasis on each of their own ego identities, we will conclude that Paula and Brad are not in a double-bind situation. Rather, their situation is a simple bind, a problem that can be resolved.

Paula and Brad are in a bind that affects many marriages. It is an individual identity versus a couple identity bind. In Chapter 2 I discussed A-frame, H-frame, and M-frame marriages. The A-frame marriage obliterates individual identity in favor of a strong couple identity. The H-frame marriage rejects couple or marital identity almost entirely in order to preserve a fierce independence of one's own ego identity. The M-frame is a true blending of both A-frame and H-frame so that individual ego identity is preserved within a meaningful couple relationship.

Essentially, the A-frame is absolute dependence, the H-frame is fierce independence, and the M-frame is a genuine *interdependence*. Brad and Paula have not yet discovered a workable interdependence. Perhaps neither of them is secure enough in his/her own identity, and therefore each is easily threatened whenever the other makes a claim or request. Only the reasonably autonomous person can voluntarily relinquish a measure of his/her freedom in order to commit to a meaningful and workable dyadic relationship. If we are not sufficiently autonomous we will more likely cling to our autonomy in a tenacious manner and will likely interpret any claim or request on us as a threat to our autonomy and independence.

It is hoped that as Brad and Paula grow in their own autonomy, they will find it easier to give up some of their prized individual identity in favor of a nonthreatening marital or dyadic identity. However, if they continue to be threatened by even the slightest request or claim on each other they may never be able to make it together.

The Growth Bind

SELF-FULFILLMENT VERSUS SECURITY

The growth bind is made up of two opposing forces. The attractive appeal is to one's desire for self-fulfillment and self-actualization. This attraction relates to the quest for being, aliveness, spontaneity, vitality, and wisdom. The opposing force is the quest for security, the desire to maintain the status quo. Any change is threatening, even if the change is only contemplated. The psyche seems to resist change because of a need for certainty. And so humans often seek absolutes, finality, answers, and a wedding service that extracts the promise of love and fidelity "till death do us part."

Each individual also wants to be secure about his or her identity. Identity is partly a function of our roles as men and women, husbands and wives, fathers and mothers. The growth bind occurs because every step in growth is accompanied by some corresponding change in the individual's security system. Likewise, any change within one person in a relationship produces a change of some type in the other person. And that change may be discomforting or painful.

Those who seek to grow are threatened by the risk of the loss of people, values, and things they hold to be precious or important. Yet, not to grow may be an even greater risk. This basic dilemma is typical of growth-oriented people. They are anxious for growth, but when the opportunity for growth occurs, they are tempted to step back and choose the security of the status quo.

EXTERNALIZING THE OLD, INTERNALIZING THE NEW

I know of few growth-oriented people who have not, sooner or later, encountered a moment of terrifying dread. When that happens, the growth that has been gained through pain and self-discovery is threatened, and the individual is terrified at the prospect of what he or she may lose. This is called a failure of nerve, and it may be temporarily immobilizing. Most people who have doggedly fought their way to this point are not going to be sidetracked for very long. They pause to breathe in new courage and new determination to continue. The growth-oriented person may make mistakes, but eventually even those mistakes will be woven into the fabric of the person's being.

Learning on the "gut" level is not easy. If we are to avoid binds, we need to unlearn many of the directives, preachments, and exhortations with which we have been socialized. We need to go back into the many relationships within our family of origin and rework them from our present-day adult perspective. To unlearn is to externalize. To learn is to internalize. The challenge of growth is to unlearn all the unproductive and self-defeating beliefs and attitudes that we have internalized since birth. Then the new learning, the relearning, or the new internalizing can begin. Actually, externalizing and internalizing are constantly interwoven because the old is more easily washed away and replaced as the new comes along. Some individuals find they must firmly establish the rationality of their new position before they can even consider expurgating old beliefs and ideas. Even after a new approach has been learned and confirmed in the mind, it may not be truly internalized and integrated into one's being and accepted in one's "gut" because internalization is an *emotional* rather than an intellectual process.

SALLY AND MARK

SALLY: My dream for Mark and me was to grow together. I don't mean exactly alike or always together, but we seem to be oriented in different directions. I want to make sense of life. . . . I want to try and understand different solutions to problems. I want my own career—to work alongside Mark—to be able to share our problems and explore together for possible solutions. Mark just seems to want to stand still. He says I make too much work out of trying to understand life. He just sees everything as black and white. He applies his simple values to everything. It seems to work for him, but it doesn't work for me.

MARK: Sally creates problems for herself because she does not have a firm hold on basic values. You work, earn money, save money, have children, train them in the right way, keep your nose clean, and that's all there is to it! Sally's problem is that she sees things in shades of gray.

Mark and Sally illustrate the contrasting forces in **deductive differentiation** and **inductive differentiation.** Mark tends to see all of life in terms of the values and viewpoints he internalized as he was growing up. Sally, although internalizing also, now allows new problems, experiences, and situations to mediate her old views. She has not thrown out the old values, but she is constantly adapting and redefining them. She induces from the old to the new. She is probably less secure than Mark, but she seems able to tolerate more insecurity in her attempt to discover and define life's meaning for herself. Mark finds his security in redoubled commitment to values and principles that he learned as a child and as a youth, and through which he continues to interpret his world. He deduces from what he has known to what he now holds as right for him. It should be obvious to the reader that inductive differentiation is the more risky, growth-oriented approach, whereas deductive differentiation is the safer, more secure approach.

The perception of experience, and then the consequent interpretation placed on that experience, is what separates deductive from inductive differentiation in the development of identity.[13] Sally is much more inductive than Mark, which means she is more open and more receptive to growth and change. Mark is much more deductive than Sally, which means he is less open to placing new or revised interpretations on his experiences. He will be less open to the concept of growth for himself, Sally, and the marriage. Sally and Mark view themselves and the challenges of life in very different ways. Although this may add to the difficulty of achieving marital satisfaction, it may also pave the way for a mature love based on genuine respect for the unique individuality of both partners. In the long run it will be easier for Sally to externalize archaic and outdated material than it will be for Mark. Likewise it will be easier for Sally to internalize new meanings and revised interpretations than it will be for Mark.

The Double Standard Bind

A double standard is any situation in which one behavioral response or stimulus is acceptable for one partner but not for the other. Western tradition has long embraced different standards for women and men regarding sex mores, sex behavior, and marital obligations. If we are to free ourselves from the powerful influence of the double standard we must be clear in our beliefs about this complicated and controversial issue.

Not all people believe the double standard is wrong. In our society the Judeo-Christian tradition has long been a very strong force perpetuating the double standard. According to the double standard, women are supposed to be subservient to men. The male derives his authority from his supposed strength and superiority, from ancient creation myths, and from the biblical account of Adam and Eve (Genesis 2:4b-3:24). (The biblical account of Genesis 1:1-2:4a is a far more sexually equal document compared to Genesis 2:4b-3:24. Genesis 1:1-2:4a tells us: "So God created man in his own image, in the image of God he created him; male and female he created them.") Regardless of how we may choose to interpret biblical accounts, the cultural tradition has evolved from them. If a person interprets these accounts as mythological accounts of the creation rather than as literal truth, then he or she will probably have great difficulty with the sexual double standard.

The double standard for males and females takes many forms and has many ramifications. Several obvious ones are as follows:

Males should be free to sow their wild oats before marriage, but females must remain virginal. This means that men should be experienced prior to the wedding night, but women must be virgins.

Males are expected to flirt, be they married or not, but females, especially married females, are not permitted to do so.

Males are not held responsible for an unwed pregnancy. The female is saddled with the burden of the pregnancy as well as with the social and familial stigma.

Birth control and contraception is the female's responsibility.

The following vignette illustrates the classical double standard of premarital sexual behavior.

Dear Dr. Crosby,

I was engaged to be married to this great guy. At least that's what I thought! We had set the wedding date and everything was going fine. That is, until one night after we had sex! He said I was the best lover he had ever had and that none of the others could come close. I accepted this as a compliment. Then he said he was glad I was a virgin. After he said this I became very anxious because I have never intended to misrepresent myself. (I had been intimate with several other guys.) The next day on the phone I told him I wanted to talk with him that evening. So when we got together I reminded him of what he had said about how he was glad I was a virgin. Then I told him! Wow! You should have seen him. At first he seemed to be stunned . . . and

then SLAM CITY! Was he ever mad! I thought he was going to
bust a gut. Well, it's all over now. No wedding, no engagement, no more telling the truth about previous lovers for me!
Can you believe this guy?

Your former student,

Lucia

The problem develops when we wish to be done with the double standard
but discover that, when face to face with it in operation, we are not as far
removed from it as we had thought. Many men insist on their right to sexual
activity before marriage, and they might even say that women have the same
rights as men in this regard. They say this until they meet someone special, and
then the good-girl/bad-girl syndrome takes over. A good girl is a virgin and is
for marrying, whereas a bad girl is fun-loving and promiscuous and is for the
purpose of having sexual pleasure.

In some societies, if husbands have a fling or brief affair they may be
reprimanded, but they are not judged as severely as wives who do the same
thing. Some men say they accept behavior in women that is similar to the
behavior of men, but I have known few men who accept such behavior in
women *to the extent women are expected to accept it in men.* There have been many
claims that the double standard is dying. If it is true that the double standard is
dying, then we must conclude that it is dying very slowly.

The Sex-Role Bind

TRADITIONAL SEX-ROLE STEREOTYPING

With rare exceptions, the roles that men and women play in society have been
determined largely by the fact of **gender** at birth. Boys and men are socialized
to become the protectors, the breadwinners, and the providers. Girls and
women are socialized to be the homemakers, the bearers of children, the givers
of love and nurture. This follows symbolical interactionism (see Chapter 2). The
sex-role bind occurs because individuals are capable of a wider variety of roles
than the narrow sex roles that society has prescribed. "Male" and "female" are
not either-or concepts. Masculinity and femininity are psychological **con-
structs** referring to behavioral and psychological-emotional traits allegedly
belonging to both females and males.

ANDROGYNY

People used to believe that if a male was "high in feminine traits," he was, by definition, "low in masculine traits." Likewise, if a female was "high in masculine traits," she was, by definition, "low in feminine traits." This is *not* the case. **Androgyny** does not mean a person is half female and half male, nor does it mean a person is half feminine and half masculine. A male may be any and all degrees of masculine and at the same time any and all degrees of feminine. Likewise a female may be any and all degrees of feminine and at the same time any and all degrees of masculine. The truly androgynous person possesses a goodly measure of both masculine and feminine traits and characteristics. Androgyny is a psychological construct that becomes part of the self-concept or self-image. Androgyny implies a complete freedom to be, to feel, and to behave in the manner in which one feels at home, comfortable, and "at-one-with self."[14]

Biologically it is a certainty that only males can impregnate, and only females can menstruate, gestate, and lactate. Although the question of sex roles is still very much subject to debate, it seems likely that most other differences are due to role learning rather than to inherent physiological differences. In a society where sex roles are rigidly defined, there is bound to be a great deal of frustration for those individuals who wish to engage in behavior that is societally defined as limited to individuals of the opposite sex. Today we are seeing men and women in many roles that were formerly considered to be appropriate for only one sex. Indeed, this role revolution undergirds both the so-called sexual revolution and the women's liberation movement.

KEN

"When I was in college I lettered in basketball. I was elected team captain my senior year. I married just after college, and we have two daughters and one son. I'm here because my job is threatened. I am a regional manager for a life insurance company. At my recent evaluation they said I was too soft, not tough or competitive enough! They said I was too sensitive and too caring. They said I got too emotionally involved with the problems of my policyholders. They expressed disappointment over what they call my lack of aggressiveness, although my sales for the past 12 months were at an all-time personal high and second highest in the office sales force. When I expressed confusion about what they were complaining about—this was later, during the oral part of the evaluation—they simply said that I projected a weak male image, and this was contrary to what they had expected of me.

"Lately I've done a lot of soul searching. As I look back, the truth is that I've always been sensitive! I have always placed people above winning, above money, and . . . you know . . . success. I've always been emotional too—hell, I feel things—deeply! I feel a lot of pain for some of my friends."

Ken's marriage appeared to be both stable and vital. There was mutual support and high-quality intimacy. The two daughters were very athletic, and the son was somewhat of a loner and an introvert, yet this was not upsetting to the parents. After several therapy sessions Ken decided that the only thing in his life that really needed to be seriously confronted and reevaluated was his relationship with his employer. Several months after he confronted his employer about the negative evaluation he resigned from the company. His wife continued in her career as a real estate broker, and for a while Ken was a house husband. Later Ken became owner and manager of a small business of his own.

The alternative to the sex-role bind is androgyny. Androgyny permits the individual to escape the bind of rigid sex-role stereotyping because it removes the effectiveness of the societal mandate to feel and to behave in a prescribed manner. In Chapter 8 we will note the crucial linkage of androgyny with equalitarian monogamy. For now let us simply note that equalitarian monogamy is extremely difficult to achieve unless or until the partners are at least somewhat androgynous.

The Ownership-Fidelity Bind

Implicit in the marriage customs of our culture is the idea of possession or ownership of the mate. This is a logical outgrowth of the feudal concept of the female as chattel (property), just as an automobile or a parcel of land is property that one possesses. The concept has evolved into the belief that she belongs to him and he belongs to her. Nena and George O'Neill point out that a simple change of prepositions can make a big difference. He may belong *with* her but not *to* her. She may belong *with* him but not *to* him.[15] The O'Neills are talking about belonging with, not in terms of the couple front but in terms of a mutual choice of primary-bond partner.

The concept of ownership leads us into a sense of security based on negative prohibition rather than on positive commitment to the other's welfare. We learn security from mate possession because from birth we have been taught that possessions provide security. And it is only a small step from physical possession to emotional possession—from owning things to owning people! We would be wise to remember that people are for loving and things are for possessing. But many of us have been socialized to believe that things are for loving and people are for possessing. The very essence of love, as set forth by Fromm, Horney, and May, is the desire to impart the self to the other, to give rather than to take.

Sexual **fidelity** is one of the cornerstones on which marriage is built. If the two partners define their marriage as a sexually exclusive relationship and if they commit themselves to each other in this endeavor, then it behooves both of them to maintain the trust of the other.

However, although sexual fidelity is an important cornerstone, it is not the only cornerstone on which marriage is built. *Nor is sexual infidelity the only kind of infidelity.* It is but a small step from the old-fashioned chastity belt to the present-day emphasis on sexual infidelity as the prime abrogation of marital trust. Unfortunately, marital fidelity has taken on an almost totally sexual connotation. In my view, and in the view of many marriage therapists, too much is made of sexual infidelity to the exclusion of subtle, less obvious infidelities. For example, a husband and wife may have stopped meaningful communication years ago. Is not this an infidelity? Or one partner may withdraw into a private mental chamber. Is not this an infidelity? Unwillingness to listen, to commit oneself, to explore, to attempt to understand, to learn to fight fairly, to learn to express negative feelings constructively, to learn the art of genuine compromise, to provide nurturance, and refusal to self-disclose are all acts of infidelity. They are acts of unfaithfulness. One of the worst infidelities is bad-mouthing your mate to other people. The point here is that there are many marriages wherein there has been no sexual infidelity, but other infidelities abound. Many a wife feels betrayed by her husband who gives her nothing but the silent treatment. Many a man feels betrayed when his wife pays more loving attention to the pet cats than to him. Why do so many husbands feel like meal tickets? Why do so many wives feel like sexual receptacles?

PHYLLIS AND BEN

BEN: She was asking for trouble and she got it! I told her if she was ever untrue to me that it would be the end. Well, I don't see any hope of staying together.

PHYLLIS: Big deal! Yes, I had an affair! And I'd do it again. I was angry. The sex was no big deal—it just sort of followed what we were feeling for each other. He was warm and kind. He listened to me and was attentive. He cared! He didn't shut me out! He didn't act like I was some sort of permanent fixture. Before we had sex we had been seeing each other for over a year. Just talking and sharing. I felt alive! I felt real!

This couple had been unfaithful to each other for a very long time. If I were the therapist I would not be interested in trying to pinpoint a first cause. It would be a waste of time to worry about "who started it." My approach would be to attempt to reopen the doors of communication and self-disclosure. Perhaps we would have to wade through a lot of pent-up anger that had never been dealt with. We would have to deal with a lot of unfinished business from the past—the past with each other and then the further past of the families from which they came. We would challenge the beliefs and assumptions about what marriage means to them and the meaning they attach to trust and fidelity.

Faithfulness, the fulfilling of faith, appears to have been absent for a long time. The penile-vaginal event between Phyllis and her extramarital partner is the least significant of all their interaction. The social-emotional intercourse between Phyllis and her partner led to sexual intercourse. The *lack* of social-emotional intercourse between Ben and Phyllis led to perfunctory sexual intercourse (or perhaps to no sexual intercourse). The dynamics to be considered are those forces and situations that led Phyllis to meet her psychological-emotional needs with an extramarital partner. Would Ben have called Phyllis "untrue" if she had a continuing psychological-emotional relationship outside the marriage *without* sexual relations? The exclusively sexual definition of infidelity is one of the most limiting, most cruel, and most deceptive beliefs our culture embraces regarding marriage, not because it condemns sexual intercourse outside of marriage but because *it fails to condemn the other acts of infidelity and unfaithfulness*. It is these other acts of infidelity and unfaithfulness that usually serve to kill the marriage.

The Good Girl–Bad Girl Bind

Good girls are for marrying. Bad girls are for sexual fun. Everyone knows that! Males know it and have lived by it for generations. Females know it all too well, for it puts them in a bind. Boys want to make out with them, but if a girl becomes too free she reduces her chance of marriage because guys want to marry good girls. This belief into which both sexes have been thoroughly socialized has prevented many females from accepting their sexuality. Good girls are really not supposed to enjoy sex, nor are they to show much interest in it. When a female shows interest in sex, the male concludes that she has "been around." She may, therefore, be a fun partner for a one-nighter, but she is ruled out as a potential mate. She represents "spoiled goods" or "used merchandise." Of course, as we have noted in our discussion of the double standard, it's OK if *his* goods have been used.

The good girl-bad girl syndrome has been thoroughly socialized into males and females for hundreds of years. Although it is much less prevalent today than in Victorian times of the late 19th and early 20th centuries, it is still very powerful.

Another name for the good girl-bad girl syndrome is the madonna-harlot syndrome, a phrase polarizing the ideas of good and bad in a more dramatic and poetic way. The madonna symbolizes sexual innocence, whereas throughout history the harlot is the fallen woman. (Of course there are no fallen men! That old double standard again.)

The effects of the good girl-bad girl bind are devastating to many marriages. When sex as intimate fun and communication is lost, it often becomes only a physiological release for the male and a duty or obligation for the female. Her orgasm and sensual pleasure are of no importance. Soon the husband experiences his mate as boring, passive, and nonstimulating. He experiences occasional impotence and worries about it more than he will admit. With a decrease in sexual interest (to protect himself) comes a general decrease in vitality, including diminished enthusiasm for his marriage. An affair may or may not be in the offing. Another man's wife or a pickup or a prostitute will *not* find him impotent. Another woman's husband may recover his potency with the first man's wife.

The sad result of the good girl-bad girl syndrome is that the male resents his wife's lack of sexual enthusiasm and spontaneity, yet she is this way because he insisted she be this way. He used other women (the bad girls) to have his fun with and then deliberately bought into the myth of the "good girls are for marrying" scenario. If all of a sudden his wife should come onto him and show great enthusiasm and passion, the typical male's first thoughts would likely be, "Where have *you* been?"

JOANNE AND HARVEY

Consider Joanne: She was socialized to save sex for marriage; if that didn't work, it must at least be an expression of endearment and affection, with, she would hope, commitment toward permanence. She was taught that men are after only one thing, so "forewarned is forearmed." Under no conditions should sex be easy or just for fun.

Consider Harvey: He was socialized to marry a woman who would be a genuine helpmate and supportive companion, as well as a loving and devoted mother. Harvey knew what he was looking for in a mate. In the meantime, he did a bit of carousing. He had a good time, yet none of his "playmates" would ever be acceptable as a "helpmate."

Consider the Marriage: Several months after Joanne and Harvey were married, Harvey begins to feel that Joanne is dull and unexciting in bed. She is no fun. She isn't sexy! She isn't alluring! She isn't seductive. Joanne begins to feel betrayed. Harvey doesn't take time with her. Harvey doesn't engage in foreplay, doesn't show affection, doesn't seem to enjoy anything nongenital such as holding or caressing or fondling.

Reconsider the Situation: Harvey really doesn't want Joanne to be the initiator or the assertive partner. If she came on to him he would suspect her of having been involved with somebody else. He would be suspicious and maybe jealous. So Joanne cannot, even if she wanted to, take the lead or give any signals that she is a capable seductress. In the meantime Harvey continues to fantasize about the fun and frolic he used to experience with his playmates.

Slowly Harvey beings to have trouble getting erections when he makes love with Joanne. Joanne is confused by this, but she doesn't feel free to change her own patterns or attitudes.

Joanne and Harvey are both imprisoned by their own erroneous beliefs and attitudes. Neither has risen above the effects of the good girl-bad girl syndrome. Nor will they rise above it, unless or until they give themselves and each other permission to integrate eros and libido within a supportive context of philos and agape. Translated this says that fine, wonderful, and highly moral young (and old) women can be seductive in their intimate relationships; males can be highly principled young (or old) men who, if they will allow it and accept it, can discover the stars of their most libidinous dreams to be none other than their wives and the mothers of their children.

The good girl-bad girl bind resolves only when men and women alike give themselves permission to own the polarities within their own hearts, minds, bodies, and souls. To own the polarity means that I can fully accept and integrate my erotic passions and my feelings of philos and agape with my libidinous desires. Once again the answer is in the integration of eros, libido, philos, and agape.

The female who internalizes "goodness" as the absence of sexual passion and playful experimentation will not be able to experience her own sexual potential. When the good girl and bad girl images are cast aside, she can be free of the deadly cultural stereotypes regarding the innocence and purity of good girls and the depravity of bad girls. Likewise, the male can rejoice because he will no longer be enslaved by the belief that his wife, supposedly a good girl, is not able to participate in sex replete with adventure, experimentation, and abandon. When this happens, both sexes are winners and there are no losers. [16]

The Transference Bind

Transference is experienced as a bind by the object or target of the transference, not by the person doing the transferring. The person doing the transferring is rarely, if ever, aware of the fact of his/her using transference. The object of the transference doesn't really know or understand what's going on. All he or she knows is that it is risky to speak, act, or react. In short, it is a confusing and risky business just to be around a person who transfers a lot. The transferring partner says things to you (the object) that you don't deserve. He or she treats you as though you are somehow responsible for things far beyond your control. The transferring partner seems hypersensitive to your slightest move, your mildest comment, your most tactful reply.

Transference is the expression of emotion or affect, stemming from unresolved relationships with early authority figures, onto significant others in present-day interactions. We may react to a husband as if he were father, or to a wife as if she were mother. We may react to a schoolteacher, a professor, a physician, a lawyer, or even a police officer as if he or she were one of our parents. If we have unfinished business left over from our family of origin—broken lines and patterns of communication, blockages of affection, unresolved conflict, and lingering resentment—the residual will be played and replayed in our primary bonding patterns with our mate and our children.

The object or target of transference is someone who in some way is symbolic of an authority figure or a significant other from our past. Augustus Napier describes an episode where a wife reacts to her husband as if he were her mother and she was a little girl.

> "One moment he was your angry husband, and you were his angry wife. Then he became angrier, and it was like turning a switch. He became Mother, and you became a little girl." Carolyn, you see, was responding to David as a transference figure, as a symbolic person. Transference occurs in every marriage, but when there is significant trauma or difficulty in the family of origin, seeing the partner as parent can seriously interfere with the marriage. . . . Actually, we project so many symbolic images onto our spouses that we do see him or her alternately as mother, father, brother, sister, even grandparent. [17]

ACTIVE AND PASSIVE AGENTS IN TRANSFERENCE

The transference bind places extraordinary strain on the person who is targeted as the object. This is the result of the object or target, the *passive* agent, of the transference not being able to understand or comprehend the statements and actions of the *active* agent, the one who is doing the transferring. How can you know that at any given moment you cease to be what you are—mate or child—and become a symbolic target for your mate or parent's unresolved conflict stemming from past relationships?

Even when we are functioning at our best there is bound to be some minimal degree of transference. Each of us has some residual of unfinished business. Most often this minimal transference is laughed off or shrugged off in a lighthearted and forgiving manner by the passive recipient. After all, neither the active nor the passive person knows what's going on, let alone give it a label. However, when a person consistently and persistently treats his or her mate or children as objects of transference, there is bound to be a growing sense of frustration and confusion on the part of the person being thus targeted.

In order to get out of the transference bind, the active agent needs to come to terms with the unfinished business stemming from earlier authority figures. The object or target of transference can do very little to help! Most important, the *passive agent must not play amateur therapist*. However, the passive agent *can refuse to be dumped on.* This is best done by placing a *label* on what one perceives to be the "game" of the active agent. "Oh, I see! You want to play the DUMPING game! Well not today—not me, no way!" Humor can be a valuable asset in the labeling of transference: "I wish your mother were here. . . . It's about time she heard this from you!" The trouble with this approach is that when one is deeply embroiled in an angry exchange, it is very difficult to extricate oneself sufficiently to be tactful or creative in the use of humor.

Transference is one of the greatest barriers to fulfilling and satisfying intimate relationships because even though we can emphasize the central role of constructive communication in fair fight styles, in transference the communication is contaminated by unresolved conflict from our earlier years. Transactional analysis, which we shall discuss in Chapter 5, is one of the best and most accessible tools for dealing with transference.

The greater our sense of autonomy the less we are likely to transfer. As Napier says, "People can't risk being close unless they have the ability to be separate—it's too frightening to be deeply involved if you aren't sure you can be separate and stand on your own."[18] This polarity between separateness and togetherness, distance and intimacy, autonomy and dependency, disengagement and enmeshment, and differentiation and fusion is a recurring theme in the study of intimate relations.[19]

The Future Security Bind: Guarantees Against Change

The future security bind is concerned with the human desire for guarantees regarding the future. There is something pervasive about our quest for certainty, for absolute assurance about the future as well as the present.

Think about the traditional wedding service and its binding words, the promise to love "for as long as we both shall live" or "until death do us part." How can a person of sound mind and moral character promise to love someone even into the distant future? Isn't this asking both to perjure themselves by extracting a promise that they may or may not be able to keep? If the promise were "to work at this love, to nurture it, and to tend to its ongoing growth," then I would have no quarrel. But a promise about one's future feeling of love seems to me to be something we may not be able to deliver. If our premise is accurate, as stated earlier, that we are the ones who kill love, marriage, and sex, then it is foolishness to expect these words of future promise to mean anything.

HELEN AND IRV

IRV: But you stood up there in front of all those people and promised that you would always love me: How can you even think of separating?

HELEN: Well how was I to know what would happen? I felt then that I really loved you.

IRV: Well, don't you?

HELEN: Don't I what?

IRV: Love me?

HELEN: I don't know. I suppose. But it's different. Things have changed. I am deeply involved in my business, and you seem to be content with your dull routine. Get up—go to work—come home—eat—watch TV—go to bed.

IRV: Why are you so restless? We're doing fine the way we were.

HELEN: You may be fine, but I'm not. I'm bored! We lead dull lives. Nothing is exciting. There must be more to life than this!

IRV: There isn't. This is it. You should be satisfied. You should be content. We have all we need—health, house, cars, security.

HELEN: I've changed.

IRV: You can't change! You promised—we discussed this years ago. You said you would always love me the way you did then.

HELEN: You were so sure of my love that you just took me for granted. I'm tired of being a fixture in your life.

Helen and Irv lost it years ago. Perhaps Irv, more than Helen, wanted the security of routine and constancy. Helen has now admitted that she feels trapped. Irv accuses her of breaking the love contract. In the name of creating and maintaining security, this couple found themselves imprisoned by it. Irv has guarded himself against changes of any kind. Helen, finally breaking through the crippling effects of being bound to security, now isn't sure she loves Irv. But Irv had wanted a guarantee that Helen would love him forever, in spite of anything he did or did not do.

Here again we see the abuse of agape love: "Love me, even if I don't deserve it." And so Irv refused to grow or to change in any way. He settled into a ho-hum type of daily existence. As a defense against the risk of change, he had, until now, shut down his capacity for growth.

THE QUEST FOR SECURITY

When it comes to love we are motivated by a desire for reassurance. We want the security of knowing that we will feel the same about each other in 10 or 30 years as we feel right now. We want to freeze the present moment so that it will last and endure forever, as if that is the only way we can experience the validation of the present.

The basic dynamic is not love as much as the desire for security. We want to believe that we can count on this present feeling in all future circumstances. "Validate me and promise never to change." This is impossible! Further, the effort to keep the promise not to change would have a disastrous effect on future growth. The promise is self-defeating because it encourages behavior that fosters decay and apathy. Such a promise encourages marital partners to take each other for granted, although nobody likes to be taken for granted.

The only workable answer to the future security bind is to diminish the demand for security obtained from others. The antidote is increased intra-psychic growth, increased autonomy, and increased differentiation. Dependence on a loved one will not do for us what we have not been able or willing to do for ourselves.

This is not to deny the value and validity of an authentic faith in God or in an Eternal Mind or Spirit. It is to say that we must accept anxiety and insecurity as part of our human condition. If we believe that creation is good, then we can find strength in our innate abilities to cope with our anxieties and our problems and to live vigorously in the present. We can trust that when tomorrow becomes today the same inner resources will enable us to endure and grow. There is a "wisdom of insecurity."[20] Paul Tillich suggests in *The Courage to Be* that it is only as we learn to take our insecurity into ourselves, as a fact of our existence, that we can truly unlearn the crippling and self-destructive dependencies.[21]

The Attraction-Reversal Bind: What We First Admired We Later Resent

The attraction-reversal bind is a phenomenon that seems to occur in many marriages. One of the traits that had the most powerful quality of attraction in the eyes of the partner early in the relationship has now become the very trait that is most resented by this same partner.

HUSBAND (THEN): One of the things I am most attracted to is her independence. I admire her strong sense of self-confidence and her self-assuredness. She seems so in control and able to handle herself in any situation.

HUSBAND (NOW): I really resent her independence. She doesn't need me. She doesn't seem to want to lean on me or depend on me for anything. I wish she needed me more. I feel unneeded, unwanted, and unloved.

WIFE (THEN): One of the things I am most attracted to is his liveliness. He is always the life of the party, and he enjoys the respect and friendship of many people. He is such an interesting conversationalist that people just seem to look up to him.

WIFE (NOW): I can't stand his damn big ego! He always has to be the center of attention. He feeds on people hovering around him. I feel absolutely devastated because I rarely get to talk when we're in public. He does all the talking and all the showing off. He controls every conversation. What gets me is how gullible these people are.

The bind here is that if we do not find another person to be attractive in some special way we will likely never be drawn to another and hence will never marry. Yet marriage therapists have long observed that often the thing we are most upset or resentful about today is the very trait or characteristic that we found to be so charming and attractive early in the relationship.

ANALYZE WHAT ATTRACTS YOU TO ANOTHER

The attraction-reversal bind can be dealt with most efficiently during the process of early dating. Simply list all the positive traits you can think of that attract you to your partner. Then rank in order the five most attractive traits on your list. Finally, write down your *projected feelings for each of these traits, assuming the trait is exaggerated to an extreme degree.*

Positive Trait	Exaggerate the Trait and then Project Your Feelings
He is the life of the party.	Everybody must bow at his feet.
She is a beautiful woman.	Everybody flirts with her.
He is strong and self-confident.	He won't trust me to do anything without his supervision.
She is so jovial and light-hearted.	She thinks everything is funny and won't take anything seriously.

After marriage the attraction-reversal bind is much more difficult to work through because people generally resist change. If the request for change comes from a mate who is reacting negatively to one of your personal characteristics, it can be especially difficult. The situation calls for leveling statements and skill in conflict negotiation. Often we learn much about ourselves as we examine the traits we find attractive in another person as well as those traits we find annoying or obnoxious in another person. It certainly behooves us to consider carefully the things we say we like about our partners as well as to be clear about the things we think we do not like about them.

Often a trait may assume importance because it covers or hides our own vulnerability. (Scenario) "Something about her independence threatens me. Although I used to admire her for her independence I now feel she doesn't need me. I didn't realize that I wanted her to be at least a little bit dependent on me!

I wonder why I wanted her to be like that?" (Scenario) "Apparently I have a need to be the life of the party because this gives me a lot of ego strokes, attention, and validation. I guess I'm not as secure and self-confident as I thought I was." Thoughtful persons can learn a great deal about themselves if they are willing to ponder their own feelings and traits in a nondefensive manner.

Double Binds

Be spontaneous! Be autonomous! Be your own person! Take control of your life! These statements sound like good advice. In truth they are double-bind statements. If I do what you tell me to do, I can hardly call myself spontaneous, autonomous, or my own person, controlling my own life. If I refuse to take your advice I remain, according to you, nonspontaneous, stunted, and stuck in the mud. This classical double bind puts us in a no-win situation. If we go in one direction we lose, and if we go in the other direction we lose.

CHILDREN WALKING INTO A PARENTAL TRAP

When parents put children in double-bind situations the stage becomes set for intrapsychic and interpsychic confusion. If a child is frequently put in a double-bind situation, the child may become so conflicted and torn apart that severe mental-emotional problems arise. When a child is bombarded with double-bind messages it becomes impossible for the child to discern his/her own sense of reality and identity. The contradictory messages cause such confusion that it becomes impossible for the child to communicate in a direct or straightforward manner.

FATHER: Come on now Tommy, you know you can tell daddy what happened behind the garage.
TOMMY: Jimmy and I were smoking cigarettes.
FATHER: You were what? I thought I told you never to smoke! This is very serious. You're grounded without allowance for 2 weeks.
FATHER: (A little later) Tommy, how would you like to go fishing with me?
TOMMY: I wou . . . I would'n . . . I don . . . I'd rath . . . Okay.

The parental ploy is to give the child at least two messages at once. Spoken: "It's okay, Tommy. Just tell us what happened behind the garage." Implied: "You know you can trust that when you tell the truth and are honest I'll be fair and square with you." So Tommy responds to the implied pitch, "I'll be fair and square." Later, Tommy clearly does *not* want to go fishing with his father, but Tommy is afraid to decline because of fear of how his father will react if Tommy declines.

MOTHER: Billy, come give mommy a big hug.

BILLY: Okay. (Billy goes over to mommy and puts his arms around her neck.)

MOTHER: (Cold and rejecting) You don't need to hug mommy! Mommy knows you love her.

This interchange between Bill and his mother is a variation on the theme "Come closer my dear so that I may reject you." The double bind is the most harmful (psychologically) of all dirty-fight techniques. It puts the receiver into a situation wherein he or she is bound to become so thoroughly confused and hence insecure that ego identity will be impeded and diffused. In poorly functioning families it is not uncommon to find a high frequency of double-bind communications.

MARRIAGE PARTNERS IN DOUBLE BIND

Marriage partners sometimes relate to each other in double-bind patterns.

ILSA: Well, you just don't give me affection! You never hug me or hold me or caress me.

FRED: I do so! Just last night I held you and . . .

ILSA: You just wanted sex!

In this very brief interchange Fred is in a double bind. If he does not give nongenital affection, that is, holding and caressing, he is guilty of being a noncaring cad. However, if he does reach out in an affectionate manner, he is immediately labeled as "just wanting sex." He is damned if he does and damned if he doesn't, and he can't leave the field. What is Fred to do?

HE: Tell me what you're thinking dear.

SHE: Oh—Just daydreaming.

HE: About what? You can tell me.

SHE: Well, I was just thinking how nice it would be if we could go out to dinner once in a while.

HE: (With a sharp and angry facial grimace) There you go again! Is that all you can think of—spending money on clothes, movies, dinner, vacations?

The next time that this man says, "Tell me what you're thinking dear," we can be pretty certain that she will be unwilling to tell him. We quickly learn these kinds of lessons.

THE DOUBLE BIND AS SELF-DEFEATING

In other types of situations there is a way of putting the partner (or the child) into a double bind by phrasing messages in such a way that the recipient is in a hopeless no-win situation.

SHE: I wish you would talk more and share your feelings with me.
HE: OK, I'll try. What is it in particular that you would like for me to share with you?
SHE: Oh, you know, just be more communicative!
HE: Well, I would like to share with you some of my ideas on what I think is going on between you and the kids.
SHE: There is nothing going on between me and the kids, and I resent your bringing it up!

This type of exchange features the request, the attempt at compliance, and then the censure for the attempt at compliance. The end result will be increased withdrawal and silence on the part of the "bound" person.

HE: I want you to like sex the way I do.
SHE: OK, I'll try.
HE: (During sex) You're just into it more because I asked you to.

A translation of the above would indicate that he really wishes that she shared his sexual feelings and desires. He asks her to be more like him. She attempts to comply. She honestly tries to be more in tune with the way he wants her to be. And when she does, he puts her down. He cancels out her changed attitude and performance by denigrating her. "You're only into it more because you know I want you to be this way. . . . You really don't *feel* any differently." Not only is this a quick way to defeat one's own request for change, it is also a guaranteed way to torpedo the relationship. Not many healthy people will long tolerate such behavior.

STRUCTURE AND TREATMENT OF DOUBLE BINDS

The structure of one common type of double bind is:

1. There is request for change or for a certain behavior or attitude.
2. An effort toward compliance is forthcoming.
3. The person who attempts to comply with the original request for change is condemned or denigrated. "You're only doing this because I asked you to, *not because you really want to.*"

There are three conditions for a double bind.

1. A primary statement. (I wish you enjoyed sex more.)
2. A secondary but unspoken statement conflicting with the primary statement. (You're only doing this because I asked you to. You're not doing it because you want to.)
3. An understood (but unspoken) prohibition against leaving the field.[22]

For a double bind to exist there need to be at least two persons who are closely involved with each other. There must be communication around some recurring theme. There must be at least two messages with the secondary message somehow contradicting the primary message. In order to be a genuine double bind there can be no means of escape. This means that the person who is in the double bind cannot leave the field.[23]

Breaking the double-bind pattern is extremely difficult. Some of the double binds that we used for illustrative purposes in this chapter can be broken, providing the "bound" person is able to comment on his/her predicament by *labeling* the double bind as a double bind. "I refuse to respond to you because you have just put me into a double bind." Only when the "bound" person is quick enough and alert enough to actually label and immediately *confront* the "binder" is there any chance to break out of the pattern. Ideally, only when partners and parents are willing to risk becoming vulnerable can there be any real possibility of breaking the pattern. Without professional help it is extremely difficult for the "bound" spouse to help the "binding" spouse relinquish the use of double binds. A double binder is a dirty fighter because he/she keeps the "bound" person on the defensive, putting that person into a quandary of confusion and bewilderment.

Summary

This chapter has been concerned with the demands, binds, and double binds that we create in the name of love. Implicit is the resulting disillusionment when we abuse the concept of love by creating such binds and demands. In the name of love we learn to exercise power over our mates by using subtle logic and reasoning. We often attempt to control our closest intimates and friends by coercing them to yield to our expectations. We do this by using an "if . . . then" form of reasoning: *If* you really love me, *then* you will. . . ."

The ABC method of rational emotive therapy (RET) was discussed as a means whereby we may challenge our beliefs. When our beliefs are irrational or fallacious we will reap unwelcome consequences from them. Each of the several imperatives that were discussed in this chapter is based on irrational beliefs, attitudes, and assumptions. When we fail to examine these beliefs and assumptions, and instead simply accept them as true and accurate, we set ourselves up for frustration. There is no way our partner can measure up to our irrational expectations. Therefore, both the partner and the giver of the imperative are confused and frustrated at the same time.

In all of the imperatives there is a strong element of manipulation wherein the initiator attempts to get his/her partner to comply with his/her request. This element of manipulation makes the imperative into a fraudulent and "dirty" method of interaction.

This chapter further considered some of the more powerful binds and double binds that are often employed in the killing of marriage. A bind is a situation from which we may extract ourselves by the application of sound reasoning and determined action. By technical definition a double bind offers no way of escape because it prohibits leaving the field. It was suggested, however, that there are ways to deal with imperatives, binds, and even double binds. Among these are the use of RET and the challenging and confronting of our beliefs, attitudes, and values. Second, the *labeling* technique may be used, whereby a name is given to the partner's maneuver so that the partner is confronted with his/her own behavior in a very direct and immediate way. Third, the partner may employ the countermaneuver of refusing to accept the terms of the bind by turning the tables in the manner of a second-order change. This entails a retort such as "To which question do you wish me to respond?" or "Which part of your message do you wish me to answer first?"

Sometimes it is impossible to forge a mature negotiating stance with a partner if the partner persists in using the manipulative devices and ploys we have considered in this chapter. If there is no improvement or change even after repeated efforts to use sound and nondefensive reasoning, leveling, and other fair-fight tactics, then perhaps the relationship is beyond repair. Ordinarily, however, a couple with sufficient commitment and willingness to learn the skills essential to conflict resolution can work through most of these imperatives, binds, and double binds. It is to this subject, the constructive resolution of conflict, that we turn in the next chapter.

Reading Suggestions

Branden, Nathaniel. *The Psychology of Romantic Love.* New York: Bantam Books (Tarcher, 1980), 1981.

Charney, Israel. *Marital Love and Hate.* New York: Macmillan, 1972.

Fromme, Allen. *The Ability to Love.* North Hollywood: Wilshire Books, 1971.

Gordon, Sol. *You Would If You Loved Me.* New York: Bantam Books, 1978.

Gordon, Sol. *Why Love Is Not Enough.* Boston: Bob Adams, 1988.

Lepp, Ignace. *The Psychology of Love.* New York: The American Library, 1963.

Napier, Augustus V. and Carl A. Whitaker. *The Family Crucible.* New York: Harper & Row (Bantam), 1978.

Satir, Virginia. *The New Peoplemaking,* Mountain View, Calif.: Science and Behavior Books, 1988.

Weeks, Gerald R. and Luciano L'Abate. *Paradoxical Psychotherapy.* New York: Brunner/ Mazel, 1982.

Notes

1. Paul F. Dell, "In Search of Truth: On the Way to Clinical Epistemology," *Family Process,* Vol. 21, no. 4 (Dec 1982), 413.

2. Albert Ellis, *Growth Through Reason* (Palo Alto, Calif.: Science and Behavior Books, 1971),1–14; and Albert Ellis and Robert A. Harper, *A New Guide to Rational Living* (North Hollywood, Calif.: Wilshire Books, 1975), 216–219.

3. *Op. cit.* Ellis, *Growth Through Reason,* 1–14.

4. Karen Horney, *Neurosis and Human Growth* (New York: W. W. Norton, 1950), Chapter 3, "The Tyranny of the Should," 64–85.

5. Myron F. Weiner, "Healthy and Pathological Love—Psychodynamic Views," In *On Love and Loving,* Kenneth Pope, ed. (San Francisco: Jossey-Bass, 1980), 123.

6. Sol Gordon, *You Would If You Loved Me* (New York: Bantam Books, 1978), Introduction.

7. Nena O'Neill and George O'Neill, *Open Marriage* (New York: M. Evans, 1972), 55.

8. Laura J. Singer, with Barbara Lang Stern, *Stages: The Crises That Shape Your Marriage* (New York: Grosset & Dunlap, 1980), 35–39.

9. Fritz B. Simon, Helm Stierlin, and Lyman C. Wynne, *The Language of Family Therapy: A Systemic Vocabulary and Sourcebook* (New York: Family Process Press, 1985), 272–273.

10. *Ibid.,* 108–109.

11. Israel Charney, *Marital Love and Hate* (New York: Macmillan, 1972), 35.

12. *Op. cit.* Simon, Stierlin, and Wynne, 96–99.

13. Susan Krauss Whitbourne and Comilda S. Weinstock, *Adult Development: The Differentiation of Experience* (New York: Holt, Rinehart and Winston, 1979), 94–99.

14. Carolyn G. Heilbrun, "Recognizing the Androgynous Human," Chapter 6 in *The Future of Sexual Relations,* Robert T. Francoeur and Anna K. Francoeur, eds. (Englewood Cliffs, N.J.: Prentice-Hall [Spectrum], 1974).

15. *Op. cit.* O'Neill and O'Neill, 248.

16. John F. Crosby, "Intramarital Sex: Wasteland or Playground?" In *Choice and Challenge: Contemporary Readings in Marriage,* 2nd ed. Carl E. Williams and John F. Crosby, eds. (Dubuque, Iowa: William C. Brown, 1979), 140–147.

17. Augustus V. Napier with Carl A. Whitaker, *The Family Crucible* (New York: Harper & Row [Bantam], 1978), 113, 118. Italics added.

18. *Ibid.*, 92.

19. *Op. cit.* Simon, Stierlin, and Wynne, 39–43, 366–367.

20. Alan W. Watts, *The Wisdom of Insecurity* (New York: Random House, 1951), 9–11.

21. Paul Tillich, *The Courage to Be* (New Haven: Yale University Press, 1952), 181 (see also all of Chapter 6).

22. *Op. cit.* Simon, Stierlin and Wynne, 96–100.

23. Gerald R. Weeks and Luciano L'Abate, *Paradoxical Psychotherapy: Theory and Practice With Individuals, Couples, and Families* (New York: Brunner/Mazel, 1982), 5–6.

Chapter 5

Love and Anger: Dynamics of Intimacy

It is our job to state our thoughts and feelings clearly and to make responsible decisions that are congruent with our values and beliefs. It is not our job to make another person think and feel the way we do or the way we want them to.

HARRIET GOLDHOR LERNER
THE DANCE OF ANGER

LEARNING TO EXPRESS ANGER

Dear John,

Six months have passed since our therapy. I am writing because I want to tell you that I have finally learned how to express anger. As you know, we got to the point where our marriage was beginning to fall apart and I really didn't care about much of anything. I kept my feelings to myself—thinking they would go away. But they never did—not for very long anyway. My mother and father were dirty fighters. They used all kinds of tactics, from screaming and shouting to slamming doors and giving each other the silent treatment. I vowed I would not have their kind of marriage.

I hated the anger I felt—it was repulsive to me. So you know what I did. I was the model wife. Whatever Sam wanted Sam got. I gave in to him on almost everything. You name it— house, car, furniture, sex, friends, vacations—wow, did I ever avoid conflict. I squished my own feelings on just about everything. And it worked fine for a while. Then slowly I began to have these queer feelings. They'd come out of nowhere—feelings like wanting to run away as I screamed at the top of my voice, or like wanting to cry and cry. One time I gave in to Sam on some little thing, and all of a sudden I felt sort of nauseated inside, like I was sick to my stomach.

It has taken a long time to get from there to here, but now I'm not afraid to let my anger out. I still don't want my parents' kind of fighting, but I have learned to respect anger as an OK emotion that can be expressed and handled in lots of good ways. First I had to see that anger was OK, that it was normal and that it was OK for me to express my feelings. I had seen myself as a superhuman person of some sort—one who looked on herself as some sort of "Miss Goody Two-Shoes," always ready to please, taking no thought for myself. It was very important to me that people see me as friendly, accommodating, and easy to get along with. Wow! How stupid can a person get? I guess I was afraid that if I let my real feelings out no one would like me.

I have learned to own my feelings, whatever they are. I've learned to be assertive and sometimes aggressive. But the most important thing is that I feel fairly safe when I express my anger to Sam or the kids. I guess they've learned that I love them even though I get mad at them, and Sam has helped me by learning to fight right back. We both can deal pretty well with our feelings as long as we don't attack each other. You know what I mean—we express our own feelings first and then ask for input or reaction from the other. We also learned that when we let out our negative feelings positive feelings return quickly.

Thanks for your help.

Beth

The Anger Taboo

What is it about negative emotions that makes intimate partners so afraid of them? No one is immune to feelings of anger, resentment, disgust, disdain, hurt, bitterness, and hatred, yet many people sincerely believe these feelings should be suppressed. **Suppression** is the conscious, intentional exclusion of a thought or a feeling from consciousness. These people believe that feelings should be denied, or at least pushed downward and inward, swallowed and digested.

WHY DO WE SUPPRESS NEGATIVE FEELINGS?

There are two predominant reasons for suppressing negative feelings. One is sociological and the other is psychological. The sociological reason is concerned with a cultural transmission of a taboo against the expression of anger. The cultural tradition has imparted the message that nice people do not show anger. Anger is wrong, bad, sinful, a sign of impure thoughts, and an indication that maybe something is terribly wrong in a relationship. The folklore tells us that in good relationships the partners do not have conflict or feel anger. This tradition encourages a separation or alienation within ourselves because we must then either deny the anger or in some other way prevent ourselves from being in touch with what we are experiencing. When this happens we deprive ourselves of a significant part of our selfhood.

The cultural tradition and folklore are partly the result of an ecclesiastical tradition that often considers anger and conflict to be wrong, evil, or sinful. This is a curious belief that is often defended in the name of the Bible and especially Jesus. However, the taboo against anger is certainly not biblical nor Jewish nor Christian in its origins. Consider the anger of the prophets. Jeremiah, Ezekiel, Amos, Hosea, and Isaiah were certainly not placaters or appeasers. They spoke out in anger about the evils and injustices of their day. Jesus upbraided the scribes, the pharisees, and the Sadducees. He scourged the money changers in the temple and challenged the authority and behavior of the elders and the members of the Sanhedrin. He attacked hypocrisy and religiosity.[1]

The reader familiar with either the prophets or the words of Jesus may say, "Well, this was righteous indignation!" Of course it was righteous indignation! Almost all anger is righteous indignation! When was the last time you were angry about something and did not feel a sense of righteous indignation? We rarely feel anger with our intimates without a feeling that we have somehow been wronged or mistreated, let down, or betrayed. If we did not believe there was an injustice of some kind or that we were right about some issue and the partner was wrong, we would likely not be angry.

The religious taboo against anger stems more from the *tradition* of the early church and the early church fathers. This tradition has been transmitted as if it were of divine authority. The anger and conflict taboos reached their highest zenith during the Victorian era, 1840 to 1940.

The second major explanation for the suppression of negative emotions is psychological in origin. We feel very insecure in expressing these feelings. The insecurity is caused by the unexpressed but underlying fear that if we let other people know what we are really feeling or thinking they won't love us anymore. *Why Am I Afraid to Tell You Who I Am?* is the title of a book that speaks directly to this fear.[2] This title asks a relevant and important question.

When we were in diapers we learned to be afraid of big people who could hurt us or who could withhold things we needed or wanted. We learned to be afraid to display anger and rage toward those on whom we were dependent for our sustenance. After all, we needed their nurture, their stroking, their caring, and their feeding. Karen Horney has pointed out that the most crucial struggle of our lives takes place at a very young age that most of us can no longer recall.[3] When the truly dependent child has negative feelings, these are often followed by anxiety. Terrified of opposing the benefactor, the infant represses hostility. This leads to internal conflict and its eventual manifestation as anxiety.

Forces of dependence, independence, differentiation, and individuation form the major schema of psychosocial development. When we become adults the emotions and feelings that we experienced in early childhood often recur. This happens whenever a present event triggers a similar feeling experienced in the past. During childhood, when we felt anger toward someone we loved, we might have reacted by pouting or sulking or withdrawing. Now, whenever we feel anger toward someone we love, we react the same way we reacted then. Anger is still too frightening to be dealt with, and so it is suppressed, displaced, or otherwise denied.

Our **primal** fear is the fear of abandonment and with it the ongoing anxiety that results from our sense of insecurity. We have great difficulty seeing that anger and love are inseparable, that both are necessary if we are to retain our dignity as unique human beings and our capacity to love. Jay Kuten has written of the paradox of anger and love.

> The fact is that were it not for this pattern, one of undulation, of change, of backing and filling in our loving, no relationship, however apparently loving, would go anywhere. No growth would be possible in the two people or in the relationship that represents what is between them. Just as with individual development, where conflict and its resolution are a necessary catalyst for learning, so in couples and more extended involvements, the failures in loving, its lapses, its opposite, hating, are part of the yeast of growth.[4]

The Conflict Taboo

CONFLICT AS AMORAL

All interpersonal relationships are potentially conflict laden. As I discussed in Chapter 4, a cultural tradition that, for whatever historical reasons, considers conflict morally wrong will encourage the suppression and repression of conflict and so lay a foundation for misunderstanding, resentment, anger, hostility, bitterness, hatred, and displaced aggression.

Many cultures, as well as our own, endow conflict with moral or immoral connotations. On the contrary, I take the position that conflict is amoral. Conflict is a neutral phenomenon. It is how one looks on conflict and how one handles it that gives it a positive or negative value.

Imagine a married couple socialized to believe that all disagreement is wrong, that the voicing of differing points of view is wrong (it is called arguing), and that the essence of marriage is to create and maintain harmony at any price. This couple will probably claim that neither of them remembers an unkind word between their parents, and they will feel guilt that their own marital relationship is not beautiful or perfect. They will probably feel conflict and will sense their underlying hostility, but they will not be able to do anything about it except be miserable. After all, conflict implies quarreling and disharmony. Quarreling is a type of fighting, and fighting is wrong! Perhaps the most unfortunate result of this kind of socialization is that the children of this couple will in turn be deprived of useful models of how to face and deal with conflict in a positive, creative, constructive, growth-producing, love-filling way.

The Opposite of Love and Hate: Indifference

The root of this negative attitude toward conflict is the popular assumption that love is the polar opposite of hate. At times it may be. Much hatred is characterized by the degree of the perceived injury or harm inflicted on oneself by some outside person, force, country, group, institution, corporation, business, industry, judicial body, or governmental agency.

Nevertheless, when we are discussing the interpersonal dynamics of human intimacy, the polarity between love and hate becomes intensely personal, and the fact of love always precedes the experience of hate. Rather than being polar opposites, they are more like two sides of the same coin. The line between love and hate is very thin, and until the negative feelings are allowed expression there is a dwindling and erosion of the positive feelings. This leads many couples to conclude, "We feel nothing toward each other, neither love nor hate." This happens because when the negative is suppressed the positive will disappear with it. Marriage therapists often hear the expression "Our love has died." The experience of "dying love" is in part the experience of the denial of feelings, first the negative and then the positive. Rollo May has described this dynamic:

> A curious thing which never fails to surprise persons in therapy is that after admitting their anger, animosity, and even hatred for a spouse and berating him or her during the hour, they end up with feelings of love toward this partner. A patient may have come in smoldering with negative feelings but resolved, partly unconsciously, to keep these as a good gentleman does, to himself; but he finds that he represses the love for the partner at the same time as he suppresses his aggression . . . . [T]he positive cannot come out until the negative does also . . . . Hate and love are not polar opposites; they go together, particularly in transitional ages like ours.[5]

In their book, *The Intimate Enemy*, Bach and Wyden call attention to dirty fighters, sick fighters, and training lovers to be *fair* fighters. Bach and Wyden say:

> Contrary to folklore, the existence of hostility and conflict is not necessarily a sign that love is waning. As often as not, an upsurge of hate may signal a deepening of true intimacy; it is when neither love nor hate can move a

partner that a relationship is deteriorating. Typically, one partner then gives up the other as a "lost cause" or shrugs him off ("I couldn't care less"). Indifference to a partner's anger and hate is a surer sign of a deteriorating relationship than is indifference to love.[6]

Indifference is often the polar opposite of both love and hate. Outright rejection is often easier to accept than being ignored or treated as though one were not there.

Clearly, facing conflict creatively is an absolute necessity in marriage. Previous generations embraced the ethical and moral concept of honesty. But one cannot help wondering how honest our ancestors really were inasmuch as they made such an effort to avoid conflict and even the appearance of conflict. Perhaps their dishonesty can be excused because they were socialized to believe that conflict was evil and bad. Nevertheless, for modern men and women, the avoidance of conflict is akin to dishonesty in intimate relationships.

KATHY AND JOHN

JOHN: I am afraid I don't love Kathy. I don't know how or why, but the feelings I used to have are gone. I try to re-create them but . . . well, it just doesn't work. Sometimes I force myself to be loving, but then it seems like . . . pow! . . . she turns around and does something to really turn me off! One of these days I'm afraid I'm really going to unload on Kathy.

KATHY: Unload what?

JOHN: Well, just . . . oh forget it!

KATHY: No! Unload what? I suppose you think I'm just feeling good about you all the time. Well, I'm not! You've got me so mixed up and confused I don't know how I feel or what I think. Lately, you just make me sick—acting like a hurt little boy if you don't get your way, clamming up, pouting, and sulking.

JOHN: You sure put your finger on it. How else am I supposed to feel when you put me down? You're the one who seems to have to get her own way. You act like no one can handle the money as well as you. You insist on doing things with your friends. You act like sex is a bore, and you parcel it out like it was rationed. You undermine everything I try to do with the kids. The fact is, I think sometimes your judgment in handling them stinks.

KATHY: I suppose you're an expert!

JOHN: I think you're too easy on them.

And on and on goes the gunnysacking—the unloading of past grievances that have been carefully saved up for just such an explosion.

Gunnysacking

At best, gunnysacking provides a release of pent-up feelings, an unleashing of the negative feelings that have been put in the "gunnysack" for safekeeping but that end up being used as ammunition at some later time. At worst, gunnysacking provides a way to get the dammed-up negative feelings out in the open. This is what happened to John. Once Kathy speaks her mind, John is able to express some of the pent-up anger he has been feeling. Actually there is a lot of hope for Kathy and John once they learn how to deal with their complaints *as they occur, instead of letting them pile up.*

Gunnysacking is one of the most vicious types of intimate fight styles because it is based on a saving up of grievances by the offended partner *without the other partner knowing about it.* The offended partner smiles as though nothing whatsoever is wrong while at the same time making special note of the offense. In a sense the gunnysacker catalogues the offense by noting the date, the circumstances, and the degree of hurt; then the gunnysacker wraps it in a special wrapping paper, ties it up with ribbon, and places it deep down in the gunnysack. Days, weeks, months, or years later there will be a slight provocation. This provocation will be trivial: It will be like the straw that broke the camel's back. Nevertheless, this trivial offense will spark the gunnysacker into action. He/she will go right to the storehouse of carefully wrapped packages of anger, resentment, and hurt. The gunnysacker then begins to unload the entire sack, bit by bit and piece by precious piece. The ensuing bombardment is much like an enemy unleashing its entire arsenal in one devastating fusillade.

The gunnysacker is dishonest in that he or she deliberately misrepresents himself or herself. Despite the pretense that all is well, all is *not* well, but *the partner doesn't know it*! Consider how many divorces begin by one mate surprising the other by saying: "I want a divorce. I have been unhappy and miserable for years." Surprise, Surprise!

The cure for gunnysacking is for the partners to commit themselves to dealing with issues as they arise. The goal is negotiation, compromise, and closure. If Kathy and John are encouraged to unload on each other on deeper levels, they may succeed in getting at the heart of their resentments. These negative feelings have been dammed up so long that the positive love feelings have diminished. No therapist would be surprised if at one of the next sessions John would say, "I'm beginning to feel love for Kathy again. I don't seem to have as much resentment, and I'm not even trying to make myself be loving." Often after a lot of negative garbage has been verbalized, it is not at all unusual for the couple to recount at a future visit to the therapist, "And that night after we unloaded all our garbage we made love like we hadn't made love for years!"

Self-Awareness

VULNERABILITY AS NECESSARY

Probably the greatest threat to a vital, growing relationship occurs when one partner is hurt or threatened by the mate. The temptation is to protect oneself from further hurt. This is accomplished by shoring up one's ego defenses, withdrawing **ego investment** (decreasing the amount and degree of our caring and commitment), and generally taking steps to make oneself less vulnerable. However, we need to realize that when we are no longer vulnerable to hurt, we also become hardened to the effects of love and receptivity. We become too hardened to feel anything positive. *Vulnerability to hurt and pain is an absolute prerequisite for the development and ongoing sustenance of love.* When we protect ourselves from being vulnerable, we likewise reduce or prevent the experience of love.

To avoid indifference and to maintain our vulnerability, we need to increase our awareness of our feelings and then learn how to express these feelings in a loving manner that is not devastating or deliberately hurtful to the mate.

FEELINGS ARE NEITHER RIGHT NOR WRONG

Much has been written in recent years about self-awareness. Self-awareness is being able to identify and describe your feelings, whatever these feelings may be. Self-awareness is being tuned in to one's inner state of being, to one's thoughts and one's feelings. Many people escape from self-awareness because they do not like themselves for the feelings they have. Or they simply do not like their feelings. These people have a belief (at level B) that we need to censure our negative or bad feelings.

Feelings are neither right nor wrong. How a person acts or fails to act on a feeling is a matter of ethical choice, and these actions can be judged as right or wrong, good or bad. However, the feeling itself is not subject to ethical or moral judgment. *We are absolutely responsible for our actions and our behavior regardless of the feelings underlying our actions or behavior. We are not, however, responsible for the feeling itself.*

Many people play games by holding others responsible for what they feel: "You make me feel like . . . ." Others attempt to make anybody else except themselves responsible for their actions and behavior: "Look what you made me do!" The mature person will learn that (1) feelings are a natural and normal part of the self and are not subject to ethical or moral censure or judgment; and (2) behavior, including the behavior of thinking, is an activity for which we are accountable, that is, for which we are responsible. Another way of saying this is *how we choose to act on our feelings is very much within the realm of ethics, but the feelings themselves are not.* The crucial point is that our feelings simply are not right or wrong, good or bad. Feelings are subject, in part, to past experience and the sensory input that we receive from our environment. Feelings come to awareness and expression within our being as a part of our emotional makeup.

Once we realize that feelings are neither right nor wrong, our ability to be in touch with all of our feelings is greatly enhanced. When we truly believe that it is all right to allow ourselves to feel our feelings, we will experience a great deal more freedom in permitting ourselves to be in constant touch with what we are feeling. We will be free to experience ourselves and to become truly self-aware.

Relatively fev· people are aware of their authentic feelings. But once we grant ourselves permission to feel, there is no limit to the growth and self-development that can occur. Many people experience great anxiety and fright as they slowly grant themselves permission to feel joy, sorrow, hurt, disappointment, sexual desire, anger, pain, resentment, envy, hatred, shame, and despair. To feel abandon and the satisfaction of commitment. To feel inner power and the futility of helplessness. To feel the weight of crushed dreams and the joy of unexpected pleasures. We live in a culture that does a good job of teaching us not to feel! We learn early on to be schizoid—to be alienated from our feelings and emotions. We are a thinking culture, not a feeling culture.

MIND AND BODY TEAMWORK

I am not suggesting that we should not pay attention to our mind and its thought processes. A mind-body synthesis that combines the mind and the body in one coherent complex is clearly called for.

The mind, guided by ethical principles and standards, processes and evaluates data. This data can be information from the environment, daily experience, our senses, and the entire emotional system of our body. The body experiences itself by permitting feelings to be received and felt. The body is the receptor organism of the impulses that permeate the individual. As such, the body is a gigantic sensory mechanism that constantly transmits feelings, impulses, gut reactions, and sensations to the mind. The mind processes, evaluates, studies, considers, and weighs various alternatives and courses of action: To do or not to do, to be or not to be, to act or not to act, to act this way or to react that way, to seek advice or handle it alone, to fight or not to fight, to take flight or not to take flight, to accommodate or placate, to compromise, to erect barriers or to remain open to growth.

Some readers may fear that if we allow that feelings are amoral, neither good nor bad, right nor wrong, this will allow people to become barbarians without moral codes or ethics. These readers miss the point that ethics begin once the feeling has been received, acknowledged, and owned: "Yes, this is my feeling. I own it. It is me. Now I must decide what to do about it." This is the beginning point of ethical-moral responsibility.

Self-Disclosure

EXPRESSION INCREASES AWARENESS

Conscious disclosure of ourselves to others is partially dependent on self-awareness. Yet, paradoxical as it may seem, self-awareness is somewhat dependent on **self-disclosure**. I am referring to conscious processes only. Unconsciously we are continually transmitting nonverbal messages that reflect our inner feelings and state of mind. According to Sidney Jourard:

> It seems to be another empirical fact that no man can come to know himself except as an outcome of disclosing himself to another person. This is the lesson we have learned in the field of psychotherapy. When a person has been able to disclose himself utterly to another person, he learns how to increase his contact with his real self, and he may then be better able to direct his destiny on the basis of his real self. . . . Self-disclosure, letting another person know what you think, feel, or want, is the most direct means (though not the only means) by which an individual can make himself known to another person. . . . A self-alienated person—one who does not disclose himself truthfully and fully—can never love another person nor can he be loved by the other person. . . . Every maladjusted person is a person who has not made himself known to another human being and in consequence does not know himself.[7]

Jourard has successfully pinpointed the issue of the relationship of self-disclosure to self-awareness, and the related issue of mental health and wholeness. One of the tragedies of primary-pair intimacy is the lack of self-disclosure by the partners to each other. Here are several techniques that are available to everyone.

THIS IS WHERE I'M COMING FROM . . . THIS IS WHERE I AM

If we assume that the anger and conflict taboos have been dealt with and the gates to self-awareness are opened at least a little, then what is the next step? To achieve self-awareness you must be willing to make first-person (I) statements that reveal your state of being or frame of mind. You must be willing to share such personal data as where you "are coming from" or where you "are at." Frequently we are puzzled in everyday situations because we have no hint of the immediately preceding circumstances. We do not know where the other person has been (figuratively or literally), and so we do not know this person's mindset or frame of reference. We do not know what he or she is thinking or feeling.

CHERYL

"I just came home that day, looked at him, and told him our marriage was over. He looked at me in utter amazement as if he didn't have the least idea what I was talking about. He knew what I had been feeling and struggling with. He knew I believed in women's liberation and that I was feeling really imprisoned by our marriage. He knew I thought marriage was created and maintained by a male chauvinist philosophy.

"What he didn't know (How could he? I never told him.) was that I had just finished reading *The Dance of Anger*[8] for your course and that it really opened my eyes. He didn't know I had been boiling inside myself because of our division of labor. He didn't know I had been wallowing in self-pity for about 5 weeks.

"He didn't know where I was coming from, and he didn't know where I was now! How could I have expected him to understand me? I never let him in."

This episode is probably repeated thousands of times daily, not in content but in its dynamics: the expectation that the other person will somehow magically know where I am coming from, where I am right now, and where I intend to go and why.

CONGRUENT MESSAGES

Self-disclosure is much more than just letting the other person know where you're coming from and where you are. It is a **leveling** process through which we attempt to be congruent in our communication. To be congruent is to be in agreement, fitting together or flowing without conflict. Much of the time we are noncongruent: We feel one thing, think another, and say something else. You may be feeling put out with someone, perhaps a roommate, and your conscious thought is that you wish he/she would move into another dorm. You then say to him/her "I'm so glad we're living together." When what we are feeling is in line (congruent) with what we are thinking, and when what we are thinking is in line with what we are saying, then we are congruent. At least we now have a chance to send a clear message, without static or double meaning or **metacommunication**. Metacommunication is a message within a message: One message is beneath, about, or beside another. Now I really like *that* dress on you! You really did a good job on *that* term paper. I telephoned you last night but no one answered. In each of these statements there are two messages, one stated and one implied. The implied message usually qualifies the stated message in some way or gives additional information, indicating I didn't like your other dress, your other term papers were lousy, and you should have been there when I called last night. (Were you out with somebody else?)

Noncongruence

TO ONESELF: I feel angry. I think these arrangements are ridiculous!

   TO LARRY: Oh, Larry, how nice of you to arrange everything and do all this!

Congruence

TO ONESELF: I feel angry. I think these arrangements are ridiculous.

   TO LARRY: Larry, I'm feeling angry about these arrangements. I think they are uncalled for and unnecessary. I wish you had checked with me.

Have you ever noticed the "painted smile"? Some people never leave home without it. The painted smile is a nervous habit. It probably stems from the command that we should always be smiley, rosy-cheeked, friendly, and amenable and that we should never say what we're really feeling or thinking. Often the painted smile reflects an uncertainty, a conflict, a contradiction, an insecurity, or a desire to give a negative message in a sweet and nonoffending manner. When you are really angry or upset with someone you should not be smiling as you level with him or her about what it is that's bothering you. If you smile as you give your angry retort you are giving a noncongruent message. Your facial smile says one thing, but your words say quite another. The painted smile is the very essence of noncongruence. It delivers two messages at once. The listener or recipient is bound to be confused because he/she doesn't know to which message he/she should respond, that is, to the message of the spoken words or to the smile.

"YOU MAKE ME" VERSUS "I FEEL"

The leveling process requires a determination not to play **games.** One of the most common games or ploys is the use of "you" statements. "You make me angry." "You disappoint me." "You hurt me." A rule concerning "you" statements is that if the content of the statement is negative (critical, condemning, judgmental, scolding), then it is important to avoid beginning any sentence with *you.* The reason for this is that when *you* is used to introduce a negative statement or sequence, it is usually received as a word indicating or introducing an attack or accusation. The partner receives the message as an attack and is immediately put on the defensive.

When we feel falsely attacked or accused we will invariably do two things: We will defend ourselves, and then we will counterattack. This gets us into either a nonproductive exchange or a destructive fight. The reader will note that if the word *you* is used in a positive manner there is no problem. We like it when people say to us "You are pretty." "You are good looking." "You did a good job." "You are really talented." "You were great." "You played a great game." When *you* is used in a positive way, there is no need to be defensive or to counterattack.

The reader may reply, "But there are times when you *do* make me angry, or you *do* disappoint me." Yes, there are many instances when you will choose to express your anger about the behavior of another. However, it is far better to learn to use "I" statements to own your angry feelings. "I am feeling angry." "I am feeling very disappointed." "I am hurt." The reason for this is that these feelings are your feelings. Own them as yours. They are not right or wrong. This involves cutting through self-protecting cover-ups, rationalizations, and intellectualizations.

Your responsibility is not to blame the other or to hold the other person responsible for what you are feeling. Rather, your responsibility is to own your feeling—to acknowledge it and claim it as your own. It is your feeling and not someone else's. You could choose to feel elated, happy, sad, encouraged, jubilant, joyous, disgusted, or even amused, but you have instead chosen to feel angry. Very good. Now make a series of simple and straightforward statements.

I feel angry and terribly hurt.
I think this kind of behavior is thoughtless.
Let's deal with this thing right now. (Or tonight or tomorrow—but deal with
    it as soon as possible. If you wait too long you'll find reason not to deal
    with it, and then you never will resolve it . . . until it comes up again.)

FEELINGS VERSUS THOUGHTS

We must make sure we differentiate between feelings and thoughts. If you can substitute the words *I think* for the words *I feel* and the sentence still makes grammatical sense, then probably you have expressed a thought, not a feeling.

I *feel* that spectator sports are not as rewarding as participant sports.
I *think* that spectator sports are not as rewarding as participant sports.

The preceding sentence makes sense either way. Hence it is a thought, not a genuine feeling. Try these.

I *feel* angry as hell.
I *think* angry as hell. (This doesn't make sense grammatically. Therefore we can
    be certain that it is not a thought; it is a feeling.)

I *feel* warm and cuddly.

I *think* warm and cuddly. (This doesn't make sense grammatically. Therefore we can be certain it is not a thought; it is a feeling.)

I *think* I am *feeling* comfortable about the decision we made. (This mixture of thought and feeling is sometimes appropriate.)

Generally, the words that follow are feeling words.

Negative	*Positive*
mad	glad
sad	happy
irked	good
scared	loving
crummy	warm
hurt	tingly
angry	inspired
spiteful	jubilant
cold	ecstatic
distant	sexy
rejected	sensuous
jealous	beautiful
numb	accepted
cranky	close
picky	tender
anxious	whole

None of the above words make sense if they are preceded by the words *I think*. All of the above words make sense if they are preceded by the words *I feel*. Therefore, the above words can be described as *feeling* words. Remember, if you use the words *I think* and the sentence or phrase still makes sense, then you know that you are expressing a thought, not a feeling.

COMPROMISE: YES—ACCOMMODATION: NO

The leveling process and self-disclosure require a determined resistance to accommodation. Accommodation is not the same as genuine **compromise**. Compromise is absolutely essential to all human relationships. In a compromise both individuals state their positions honestly, negotiate the issues, and are willing to give and take as a workable solution is hammered out on the anvil of constructive bargaining. In accommodation, however, one individual "gives in" to the other in order to keep peace, placate, please, or appease.

People accommodate to their own peril. The individual who accommodates tends to obliterate genuine feelings and thoughts in order to keep peace or to avoid conflict. People who are fearful of negative emotions and conflict are more prone to accommodate because it protects them from the anxiety of self-assertion and self-disclosure.

My students and clients have often asked me, "But aren't we supposed to please each other?" "Isn't pleasing each other what marriage is all about?" "Shouldn't we be there for the other?" My response to these questions is "Yes—to a point." The basic thought of wanting to please each other is good. The intent is good. And certainly if we are not committed to pleasing our partner, our marriage will be in great danger of falling into a self-centered narcissism.

However, many people overdose on the idea of pleasing their partner, and in this process they have lost their own identity. These people have obliterated their selfhood in the name of pleasing their partners. In the name of pleasing they have become accommodators. Some therapists call accommodators *placaters.* To accommodate once in a while with fairly equal reciprocal accommodation by the partner is okay. However, when accommodation becomes the modus operandi of one partner, the marriage is probably unequal and perhaps unstable. The very heart of the meaning of compromise implies self-assertion, clear statements about where each partner stands and what each partner wants. Compromise is the result of honest negotiating that assumes that the parties to the compromise have stated their original positions clearly and without ambiguity. Then, each person gives up a portion or a part of his or her original stand. This is often done with a quid pro quo, something for something. In a genuine compromise there are no losers. We must also recognize that rarely does either partner get everything he or she originally wanted.

A common mistake in negotiation is to give in or to concede without making your position and your requests clear and emphatic. Giving in *prematurely* is the essence of accommodation. *To simply give in and then think that we have compromised is an exercise in self-deception.* Eventually the accommodator will wonder why his/her mate is so demanding and controlling, always in charge and acting as the powerful partner. The answer is that the accommodator has been the inadequate one by always giving in and permitting the other to get his/her way in almost everything.[9]

THE PRICE OF SELF-DISCLOSURE

Because self-disclosure is a risk-taking behavior, it is learned only as one is able to endure anxiety and discomfort. We only take risks when we feel secure enough to withstand the counterattack of anxiety. Rarely can we accomplish this entirely.

Self-disclosure is risk taking because the person has summoned enough courage to reveal his or her inner feelings and emotions. In secondary relationships this may be uncalled for and unnecessary. But in primary or intimate relationships it is the key to growth and joy, to spontaneity and vitality, to depth and meaning. The risk involved in self-disclosure is great. Each person has his/her own private risk threshold—that point beyond which he or she is afraid or unwilling to go. Some people overextend themselves and then retreat. I suspect the majority will never experience the growth of intimacy because they cling to a relatively low-risk threshold in order to maintain their emotional security, that is, in order to feel safe.

Intrapsychic and Interpsychic Conflict

INTRAPSYCHIC: GEORGE AND GLORIA

George and Gloria have been going together for almost a year. Their relationship has been a deep and rewarding experience for both of them. Lately, however, George has become picky, hypercritical, and oversensitive to things Gloria says and does. George has decided to talk to a therapist about his relationship with Gloria.

> I don't know what it is, but everything she does bugs me. I get angry when she tries to plan an evening or weekend. Then when she doesn't offer her opinions about what we're going to do, I feel she doesn't care. We're saving money for our marriage, and then she comes up with expensive ideas on how to spend it. Lately, no matter what it is, I react negatively. The other day for instance, we were walking downtown and she started window shopping—you know, saying how much she'd like this dress or that coat. I found myself getting critical and hostile. I felt like . . . well, like here was a person who was never going to be satisfied with what she had . . . (pause) . . . .

> A couple of weeks ago I wanted her to fuss over me a little. I had seen some girl really pouring a lot of affection onto a guy, and it struck me that Gloria never fusses over me that way. So when I saw Gloria I noted her reactions. She sure was a loser compared to the girl I had seen making a fuss over the guy.

> And we argue a lot—no matter what we are discussing I end up disagreeing with her. You know—like if she says it's a good movie I'll take the opposite stance. Yet I love her! I still want to marry her. Why do I keep reacting to her the way I do?

There is no simple answer to George's question. Every couple needs to work through their interpersonal reactions, and no relationship is entirely free of personality quirks or idiosyncrasies. However, it may be that George's basic conflict is intrapsychic, or inside himself. He fears that he will be controlled by Gloria and that she will never be satisfied. He wants to be fussed over, yet instead of facing her with his request or desire he creates a test for her as if he says to himself, "I'll watch her every move and see how she performs." Under these conditions Gloria will always come out a loser. She doesn't know the name of the game George is playing.

I would suggest that the primary conflict is within George and only secondarily in the relationship with Gloria. We must remember that George is a subsystem of the family in which he grew up. Almost everything George is to this point in his life is the logical end result of his experiences within his **family of origin** and the social interactions with his peers and elders as he was growing up. George has a lot of deeply hidden anxiety and hostility. He is not nearly as autonomous and self-directing as he probably pictures himself to be. George is probably transferring emotionality that was never dealt with in his family of origin. He is interacting and responding to Gloria as if he were still fighting his mother and/or father. George appears to be easily threatened by Gloria and wants her to display more open affection, perhaps to reassure him that he is OK. We don't know much about the family of origin, but we may surmise that there is a lot of unfinished business. What was his relationship like with his father, his mother, and his brothers and sisters? Did people form coalitions against each other? (That is, did two or more join together and gang up on another sibling?) Was George triangled by his parents? With whom is George really angry? Gloria? Siblings? Parents?

Before George gets married, it would be an excellent move for him to delve into his family of origin relationships. The extent to which George accepts himself and is able to handle his unfinished business from the past will determine, in large part, the kind of quality of relationship he has with Gloria or any other potential partner.

INTERPSYCHIC

Interpsychic or interpersonal conflict is a more obvious kind of conflict. Interpersonal conflict between lovers and partners may focus on trivial, inconsequential things, or it may focus on major issues. Inconsequential things may serve as decoys for the actual source of conflict. Much of the pent-up hostility of marital partners is expressed in passive ways or is displaced to inappropriate objects. The designation **passive-aggressive** is given to those who aggress passively, perhaps by being unduly critical or by nit-picking. When aggressive, hostile feelings are displaced, we see a form of scapegoating. There is a well-defined pecking order in our society that designates the legitimate objects of our displaced hostility feelings (that is, father picks on mother, mother on oldest child, and so forth down the ladder until somebody has only a cat or dog on which to take out their feelings).

Theories of Conflict

THEORIES OF INTRAPSYCHIC CONFLICT

Intrapsychic conflict is conflict within the self that arises from our drives and values pulling against each other. Classical Freudian psychoanalytic theory posits the fundamental conflict as one between the **id** and the **superego**. (The id or basic life energy would go wild were it not for the constrictions imposed by the superego.) Classical theory does not deny the fact of conflict between (inter) people. The concern here is where does the conflict *originate*—from within the self or between people, intra or inter? **Neopsychoanalytic theories** (the theories of Karen Horney, Harry Stack Sullivan, and Erich Fromm) stress the centrality of intrapsychic conflict as being between the child and the restrictiveness of the parents. This can take the form of fear of parental disapproval (Sullivan) or fear of parental abandonment (Horney).[10] According to Horney, all later anxiety is due to the early infant-parent struggle.[11]

Most object relations theorists hold to the conflictual theory between the id, ego, and superego.[12] The id, ego, and superego do not refer to actual phenomena or entities existing within the self but are meant to be symbolic references to libidinous (instinctual) energy, the reality principle (ego), and the internalized voice of parents and society (superego). Ideally, the ego is strong enough to be the arbiter between the id (which seeks pleasure) and the superego (which demands compliance). The ego takes account of the reality of the basic or core self of the person. The degree of strength and maturity of the ego determines the degree of control the superego is allowed to exercise over the instinctual libidinous drives.

Viktor Frankl has pointed out another kind of conflict, in contrast to the conflict between drives and social compliance. Frankl suggests that anxiety arises from "conflicts between various values; in other words, from moral conflicts or, to speak in a more general way, from spiritual problems."[13] Frankl believes that much of our internal conflict arises when we are unclear about our goals, values, and purpose in life. Frankl believes that neurosis is caused by a lack or loss of meaning in one's personal existence. When this happens there is an inner emptiness that Frankl calls the existential vacuum: The existential vacuum is an emptiness or void in one's inner being. It is this inner emptiness that becomes the fertile soil for the development of neurosis, especially anxiety neurosis. Frankl believes that the more we can define for ourselves the specific meaning of our own existence and commit ourselves toward fulfillment of those goals and purposes the less we will be tormented by anxiety, confusion, and neurosis.

INTERPSYCHIC CONFLICT: SYSTEMS THEORY

Systems theory says that intrapsychic conflict may be better understood and explained as learned behavior within the developmental framework of the familial interaction processes in the family of origin.

Whether the conflict is *intrapsychic* in manifestation or *interpsychic* does not really matter inasmuch as these are only labels indicating struggles within oneself versus struggles with one's intimates. Systems theory claims that the origin of conflict is in our relationships with significant figures from our past and present. Systems theory holds that the developmental process within the family of origin is the basic proving ground for the forming of personality and character; that is, it is what makes us what we are (Appendix A).

We learn to be inwardly conflicted because of the communication patterns surrounding the myriad of familial situations that we experienced as we grew up. This "growing up" reaches through middle and late adolescence and extends even into adulthood. Sometimes we are in our forties and fifties before we are able to free ourselves from many of the destructive communication and expectation patterns and destructive coalitions and triangulations stemming from our upbringing.

To say that a person suffers from intrapsychic conflict does not say anything about the origin or cause of the conflict. Family systems theory parts company with the classical and neoclassical belief in the id, ego, and superego. Instead, family systems theory claims that our internal conflicts are the logical result of having been placed in communication binds, double binds, coalitions, triangles, and neverending circular feedback loops wherein we are imprisoned by the covert operating rules of our family. (See Appendix A for a more detailed explanation of these terms.) These patterns of communicating and relating have a powerful negative impact on our development. When we are not able to break away or break out of these patterns we are bound to reproduce them within our marriage and our **family of procreation.** Within the family systems framework the circularity never ends in that what we are is the result of what we were in terms of the family of origin. Thus the between-persons dynamic (inter) causes the within-the-self dynamic (intra), which then is joined in marriage with another person. Between the two of them there develops a new system (inter), which will then have children and repeat the cycle. Thus the inter causes the intra, which causes the inter and so forth. As we noted in our discussions of family systems theory, inter and intra are circular in that they continue to cause each other. It is useless and irrelevant to attempt to determine which comes first because neither could exist without the other.

Methods of Avoiding Conflict

An internal **conflict** can focus on anything that encounters resistance when attempts are made to incorporate it or make it acceptable to the self. Because facing conflict creates unpleasant feelings of tension and anxiety, individuals develop conscious or unconscious methods of handling conflict. One method is suppression. To suppress is to consciously put it in the back of one's mind and deliberately decide not to deal with it. The person tries to think, feel, and act as though whatever is suppressed never happened. **Repression,** on the other hand, is an *unconscious* process of blocking out the conflict so that it does not come into consciousness. Repression is part of the Freudian schema. As such it is a basic term in classical theory, but it is not necessarily accepted by systems theorists, behaviorists, or learning theorists. Classical theory holds that repressed material exerts a powerful influence on us because repression causes the conflictual material to be expressed in the form of compulsions, obsessions, anxiety, and depression.

A person who is torn within, consciously or unconsciously, will have difficulty dealing with conflicts on the interpersonal (interpsychic) level. On the other hand, people who have dealt successfully with their inner conflicts are able to address interpersonal conflict in a reasonably creative, autonomous, and spontaneous manner. Let us caution, however, that to experience internal conflict is to be human and that no one is conflict free. Our humanity is such that we are capable of emotionality and rationality. We experience drives, desires, feelings, and pleasures; we also experience meaning and meaninglessness, value and worthlessness, intelligence and stupidity, joy and despair, hope and sadness.

Our intellect can serve us in conflict avoidance as well as in **conflict resolution.** For example, through rationalization one can refer to plausible reasons for one's behavior and thus avoid facing the real reason. Or one can project one's own traits, likes, and dislikes onto another person so as not to have to own them in oneself. Or, as we have seen, through transference one might transfer feelings stemming from conflict with early authority figures within one's family of origin toward a significant person in one's present environment.

All of the methods just discussed are means by which we may avoid the facing of both internal conflict and conflict existing between ourselves and others. *Perhaps the most important point for our purposes is to understand clearly that conflict that remains unfaced and not directly dealt with will always serve to have a negative and contaminating effect on ongoing present-day relationships with intimates as well as with people with whom we work and have ordinary dealings.*

Transactional Analysis

Transactional analysis (TA) is the study of the characteristics of the various ego states that all human beings experience. Eric Berne's first book on TA, *Games People Play*, became a bestseller. Unfortunately its popularity seemed to be based on public fascination with the games rather than with the interpersonal dynamics underlying the games.[14] Thomas Harris worked closely with

Berne as one of the original members of the San Francisco Social Psychiatry Seminars. Harris's book is entitled *I'm OK—You're OK.* [15]

As we have seen, psychoanalytic theory is based on the concept that we have three parts or structures within ourselves. These are the id, the ego, and the superego. Transactional analysis also posits three basic structural divisions within the self. These are not real entities, but they are symbolic of the material that each incorporates. Each structure is called an ego state. The three ego states are the Parent, the Adult, and the Child. (Henceforth, the *capitalized* Parent, Adult, and Child will refer to the ego states symbolized by each term.)

> Continual observation has supported the assumption that these three states exist in all people. It is as if in each person there is the same little person he was when he was three years old. There are also within him his own parents. These states are audiovisual recordings in the brain of actual experiences of internal and external events, the most significant of which happened during the first five years of life. There is a third state, different from the first two. The first two are called Parent and Child, and the third, Adult. [16]

THE PARENT

The Parent is like a videotape recorder that recorded all the information available to it throughout childhood without editing or scrutinizing. Thus, the Parent is the "taught" way of life in which we were carefully indoctrinated during those early years.

> The Parent is a huge collection of recordings in the brain of unquestioned or imposed external data perceived by a person in his early years, a period which we have designated roughly as the first five years of life. . . . The name Parent is the most descriptive of the data inasmuch as the most significant "tapes" are those provided by the example and pronouncements of his own real parents or parent substitutes. Everything the child saw his parents do and everything he heard them say is recorded in the Parent. [17]

The Parent is the source of rules, laws, rituals, standards, proscriptions, prescriptions, frowns, smiles, praise, approval, and disapproval. According to Harris,

> The significant point is that whether these rules are good or bad in the light of a reasonable ethic, they are recorded as *truth* from the source of all security, the people who are "six feet tall" at a time when it is important to the two-foot-tall child that he please and obey them. It is a permanent recording. A person cannot erase it. It is available for replay throughout life. [18]

THE CHILD

The Child is also a recording, which is made simultaneously with the Parent recording. However, it is a recording of feelings. These include the sensations associated with what the child feels as he or she sees, hears, experiences, understands, or doesn't understand. The 2-foot-tall child absorbs and responds to his or her 6-foot-tall parents. "Since the little person has no vocabulary during the most critical of his early experiences, most of his reactions are *feelings*. We must keep in mind his situation in these early years. He is small, he is dependent, he is inept, he is clumsy, he has no words with which to construct meaning."[19] Just as the Parent is the "taught" way of life, the Child is the "felt" way of life. The child felt many positive feelings, which became the basis of later feelings of joy, pleasure, fun, and spontaneity. The negative feelings, however, are the ones that seem to cause later difficulty.

Harris claims that there is a residue of unhappy feelings resulting from the fact of being a child regardless of the good intentions and well meaning of parents.[20] All the child's feelings are permanently recorded in the brain and cannot be erased. Just as with the Parent, something can happen today or right now that will transport the child back into the Child ego state where he/she feels painful emotions. Thus, whenever any painful situation of childhood is somehow replayed or re-created in the present, the feelings we felt then we will also feel now.

THE ADULT

The third ego state is called the Adult. The Adult is labeled the "thought" way of life. The Adult is like a data processor that gathers and processes data fed through it by the Parent and the Child, when and if the Adult chooses to do so.

> Adult data accumulate as a result of the child's ability to find out for himself what is different about life from the "taught concept" of life in his Parent and the "felt concept" of life in his Child. The Adult develops a "thought concept" of life based on data gathering and data processing.[21]

The Adult does reality testing and probability estimating. The Adult checks out the Parent data to see if they are valid or invalid, applicable today or outdated, and in this light determines how to accept and handle the feelings of the Child. The Adult attempts to process the situations of early childhood and in the light of increased wisdom and insight over the years is able to counter the negative feelings of the Child. Although the recordings cannot be erased, the Adult can make a conscious decision not to replay them and not to permit the archaic situations of the past to contaminate the present and the future.

Thus, the insight of self-understanding needs to be followed, sooner or later, by a conscious choice—a firm decision. Each of us must decide either to live our life under the tyranny of the " shoulds" and "should nots," "dos" and "don'ts," "oughts" and "ought nots," or to put reason and feeling to work, evaluating how it came to be that our *taught* way of life affected our *felt* way of life and thus influenced our present state of happiness or unhappiness, spontaneity or depression.

THE GOALS AND PURPOSES OF TRANSACTIONAL ANALYSIS

Transactional analysis is a tool or a method of looking at the verbal and nonverbal transactions between people in order to determine in which ego state the transactions originated. Some transactions originate in the Parent, some in the Child, and it is hoped, many in the Adult. TA is a method of self study that can help us pinpoint why we feel the way we do and why we think and behave the way we do. TA makes it possible to discover our own games and thereby consciously choose the Adult position. *This is not easy to do!* Nevertheless, when we realize that the Not-OK feelings will never be magically erased but that as Adults we can refuse to listen to them, then our Child and Parent game-based strategies can be discarded. We can choose to build a repertoire of positive scenarios and outcomes based on our experiences in the real world. These positive recordings will help us fill our own cup! It may be surprising to us to discover how much of our defeatist and self-destructive and self-incriminating feelings and attitudes have come to us by way of our Parent constantly beating on our 2-foot-tall Child.

A second major goal of TA, in addition to helping us pinpoint which ego state we are in at any given moment, is to enable us to communicate and negotiate on an Adult-Adult level. Figures 5-1, 5-2, and 5-3 illustrate three

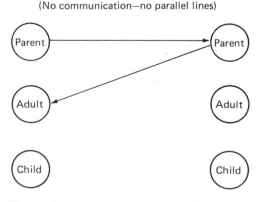

(No communication—no parallel lines)

Figure 5-1 Noncomplementary Transactions

(Communication—parallel lines)

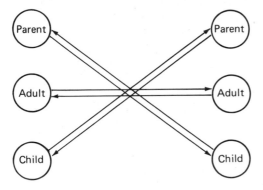

Figure 5-2 Complementary Transactions

different types of communication. Figure 5-1 shows very poor or *crossed* communication. Notice how the messages go from Parent to Child or from Child to Parent. This kind of communication always features crossed lines. Figure 5-2 shows somewhat better communication, but notice that it is strictly *complementary* and *parallel*. If one partner is communicating Parent to Child, the other will be communicating Child to Parent. Some relationships are characterized by Child-Child transactions, and some are characterized by Parent-Parent transactions. The ideal goal, the purpose of TA as it affects intimate relationships, is to establish and maintain, insofar as humanly possible, Adult-Adult transactions in the process of conflict resolution. This is illustrated in Figure 5-3. Notice that the transactions are *Adult, complementary,* and *parallel.*

Adult-Adult communication is an absolute prerequisite for the constructive resolution of conflict. Obviously, no one can relate as an Adult all the time.

(Communication for effective conflict resolution)

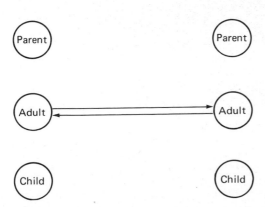

Figure 5-3 Complementary Adult-Adult Transactions

There will be times when we may choose to be in our Child ego state or in our Parent ego state. There will be other times when we backslide and momentarily regress into the Parent position or the Child position. However, only when partners are free to be themselves, free from the tyrannical Parent that beats on and threatens the helpless Child, can there be a truly fulfilling and vital relationship. Freedom "from" is a prerequisite for freedom "to." We cannot be what we are until we are somewhat at peace with what we were. It is at this point that TA can become a tool for working through many of our early relationships within our family of origin. (See Appendix A.)

Ground Rules for Fair Fighting

FEELING SAFE WHEN DEALING WITH CONFLICT

The purpose of outlining the following fair-fight rules or standards of behavior is to help us feel secure in accepting criticism of ourselves, especially as we attempt to deal with conflict in a constructive manner. The key premise is that if we feel *safe* we will feel less threatened by the process of conflict resolution. If we can trust—really believe—that our partner will not abandon us or take advantage of our vulnerability, we can then learn to interact in an aboveboard, straightforward manner. We can never feel safe when we are being accused or are under attack. We can never be under attack without being defensive, even if our defensiveness is hidden by a strong counterattack. I believe this trust to be the bedrock type of trust without which we will never feel safe or secure in marriage or in any intimate relationship, and without which we cannot really learn to handle conflict constructively.

Paradoxically, if we wait until we feel safe before we attempt to implement the following principles, we will prevent ourselves from internalizing the sense of safety that the rules are designed to help provide for us. Therefore, regardless of our internal safety level, we will internalize increased security and confidence as we attempt to build these fair-fight rules into our everyday routine. Most of the rules are applicable to primary interpersonal relationships, including marriage, parents, children, brothers, sisters, and work colleagues. Also, many of the rules are applicable to secondary relationships such as clerks, bureaucratic office staff, and restaurant personnel.

Sixteen principles are basic in the handling of negative emotions and conflict.

ONE: NEGOTIATE FROM THE ADULT

Each partner must make a firm commitment to negotiate from the Adult rather than from the Child or Parent (using transactional analysis terminology). All fighting, arguing, or disagreeing will remain woefully ineffective until this most basic commitment is made. There is no way the Child can truly negotiate because it is always vulnerable and often feeling hurt or threatened. The Parent tends to defend the archaic positions of the past, making it almost impossible to move beyond a rigid stance that impedes the responsible sending and receiving of messages. Furthermore, the Parent is too full of *shoulds, oughts,* and *musts,* which are not good words to use in fair-fight negotiation.

TWO: AVOID ULTIMATUMS

We list this rule early because many dirty fights occur because one or the other partner gives an ultimatum. (Either you do thus and so or it's over!) We need to avoid statements that leave the other no room to move around. No one likes to be attacked. No one enjoys being backed up to a wall or being put in a corner with no space for dignified response. Negotiation is the tool of compromise and constructive conflict resolution. What many people call negotiation is not negotiation but rather is ultimatum and counterultimatum. When no room is allowed for authentic communication, we have effectively obliterated the other—we have put the other in the Child position because we have assumed the Parent position.

THREE: IF ONE LOSES, BOTH LOSE

In our highly competitive society we are all socialized into the idea of winning as good and losing as bad. But in intimate relationships, when one wins and one loses, both lose. Whoever wins may feel good, superior, or vindicated. The winner may even feel guilty or remorseful about winning. Whoever loses will likely feel defeated, stamped down, rejected, and/or manipulated. Strangely, the loser may feel good because it was once again demonstrated that he or she is a loser or a victim. Because it is the two partners, the winner and the loser, who form the relationship, the relationship is the thing that suffers most, and usually it suffers more than we ever realize. Do you know any persons who always seem to be on the losing end who feel good about themselves and/or good about the relationship? The truth is that unless someone is suffering from some kind of martyr complex or victim complex, no one really feels good about losing! Eventually the relationship will break down simply because the loser will have been driven out, emotionally if not always physically.

Once we succeed in dealing with feelings by becoming self-aware and self-disclosing, by leveling and permitting ourselves to accept our vulnerability, we are able to place the health of the relationship above the individualized fact of winning or losing. When we see clearly that the relationship always loses when winner is pitted against loser, we can begin to commit ourselves to authentic negotiation instead of allowing ourselves to be manipulated into frontal attacks or accommodations. Even though we live in a very competitive society with great emphasis on winning, we do well to throw these two words, *winners* and *losers,* out of our fair-fight vocabulary. There is no room in marriage for the concept of winning and losing.

FOUR: SAY WHAT YOU REALLY MEAN

Never say yes if you mean no, and never say no if you mean yes. If at all possible, any reservations should be stated at the time of the response, not later. Grave harm is done by premature accommodation and by false representation of one's true feelings and thoughts. Here again, it is vitally important that we are aware of what we are really feeling.

A common reason people give for being dishonest—for not saying what they really feel or think or want—is that they want to protect the other person from being hurt. To this I must reply that people often find that whenever they protect someone they care about, in the long run the situation becomes worse rather than better. We need to ask ourselves, Who are we really trying to protect? The other person or ourselves? Often we are really protecting ourselves, but we do so under the pretense that we are protecting the other. We protect ourselves because we want to shield ourselves from the feelings of our own pain, fear, fright, shame, or embarrassment.

One of the best methods for determining where both you and your partner stand on any given question (Do you want to go to the movies tonight? or Do you believe in capital punishment?) is the 1–10 scale. On a scale of 1 to 10, where are you on the question of going out to dinner (visiting parents, having sex, wanting children, and so on)? If you feel strongly negative on any issue, that is, 1, 2, or 3, then you had better not say yes if you mean no. On the other hand, if you feel strongly positive on any issue, that is, 8, 9, or 10, then you had better not say no if you mean yes. It is at these two extremes that we are most likely to misrepresent ourselves in order to protect ourselves from having to explain our position. Also, at the extremes we sometimes misrepresent ourselves in order to please the partner. *However, under these conditions we should not try to please the partner.* Please yourself by being true to your feelings. If our score on any issue is a 4, 5, 6, or 7, then we are in legitimate compromise territory. Here is the safe range for giving in to the other, for taking turns in choosing what to do for recreation or entertainment, in deciding whose parents to visit at the holiday season, and so on. A 4, 5, 6, or 7 is also legitimate "giving-in" territory, where we need to negotiate a little and then give in to each other to please one another. There is nothing wrong with "giving in" and attempting to please the partner as long as it is fairly equal and balanced.

(1	*2*	*3)*	*(4*	*5*	*6*	*7)*	*(8*	*9*	*10)*
No territory				*Compromise territory*					*Yes territory*

FIVE: AVOID ACCUSATIONS AND ATTACK

The threatened self (the Child in us, the source of dependency feelings and excessive feelings of jealousy) is likely to spring to the attack. As I have noted, "you" statements are often implicit or explicit attacks. "You make me angry." "You never do anything right." "You made me do this." "You always act that way." I caution against using these accusations because they are usually interpreted as attacks. Attack puts the other person on the defensive and provokes counterattacks. Rare is the person who does not become defensive when attacked or accused.

HE: You always belittle me. You put me down. Every time I say something you have some way of canceling it out. (Attack)

SHE: You're damn right—because your ideas are stupid! You haven't had a good idea since you were born! (Counterattack)

SIX: OWN YOUR OWN FEELINGS FIRST

Begin with "I." "I feel." "I feel angry." "I feel disappointed . . . hurt . . . rejected . . . resentful . . . betrayed." This is not just playing with words. It is important because it is "my" feeling, not yours. You did not give it to me or make me have it. I chose it. I could have chosen to laugh, jest, ignore, or overlook. Instead, I chose to feel badly, and, in my opinion, I feel badly for good reason.

HE: I feel very badly when everything I say is rejected.

SHE: I don't mean to reject you. I sometimes think you don't really grasp the problem I'm dealing with.

The reader may wonder if this small distinction is important. After all, is it not true that the charge still stands? Yes, the charge still stands, but it does not *demean* the partner. It does not run the partner down by accusing and putting down. This is of great importance in conflict situations because the possibility of negotiation and resolution depends largely on the *absence of defensiveness.* Raising an issue, airing a criticism or complaint, or stating a hurt or a deeply felt grievance can always be done honestly and forthrightly without any words of attack. Our goal is to create the *conditions* for fair fight. One of these conditions is to avoid accusation and attack. Raise the *issue.* Stay on the *issue.* Discuss and negotiate the *issue.*

If we take the time to recognize, label, and accept our feelings, and then raise the issue of the other person's behavior that bothers us, we increase the possibility of resolution because we have not let the fight degenerate into personal attack. We may still end up feeling hurt or angry, but that is all right because these are genuine feelings. We express our feelings and then allow the other to respond.

None of this will work, however, if the fighters are triggered by a hidden or secret agenda. If there is a hidden agenda, then no fair-fight rule will help because the person with the hidden agenda is already involved in dirty fight by nature of the hiddenness of his/her agenda. Sometimes these persons are called provokers because they provoke and taunt the partner and the partner cannot possibly know from where the attacker is coming.

In sum, focus on the feeling first, own it, and then focus on the behavior that is related to the feeling. Do not focus on the other person, only on the problem or issue. This is impossible in direct attack because in direct attack the one who is attacked is bound to become defensive, and then the stage is set for a downhill, dirty fight.

SEVEN: ALWAYS CHECK OUT YOUR PERCEPTIONS

Checking out one's perceptions means that we need to ask the partner whether your perception of him or her or the present situation is accurate. Very often our perceptions seem accurate and on target to us, but when we ask the other about it we get a completely different response.

SHE: I sense you're angry as hell about something—is it me?

HE: It's not you—not really.

SHE: Then what is it? Is there anything I can do?

HE: Yes. Just leave me alone.

SHE: Okay. I'm here if you need me.

Assuming he means what he says, she can now leave him alone, trusting that whatever is upsetting him does not involve her. If, however, he broke ground rule four (never say no if you mean yes) and he does not really mean what he says (It's not you—not really), then he will probably resort to increased passive-aggressive behavior. That will probably lead to an explosive barrage: "What the hell is wrong with you? You know damn well what I'm upset about—at least if you really loved me you'd know." This will of course provoke the partner, and we're off and running in a dirty fight.

A corollary to the checking out rule is the warning against *psyching out* the partner. Psyching out a partner goes beyond the rule of checking out your perceptions. Psyching out is the extremely dangerous practice of assuming that we know what the other person is thinking and feeling. Further, it usually involves the attribution of motive and purpose. When we are the objects of this kind of behavior we usually feel as though we have been invaded or violated. Psyching out is sometimes referred to as mind raping. It is often an attempt to control the partner by claiming to know what and why the partner is thinking, feeling, or doing a particular thing.

JIM: I know why you always dress extra sharp when we go to one of my office parties.

GINNY: I don't dress up any more for your friends than for mine.

JIM: You have a crush on Steve Mason.

GINNY: I most certainly do not!

JIM: Oh yes you do! You may deny it, but I know you do.

CHRIS: (To therapist) Andy always seems to feel he has to please me.

ANDY: I most certainly do not!

CHRIS: Yes you do. You're afraid to assert yourself.

ANDY: (To therapist) See that? She's always telling me what she thinks I'm feeling. I'm tired of it.

EIGHT: STATE YOUR WISHES AND REQUESTS CLEARLY AND DIRECTLY

Ask for what you want. A kindly, direct request, even if met with refusal, is far better than manipulative game playing. The attempt to change your partner by manipulating or by "conning" or by playing mind games creates ambiguity, confusion, mystification, and further defensive resistance.

SHE: Will you make love with me?

HE: No! I'm in a dumpy mood, and I don't feel good about anything right now.

Often our pet cats or dogs do a better job of communicating to us their wants and needs than do we human beings. There is nothing wrong with being open and direct in our requests. The reason many people are devious and manipulative is because they are afraid of being turned down or rejected in their requests. This then needs to be confronted and discussed.

NINE: NEVER USE SEX TO SOOTHE OVER A DISAGREEMENT

Never use sex or the lure of sex as a means to soothe over bad feelings or to seduce your partner into a "lovey-sexy" mood in order to get him or her to agree with you on some issue. When sex is used in this manner it is a manipulative ploy.

SHE: (To herself) All I need to do is to get him in bed, and he'll see it my way.

HE: (To himself) All she needs is a little bit of affection and loving, and then she will agree with me.

The immediate aftermath of a romp in bed may feel very pleasant, but the long-term effect of such a ploy is harmful. When people use sexual persuasion to get their mate to agree with them, the end result of the issue or the conflict remains unresolved. Or, if the disagreement is over some immediate decision, it is very likely that the sex is so persuasive that the issue is always decided in favor of the seducer. When this ploy is seen through or wears itself out there is a great risk of resentment of having been manipulated. Decisions requiring joint agreement should be arrived at honestly and forthrightly. Such decisions should not be bypassed or short-circuited, or otherwise avoided and coated over with a layer of sexual fun time because this increases the likelihood of later gunnysacking and passive-aggressive behavior.

TEN: REPEAT THE MESSAGE YOU THINK YOU RECEIVED

Repeat back to your partner what you think you heard him or her say. This is called "active listening." I call it football. You can't throw the ball (the message) back to your partner until you prove to your partner that you caught the ball (the message) he or she threw to you. You prove you caught the ball by stating back to your partner what you think you heard him/her say. The message you repeat back does not have to be word for word, but it must capture the gist or main point of the partner's message.

Football forces us to do three things. First, it forces us to listen very carefully. The greatest weakness in most communication is the failure to listen actively and attentively to the other. Most of the time we only half listen because we are intent on what we are going to say back. Second, active listening tends to slow us down in our reaction, especially if we perceive the comments as an attack or accusation of some kind. Third, repeating back what we think we have heard provides a check on the sender and on the receiver. The sender is the "encoder," and sometimes the message is not clear or is too long and drawn out. Repeating back is also a check on the receiver who is the "decoder." The decoder is required to paraphrase the content of the message and sometimes to reflect back the feelings that were expressed. If the sending partner says that you have not caught the message, then the sender must re-encode the message and send it again. The sender must re-send the message until he/she is convinced the partner has caught the message in its entirety. If the sender says that the receiver has caught only part of the message, the message must be re-encoded and re-sent. This is because no one can half catch a ball! You either catch the football or drop it! If you are juggling it as you run out of bounds, it is alway ruled an incomplete pass. When the sender says that the receiver has caught the message, then, and only then, can the receiver reply to the message. Now the receiver becomes the sender and the process is reversed.

This is always a good exercise to use in ordinary misunderstandings. I have used it with couples, parents and children, parents and teenagers, and even with employers and employees. Actually anybody can play this game without ever telling anyone what he/she is doing.

TEACHER: (To student) Now let me see if I have this straight. You are saying (wondering, asking) that you would like to drop Psychology 403 and add Physics 538.

STUDENT: (To teacher) No. I want to drop Psychology 403, take an incomplete in Psychology 529, and add Physics 538.

BOSS: (To employee) Let me see if I have this straight. You are asking (saying, wondering) if you can work overtime this week so that you may take an extra day over the long Labor Day weekend.

EMPLOYEE: (To boss) Yes, you have it right.

ELEVEN: REFUSE TO FIGHT DIRTY

Hitting below the belt will invariably produce counterattack. Gunnysacking, engaging in passive-aggressive behavior, using the silent treatment, and name calling are dirty fight tactics. The worst of all dirty fighting is, of course, physical abuse. Physical abuse is such a severe form of attack that it is labeled pathological. I will restrict our treatment of dirty fighting to the nonphysical.

When we attack an intimate it is usually a sign that we are inept at dealing with a particular problem. Whenever we attack our partner's tender spots or vulnerable areas we are revealing our own inability to cope with the problem or issue at hand. Dirty fighters are losers even before they attack. Often a dirty fighter gets to a certain point in an interaction and then he or she feels ineffective and trapped. At this point he/she strikes out in rage and uses all sorts of dirty fight styles. As mentioned, physical fighting and abuse is the worst, but the nonphysical styles include the silent treatment, gunnysacking, passive aggression, the throwers, the yellers, the pouters, and the sulkers. There is also the rapid-fire questioner who asks one question after another and never permits the partner to answer. [22]

TWELVE: RESIST GIVING THE SILENT TREATMENT

Keep the lines of communication open. Avoid the silent treatment. Many people have a history of dirty fighting in their family of origin. These people often are adamant that they will not fight with their mate under any conditions. They tell themselves that because it takes two to fight there will be no fight, since I refuse to fight. These people have good intentions by refusing to fight, but their reasoning is fallacious. They assume that if they refuse to fight (attempt to resolve the conflict constructively), there will be no fight and that will be the end of it. To these people peace is the absence of conflict. They therefore embrace the silent treatment. They are the avoiders, the silent noncombatants who think of themselves as peacemakers. They are wrong! Thinking that there will be peace if they refuse to interact, they inevitably make the situation far worse. Silent treatment tends to increase the frustration and anger of the partner, who can now do nothing except fume at having been shut out. Let's assume you are very upset about something that is going on between you and your partner. OK—you're upset and that's a frustrating feeling! Now let's assume that your partner absolutely refuses to discuss the situation with you. He/she turns away from you and won't talk. Now how do you feel?

Most people who are on the shut-out side of the silent treatment end up with a double dose of frustration. Originally they were upset or angry over a situation, but now they are much more enraged because they are left with no way to work out a solution. The silent treatment doubles and then redoubles the frustration. The silent treatment will ensure that issues begging to be dealt with will fester and seethe with infection. Although the silent treatment ensures the absence of unpleasant overt exchanges, it also ensures the stunting of marital growth. Finally, the marriage dies.

THIRTEEN: FOCUS THE ISSUE AND FOCUS THE PRESENT

Constructive resolution of conflict demands that the partners stay on target, focused on the problem or issue at hand. Further, the partners must remain in the here and now, not the there and then. Bringing up a host of past grievances, previously undealt with, in rapid-fire succession is gunnysacking. Bringing up past issues that have never been dealt with will simply escalate any present disagreement into a barn burner. If the past is so full of unresolved garbage then professional marriage therapy is probably necessary. Before many issues of the present can be dealt with there often needs to be a clearing of past resentments.

Issue hopping occurs when one partner begins to feel pinned down in the argument. The tactic is to argue in a circular fashion. "If you pin me down on this issue I will switch issues in order to continue the fight, and you will never win. I will keep hopping from one issue to another to another until you become exasperated with the whole thing." Of course, the more this kind of thing goes on, the greater will be the frustration and resentment of the partner.

The most common mistake most of us make is changing our focus from the issue to the person. We have already discussed this. Suffice it to say that constructive fighting and interacting demands that neither party attack the other. Sometimes, especially when we are angered, it is very difficult to stay on the issue. When this happens we need to condition ourselves to call time out.

FOURTEEN: CALL "TIME OUT" AND "FOUL"

In order to carry out all of the above fair-fight rules and techniques we need to be able to recenter ourselves. Partners need to l~arn to call "time out" from the intensity of the **dialogue** when things get heavy. Sometimes the interlude may be a short 60-second breather, and sometimes it may need to be 5, 10, or 60 minutes. Sometimes it is better to postpone the interaction until cooler heads prevail. *Note:* If postponement is agreed on, do not make the mistake of failing to renew the interaction at the agreed-on time. If the interaction is not renewed, there can be no mutually satisfying closure to the conflict. Too many people postpone and then later, when they are feeling better, resist resuming the dialogue over the conflict. This is a mistake because there is no definite closure to the issue.

People who have learned to handle conflict constructively report that when they label a move by the partner as "foul," there is a quick return to issue-based interaction. This is because both partners have committed themselves to fair-fight rule number one: Negotiate from the Adult ego state. All statements that we consider to be out of bounds or foul come either from the Child or from the Parent but not from the Adult. Therefore, crying "foul" is a good method whereby each partner is responsible to help the other remain in his/her Adult ego state.

FIFTEEN: USE HUMOR AND COMIC RELIEF

Laugh at yourself and the situation but never at your partner. Humor is one of the greatest stress reducers known. Humor is especially important in our attitudes toward ourselves. Learning to take ourselves less seriously and with less self-criticism and self-judgment can have a healing effect on our fight style. The ability to sense, feel, and label contradictions within ourselves and to see the absurdity and ridiculousness of many of our conflicts is very helpful in learning to fight fairly and deal with conflict constructively. Many disagreements and severe conflicts are brought to closure as soon as one or both partners can cut through the icy seriousness of the situation and redefine or relabel the problem or issue in a delightfully humorous vein. This does *not* mean that we make jokes at the expense of the other, nor does it mean we use a humorous sarcasm, which can be extremely deadly.

Many people say they wish they could learn to take themselves less seriously. Because most intimate quarreling is over trivial issues that are transformed into serious clashes of will, it is desirable for us to be able to bring a touch of humor to the situation. A few seconds of comic relief may go a long way toward giving us a more reasoned perspective on the situation and on ourselves.

SIXTEEN: ALWAYS GO FOR CLOSURE

Strive for closure as soon as possible or practical after an altercation, misunderstanding, or disagreement. This prevents gunnysacking, passive-aggressive behavior, and the silent treatment. More important, it holds the partners to their commitment to negotiate until the issue is either resolved or defused. The earlier and clearer the closure, the stronger the feelings of reconciliation and the experiencing of positive bonding and feelings of love and respect.

Closure will never happen if we refuse to assert ourselves and confront the situation. Closure will never happen if we continue to "save up" the beefs and gripes and unleash them only when the sack is too full to contain them. We will never bring closure as long as we punish the partner by using safe ways to "spite" him or her in passive-aggressive style. And certainly the silent treatment never brings closure to anything. When things are brought to closure they can no longer hurt or cause dissension. Closure allows us to get on with our living in a more spontaneous manner.

There are other ground rules that might be helpful. But too many rules block effective use of the basic ones. There is no substitute for reality testing. Dealing with actual interpersonal conflict is the only way to learn to fight fairly and constructively. It is the only way to build one's self-confidence and sense of security. The only way to discover for yourself the validity and helpfulness of these ground rules is to test them. As we practice the basic principles of fair fight we will grow in our sense of personal psycho-emotional safety. As we learn to trust that our partner will not abandon us or abuse us, we will grow in our ability to be assertive and nondefensive. Unfortunately there is little chance of achieving increased levels of security without taking the risk of learning to fight fairly.

Conflict Defused but Unresolved

Conflict resolution requires a relationship between mates who are communicating in their Adult-Adult ego states. Yet even good communication between Adult-Adult partners is no guarantee that a conflict will be resolved. There are times when conflict is not resolvable. There are times when the partners can go no further. If the unresolved conflict is being handled in the Adult-Adult ego state, and if the nature of the conflict is sufficiently important to each person that living together or remaining married is no longer feasible, then sometimes separation/divorce is the only acceptable alternative.

On the other hand, if the conflict is not resolved and if it is defined as *not* being of absolutely crucial importance, then two mature adult people may simply have to accept their differences on the matter. If resolution appears to be impossible and the nature of the conflict is not all that serious, then we at least have a *defused* situation. Defused means that the conflict no longer has the power to divide. If the conflict has been adequately discussed and dealt with over a period of time and there seems to be no meeting of the minds, and if the nature of the conflict is defined as not being of absolutely crucial importance in one's scale of values, then we may say that the conflict is defused. It can no longer hurt our relationship.

Far too many people hold the irrational beliefs that they must resolve all conflict and, further, that all conflict is resolvable. Couples need not resolve all conflict! And not all conflict is resolvable! When conflict remains unresolved, yet defused, there remains the task of expressing agape love by respecting the partner's position and graciously accepting the fact that the two of you will likely never agree on that particular issue. If the issue is defined as being absolutely crucial for the relationship to survive, then the relationship may have to terminate. *Most issues, however, can be redefined, relabeled, or reframed so that they are not make or break issues.*

SHE: Either you learn to put the toilet seat back down when you're finished or I'm getting a divorce.

HE: It's a good thing you keep noticing the toilet seat. It keeps you from seeing all my other faults.

This response does not attempt to evade the issue by denial or by starting a useless fight wherein nobody wins. The response is a reframe where the situation is viewed in a completely different light.

HE: I'm embarrassed to be driving such an old junker to work every day.

SHE: It's not an old junker! It's an antique with both practical and sentimental value. It's something of value. It really makes a statement!

This is a redefinition. To him it is a junker. To her it is an antique that continues to say something important.

Defused conflict need not be harmful to future intimacy and quality. *This is because defused conflict has not been placed under the table or driven underground.*

The Adult-Adult couple will not insist that the other "believe as I believe," "do as I do," or "see it as I see it." Rather, each partner will attempt to clarify his/her own position and to understand the partner's position. When we are truly able to accept our differences, even when we do not agree or approve of the partner's position, we have arrived at conflict defused but unresolved. This is also a type of closure.

Coda

There are many situations wherein good communication is virtually impossible because of the fact that there are too many barriers or negative feelings. These include transference, an imbalance of power within the relationship, and the belief that the female sex is not truly equal to the male sex in terms of authority and power. The issues of power and equality will be considered in Chapter 8. For now, it is enough to say that if there is a severe imbalance of power, authority, and decision making, and especially if this imbalance reflects a belief that men and women are not equal, there will be little likelihood of satisfactory communication and constructive resolution of conflict. This is because ideology and belief are extremely powerful forces in preventing the dialogue from progressing to genuine compromise.

Summary

This chapter emphasized that protection of the self against pain and hurt creates much of the disillusionment with marriage by blocking individual growth and growth of the relationship. Growth is facilitated by an open attitude toward anger and conflict and by the realization that any dynamic love involves acceptance of negative feelings.

Sociological and psychological reasons for the anger taboo were considered. The cultural belief gives people an excuse to continue in their refusal to express negative and potentially hurtful feelings. The psychological-emotional basis for the anger taboo states that we learned to suppress anger when we were very young because it was too frightening to express our hostility toward our parents. The fear of losing love and the fear of abandonment are very powerful reasons for being reluctant to express our negative emotions, even with someone we trust very much.

When feelings are denied and suppressed there is an inevitable deterioration of the relationship, largely because the spontaneous good feelings are felt less and less often. The positive feelings fade away to the same degree that the negative feelings are denied or pushed down. The difference between accommodation and compromise was emphasized because some people obliterate themselves by always attempting to please the partner.

This chapter emphasized that the constructive handling of conflict is the most important skill in the total communication process. Intrapsychic conflict can be the cause of interpsychic conflict, and interpsychic conflict can be the cause of intrapsychic conflict. Whenever one has disharmony or a raging conflict within oneself, this internal frustration is bound to carry over to interpersonal relationships. Likewise, whenever one has strong and constant turmoil in his/her interpersonal relations, there is bound to be a powerful impact on one's intrapsychic makeup.

The basic assumptions and premises of transactional analysis were reviewed in order that the reader might have some specific method for better understanding his/her own self. The chapter then outlined 16 basic principles for the constructive resolution of conflict (fair-fight techniques). These basic rules are intended to increase our sense of self-confidence and inner security as we attempt to verbalize our innermost thoughts and feelings in a constructive manner. The chapter ended with a coda that disclaims that all conflict is resolvable and that all conflict must be resolved for the relationship to be of high quality.

Reading Suggestions

Bach, George and Peter Wyden. *The Intimate Enemy.* New York: William Morrow, 1968.

Broderick, Carlfred B. *Couples: How to Confront Problems and Maintain Loving Relationships.* New York: Simon & Schuster, 1979.

Compos, Leonard and Paul McCormick. *Introduce Your Marriage to Transactional Analysis.* Berkeley, Calif: Transactional Publishers, 1972.

Elgin, Suzette Hayden. *The Last Word On the Gentle Art of Verbal Self-Defense.* New York: Prentice-Hall, 1987.

Fitzpatrick, Mary Anne. *Between Husbands and Wives.* Newbury Park, Calif.: Sage Publications, 1988.

Harris, Thomas A. *I'm OK—You're OK: A Practical Guide to Transactional Analysis.* New York: Harper & Row, 1967.

Kuten, Jay. *Coming Together—Coming Apart: Anger and Separation in Sexual Loving.* New York: Macmillan, 1974.

Learner, Harriet Goldhor. *The Dance of Anger.* New York: Harper & Row, 1985.

Learner, Harriet Goldhor. *The Dance of Intimacy.* New York: Harper & Row, 1989.

Miller, Sherod; Daniel Wackman; Elan Nunnally; and Carol Saline. *Straight Talk.* New York: Signet, Rawson, Wade Publishers, 1982.

Notes

1. Matthew 23:2–38.
2. John Powell, *Why Am I Afraid to Tell You Who I Am?* (Niles, Ill.: Argus Communications, 1969).
3. Karen Horney, *The Neurotic Personality of Our Time.* vol 1, *The Collected Works of Karen Horney* (New York: W. W. Norton, 1937), Chapters 4 and 5.
4. Jay Kuten, *Coming Together—Coming Apart: Anger and Separation in Sexual Loving* (New York: Macmillan, 1974), 177–178.
5. Rollo May, *Love and Will* (New York: W. W. Norton, 1969), 148. Quotation reprinted by permission.

Sexuality: the quest for value and meaning

Sexuality versus sex

Hedonism versus Victorianism

Congruency and configuration

Anxiety about sex

Owning our sexuality

The single-identity myth

The "if you feel it, you will do it" myth

Summary

Reading suggestions

6. George R. Bach and Peter Wyden, *The Intimate Enemy* (New York: William Morrow, 1968), Chapter 1. Quotation reprinted by permission.

7. Sidney Jourard, *The Transparent Self* (New York: D. Van Nostrand [Insight Book], 1964), 5, 24–26. (Copyright 1971 by Litton Educational Publishing, Inc. Reprinted by permission.)

8. Harriet Goldhor Learner, *The Dance of Anger* (New York: Harper & Row, 1985).

9. *Ibid., 189–221.*

10. Karen Horney, *Our Inner Conflicts* (New York: W. W. Norton, 1945), Chapter 2.

11. John F. Crosby, "Theories of Anxiety: A Theoretical Perspective," *The American Journal of Psychoanalysis,* Vol. 36, no. 3, Fall, 1976.

12. Michael St. Clair, *Object Relations and Self Psychology* (Monterey, Calif.: Brooks/Cole, 1986), Chapters 3, 4, 5, 7, 8.

13. Viktor Frankl, *Man's Search for Meaning* (New York: Beacon Press, 1959), 103.

14. Eric Berne, *Games People Play* (New York: Grove Press, 1964).

15. Thomas A. Harris, *I'm OK—You're OK: A Practical Guide to Transactional Analysis* (New York: Harper & Row, 1967). (Copyright © 1967, 1968, 1969 by Thomas A. Harris, M.D. Quotations reprinted by permission of Harper & Row, Publishers, Inc.)

16. *Ibid.,* 18.

17. *Ibid.,* 18.

18. *Ibid.,* 18–19.

19. *Ibid.,* 20.

20. *Ibid.,* 26.

21. *Ibid.,* 29.

22. *Op. Cit.,* Bach and Wyden.

6

Sexuality, Value, and Meaning:
Owning Ourselves

Human sexuality begins at birth and ends at death. It is not a facet of humanity that exists solely during the years from sixteen to sixty, as some would like us to believe, but is rather as much a part of being a person as breathing is, and lasts just as long as breathing does.

JAMES LESLIE McCARY,
FREEDOM AND GROWTH IN MARRIAGE

RUSSELL'S LAMENT

"To the amazement of my friends, I am honestly able to pick up the phone at any time and get a bed partner. I can vary my partners. This sounds so smug on my part, yet I say it in amazement. I have sought sex as an avenue to status and find it empty. Do not misunderstand me: sex, even without passion, has its rewards. Yet those rewards are no longer enough. Sex has proved to be a momentary, passionless thing. It has become rewarding only in the short run. At times, I find myself using it as a sleeping aid! I am dissatisfied with passionless sex and dissatisfied with a relationship devoid of sex. I seem unable to find what I want in one person. I am looking for a total communication that will make someone unique to me and me unique to that person. I seek to have a great value placed on my existence and to place an equally great value on that person's existence. I hope to raise a family. I want to experience what must be the great joy of realizing that this communication of two people has created a third individual; different from both, yet the product of both."

Sexuality: The Quest for Value and Meaning

A popular brand of cigarettes used to advertise: "Are you smoking more and enjoying it less?" Let us change the subject of this ad from smoking to sex: "Are you having more sex and enjoying it less?" Has sex been oversold? Is it likely that the easy-sex ethic can deliver on its promises?

This chapter is based on the premise that what we value in life produces meaning. Therefore, if we value sex it is potentially one source of meaning in our life. Yet many, like Russell, who claim to value a hedonistic or pleasure-motivated sexual ethic are experiencing boredom and meaninglessness. Why? Do they not really believe in the value they claim to embrace? The position I take in this chapter is that sexual attitudes and behavior cannot be separated from the basic and ultimate questions of life. Indeed, in this age of anxiety, the search for meaning and the need for affection, reassurance, security, and succor often masquerade as the sexual drive. Thus, the search for meaning is central to our understanding of the role of sexuality in our existence.

188

EXISTENTIALISM

Existentialism focuses on our responsibility to define the meaning of existence and to take responsibility for our own lives. The **existential** point of view, stated quite simply, is that our existence as human beings precedes our essence—our meaning and our purpose. Existence contains essences, or meanings, to be discovered. An opposite and more traditional viewpoint states that the meaning of one's life is automatically given at birth (or conception). Thus, according to this view, essence (meaning and purpose) precedes existence.

One can believe in a Divine Persona who creates and gives life and also believe that each individual is ultimately responsible for giving meaning and purpose to that life. Phrases such as *self-fulfillment, self-realization,* and *self-actualization* imply that the essence or meaning of life is something each of us must arrive at for ourselves, each in our own way. I cannot do it for you, and you cannot do it for me. We can do it within a religious or a nonreligious framework. However, if we do not find that meaning, we experience an inner emptiness that produces despair, dread, ennui, and malaise.

Viktor Frankl claims that when an individual fails to experience meaning in life, that individual is caught in an "existential vacuum"—an inner void. Frankl claims that each of us must confront this void in order to discover meaning and purpose for ourselves. [1] Frankl opposes Freud's **pleasure principle** and Adler's **power principle** (briefly, the ideas that pleasure alone or power alone motivates human behavior). Frankl claims that we are motivated primarily by a deep desire to make sense out of our existence by discovering and creating meaning in our daily lives. Frankl's theory of psychotherapy is called **logotherapy** (from the Greek word *Logos,* signifying meaning).

> Logotherapy . . . focuses on the meaning of human existence as well as on man's search for such a meaning. According to logotherapy, the striving to find a meaning in one's life is the primary motivational force in man. . . . Logotherapy deviates from psychoanalysis insofar as it considers man as a being whose main concern consists in fulfilling a meaning and in actualizing values, rather than in the mere gratification and satisfaction of drives and instincts, the mere reconciliation of conflicting claims of id, ego, and superego, or mere adaptation and adjustment to the society and environment. [2]

SEX AND PSYCHIC RESTLESSNESS

To determine how much of the current preoccupation with sex is an attempt to overcome feelings of impotence in the face of the existential void is a nearly impossible task. However, it is apparent to many psychologists, psychiatrists, marriage and family therapists, and sexologists that many people seem to seek out sexual activity that gives them little pleasure and joy. In line with this observation, it has been suggested that sex becomes a cover for various kinds of psychic distress and unrest.

Karen Horney has suggested that "all is not sexuality that looks like it." Horney claims that sex is very often "an expression of the desire for reassurance" and that it is often "regarded as more a sedative than as genuine sexual enjoyment or happiness."[3]

Erich Fromm makes a similar point: "An insecure person who has an intense need to prove his worth to himself, to show others how irresistible he is, or to dominate others by 'making' them sexually will easily feel intense sexual desires, and a painful tension if the desires are not satisfied."[4] However, as Fromm points out, these desires, although interpreted by the person as genuine physical needs, are merely stand-ins for less obvious psychic needs. A healthy sexuality is not based on such needs.

Free-floating anxiety will readily attach itself to the sex drive in such a way that the subject is totally unaware of the inauthenticity of his or her sexual desire. Sexual preoccupation may be acting-out behavior stemming from repression and suppression of genuine ego needs.

Frankl has remarked that

> "There are various masks and guises under which the existential vacuum appears. Sometimes the frustrated will to meaning is vicariously compensated for by a will to power, including the most primitive form of the will to power, the will to money. In other cases, the place of frustrated will to meaning is taken by the will to pleasure. That is why existential frustration often results in sexual compensation. We can observe, in such cases, that the **sexual libido** becomes rampant in the existential vacuum."[5]

When we combine the thoughts of Horney, Fromm, and Frankl we see that they are each pointing to the same phenomenon. Each is pointing to the idea that overt sexual behavior often reflects an inner state of being that is a combination of several of the following: emptiness with feelings of malaise, highly anxious, depressed, insecure, or lacking in genuine affection. Sexual activity becomes, in transactional analysis terminology, an attempt to make the Not OK Child feel OK. It is surprising how inner psychic distress and restlessness can camouflage itself under the guise of sexual appetite and desire.

The following case study illustrates such unrestrained sexual desire.

GARY

Gary is in his early thirties, married, the father of one child, age 8. Gary has been married once before. That marriage was of short duration, and he has described it as a union of two incompatible, immature people.

I am here because I'm worried about myself. I feel tense and uptight most of the time, especially when I'm under any kind of pressure at work. My wife doesn't seem to understand and I sometimes feel resentful toward her. Several years ago I began to have sexual relations with a woman I had met at work. She was a lot of fun, although I never really had any feelings for her. . . . You'd have to understand that except for one or two occasional flings, I was pretty much on the up and up with my wife. I don't believe in extramarital sex, but now I almost thrive on it. I go crazy for women. It's so easy . . . so why not? I don't think my wife knows it, although I'm sure she suspects.

The trouble is I'm scared! I'm really worried that I'm abnormal. I feel like my sex drive is . . . well, you know . . . like I'm oversexed. I meet a woman and before you know it I'm in bed with her. Sometimes I don't even know her name or what she looks like. All I know is that I feel driven—I've gotta have her—my whole body vibrates with excitement and I act like I'm programmed to always be on the make. Then . . . well . . . I feel better for a few minutes. But then I get depressed over what I've done. I've learned to ignore my conscience. Hell, if I let screwing bother me I'd die of guilt. When I get too depressed and down on myself I make noble vows of chastity. But you know how long I stick to that. First chance I get—right back at it. I guess you could say I love it. But then I hate myself for loving it.

Gary is saying many things. He is bothered by his sexual appetite: He sometimes feels guilt, which bothers him, and at other times he successfully suppresses his guilt feelings. He wishes to be free of his compulsive behavior. He tries hard to put up a good front, but this doesn't do much for his self-image. Gary doesn't like himself. He really doesn't approve of what he is doing. Yet he may be saying something on a deeper level. He may be saying that he has an all-pervading disgust for himself, and he may be camouflaging his request for help in a request to help him curb his sexual appetite. As in all case studies, the dynamics go far beyond the material presented. It is safe to say, however, that Gary's behavior is an outward manifestation of an inward struggle of some kind. Gary appears to be compulsively driven inasmuch as he is woefully indiscriminate in his choice of partners.

Gary's situation is an example of Horney's dictum that not everything is sexual that appears to be. Gary also illustrates Frankl's emphasis on the libido becoming rampant and Fromm's emphasis on the attempt to dominate others by "making" them sexually. Sex is being used to fill the inner emptiness of the existential vacuum, as a sedative, and as a cover for deep internal pain and conflict. Gary's situation also illustrates Bradshaw's emphasis on the power of toxic shame.[6]

SEXUAL ACTING OUT

A great deal of sexual relating is **acting out**. Acting out, a Freudian term widely accepted even by non-Freudians, indicates that unresolved inner feelings, frustrations, and conflicts play through the individual such that the person's behavior becomes an outlet for unresolved material. This in no way implies that a person who is sexually active within marriage or even outside of marriage is merely acting out. It is important to stress, however, that strong identity—knowing who you are and feeling good about yourself—is the single most important ingredient in a healthy sexuality.

The relationship between the existential void and human sexual behavior is indeed valid. People are never isolated sexual creatures, nor are they isolated organisms set apart from the environment and social context in which they live, work, suffer, and love. We are exposed to great international issues and to nagging trivia. Foreign policy, national policy, the constant threat of nuclear holocaust, population crises, ecological concerns, poverty, law and order, revolutionary movements, and questions of personal and social ethics are thrust on us almost every day. These problems increase the frustration caused by our human weaknesses and impotency. Pressures from large corporations, the all-enveloping political bureaucracy, inflation, and the threat of unemployment can dwarf our individual capacities for effecting change and create in us great frustration and feelings of impotence. We start asking ourselves, What can one person do? What is the sense in it all? Where are we going? Gradually we may become apathetic! We may say we do not care. Under these conditions it is not unusual for some people to attempt to escape through the pleasures of sex.

This dilemma is due in part to a breakdown in traditional belief systems that in earlier times protected us from anxiety. Paul Tillich maintains that because we are living in a period of great change, the traditional means of coping with anxiety no longer work. The traditional symbols no longer convey the meanings that they did to former generations. Ancient formulas and creedal statements are no longer relevant to a significant portion of modern society, not because they are wrong but because they cannot be understood today in any meaningful way.[7] This leaves the individual in a frustrating and anxiety-producing situation. If the traditional religious and cultural symbols are no longer meaningful, they cannot be of much use in helping people to find security. The challenge is to discover, define, and redefine authentic values and meanings for ourselves. Tillich says "man's being includes his relation to meanings. He is human only by understanding and shaping reality, both his world and himself, according to meanings and values."[8]

And so it is not strange that our restlessness and anxiety drive us to search for concrete channels of expression. The libido is well qualified to serve as this channel. In sexual expression people often find a unique kind of security and peace, even if only fleetingly. Thus, sexual behavior may serve as an outlet for psychic restlessness and as a pseudo security-producing mechanism.

Sexuality Versus Sex

I use the word **sexuality** for the total fusion of sex with personal identity. Human sexuality includes an individual's entire sexual identity and psychic orientation. It is both a part of one's self-concept and dependent on one's self-concept. We are concerned here with our identity and our individual awareness and acceptance of the essential core of our being. Sexuality is bound up with our total sense of self, including our **self-esteem,** self-acceptance, self-confidence, and self-trust.

The word *sex* refers to our gender as male or female, to the act of intercourse and sexual relations (that is, to have sex or to have sexual relations), and usually to all matters relating to the genital differences between males and females. The reader can grasp the difference between *sex* and *sexuality* by focusing on the possible meanings of the following two questions.

1. Do we need more and better *sex education* in our families, schools, and religious institutions?
2. Do we need more and better *education in human sexuality* in our families, schools, and religious institutions?

We probably need both, but let us not think that sex education is the same thing as education in human sexuality. Let us emphasize once again that human sexuality is part and parcel of our total identity and self-concept. It is far more than the study of male and female genitalia and the facts of human reproduction. Human sexuality relates directly to the psychic core of our being and can never be separated from our total selfhood.

Hedonism Versus Victorianism

A value creates meaning only to the extent that the value is honestly and authentically held. Rollo May has insisted that "the degree of an individual's inner strength and integrity will depend on how much he himself *believes* in the values he lives by."[9] (Emphasis added.) If the so-called value is really only a pseudovalue, it will be incapable of providing meaning for any prolonged length of time.

Our consideration of value systems begins with **hedonism,** or the will to pleasure. For some, hedonism seems to offer a meaningful way to approach life. For others, it only functions superficially to provide temporary relief from the sense of inner restlessness and anxiety. Thus hedonism probably becomes an escape for many people, resulting only in redoubled attempts to obtain pleasure when the specter of emptiness raises its ugly head. Philosophers and theologians alike have called attention to the fact that humans have always resorted to pleasure as a diversion from the business of life, especially when we feel helpless in our efforts to exercise control over forces that threaten our security.

When people experience the loss of purpose, meaning, and value in their personal existence, they often attempt to fill the void with the pursuit of pleasure. It is as if they say to themselves, "I may as well enjoy what little I can. Tomorrow we may all be reduced to rubble!" Is not this the source of much hedonistic preoccupation today? Is it not true that we have experienced, in a deep and profound sense, a loss of meaning and value? Failing to make sense of this loss, we have opted for a shallow hedonism, or we have repressed our existential doubts in order to remain faithful to the traditional symbols, creeds, and dogmas within the traditions of Western thought. Some have opted for Eastern thought, but they, too, face a dilemma because the Western mind is socialized in a Western pattern and can internalize Eastern patterns only with great difficulty.

Liberation from the narrow antisensual and antisexual bonds of Victorianism is a positive development. Who among us would wish for the return of a rigid, repressed sexual orientation? In vain this tradition has protested that sex is good, only to have the message contradicted by warnings, limits, and preachments that give a metacommunication, a message within the message. The primary message states, "Sex is good." Then the secondary message that qualifies the primary message states, "But be careful because it is also dirty and essentially enjoyable only through the lower instincts. Furthermore, it is acceptable and permissible only for married people." As Rollo May says, "In Victorian times, when the denial of sexual impulses, feelings, and drives was the mode and one would not talk about sex in polite company, an aura of sanctifying repulsiveness surrounded the whole topic. Males and females dealt with each other as though neither possessed sexual organs.[10]

If Victorianism is hypocritical, does it not follow that hedonism is more desirable because it is honest? No, not at all. I suggest that a moment-to-moment pleasure orientation fails to satisfy the human quest for meaning. Many, undeniably, take the hedonistic road and sing its praises. Others attempt to travel the hedonistic road but finally confess that they are no happier and are even more restless and anxious than before.

I reject hedonism. Hedonism is an unsatisfactory way to fill the existential void or to compensate for not being able to fill it. Hedonism fails not because it emphasizes pleasure but because it has no purpose or meaning beyond the immediate pleasure. With equal conviction but for precisely the opposite reason, I reject the nonsexual, antisexual, repressed-sexual stance of Victorianism. Victorianism proclaims sex as symbolically meaningful, yet it denies the meaning inherent in pleasure.

A SYNTHESIS

If we reject both the antisexual emphasis of Victorianism and the prosexual emphasis of hedonism, what is left? What would a viable synthesis entail? How can people fulfill the quest for meaning and value as well as the desire for pleasure, enjoyment, and fun? What would a synthesis accept and reject from these polar approaches to sexuality? My synthesis would reject the essential tenets of the two traditions. I would reject the hedonistic position with total emphasis on immediate pleasure, and I would also reject the Victorian position that pleasure is wrong, evil, or sinful.

An effort to synthesize these two traditions would logically start with an examination of the idea that pleasure is or has the potential to be a value and is not merely a means to some other end but is an end in itself. Pleasure is its own reward, and as such pleasure is its own meaning. Because pleasure is meaningful it is also valuable and hence is something of value and of worth. It does not need to be rationalized, nor does it need some other form of justification to make it worthwhile.

Pleasure has always been valued for its own sake, regardless of philosophical, theological, or moralistic reservations about the dangers of hedonism. Sometimes we break rules in order to experience pleasure. The usual price we pay is guilt. Some people have guilt attached to every pleasurable activity imaginable.[11]

The greater the taboo against pleasure, the greater the possibility of guilt if the taboo is violated. The taboo against masturbation is a case in point. The taboo against masturbation triggers guilt even in those who only daydream or fantasize about it. If the guilt outweighs the pleasure, then one concludes that the pleasure was not worth the price. If the pleasure wins over the guilt, then the mental pain (guilt) was more than offset by the pleasure.

We do not need to confine ourselves to explicit sexual activities in illustrating the value of pleasure. Fear of pleasure has led to prohibitions against cosmetics, movies, television, eating, drinking, dancing, sports, and card playing. According to some moralists, if men and women are creatures with a higher, godly nature and a lower, demonic nature, then activities that feed the desires of the lower nature need to be forbidden.

Yet people have always succeeded in flirting with pleasure despite the threat of punishment or guilt. We all seek pleasure whether by enjoying the company of good friends; eating at a gourmet restaurant or at a fast-food franchise; watching TV or videos; going to the theater or to the movies; listening to music; watching and playing sports; and enjoying numerous leisure time pursuits. We do these things primarily because we *enjoy* them. They are pleasurable! Therefore, if we are to resolve this dilemma, we must reject an ethic that claims that pleasure is wrong or evil, and we must then determine the appropriate role for pleasure to play in a revised value system.

Figure 6-1 illustrates the extremes of hedonism and aestheticism. **Aestheticism** is the cult of beauty and good taste. As used here, aestheticism refers to the pursuit, cultivation, and enjoyment of sex along lines of perceived beauty, in which sex is identified with love and affection, devotion and commitment. The synthesis of Figure 6-1 taps into a double source of value: intrinsic value and extrinsic value.

INTRINSIC AND EXTRINSIC VALUES

If pleasure is intrinsically valuable and sexual relations are pleasurable, does this imply that the value of sexual relations is exclusively in the sexual act? Not at all. A clear distinction should be made between *intrinsic* and *extrinsic* values. An intrinsic value is inherent to the object that is valued. Intrinsic valuation is philosophically considered to be *objective* in that the value resides within the object itself. An extrinsic value is external to the object and lies in the mental attitude or mind of the person doing the valuing. Philosophically, it is considered a *subjective* value. (Beauty is in the eye of the beholder.)

I would like to contend that sexual relations may be intrinsically pleasurable in and of themselves. Likewise, I would like to contend that if the sexual relations are set within a context of affection and love, these sexual relations are also extrinsically valuable. It is my position that hedonism can give *only* intrinsic meaning and aestheticism can give *only* extrinsic meaning. Hence, our synthesis, a mixture of intrinsic hedonistic pleasure and extrinsic aesthetic pleasure, gives a double dose of meaning because we are embracing both values,

Extreme Hedonism	Synthesis	Extreme Aestheticism
Intrinsic Value:	The blending of Intrinsic and Extrinsic:	Extrinsic Value:
Pleasure is its only goal and reward. A denial of love and affection as necessary for sexual pleasure.	Hedonistic and Aesthetic values interact to create a configuration of value.	Only love justifies sex and gives it meaning. A denial of pleasure as a value in itself.

Figure 6-1 A Hedonistic Aesthetic Synthesis

the intrinsic value of sex itself as fun-filled pleasure and the extrinsic value of sex as a means of expressing love and affection. In extrinsic valuation of sex the value is not in the actual act of sex but rather is in the *symbolic nature of the intimate bond* as an expression of affection, love, commitment, and devotion.

A synthesis of intrinsic hedonism and extrinsic aestheticism gives added meaning because we are embracing both sources of value rather than just one as the hedonists do on the one side and the aestheticists do on the other side. I am saying, "Hey look, sex is wonderfully pleasurable *and* it is even more so when it is experienced in the context of two persons who are deeply and lovingly committed to each other." In short, when the intrinsic value is combined with the extrinsic value we have the best of both worlds. Sex becomes filled with a double dose of meaning because it has two sources of value instead of one.

Congruency and Configuration

WITHOUT VALUE THERE CAN BE NO MEANING

I have developed the theme that meaning is the end product of what we value. And what we value can arise either intrinsically or extrinsically, or both. When value arises from both sources it yields double meaning. When people have an authentic belief (rather than an inherited or conditioned belief) in the values they embrace, they are likely to experience meaning and purpose in their daily living, devoid of excessive anxiety, depression, or psychic restlessness. They probably experience joy and happiness in reasonable measure. We can say that pleasure is a value in and of itself and therefore is its own meaning, but we should also point out that much greater meaning is possible when extrinsic value is combined with intrinsic value.

Now we need to ask: Can something be of value even if it is not pleasurable? The answer is definitely yes. Suffering is certainly not pleasurable, but it can have great meaning. Bereavement is not pleasurable, but the experience of the loss of a loved one may be very meaningful. Death of another is often a meaningful experience, even though it is painful and nonpleasurable. Doesn't contemplation of our own eventual nonbeing give new meaning and importance to our being? If we knew that we would never die, would time be as important to us and would the events in our lives have as much meaning for us? Studying for an exam may not be our idea of pleasure, but this does not mean that studying is without meaning. It is meaningful precisely because it is purposeful and valuable, both intrinsically for what we learn and extrinsically for the progress any given course makes toward our degree and future employment.

DEFINING YOUR VALUES:
GIVING MEANING TO YOUR EXISTENCE

The existential challenge, that is, the challenge of discovering and defining meaning for our own existence, is a challenge that each person must meet alone. No one person can ever define or fulfill the meaning of another person's existence. Unfortunately, some try. Unfulfilled parents sometimes look to their children for the fulfillment they never achieved for themselves. Husbands sometimes look to their wives for fulfillment, and wives look to their husbands. Children sometimes yearn to remain emotionally dependent on their parents, wanting the parents to help them give their lives meaning and purpose. Parents can give direction, guidance, and a framework for the structuring of values, but they cannot define or fulfill the meaning and value of their children's lives.

The establishment of meaning is also thwarted if one adheres to only one source of value. When meaning is confined to one kind of value it becomes narrowed and constricted. This is the fallacy of hedonism, which focuses solely on the value of pleasure. Similarly, to restrict one's definition of a person to one's so-called higher nature or lower nature dehumanizes that person.

Eastern thought teaches us a great deal about paradoxical logic, whereas Western thought has rigidly followed the cause and effect of Aristotelian logic. Paradoxical logic teaches us that there would be no cold without heat; there would be no joy without sorrow or pain; there would be no good without bad; there would be no love without hate and anger; there would be no faith without doubt; there would be no passion without stoic dispassion; there would be no security without anxiety; there would be no possibility of "being" without the possibility of "nonbeing"; there would be no meaning without the possibility of meaninglessness; and there would be no value without the possibility of worthlessness.

When values, however paradoxical they may be, form a configuration, and when they are congruent with each other, life takes on its own meaning in the sense that the meaning of human existence is intrinsic to the very process of living. When values are congruent they may be quite different and include a wide range of possibilities, but they are not in conflict. They are compatible; they fit in with each other and form a configuration that consists of many parts. A true configuration of values allows for human diversity, spontaneity, and growth. Thus, the meaning that one chooses to give to one's existence is greater than the sum of the several parts because these parts interact, complement, and otherwise feed into each other, forming a holistic pattern.

Consider sex. It can exist as a meaningful configuration. Sex, sexuality, and sensuousness are values, not in isolation but in relation to each other and to the whole. Similarly, pleasure is a value that takes on greater meaning when it is congruent with other values within the configuration. Personal life meaning

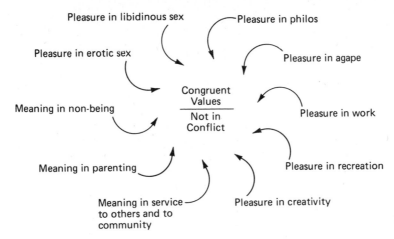

Figure 6-2 A Configuration of Congruent Values

and fulfillment arise from a configuration of values, each different, yet each congruent and not in conflict or contradiction to other values.

Figure 6-2 illustrates a configuration of values that are congruent. The concept of value congruence is quite similar to the ancient Greek concepts of the balanced life and eudaemonism or "well-being." It is a recognition that human beings derive meaning from a wide range of pursuits, interests, and relationships. Each of the several factors in the configuration delivers an intrinsic value; that is, each factor has an inherent value in itself, providing that the individual has an authentic belief in that value. These several intrinsic values have a very significant cumulative effect when they are congruent. This is what we mean when we say that the whole is greater than the sum of the parts.

It needs to be emphasized that when our sexuality is separated from a meaningful framework of values it can quickly become dull and meaningless, lacking any payoff beyond momentary orgastic satisfaction.

VIVIAN

"Well—this is going to be hard for me. When I was in high school I was a good girl. I hardly did anything except make out a little. My senior year I met Gene and he kept pressing me. He was patient for a while, but then I started to worry about losing him—and after all, what's so big a deal about having sex? So we did. We went on like that until I went to college.

"College almost blew my mind. I mean guys just expected it—like it was some sort of payoff for taking me out. Anyhow, I started enjoying it. I guess I had never realized how sensuous I was. For a while I couldn't stay out of bed. If a guy even looked at me—well, you know, a kind of penetrating, inviting look—well there I was . . . ready to go for it. Usually I would see the guy 2 or 3 weeks, and then the whole thing would sort of die out. This went on for about 2 ½ years, and it was always the same story. I'd get real interested in a guy and then we'd ball for hours. It was great! I was on the pill, and I was always on guard against AIDS and stuff.

"Then—I guess it was back in February, I was in bed with this dude, and after I had an orgasm I looked at him and all of a sudden I started to feel nauseated. . . . like I wanted to puke. I was scared I was really sick with something. I got over it OK, but then 2 or 3 weeks later I was with this other guy who was just beginning to get it on when I started to cry. He got real scared and asked me if I was a virgin or something and did I want to go home to Mommy. I told him to stick it up his ass . . . but that bothered me because I sort of really did want to go home to my Mother. Mom and I usually got along pretty well—the usual fights about clothes and boys and stuff—but basically I never had much flak from her. . . . I just never told her anything important.

"What I should have done was get someone on campus to talk to, but I thought I could handle it. Well, one day I was listening to you in class—talking about that value configuration stuff—and it really grabbed me. It's like a part of me wants sex but another part of me wants something more than that. I don't like this part of me, and I used to keep wishing I didn't enjoy it so much because then there wouldn't be any problem. Then I met Fred. Fred's the greatest! We started the way I always started, but in a short time the sex bit changed into sort of . . . an ego trip you might say. We started really digging each other. We talked by the hour, we played together, we laughed and joked with each other. We even studied together!

"Well, I'm about to graduate, and I'm feeling better about myself than I can ever remember. Fred and I will probably go our separate ways, but I know I'll never settle for just sex again. I think I must have been trying to prove something to myself—or something like that. Don't get me wrong—I still like sex—it's great fun—but a steady diet of that without all the other aspects of a relationship just isn't worth the bother. Of all the men I've been with, Fred is the only guy who has ever been a person to me. All the others are dim blurs—bodies with erections. Well—Ann Landers wouldn't approve . . . but who cares? I feel really together. I think my body was telling me something. I'm glad I listened!"

Vivian will never again need to wonder if there's anything more to sex than two naked bodies getting all tangled up together. She knows better. She will probably invest her psychic and sexual energy in places where the rewards are both intrinsic and extrinsic. This is the main theme of an existential approach to sexuality.

We are a strange mixture of body, mind, and emotions, and it is a form of self-mutilation to pretend that the genitals can be separated from the emotions or the emotions from the mind. Perhaps all of us, in different ways and in different ethical-moral terms, must make sense out of who we are and what we do. We may poke fun at the values of our parents or our forebears or at the teachings of the church or the synagogue. But unless and until we discover meaning in our own authentic values, sexual and otherwise, we are likely to live in our own existential voids. [12]

Anxiety About Sex

SEX EDUCATORS ARE DEGENERATES

Sex education is a new scheme designed to demoralize our youth, all part of a giant conspiracy to rape the people, weaken their wills and make them sensuous, atheistic slaves. . . . The sex educators are in league with the sexologists. . . . They represent every shade of gray morality, ministers colored pink, and camp followers of every persuasion; offbeat psychiatrists to ruthless publishers of pornography. The enemy is formidable at first glance, but becomes awesomely powerful when we discover the interlocking directorates and working relationships of national organizations which provide havens for these degenerates. [13]

When we examine this piece of rhetoric we see several themes. The writer is obviously irate about sex education in the public schools. Sex education is a plot, probably a communist plot since the writer calls ministers pink. The object of the plot is to make young people sensuous and atheistic slaves. Psychiatrists are linked with pornographers, pink ministers, and sexologists. The sex educators are gray in their morality.

As is often the case, such statements reveal more about the fears and anxieties of the writers than about the merits of sexuality education in the public schools. This theme is not new. It has recurred in past history, and it is fashionable today in the United States. Opposition by the Moral Majority and the far right to sexuality education in the public schools is very much alive. The claim is that sex education should be taught at home and in places of religious worship. Of course they are absolutely right on this point. There are few educators in the field of human sexuality who would disagree with the need for sex education to be taught at home and in churches or synagogues. The trouble is that the job just isn't getting done.

As mentioned earlier, our society seems to be very reluctant to teach about human development, interpersonal relationships, family relationships, and sexual and marital relationships. Some people oppose these subjects being included in public education curriculums because "really, these things just come naturally." Others are opposed because they claim this is a question of values, and evidently they are against any teaching of values in the public schools. Never mind that teaching children not to cheat and to be trustworthy and honest are values! Still others claim that if we teach about sexuality young people will want to go out and experiment. This is like saying that courses in driver education increase automobile accidents, that courses in water safety increase drownings, and that courses in home safety increase carelessness.

SOCIALIZED TO BE UPTIGHT

The question I want to address is Do we Americans feel comfortable with our sexuality? Do we incorporate our identity as sexual creatures into our total self-concept, or do we alienate our true selves from our genitals?

Ours is a highly sexually anxious culture. We were born into a transplanted antisexual ecclesiastical tradition that claims that sex is good—but only within marriage—and certainly it is not to be enjoyed for its own sake. These concepts were stressed by the Victorianism of the late 19th century, a period considered to be the age of prudery. Sex as a legitimate topic of conversation has been a cultural taboo for over 150 years. Under these conditions how can we expect the American population to be anything but anxiety ridden?[14]

One of the strongest themes running through our cultural heritage is the good girl-bad girl syndrome that we have already discussed in some detail. Yet we wonder why some men are impotent with their wives but aren't with pickups, bar girls, hookers, mistresses, or even other men's wives. We wonder too, why some women are so sexy in their appearance and mode of dress and yet so nonsexual in their marital sex relations. The answer to these questions is, of course, that we have been thoroughly programmed and conditioned. We behave and react the way we have been taught to behave and act.

How many of us can close our eyes and imagine our parents having a rip-roaring good time in bed? Is it too much to say that a great number of our population were brought up as if our fathers and mothers ignored their genitalia except during private sanitary ablutions? We are, after all, a culture that bundles its babies so that there is no way a baby can touch its genitals. We are a culture that passes along tales about the consequences of masturbation. We are a culture in which everyone knows that the real meaning of sin is s-e-x and that morality refers first of all to sexual morality. We act as though hardly anybody has sex before marriage in spite of strong evidence that the rate of premarital sexual intercourse has risen to the point of nearly all presently married men in America having had at least one episode of premarital sexual intercourse. According to Bowman and Spanier, "Virtually all married men in contemporary America have had premarital intercourse, but the experience of females has traditionally been more limited."[15] A conservative current estimate of at least one episode of premarital sexual intercourse for males is between 85 and 90 percent and for females 70 to 75 percent.[16]

Robert Seidenberg has pinpointed this issue. He says:

Somehow our preoccupation with sexual behavior in general has distorted our moral sense. We have judged the morality and worthiness of people almost solely on their sexual behavior and proclivities. Ergo, a young girl is worthy or valuable because she is a virgin although completely corrupted in values of charity, consideration for others, or ability to love. Similarly, a husband is moral if he has observed fidelity but has enslaved his "loved-one" and kept her mindless. The preoccupation with sex has kept us from exploring and defining more sensible and authentic calipers for worthiness—better things to measure a man or a woman by—One shudders to think of the number of reputations and lives that have been destroyed throughout our history by our largely irrational attitudes toward sex. It is not at all difficult to understand sexual fears and abhorrences. There are optimists among us who feel that mankind can make judgments of a person's worth in factors other than sexual. Perhaps demoralization of sex is a logical contemporary project. [17]

Although I am not advocating a demoralizing of sex, there is much in Seidenberg's statement that rings true. Each individual needs to create an authentic **sex ethic** that upholds the dignity and worth of the self, the other, and the relationship without compromising the blending of hedonism and aesthetics. This is a tall order and probably impossible for those with rigid ethical systems. Nevertheless we do have a right and a responsibility to work through our sexuality, including our feelings, desires, and ethical priorities and responsibilities.

In doing so, we will be facing the omnipresent anxiety about sex so carefully hidden by so many people. This anxiety is usually signaled by an attitude toward sex that indicates, among other things, that "I would just as soon not discuss it; I think sexual talk or discussion is in bad taste; cultured people need not talk about such undignified matters; the antisexual people are right . . . sex really is not compatible with motherhood, the flag, God, apple pie, or baseball." This anxiety is not easily put to rest, for it usually protects the self from its deepest feelings and desires. Yet there simply is no way for us to achieve a strong and total identity without dealing with our sexual identity; *the two cannot be separated.*

Owning Our Sexuality

What does it mean to own one's sexuality? Basically, it means to acknowledge and internalize the fact that we are sexual creatures and that sexuality is a vital and dynamic part of our identities. To own our sexuality is to acknowledge it and then incorporate it into our self-concept or self-image, to possess it, to accept it as natural, to rejoice in it, and to enjoy it. It is to affirm, "This, too, is me—really me—and I like it."

Again, a careful consideration of terminology is important here. By *sexuality* I mean the total panorama of emotions, behavior, and experiences associated with maleness or femaleness. I do *not* mean simply sexual relations, coitus, or orgastic experience. It is a gigantic self-deception to think that we are not instantly aware of the gender of whomever we see, meet, talk with, or touch. For example, if I say that I need meaningful friendships with females as well as males and then deny that there is a difference between these male-female and male-male friendships, I am being naive and self-deceiving. I am trying to place the male-female friendship on a platonic or sexless level, denying that I am also enjoying the femaleness of women friends. These are psychic relationships, but they are also obviously sexual in that they meet my sexual need to relate to females in a meaningful way *even if there is no flirting or physical contact involved.* Sex is never limited to our genitals!

There does not need to be any genital or orgastic sex for a relationship to be sexual. When males and females deny their gender and attempt to relate to each other as if they were sexless or genderless, it is safe to assume that their conscious anxiety level is kept at a minimum by such denial. They dare not admit to themselves any conscious awareness of the other's gender, for if they did they would feel uncomfortable and ill at ease. For these people the safest course of action is to live their daily lives as if they are totally unaware of maleness and femaleness.

SELF-AWARENESS AND SELF-ACCEPTANCE

If we own our sexuality, we are determined to stop running away from our obvious sexual differences. The first step, therefore, toward accepting or owning our sexuality is to be willing to take the risk of discovering that the male human being and the female human being are both highly sexual creatures and that there is no need to be afraid of or anxious about our own sexuality. To do this we must learn a degree of self-awareness. It is fair to say that most people who are anxious about their sexuality are somewhat afraid of it. Consequently, their security demands that they deny the presence of sexuality in human relationships.

Self-awareness implies acceptance of one's feelings and fantasies. We have all heard directives aimed at controlling our feelings. "Don't allow yourself to have such feelings." "Dirty thoughts make dirty bodies."[18] Such statements produce feelings of self-doubt and shame, the foundation stones for later sexual guilt. I cannot stress too strongly that a feeling is simply something we experience. If we fail to accept our feelings as being *bona fide me,* then we are, in effect, alienating a part of ourselves from the whole. Psychologists have more than adequately established that there is a measurable difference between an emotion and a behavior, between a feeling and acting on that feeling. Even the famous statement of Jesus that "any man who lusts after a woman in his heart has already committed adultery" needs to be taken in context. Jesus was attacking the self-righteousness of the scribes and pharisees who were competing for honors in a game called "see how pure I am." In this oft-quoted passage of scripture Jesus was simply reminding the scribes and pharisees that adultery begins in the heart and therefore they are not as pure as they like to think they are.[19]

There is a difference, at least among mature adults, between the thought and the act. If feelings were subject to moral censorship, both men and women would be immensely frustrated. Feelings of anger, resentment, distrust, hatred, hurt, and spite are not at all irrational, bad, or sinful. They are the logical result of preceding experiences. The feelings we experience are not the real issue. *The real issue is how we choose to deal with and handle these feelings.* If we deny the feelings we simply refuse to become self-aware and self-accepting adults. If we accept the feelings and integrate them into our self-concept, we are on the road to wholeness and maturity.

DEALING WITH SEXUAL FEELINGS

What are the most desirable ways for dealing with feelings? Three ways are suggested, each a useful step toward self-knowledge and self-acceptance. Pretend that you are attracted to someone and this attraction is fairly strong and persistent.

1. We can allow ourselves to feel our attraction—without evasion or denial.
2. We can choose to deal with the attraction feelings by chasing down the origin and possible meaning. Feelings, like dreams, can be clues to our innermost fears, wishes, and desires.
3. If the feelings can be acted on, we need to choose either to act or not to act. If we choose to act, then we must further choose *how* to act.

Pretend that you are married or engaged. Assume that you become attracted to someone else. How will you handle these feelings?

1. Allow yourself to feel whatever it is you are feeling. Don't deny it or brush it aside or ignore it.
2. Do some thinking about your feeling of attraction. Ask yourself questions. Does this person remind me of a past boyfriend or girlfriend? Does this person plug into my past in some symbolic way?
3a. It's a nice feeling. I feel warm about it. However, I shall *not* do anything about it.
3b. I think I'll ask him/her if we haven't met somewhere before! I know this can be risky and flirty, but I want to do it.

The point is that we are responsible to handle our feelings in self-responsible ways. We make choices. We make decisions. Our romantic society would have us use phrases such as "I just fell for her/him. I couldn't help it. It was love at first sight. I can't help it if he/she turned me on. It just happened." These romanticized and hackneyed phrases tend to create in us a feeling that *something is happening to us* and that we are powerless and not responsible for the outcome! The alternative position is our belief that *we are the ones who choose or do not choose to make things happen.*

If I feel tired, I can acknowledge the feeling, trace it down, and then decide to take a rest. If I feel angry at you, I can acknowledge the feeling and allow myself to feel the anger; then I can try to figure out the reasons for my anger; and finally I can choose to express my anger or not to express it. The point here is that I have choices. I am not the helpless victim of my feelings. If I feel attracted to a woman, I can first acknowledge the feeling and allow it to register throughout my being. Then I can try and figure out its origin and any possible meaning it may have (I may have just had a fight with my wife, or I may be feeling very high about my marriage, my work, or myself). Finally, I can decide if I will express this feeling in any manner. If I am afraid of the feeling or ashamed of it, I will either rationalize it or suppress it or deny it totally, *thus giving the feeling more power than it would otherwise have.*

Many people have been socialized to believe that any feeling they acknowledge is an omen that something is wrong. It is widely believed, for example, that a married person should never be attracted to anyone except his or her mate. And so it is that most of us, when an attraction begins to develop, deny it or suppress it. When we deny or suppress such feelings we actually endow the feeling with additional power over us.

A wedding ceremony was never a deterrent to sexual attractions. Some people believe that once they say "I Do" they will never again be attracted by a shapely vision or a handsome physique, by warmth, by fascinating conversation, or by a shared interest. This belief is, of course, irrational and naive. Fully grown adults should know better. Mature people do not need to protect themselves with such beliefs. Mature people are able to acknowledge such attractions and deal with them. The popular assumption, especially among those who are most anxious about sex, is that if you acknowledge an attraction, even if only to yourself, it is only a matter of time until you are involved in an affair. The position taken here is exactly the opposite! *When we are able to acknowledge to ourselves that we are attracted, we greatly increase our ability to deal with the situation in a mature and ethical way.*

The Single-Identity Myth

A pervasive belief in our time is the notion that each of us has a single identity and that the process of psychological development is geared to discovering this identity. I have labeled this the "single-identity myth."

WILL THE REAL ROB PLEASE STAND?

The myth is that the real Rob matches only one of the following alternatives in each pair of portraits.

I am Rob. I am a warm, sensitive, giving person. I enjoy people. I like to be friends with everyone. I take pride in being a nice guy.

I am Rob. I don't like myself when I get angry. I don't like it when I'm irritable or short tempered. Yet I often get angry and irritable.

I am Rob. I love my wife and my children. I am committed to their well-being.

I am Rob. I don't like it when I feel upset with the kids. What will they think? I really detest fighting with my wife—people shouldn't fight or quarrel.

I am Rob. I enjoy sex with my wife. We seem to meet each other's needs very well.

I am Rob. Sometimes I feel I am oversexed. At times I think I'm the world's worst adulterer, at least mentally.

I am Rob. I am a person who enjoys solitude, peace, and quiet evenings at home.

I am Rob. I love parties and gatherings, a little booze, and even flirting.

If Rob believes he is exclusively, or even predominantly, one of these personas with a social front, facade, or mask, then he is bound to be restless and uncomfortable when any of the other Robs shows up or takes over. If he acknowledges and owns only one part of himself as being "the real me," he is in fact denying and shutting out the other parts of himself.

The single-identity myth is very dangerous because it prevents us from accepting and owning all the various parts of ourselves.

MULTIPLICITY OF EGO PERSONAS

We are multifaceted creatures, and we each find our true identity by integrating our various faces, moods, and feelings into a meaningful whole. There is an identity based on the self-image and the self-concept. But the self is a multiplicity of ego personas, and to speak of a single ego persona as being the whole is to deny the other ego personas.

Our identity is restricted and narrowed if it is based primarily or exclusively on only one or two ego personas. Identity can be better understood if we see it as the degree to which we are in touch with and accepting of our several ego personas. A healthy identity is one wherein we have integrated our various ego personas and there is complete acceptance and communication between them. The person with a healthy identity accepts and owns the various parts of herself or himself even when sometimes these ego personas are in conflict or contradictory.

Rob wants to think of himself as a nice guy, and yet he has another side of himself wherein he is angry and irritable. These two ego personas are both Rob. They exist side by side, and it may be this fact that creates a tension within Rob. Nevertheless, this tension can strengthen Rob by serving to create a balance. The healthy person needs to feel anger and to learn how to express it in positive, constructive ways.

Far too many people deny or block out the fact of ego personas that they deem unattractive or uncomfortable. They say to themselves, "That fit of angry temper was not really me." But as we deny our ego personas, communication within the self becomes impossible. Hence, there can be no integration of the ego personas into a solid core of identity. Other people achieve a quasi-self-acceptance by begrudgingly acknowledging the reality of their unattractive (to them) persona states, but they accord these states an inferior or "not really me" status, thus preventing total integration. It is in this context that most people fail to own their sexuality. They dare not admit, even to themselves, that they are sexual creatures who might find great joy and satisfaction in their sexual experience. To do so would be contrary to their self-perception or their self-image. Figure 6-3 illustrates quasi-self-acceptance. When we fail to acknowledge all of our various facets, the excluded facets or personas become alienated from our conscious awareness. This exclusion then comes back to haunt us by making us more tense, more rigid, and more judgmental and condemning of others. It can also lead to projection, in which we criticize and condemn in

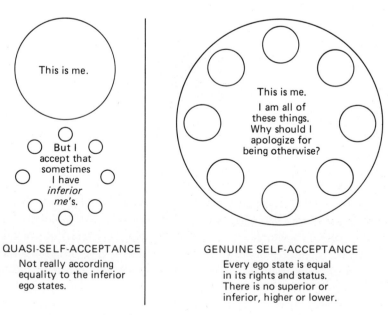

QUASI-SELF-ACCEPTANCE

Not really according equality to the inferior ego states.

GENUINE SELF-ACCEPTANCE

Every ego state is equal in its rights and status. There is no superior or inferior, higher or lower.

Figure 6-3 Quasi-Self-Acceptance versus Genuine Self-Acceptance

others what we are unable to accept in ourselves. The single-identity myth is directly related to object relations theory in that those parts of ourselves that we deem to be unacceptable are often the very parts that we unconsciously split off at a very young age. Later, in adolescence and adulthood, the unacceptable parts or facets of ourselves are the very parts we project onto others in the form of projective identification. In projective identification we induce the significant other person to take on the traits we find unacceptable in ourselves.

SHARON—A NOD TOWARD SELF-ACCEPTANCE

"I enjoy sex as far as that goes, but I think it has its place. I think people make too much of it. If my husband wanted sex every night I wouldn't cooperate. It just wouldn't have any meaning for me. Anyway, most of my enjoyment is in trying to please him, but even that gets tiresome. I think there's much more to life than sex. Sure, sex can be enjoyable—but must it be so important? You probably think I'm prudish, but compared to my parents I am very liberated. We couldn't even mention the words *sex* or *pregnant* when I was growing up. My mother never told me anything about menstruation except to give me a book to read. "Here—read this—pretty soon something is going to happen to you and you'll wonder what's going on." She didn't teach me anything. That's for sure! I accept sex. I really do. But I can't see getting all excited about it! I could just as easily do without it. One of my friends told me that I should read that book by "J"—*The Sensuous Woman* I think it's called. I can't accept that sort of thing. That kind of sex is disgusting. I think sex is meant to be a special thing between a man and a woman, but when it gets into all those perversions it loses its meaning. I can't imagine myself lying in bed fondling my—you know, playing with myself or my husband or anything like that. I'd feel like a sex pervert."

Although Sharon is far from being sexless or frigid or antisexual, it is reasonable to conclude that she certainly is not a person who feels really good about her sexuality. She has reached the point of quasi-acceptance, and she feels comfortable and secure at this level. This conclusion is not based on the fact that she finds *The Sensuous Woman* somewhat repulsive.[20] I am saying that Sharon is quasi-accepting of her sexuality because she seems to take no delight in her own body or her own femaleness. She says she could easily live without sex. Sex to her is a nuisance—necessary for her husband and for others but not really vital or exciting for her. It is just something that is OK as long as it's in its proper place and not overdone. Sharon simply has never really owned her own body. She does not dare to think of herself as a sexual person, and she does not dare enjoy spontaneous sexual playfulness. Although she appears to be far more liberated than her mother, in truth she is still very much under her mother's influence.

Sharon's ability to discuss sex is a healthy sign. Certainly her mother would never do that. Because Sharon is able to talk about it she assumes she is far more liberated than her mother. But she is wrong. Sharon's deepest feelings are actually similar to her mother's feelings. Sharon has accepted sex as a second-class facet of herself: important, but somehow not quite as worthy of status as a full-fledged, first-class facet or persona. Sharon is alienated from a part of herself. She has not rejected her sexuality, but she accords it only a *conditional* acceptance. In other words, she doesn't reject her sexuality, but she doesn't really accept it either.

Alas, joyous acceptance and ownership are entirely different from grudging or quasi-acceptance. When we speak of owning ourselves, we mean far more than a perfunctory nod! We mean accepting and enjoying all of oneself. To own is to claim for oneself or to possess. To own is not to evade or give a nod to, as if one really should not make too much of those organs and body parts that have been described as the lower part or baser (*Translate:* DISGUSTING) parts of the human body.

REEDUCATING AND RESOCIALIZING OURSELVES

We should begin to own our bodies when we are in diapers. Our parents were in control then. There is no reason why any person should grow up being ashamed of his or her genitals, sex drive, or excretory functions. Early warnings and prohibitions against touching oneself create a formidable barrier to the development of a healthy self-image. Fear is learned at a very impressionable age, and it is fear that reinforces messages about bodily taboos. The list of fears includes fear of masturbation; fear of contamination; fear of wet dreams; fear of being naughty or dirty; fear of what others might think if they knew our thoughts or feelings; fear of getting caught; fear of feelings, fantasies, and desires; and fear of pregnancy, childbirth, and menstruation. The overwhelming fear is probably fear of punishment for breaking the taboos associated with the preceding list, especially taboos relating to the body.

Our fears can lead us into ignorance, especially if we associate education about our body functions and sexually transmitted diseases with a sense of shame. We need to grow up with a respect for sexually transmitted diseases and especially AIDS. Except for AIDS and herpes most sexually transmitted diseases can be cured *if fear and shame do not prevent us from seeking medical care early on.*

It is never too late to begin to truly own and enjoy one's sexuality. None of us can go back in time and make a change here or a switch there. Instead, we must each arrive at an accurate and untainted view of human nature, including human sexuality. Then we must discard the most destructive taboo of all. This is the taboo proclaiming that owning one's sexuality means that you are an immoral or indecent person. Finally, we can reeducate and resocialize ourselves, laying to rest the inconsistent sexual beliefs we inherited. Much of our ethical heritage may be very sound. This is for each of us to determine for ourselves. But we must also consider the innuendos, the implications, and the implicit threats that were often used to drive the belief system home. It is these hidden implications that create feelings of lingering shame, guilt, self-disgust, and self-doubt. Shame remains the single greatest reason for later-life guilt and sexual hang-ups. Shame and guilt are the great twin barriers to complete self-acceptance.[21]

The "If You Feel It, You Will Do It" Myth

A companion myth to the single-identity myth is the myth that says, "If you feel it, you will do it." This myth is destructive. It is also widespread. Essentially the myth claims that if you own your sexuality or even admit to being a sexually aware person you will likely be acting on your sexual feelings in bad, sinful, dirty, or otherwise immoral ways. The fallacy of the myth is that it confuses emotions and feelings with ethics and moral/immoral behavior.

FEELING VERSUS BEHAVIOR

As we have already considered, to feel something or to think something is not the same as acting on what you feel or on what you think. A feeling is not a behavior. To indulge in **fantasy** may elicit feelings, yet even these feelings are neither right nor wrong, moral or immoral as long as they remain feelings.

Ethics is the name given to the premises, principles, and guidelines underlying behavior. Behavior, not feelings, is subject to ethical and moral scrutiny. This means that regardless of how much we may want or wish to do something, whenever we translate a feeling or thought into a behavior we then subject ourselves to ethical judgment concerning this behavior.

In short, there is a major difference between feeling and doing. They are not the same. Ethical judgment has to do with human behavior where there is at least some element of choice. If there has been no decision involved there can be no ethical application. This is why some people claim they were commanded by God; or that they were drunk, drugged, or in a trance; or that they were psychotic when they did something. To be under such a command, or to be in a trance or in a psychotic or drunken state would remove the element of personal responsibility for one's actions.

Many people assume that a person who is brazen enough to state "I am a sexually aware person" is probably also engaging in some form of immoral sexual activity. We somehow make a leap in our own suspicious minds that "to be in touch with one's sexual feelings" is related to unrestrained and immoral sexual behavior.

SEXUALLY FAITHFUL COUPLES OWNING THEIR SEXUALITY

I have seen many couples in marital therapy who chose to work together on "owning" their sexual feelings and desires. Their goals have been to grow and develop individually and as intimate couples in their personal integration of their sexual selves and their self-concepts. Prescribed exercises in mutual pleasuring and in guided fantasy served to help these persons accept and own their feelings associated with their genitals in a new and fulfilling way. All of these couples would probably resent the implication that because they had now achieved integration of their sexuality and their selfhood, they likely would be involved in extramarital sex.

The benefits of marital therapy as described above include a more alive, vital, and dynamic marital intimacy as well as an everyday wholesome, healthy attitude toward the sexuality of children. If they are or intend to become parents, however strict they are concerning their children's behavior, they will NOT attempt to use shaming techniques on their children. They will NOT lay guilt trips on them. Erik Erikson's negative steps in his developmental sequence—mistrust, shame, guilt, and inferiority—all build toward identity diffusion and negative self-concept.[22] There is no more effective way to ensure negative self-concept than to teach children that their feelings and thoughts must be justified. Virginia Satir talked much about parents who insist that their children "have only justified feelings."[23] The children who today are programmed to censor their feelings will be the adults of tomorrow who will be opposed to sex education, personal development education, and all manner of family life education in the public schools.

Virginia Satir says that "our sex, our genitals, are integral parts of ourselves. Unless we openly acknowledge, understand, value, and enjoy our sexual side, we are literally paving the way for personal pain."[24] Satir comments further:

> If you had seen as much pain as I have that clearly resulted from inhuman and repressive attitudes about sex, you would turn yourselves inside out immediately to attain an attitude of open acceptance, pride, enjoyment, and appreciation of the spirituality of sex. Instead, I have found that most families employ the rule, *"Don't enjoy sex—yours or anyone else's—in any form."* The common beginning for this rule is the denial of the genitals except as necessary nasty objects. "Keep them clean and out of sight and touch. Use them only when necessary and sparingly at that."
>
> Without exception, every person I have seen with problems in sexual gratification in marriage, or who was arrested for any kind of sexual crime, grew up with these kinds of taboos against sex. I'll go further. Everyone I have seen with *any* kind of coping problem or emotional illness also grew up with taboos about sex. These taboos apply to nudity, masturbation, sexual intercourse, pregnancy, birth, menstruation, erection, prostitution, all forms of sexual practice, erotic art, and pornography.[25]

SUMMARY **213**

THE ANXIETY MAKERS

Unfortunately for the collective health and happiness of people in our society, it is almost impossible to convince those ridden with sex anxiety that their emotional feeling state is outside the bounds of ethical and moral censorship. A person who insists on believing that emotional self-ownership of sexual feelings and genitals will lead to immorality, depravity, and debauchery will need to be sexually anxious and constantly on guard lest the slightest feeling or thought invade his or her consciousness. Defenses will need to be created and kept shored up. Eternal vigilance will be necessary. The person's energies will soon be invested with self-righteousness, and his/her demeanor will soon be characterized by a rigid fanaticism. The children will be programmed in the parent's image, and then, once again, we will have come full circle. The child is father to the man. The child is mother to the woman.[26]

The "if you feel it, you will do it" myth fails to permit total acceptance, ownership, and integration of our sexuality into our self-concept, and hence our identity. Further, it encourages the mistrust and malfunctioning of the self and prevents the self from taking full and complete responsibility for itself within society. Instead of sharpening our ethical choices and responsibilities within the social order, it encourages the individual to retreat from mature self-responsibility by imposing a fear of oneself. This fear and mistrust of our ability to make wise, informed, and mature ethical choices condemns us to be diminished in our humanity, unable to experience an integration of our sexuality with our total personality.

Summary

This chapter has focused on two main themes: The first theme emphasized that sexual pleasure is a value that is capable of giving meaning to one's life. The second theme was concerned with our need to own our sexuality as a genuine part of ourselves and our self-concept.

We said that meaning is largely a product of what we value. Within this framework a lot of sexual activity is *not* meaningful because it has lost its value base. On the other hand, much sexual activity is extremely value-filled and productive of meaning. Value in sexuality is derived from both intrinsic and extrinsic sources. Hedonism is an intrinsic value because the value of pleasure is in the joy of sexual expression. However, many people believe that the value of sex is only in the fact that sex is a means of expressing love and affection. Thus sexual value is extrinsic to the act of sex because the value is not in the pleasure of the act but in what the act of sex signifies and means.

When values from both these sources are combined they form a configuration of value within which we can experience both intrinsic and extrinsic values—both sexual pleasure for its own sake and sex as an expression of love and affection. When both types of values are present the sexual encounter takes on double meaning. When there is double meaning, both intrinsic and extrinsic, there is greater likelihood of ongoing satisfaction, shared happiness, and stability.

The second theme emphasized the relationship between sexuality and identity. A case was made for the position that our society has protected itself against anxiety about sexual matters by considering sex to be a second-class facet or persona of the individual. Sex is treated as if it doesn't really exist. This is total denial. For others it has been condescendingly accepted as being part of our "lower" nature as compared to the "higher" nature of mind and spirit. As a result, far too many people are alienated from their physical and emotional sexuality. If we are to reclaim our sexuality, we will have to welcome this alienated portion of our being into full fellowship, communication, and membership with the other parts of our selves.

Acceptance of our sexuality into the total self-concept will not happen unless we discard the fallacy that says "if we think it we will do it." This fallacy is the claim that if the individual incorporates sexuality into the self-concept, he or she will lose a sense of ethical direction. Morals will go out the window. And so we are told that if we allow ourselves to *feel* something, we will automatically *act* on what we feel. The truth is quite the opposite. The more we are afraid of our sexuality and the more we fear its consequences, the greater will be its influence over us. Covert, repressed, denied, and suppressed sexuality has much more power over us than does open acknowledgment and self-acceptance.

Once we acknowledge and accept our sexuality we have the right and the responsibility to determine if, how, when, and under what conditions we will express ourselves. Many people are frightened by this responsibility. They would rather have someone else or something else tell them what to do and when to do it. These people experience high anxiety at the thought of exercising responsibility over themselves. Nevertheless, those who seek full self-awareness and self-acceptance must accept this responsibility.

This acceptance and self-imposed responsibility are prerequisites for reclaiming our sexuality and owning ourselves. In short, how we feel about and define ourselves in terms of our sexual identity is a very important source of meaning in our lives.

Reading Suggestions

Borowitz, Eugene. *Choosing a Sexual Ethic.* New York: Schocken, 1964.

Bradshaw, John. *Healing the Shame That Binds You.* Deerfield Beach, Fla.: Health Communications, Inc., 1988.

Crosby, John F. *Sexual Autonomy: Toward a Humanistic Ethic.* Springfield, Ill.: Charles C. Thomas, 1981.

Fossum, Merle A. and Marilyn Mason. *Facing Shame.* New York: W. W. Norton, 1986.

Frankl, Viktor. *Man's Search for Meaning.* Boston: Beacon Press, 1963.

Hunt, Morton. *Sexual Behavior in the 1970s.* New York: Dell Publishing, 1974.

Masters, William H. and Virginia E. Johnson. *The Pleasure Bond.* Boston: Little, Brown, 1974.

May, Rollo. *Man's Search for Himself.* New York: W. W. Norton, 1953.

May, Rollo. *Love and Will.* New York: W. W. Norton, 1969.

Russell, Bertrand. *Marriage and Morals.* New York: Liveright, 1929.

Schaef, Anne Wilson. *Escape From Intimacy.* New York: Harper & Row, 1989.

Viorst, Judith. *Necessary Losses.* New York: Random House, 1986.

Notes

1. Viktor Frankl, *Man's Search for Meaning* (Boston: Beacon Press, 1963), 102. Quotations reprinted by permission.
2. *Ibid.,* 99, 105.
3. Karen Horney, *The Neurotic Personality of Our Time* (New York: W. W. Norton, 1937), 157–159. Quotations reprinted by permission.
4. Erich Fromm, *Man for Himself* (New York: Holt, Rinehart and Winston, 1947), Chapter 4. (Copyright © 1947 by Erich Fromm.) Quotations reprinted by permission.
5. *Op. cit.,* Viktor Frankl, 109.
6. John Bradshaw, *Healing the Shame That Binds You* (Deerfield Beach, Fla.: Health Communications, Inc., 1988), 25–112.
7. Paul Tillich, *The Courage to Be* (New Haven: Yale University Press, 1952), 50, 62. Quotation reprinted by permission.
8. *Ibid.,* 76.
9. Rollo May, *Man's Search for Himself* (New York: W. W. Norton, 1953), Chapter 6. Quotation reprinted by permission.
10. Rollo May, *Love and Will* (New York: W. W. Norton, 1969), 39. Quotation reprinted by permission.
11. John F. Crosby, *Sexual Autonomy: Toward a Humanistic Ethic* (Springfield, Ill.: Charles C. Thomas, 1981), Chapters 2 and 3.
12. For a comprehensive treatment of this theme the reader is referred to John F. Crosby, *Sexual Autonomy: Toward a Humanistic Ethic* (Springfield, Ill.: Charles C. Thomas, 1981).
13. Gordon Drake, *Blackboard Power* (Tulsa, Okla.: Christian Crusade Publications, 1968). Quotation reprinted by permission.
14. Arlene Skolnick, *The Intimate Environment* (Boston: Little, Brown, 1973), 174–177.
15. Henry A. Bowman and Graham B. Spanier, *Modern Marriage* (New York: McGraw-Hill, 1978), 92.
16. Henry A. Bowman and Graham B. Spanier, *Modern Marriage* (New York: McGraw-Hill, 1978), 86–91. (A survey of 50 studies of cumulative incidence of premarital sexual intercourse.) Also see: Elise F. Jones et al., "Teenage Pregnancy

in Developed Countries: Determinants and Policy Implications," In *Family Planning Perspectives,* Vol. 17, no. 2 (Mar/Apr 1985). The United States has the highest overall birthrate and the highest white birthrate per 1000 women under 20, compared to England and Wales, France, Canada, Sweden, and the Netherlands.

17. Robert Seidenberg, *Marriage Between Equals* (Garden City, N.Y.: Anchor Press, 1973), 238–239. Reprinted by permission of Philosophical Library, Inc.

18. *Op. cit.,* Arlene Skolnick, 167–191.

19. Matthew 5: 20 and 28.

20. "J," *The Sensuous Woman* (New York: Lyle Stuart, 1969).

21. *Op. cit.,* John Bradshaw, Chapter 5, "12 Steps for Transforming Toxic Shame Into Healthy Shame," 125–132.

22. Erik Erikson, *Childhood and Society* (New York: W. W. Norton, 1950), Chapter 7.

23. Virginia Satir, *The New Peoplemaking* (Mountain View, Calif.: Science and Behavior Books, 1988), 120.

24. *Ibid.,* 125.

25. *Ibid.,* 124–125.

26. For more complete background on this theme the reader is referred to Bertrand Russell's essays on sex ethics and marriage: Bertrand Russell, *Marriage and Morals* (New York: Liveright, 1929).

Getting In and Getting Out:

Preliminary Marriage, Divorce, and Remarriage

And I see love-hungry people,
trying their best to survive;
when right there in their hands
is a dying romance,
and they're not even trying
to keep it alive

RAFE VANHOY,
WHAT'S FOREVER FOR?

219

There are several ways of getting into marriage. One way, practiced less today than in the past, is the process of dating and courtship followed by formal engagement and then marriage. A second way is cohabitation prior to formal marriage. A third way, combining the dating of the first way and perhaps the cohabiting of the second way, is remarriage after divorce. Because divorce has become increasingly common and socially acceptable compared to the prevailing standards of the pre-1960s, first marriage may actually be a *preliminary* marriage, that is, a legal marriage but not necessarily a permanent one.

In terms of family type and structure, there is the first-marriage nuclear family, the single-parent family, the remarried family, and the stepfamily. The stepfamily can be of several combinations: a father and his biological children with a wife who brings no children into the new marriage; a mother and her biological children with a husband who brings no children into the new marriage; or, both husband and wife bring their children from previous relationships into the new marriage. There is also the single-parent family. Additionally, there are gay and lesbian marriages that are recognized by some ecclesiastical institutions but not officially recognized by the state or federal government as being legal unions. Some gay and lesbian unions include children from past marriages and/or children by adoption or foster parenthood.

I will begin our discussion of preliminary marriage by considering the types of cohabitation. Although there are several different ways of classifying and labeling different premarital and nonmarital states of living together, I will discuss them according to three different types.[1] The first type we will label *casual cohabitation*. The second type is *trial before marriage* (the colloquial term is *trial marriage;* legally speaking, there is no such thing as trial marriage). The third type is characterized by an *ideological opposition to marriage.*

Casual Cohabitation

SHEILA AND FRANK

SHEILA: You asked us what our relationship was like. Well, it's simple. We have been attracted to each other for some time. We found ourselves sleeping over at each other's places. Our personal belongings were strewn over both places. We are both career minded, and neither of us plans to get married for quite some time. The idea of living together became a practical matter of finances combined with our attraction to each other. We have no commitment to each other except for this interim time in our life. We are both seniors, and we plan to go to graduate school in different parts of the country.

Our living together arrangement will end this spring or summer. Separating will be difficult because we have been through a lot together. There have been fights and hurt feelings. There have been threats to leave and feelings of rejection. Most of these hard times revolved around our assumptions and expectations.

Neither of us has been jealous of the other's friends, although Frank claims he would not want to know if I had sex with someone else. We just took it for granted that there would be no others for as long as we stayed together. We share all household, entertainment, and food expenses equally. Each of us controls our own finances, and there is no accounting to the other.

So far this has been the easiest part of the arrangement. The most difficult part is finding time to spend with each other, you know, just for us. Before we started living together we seemed to pay more attention to meeting each other's needs. Our relationship is now more low key. Sex isn't as good as it used to be, but it's still good. We seem to have gotten into a rut. On the whole we are glad for the experience. At least I am, and I think Frank is too. We think it will have a good effect on our future choice of mates.

Casual cohabitation has as its basic feature a lack of any professed commitment to the distant or long-range future. There may be a commitment for a relatively short period of time, say a semester, a school year, or a summer. However, in casual cohabitation there is no overt planning for the future in terms of ongoing commitment, marriage, children, or career. The focus is on the present and the immediate future. Usually there is minimal or no financial responsibility on the part of one partner to the other. Likewise there is a minimal pooling of financial resources beyond the payment of rent, utilities, and entertainment.

Trial Before Marriage

LOIS AND ALEX

ALEX: I've started writing several times and have had to stop myself after several pages. It's been impossible for me to condense all my thoughts on "Why I'm happy we've lived together." Tonight I thought of a new approach—"Why I think we've lived together happily"—so I'll give that a go.

There are several things vital to our relationship, which is now over a year old. Foremost is honesty. We are totally open and honest about what bothers or upsets us, and so we avoid pent-up emotions and resentments. We have very open lines of communication.

Lois and I have remained completely independent financially. We split rent and groceries down the middle. We each have our own car and several pieces of furniture. We have gone fifty-fifty on some of the bigger items we bought for the apartment. This type of independence is very important to me. I would hate to feel tied to someone because of money.

Also, Lois and I respect and like each other and try to be considerate of each other's feelings. Our love continued to grow after we began living together, and it is still growing. By living together we've avoided a lot of romantic crap and have really gotten to know each other. Lois put it like this: "Living together eliminates game playing." We have carried on as individuals. We have separate as well as mutual friends. And we have many separate interests.

Through all this we have grown very close, and we are now planning our futures together. We think we'll make it.

Trial before marriage is more commonly known as trial marriage. Trial before marriage differs from casual cohabitation primarily in that there is a commitment beyond the present and the immediate future. There is a commitment to each other to seek an answer to the questions "Can we make it together in marriage?" "Are we good for each other?" "Do we have what it takes to make it in marriage?"

A trial before marriage is a very different entity than casual cohabitation. In casual cohabitation one of the partners may wish for more commitment or for a longer time contract, but this wish does not define the relationship. Casual cohabitation is casual and for the short term only. There is no plan for marriage. Trial before marriage is exactly that—a *trial prior to our wedding* so that we may make sure we are well suited for each other. Trial before marriage is a test run, so to speak, with full intentions of carrying through to legal marriage.

Ideological Opposition to Marriage

LOUISE AND CHARLES

LOUISE: I will never marry. Charles and I consider ourselves married in a spiritual sense but not in any legal sense. We are lovers. We are mates. We are a team. Legal marriage is not for us. First, once you get married you begin to act the social role. You know: husbands do this, wives do that. I've seen many good relationships destroyed once the couple made it legal. Second, I view marriage as a very personal experience. It is none of the state's business. I resent the idea of a marriage license. I think it's just another invasion of my privacy.

CHARLES: Louise is right. What she and I do is our business and no one else's. I do not need a piece of paper and a ceremony to prove that we are sincere and devoted to each other. My friends have said to me, "Oh yeah, but wait until there's a real fight and see how much easier it is to get out or just leave." Well, Louise and I have had some very big fights about serious matters that we disagree about. We have dealt with a lot of conflict. Our word is our bond, and we have both pledged that we will never leave each other without making every effort to resolve the issues between us. As a matter of fact, the absence of any legal tie has increased our intent to make a go of our relationship. We've been together 8 years now. Hell, what percentage of marriages break up within 3 years?

There are some cohabiting relationships that, strictly speaking, are neither casual nor trial. I classify these as extralegal unions. They include couples who choose to share their lives with each other but are opposed to the institution of marriage and its legal definition. These people are opposed to marriage on ideological grounds. Most frequently, like Louise and Charles, they are opposed to the state having anything to do with their private relationship.

Sometimes, however, the opposition to legal marriage is based on the belief that once the couple is legally married they will fall into the marriage trap of stereotypical sex-role division of labor and expectations of husband and wife **role** performance.[2] Extralegal unions often become legal after 7 years of shared living because of the laws of the state. This is called common-law marriage, and for centuries it has served as a means of giving legal status to a preexisting extralegal relationship.

There has never been a government, state, or body-politic that has not had a vested interest in the mate selection patterns of its young and in the definitions of what constitutes legal marriage. The reason for this, as we saw in an earlier chapter, is because the state holds the parents responsible for the children that are born into such a union. Legal marriage confers and confirms the responsibilities of parenthood. The state really doesn't care so much about the marriage itself, but it does care about the socialization and acculturation of the children.

Research on Cohabitation

Cohabitation research does not distinguish between the three types of cohabitation discussed previously. Further, in cohabitation research a distinction must be made between those who are *currently* cohabiting and those who have *ever* cohabited. The "currently cohabiting" rate will always be much smaller than the "ever cohabited" rate. "Between 1980 and 1988, the number of unmarried-couple households increased by 63 percent, somewhat less than the 117 percent increase in these households that occurred during the comparable 8-year period in the 1970s."[3] Thus, although cohabitation increased during the 1980s, it did not increase as rapidly as it did in the 1970s.

> It is evident that the most dramatic increase in this form of living arrangement has occurred since 1970. . . . Rarely does social change occur with such rapidity. *Indeed, there have been few developments relating to marriage and family life which have been as dramatic as the rapid increase in unmarried cohabitation.*[4] (Italics added for emphasis.)

According to the U.S. Bureau of the Census, "There were 2.6 million unmarried-couple households in 1988, representing about 5 percent of the 54.4 million couples (married and unmarried) in the United States that maintain their own households."[5] (Technically speaking, the Census Bureau counts the frequency of the occurrence of unmarried couples. Unmarried couples are defined as two *Persons of the Opposite Sex Sharing Living Quarters*, or POSSLQ. Some of these couples may *not* be cohabiting in the sexual sense, for example, a tenant or an employee.)

According to Macklin (writing in 1986), "nonmarital cohabitation in the United States serves primarily as a part of the courtship process and not as an alternative to marriage."[6] Macklin further states: "It is obvious that nonmarital cohabitation, which became highly visible less than 15 years ago, is rapidly becoming part of the normative culture."[7]

QUALITY OF MARRIAGE FOR PARTNERS WHO HAD COHABITED WITH EACH OTHER

A fairly widespread belief and hope some years ago was that cohabitation would improve the quality of marriage for those who proceeded from living together into legal marriage. Also, there was the hope that cohabitation would have a positive effect on the quality of future marriage even if the cohabitants ended up marrying someone else.[8] On the whole, current research fails to bear out either an increase or a decrease in marital quality among those who cohabited with each other prior to marriage. A study by Ganong and Coleman looked at the question of preparation for *remarriage*. They state that husbands who had not cohabited "had more disagreements, reported more marital problems, and indicated less affection for their spouses. For wives, the only significant difference was for Frequency of Disagreements."[9] Nevertheless, the value of cohabitation prior to *first* marriage remains equivocal. Macklin, in summing up a number of research studies, states:

> It is clear that premarital cohabitation does not help persons to select more appropriate partners and does little to improve the quality of the marital relationship. . . . It would appear that, as with marriage, simply living with someone does not ensure a quality relationship. . . . There has been little effort to help couples use their premarital cohabitation as a time for conscientious assessment and relationship enhancement and, hence, there is no way of knowing if such an effort would make a significant difference in the later marital relationship. . . . As noted above, there is no reason to think that premarital cohabitation will affect marital quality or divorce rates.[10]

Whether or not cohabitation has a positive influence, no influence, or a negative influence on later marital quality depends to a great extent on the persons involved, their expectations, their level of maturity, their age, their educational level, their values, their beliefs, and their ability to learn from past experience.

Contrary to what many people believe, persons who cohabit are not necessarily "liberated" or "free" or "autonomous" or "differentiated." Some of them are quite traditional in their beliefs and attitudes, especially in their attitude toward equality and the balance of power. For others, the act of cohabitation is a statement of protest directed to the families of origin or to society at large. If it is a protest, it is not likely that it will endure once it has made its point or once there is nothing left to rebel or protest against.

An exploratory study by Mark Rank focused on the transition to marriage.[11] Although Rank's sample was small (40 individuals, 31 relationships), the methodology employed was suggestive of the type of research needed if definitive answers are to be given to questions such as:

Does cohabitation lead to more careful choice of mate?
Does cohabitation decrease one's chance of the relationship terminating in divorce?
What percentage of cohabiting couples proceed into marriage?
What percentage of those cohabiting who did not get married to their cohabitant were glad for the experience and defined it as growth producing?
How does the divorce rate for those who have ever cohabited compare to the divorce rate for those who have never cohabited?

Rank compared four groups: (1) cohabited and then married; (2) cohabited and married, then divorced; (3) dated and then married; and (4) dated and married, then divorced. The results indicated that a more salient factor in determining marital quality has to do with the *congruency of expectations*. Those couples, whether cohabitants or not, who were more congruent in their expectations of each other and of marriage were able to forge a successful transition into marriage.[12]

On the whole, the research on the short-range and long-range effects of cohabitation in any form—that is, cohabitation with someone other than one's present mate or with one's present mate—fails to substantiate or give basis for the belief that cohabitation increases marital adjustment or satisfaction. *In other words, although cohabitation appears to be here to stay and on the increase, it seems to have no effect on the quality of later marriage and hence no effect on the divorce rate.* Although the experience of cohabitation may give never-married persons a growth-producing experience in **heterosexual** living-together intimacy, it apparently does not give them any edge over noncohabitants in their future ability to create a quality marital relationship.

DISADVANTAGES OF TRIAL BEFORE MARRIAGE

The breakup of a trial before marriage, as with any meaningful relationship, can be a tremendously painful experience filled with sorrow and grief. Some therapists use the term *divorce* when referring to the breakup of any intimate relationship because the severity of pain and grief is often as severe as the pain and grief experienced in legal divorce.[13]

Just as in the case of legal marriage, one or more broken relationships can take a very high toll on one's self-image, sense of self-worth, and feelings of self-esteem.

There is the danger that the partners will leave the relationship when the first really serious conflict surfaces. To leave at the first sign of serious conflict denies both partners the opportunity to learn the skills of conflict resolution, negotiation, and compromise.

There is a danger that the couple will still be less than honest and less than candid about problems and issues because they are both aware that the other could leave without any legal barriers or hurdles. Fear of "losing" the other will have the negative result of a guarded self-disclosure rather than of full and spontaneous self-disclosure.

ADVANTAGES OF TRIAL BEFORE MARRIAGE

One of the great benefits of a trial before marriage is that sex is de-idolized; that is, sex is taken off its pedestal! One of the important arguments against sex before marriage is that the sex becomes very romanticized. There may be great chemistry and electricity between the couple, but they will soon part to return to their own pad, so to speak. This tends to increase the excitement of sex and the desire to make oneself very appealing to the partner. It increases the likelihood of dishonesty and the "faking" of desire, pleasure, and even orgasm. However, in a trial relationship, sex is set within a more honest and realistic context, and the distance factor is removed, thus forcing the couple to deal with each other in a less romanticized way; that is, they see each other now with hair up, hair down; good mood, bad mood; clean body, sweaty body. Further, they now share a kitchen, bedroom, bathroom, and living room. They are under foot. They have less personal space. They have ongoing sexual access and need no longer plan their times to make love. All of this tends to de-idolize sex and place it in a realistic perspective. If the couple can manage this and deal with it creatively, it is a good sign of their ability to handle other hurdles as well.

A long-term commitment is delayed until the partners have a reasonable storehouse of practical experience in meeting each other's needs and engaging in constructive handling of conflict.

No children are brought into the world. Most trial relationships are defined as trials in order for the couple to determine if they really think they are mature enough and well suited to each other to make a go of it in the long run. Therefore there is protection against conception based on the belief that it is better to make a life for yourselves before you make another life. (We cannot ignore or deny that brief legal marriages into which children are born are emotionally costly to the children and emotionally and financially costly to the parents, sometimes to grandparents, and to society.)

The breakup of any meaningful intimate relationship may be quite traumatic and painful. A trial relationship is no exception. However, in the absence of a legal divorce process, the trial relationship affords an opportunity for a rational and dignified consideration of each other's position without agonizing feelings of guilt, failure, and mutual charges of recrimination that appear to be more prevalent when people go through a legal divorce.

A trial before marriage is an opportunity for in-depth personal growth based on the experience of a shared life-style. This growth can occur even if the trial relationship should be dissolved. Many people value this experience because they feel that it prevented them from making the mistake of entering a legal marriage that would have been destructive for them.

It is wrong to say that a dissolved trial relationship was unsuccessful. It may have been very successful in opening the eyes of one or both partners concerning the realities and responsibilities of married life. It may have been extremely successful in helping the partners know more about their own selves in terms of what they want out of life and whether or not they feel they are "ready" for marriage.

In short, although a trial relationship may not increase the quality of one's future marriage, it may provide the necessary experience that one some-times needs to decide that one is simply not ready for marriage. In this sense trial before marriage may be said to be a shock-type mechanism that serves to prevent a number of people from entering an ill-advised marital union.

LINDA AND RICK

LINDA: Rick and I were to have been married in August, but the date was postponed indefinitely. I wasn't as sure as Rick was about our future, so since we both were to attend summer school, we pooled our resources and moved into a small house for 2½ months. Now, 8 months later, I can look back through the journal I kept of those days and congratulate myself for having the courage to enter that trial marriage. Quickly, all the disenchantment of the early months of marriage set in: loss of romantic feelings, squabbling over everything, mutual feelings of being taken for granted, and sex becoming a daily routine instead of a time to really be together. It was a highly emotional time for me, as I swung from great joy and tenderness to awful depression over what seemed such a failure.

My predominating emotion was the sense of being trapped, of finality. One day I complained in my journal that I felt possessed by Rick. I felt like I was being pushed into a funnel with the narrow end being a wedding ring that I knew I didn't want! I felt trapped by love and a "duty" to return that love. Now I can see that my trap was partially self-made by my own emotional needs and insecurities. It wasn't all Rick's fault, and I don't mean to imply that it was. I just wasn't ready for this kind of life.

Our place shook with conflict—over how to fry bologna, when to feed the dog, whose turn it was to do the dishes, when to have sex—anything! I think much of the conflict stemmed from the final un-covering of our true attitudes toward ourselves, each other, and life in general—but the fights were usually about the little annoyances.

We had friends, this newlywed couple, who were experiencing much the same thing, except they were married. I'm so glad that mine was only a trial marriage because if I had been chained by a ring and a license, I don't know how I could have handled the intense conviction that we had made a terrible mistake. At the end, he left town as planned, and 2 months later I found strength to break our engage-ment. Now I see not only that we were not right for each other but also that is was not the right season of my life for the responsibility of marriage—I still have much growing to do before I will be ready. As far as the right or wrong side of what we did, I do not see how we could have been any more ethical than we were. We accepted our responsibility to ourselves, to our possible future children, and to society by trying to determine if we could build a strong marriage before we made a final commitment. If we had married, I fear we would both be very unhappy right now. Even my parents, who were very upset with me for living with Rick, now agree with me and share my good feelings about having avoided a costly mistake.

First Marriage as Preliminary

Let us now consider this current state of affairs in relation to the concept of *Marriage in Two Steps* as advocated by Margaret Mead.[14] Mead's two-step proposal stated that people would begin with "individual" marriage, which would not be what we think of as legal marriage. Individual marriage is equivalent to what we have called "trial before marriage." Mead's step two, "parental marriage," is what we call legal marriage and cannot be entered into until one has first been involved in an "individual" marriage. Mead's proposal was based on the assumption that childbirth and childraising, if not conception, were part of step two, the parental marriage.

According to Martin and Bumpass, the current state of affairs is that "about two-thirds of all first marriages are likely to end in separation or divorce."[15] Separation does not always lead to divorce, but it is an indication of breakdown and internal discord. Martin and Bumpass also point out that the drop in divorces since 1980 is misleading. Although the number of divorces per 1000 people (the crude divorce rate) has leveled off since 1980, we must also consider the number of separations that take place. When we consider separations it appears that only about one third of the American marrying population will be free of either separation or divorce. This still fails to account for those unhappy marriages where nobody does anything about the unhappiness, the so-called "grin and bear it" type marriage.

Nearly 80 percent of middle-aged, divorced individuals will remarry.[16] According to Andrew Cherlin, "the upshot of all this is that most people who get divorced remarry. About five out of six men and about three out of four women remarry after a divorce, according to the experiences of the older generations alive today."[17] The salient point is that we appear to have a serial type of monogamy (sequential monogamy or progressive monogamy) for between one third and nearly one half of the population. Therefore, nearly one half of the United States population is involved in some sort of preliminary marriage, at least in the sense that the first marriage is considered to be but a "prelim" to the "real thing," that is, the main event—the second marriage.

When we combine the remarriage figures to include the estimates of the numbers of persons who have ever cohabited, we are talking about more than 50 percent of the United States population. (Some of the "ever-cohabitants" are also counted in the number of divorces, and thus the sums cannot be additive.) My contention here is that whether we call it trial before marriage or marriage in two steps or **serial monogamy**, over half of the population of the United States has had an experience of living together, legal or nonlegal, prior to the relationship that they refer to as being "for keeps." One of the most recurring of all recent protestations on the part of divorced persons is "my first marriage was a mistake . . . the next one is for keeps."[18]

Marriage in two steps is a present reality although we don't call it that. We call it "marriage, divorce, remarriage." It is ironic that trial before marriage is criticized and condemned by moralists, but serial marriage is merely lamented as being unfortunate! Marriage in two steps is considered immoral, whereas marriage-divorce-remarriage is considered morally superior.

In any serious dyadic commitment, separation and the dissolution of the relationship is usually an experience of deep personal loss filled with pain and grief, with anger and a sense of failure.[19] Regardless of whether we are speaking of the breakup of a trial before marriage or of marriage itself, the pain and suffering may be very powerful. The cost of ending a relationship is not just to the individuals, but in a sense it is a cost to the entire society. People become distrustful. People become leery and closed and seek to reduce their vulnerability. The cost is generalized to the institution of remarriage wherein the partners are desirous of making good the new relationship, yet they are afraid and fearful of another failure.

Nevertheless, for better or for worse there appear to be three ways to enter marriage: the traditional way, the trial way, and the remarriage way. My point has been to emphasize that the traditional way ends up to be the way of less than half of our total population. The other half either enter marriage with a preliminary experience of cohabitation or enter a marriage that eventually is defined as a preliminary marriage to the second marriage, which is the real thing! This marriage is preliminary in the sense that it is prior to the main event, the second marriage, which is defined as being "for keeps."

What all of this points to is that we are doing something wrong! Trial before marriage has not really had any significant impact on lowering the divorce rate. Today third and fourth marriages are increasingly common, thus postponing the relationship that is to be "for keeps." The theme of this book has dealt with those things that are wrong in marriage by emphasizing what can be done to turn things around and to create increased marital satisfaction and happiness. Chapter 8 will emphasize the "right" things we need to do in order to achieve a vital and growth-oriented relationship. For now, let us examine more closely the issues and problems related to divorce and remarriage.

Divorce and Remarriage

STATISTICS AND TRENDS

The national marriage rate fell by 2 percent, from 9.9 per 1000 people in 1987 to 9.7 in 1988. The marriage rate, recorded since 1867, has varied between a high of 16.4 in 1946 and a low of 7.9 in the depression year of 1932. The 1988 rate is the lowest marriage rate since 1967 when it was also 9.7. This is the fourth consecutive drop in the marriage rate after a period of fairly steady rates from 1980 to 1984.[20]

The marriage rate has dropped slightly, and the divorce rate, after stabilization between 1982 and 1986, is at its lowest since 1975. Divorce statistics can be misleading inasmuch as there is a *percentage* rate that is used by the media (for example, when it is reported that there is one divorce per every two marriages). The percentage rate is really not very helpful because it compares the number of weddings per year with the number of divorces per year, but the divorces represent relationships that range from several months to 50 or 60 years in duration. Also, a low marriage rate in a given year makes the divorce rate look worse, and an extra high marriage rate makes the divorce rate look better. The *crude* divorce rate is reported above. The crude rate is the number of divorces per 1000 population. The *refined* rate seems to be more helpful. The refined rate indicates the number of divorces per 1000 married women.

Because there are only two ways to end a marriage, death and divorce, the ratio of these two numbers is very revealing. For example, if we look at a hypothetical town by the name of Middleville and discover that in 1990, 100 marriages ended by death of a mate and 50 marriages ended by divorce, then we have a relatively clear picture of what percentage of marriages actually did endure until one of the partners died compared to those marriages ended by divorce.[21] According to Spanier and Furstenberg, on a recurring annual basis since 1974, there have been more marriages terminated by divorce than by death.[22]

Although divorce statistics can be abused and used as an excuse for almost any kind of moralistic lamentation, one can hardly deny that statistics on divorce are one measure of marital failure. However, divorce statistics have never been a valid measure of marital success or marital health.[23] The point here is that many couples stay together in spite of the fact that their marriage is of low quality, devitalized, conflict habituated, or wherein there is emotional divorce but not legal divorce. Some existing marriages are pro-forma exercises in pseudomutuality and/or in-house separations. This is why Martin and Bumpass talk about a two-thirds rate in marital disruption.[24] (The quality of a vital marriage will be considered in Chapter 8.)

DIVORCE

Some people enter into divorce lightly; others travel the path of divorce with great fear and trepidation. Still others go through the divorce process in order to escape the consequences of imprisonment and abuse and therefore find divorce to be a great relief. Although divorce can be a rational, civil, and dignified process for some, the fact remains that for many people the act of filing for divorce and carrying this process through to its conclusion is an act of very great courage that requires a steadfast determination and a commitment to oneself that was previously unrivaled in their life.

Divorce is not as simple as it sometimes sounds. Although it takes two to marry and only one to divorce, no-fault divorce is no guarantee against litigation over property and child custody. You can't divorce your children, and yet in divorcing, some parents lose their children, if not for life at least for a significant part of the child's or youngster's growth toward maturity. All divorces cannot be considered to be similar in that one who divorces because his/her mate is abusive and violent will not have the same emotional responses as those who divorce because the marriage is devitalized, dysfunctional, oppressive, or simply worn out.

There are stages in the decision to divorce, and there are predictable stages in recovery from divorce.[25] In a very general sense the stages of divorce parallel the stages of grief resolution as postulated by Elisabeth Kübler-Ross.[26] Kübler-Ross outlined the grief stages of death bereavement as denial, anger, bargaining, depression, and acceptance.[27] Paul Bohannan used a different approach to describe the events and challenges of divorce. He described six different divorces: emotional divorce, legal divorce, economic divorce, coparental divorce, community divorce, and psychic divorce.[28] This last station, as Bohannan calls it, is similar to the healing that takes place in the grief resolution process.

The pain of divorce and its totality of consequences are usually underestimated. If males are the more active agents in seeking the divorce, it is likely that they have been having fantasies of what it will be like when they are single again and can "play the field." Many males look forward to their new-found singlehood and to leading the life of a playboy. Yet males often get caught up in their own denied and suppressed dependency and often tire very quickly of the swinging existence they had fantasized. The result of this is that more males remarry than do females, and they remarry sooner than do females. Just as there is "his" marriage and "her" marriage, there is also "his" divorce and "her" divorce.[29]

Perhaps the greatest sense of loss arising from divorce is the loss of children by the nonprimary caregiver. (Joint custody does not necessarily imply joint caregiving. *Custody* is a legal term referring to who has the responsibility for making educational, medical, and other major decisions for the minor child.)

Conflicts about visitation, remarriage, the birth of new children in a remarriage, and geographical distance all contribute to diminished contact between noncustodial parents and their children. An important finding is that fathers' postdivorce relationships cannot be predicted from their predivorce relationships with their children. Many previously intensely attached fathers cannot tolerate part-time parenting and become disengaged, other fathers who had little predivorce contact with their children become active, competent parents.[30]

According to Sharon Price and Patrick McKenry "the basic theoretical approaches to explaining why people divorce center around exchange theory, which accounts for divorce in terms of costs and rewards."[31] Exchange theory considers degree of attraction to mate (internal) versus outside attractions (external), barriers to divorce, costs of remaining married, cost of divorcing (including social cost, actual financial cost of the divorce now and long-range financial cost), rewards and benefits of remaining married, and rewards and benefits of divorce. Reduced to its most basic terms, exchange theory compares what you perceive you are giving versus what you perceive you are getting. Diane Vaughan says in her book *Uncoupling,* "Never will the degree of investment and commitment be identical for both. But the relationship may be sufficiently central to the life and identity of each that neither may be prepared to go on (toward divorce)."[32] In a sense, this entire book constitutes a series of responses to the questions "Why do people want to get divorced?" and "What is the bottom line in keeping couples together?"

REMARRIAGE AND REDIVORCE

TANYA AND TONY

TONY: I did not live with anybody before I got married. I had sex with several different women, and for the most part these were very good experiences. When I met Marcia I thought "This is it! This is for life!" No doubt about it. I was crazy about her, and I think she felt that way about me. After living with Marcia for 4 years things went downhill rapidly. Everything went wrong. I couldn't do anything right. She was dominating and controlling. No matter what the situation, she would tell me what to do and how to do it, and it drove me buggy. After another 6 miserable months we divorced. It was no big hassle because it was fairly mutual. Because we didn't have kids it was fairly easy to split up the stuff we owned.

I was single again. I did some bed hopping, but that got tiresome very quickly. I met Tanya about 18 months after Marcia and I got divorced. It wasn't love at first sight, but I sure was gone on her. She was a fantastic person, a fantastic lover. She was everything Marcia wasn't. We dated about 2 months and got married. That was about a year ago. Now look at us! I tell you, I can't trust her. She keeps talking to her ex-husband, Ralph. Sometimes I think I'm going crazy with jealousy. If that's not enough, she parcels out sex like it was being rationed, and she is bossy as hell. Sometimes I can't believe how stupid and blind I was. I married a woman just like my first wife. Sometimes I think I should have stayed with my first wife. At least I wouldn't have Ralph to contend with.

TANYA: I was very much in love with Ralph, but after 2 years of marriage he left me for someone else—an older woman who swept him off his feet. I guess I still loved him even after we were divorced. When I met Tony I was still hurting from losing Ralph. Tony seemed so nice. He cared about me, and he took care of me. He did little things for me. He paid a lot of attention to me, and he always seemed to be there for me. After we got married he seemed to just let me hang. He quit caring. He quit doing things for me. He quit loving me sexually. All he wanted was to come! He no longer took time with me. I guess I was mentally still married to Ralph. I hadn't realized it, but once Tony started to neglect me I retreated into a fantasy with Ralph. After a while I didn't give a hoot about Tony, so I started taking control of everything! Why not? He had betrayed me, and the only way I knew to get back at him was to dominate him and make his life miserable. As far as I'm concerned this marriage is over.

Not only has divorce become widespread in our society, remarriage has become widespread also. Remarriage may be the single most important topic of future efforts in the area of marriage preparation and family life education. In the United States, one out of three brides and grooms have been married at least once previously. The estimated annual national total of remarriages for previously divorced men and women increased almost every year from 1970 to 1983.[33] Divorced men and women marry at higher rates than singles. In 1983 the remarriage rate for divorced women was 44 percent higher than the marriage rate for single women. Similarly, the remarriage rate for divorced men was three times higher than for single men. Approximately one fourth of all divorces in the United States are dissolutions of marriages that followed divorces, that is, divorces of remarried persons.[34]

For divorced persons, marriage rates were higher for men than women for all age groups over 25.[35] In 1986, just under 120 divorced males remarried per 1000 population compared to 80 females (33 percent more males than females remarried in 1986).[36] An overall estimation of the remarriage rate has 76 percent of all divorced women eventually remarrying and 85 percent of divorced men.[37]

There are some challenges and problems faced by first marrieds that are *not* faced by second marrieds, third marrieds, and even fourth marrieds. However, most of the material in the first six chapters of this book apply to remarriages as well as to first marriages. Exceptions to this are (1) those first married who are virginal at marriage and thus face the newness of sex. Remarriages do not have to cope with lack of sexual experience. (2) Presuming they have been sexually exclusive, first marrieds have no other means of first-hand comparison. Remarrieds do not face that situation. In fact, comparison to the first marriage, which serves as a baseline, is one of the biggest potential problems of remarriage.[38] (3) Some remarrieds do not face childbirth, but then, some first marrieds do not either. (4) First marrieds face only one set of in-laws, providing the in-laws themselves do not remarry. These are some of the challenges and issues faced by first marrieds and not by remarriages. The real issues, however, are those challenges and problems faced by remarrieds that are *not* faced by first marrieds.

Before we consider these issues, we need to remind ourselves of two things. First, not all remarriages are the result of a prior divorce. Remarriage may also occur after the death of a mate. Although these two antecedent conditions of remarriage—that is, after divorce and after death of a mate— share many similarities, they are also different from each other in several crucial ways. Remarriage after death of a mate seems not to be tinged with a sense of guilt so often experienced by those who remarry after divorce. This guilt arises from a sense of failure that many divorced persons carry into their new marriage. Most of all we need to realize that death of mate rarely involves decision making except in those cases wherein decisions had to be made directly dealing with the continuance or noncontinuance of life support systems. Divorce, however, almost always involves a decision on the part of at least one partner. This decision will affect one's entire future life and the life of the partner and the children. The possibility for later guilt about this decision is a major factor separating the two conditions of remarriage. Another major area of difference between the two conditions of remarriage involves finances. Remarriage after death of one's mate eliminates the problems of support, retooling support, and child support often experienced by divorced persons.

The second thing that we need to remind ourselves about when we discuss remarriage is that not all remarriages consist of both partners remarrying. A remarriage can consist of only one partner who is remarrying, whereas the other partner is marrying for the first time. This situation can be stressful inasmuch as one partner may have extensive marital experience, whereas the other has none. Also, partners in remarriage may or may not be parents. The remarriage situation may transform one of the partners into the role of "instant" parent, even if only in title. Following is a list of some of the more pressing and crucial issues that face remarrieds that are *not* faced by first marrieds.

Remarrieds face the *ghost effect* of the partner's first spouse. For some this is no problem at all. For others it is a huge problem giving rise to jealousy, suspicion, anger, and even rage. If the ex-mate of your partner remarries, the situation may be alleviated somewhat, but not always and not entirely. Tony was in severe competition with the ghost of Ralph.

If either you or your new partner brings children into the new marriage, the new marriage becomes a special type of remarried family called a step-family. We will discuss the stepfamily in greater detail later.

Remarrieds often face severe financial problems, especially if either partner is providing financial support to the former mate. This financial support could be in the form of child support or retooling money that is awarded so that an ex-mate can prepare to enter or reenter the work force. The new partner may resent the fact of money being sent to the ex-mate.

The remarriage involves comparison with the first marriage even if this comparison is covert, implicit, and denied. Neither Tony nor Tanya was really over their first marriage when they entered marriage with each other. Both of them had unresolved feelings about their first partner, and the memories of this relationship helped contaminate their relationship with each other.

Remarried persons who were the "active agents" in their first divorce are more likely to call quits much more quickly on a second marriage once it starts to go downhill than they did on their first marriage. This is because they may feel that they waited far too long to exit the first marriage, and they aren't about to repeat the long wait a second time. Therefore, once they perceive the negative handwriting on the wall, they are more prone to get out of the relationship fairly quickly.[39] This was the case with Tony and Tanya.

Graham Spanier and Frank Furstenberg point out that often the remarried partners differ significantly in age and that this is not usually the situation of first marriage where the age differential is usually minimal. They also point out that at the time of remarriage the persons enter a second marriage cohort with different socio-cultural expectations and are usually, if not always, at a different point in their life-development process; that is, they are at a later state of development. The husband may be in his early fifties, whereas the wife may be in her late thirties.[40] Because of previous life experiences they could be out of sync in that they have different interests and different preferences in leisure time pursuits as well as different values, attributed meaning to life events, attitudes, and ways of perceiving the events of everyday life.

REMARRIAGE WITH CHILDREN

PAMELA AND PAUL

PAMELA: I never dreamed it would be like this. There is no time for us! Money is so tight I could scream. My children don't get along with his children except when my two are at it with each other. Paul won't discipline his kids. He is so damn wishy-washy and easy on them that I can't make them do anything. Then my kids get on my case about how easy his kids have it. Sometimes I actually think Paul's children, especially his oldest, Patricia, want to break us up. I can't believe the way they talk to me. "You're not my mother! You can't tell me what to do. Only my Dad can tell me what to do so get off my case! I'm going to go live with my mother."

PAUL: Pamela overreacts to almost everything. Things aren't as bad as she says. She needs to loosen up a bit and not try to be so restrictive with the kids. My kids aren't used to it, and her kids resent it. Just ask them! I'm really not bothered by the same things that bother Pam. What bothers me is that Pam and I seem to be drifting apart. We don't seem to have time for each other. Lovemaking has become perfunctory and almost boring. Pam always seems to be tired and worn out. Nobody seems to be having fun anymore. We tried to do things together for a while, but you know how that goes; after a few months we all seemed to be overdosed on togetherness.

I don't know what to do about this feeling of Pam and I slowly drifting apart. I don't have the money to take much in the way of vacations. We have two cars. We only owe on one. The mortgage payment is hefty for our large house, and food costs are killing us. The kids always seem to want this or that. We see to it that they get what they need, but there's little left over. You remember that old TV show, *The Brady Bunch?* What a crock of bull that is!

The presence of children greatly complicates remarriage. Let us pause a moment to reconsider where we have been. First, marriage itself can be very difficult and very challenging with many potential problems. This has been emphasized throughout this entire book. Second, remarriage has almost all of the problems and challenges of first marriage plus at least five more that we discussed previously. Third, when we add children, his, hers, and ours, we have created a whole new bundle of problems and challenges. If children come from both sides (as in Figure 7-1, his children and her children), it is important to remember that they do not share a common history and will initially, at least, live together almost as strangers and/or intruders.

Before we delve into these potential problems and challenges let's clarify our terminology. Paul Glick defines a *remarried family* as "a husband and wife maintaining a household with or without children in the home and with one or both spouses in their second or subsequent marriage." A *stepfamily* is a remarried family with a child under 18 years of age who is the biological child of one of the parents and was born before the remarriage occurred."[41] Keep in mind that the U.S. Bureau of the Census considers stepfamilies to be a subset of remarried families; that is, not all remarried familes are stepfamilies. In 1987

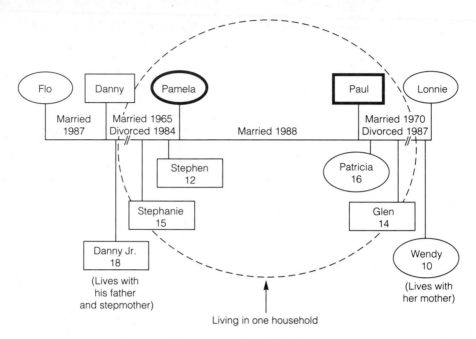

Figure 7-1 A Binuclear Stepfamily: Pamela and Paul

there were 4.30 million stepfamilies in the United States, which constituted 6.7 percent of all American families. Additionally there were 0.94 million remarried families with children under 18 who were not stepfamilies, constituting 1.4 percent of all American families.[42]

Marilyn Ihinger-Tallman and Kay Pasley use a ninefold typology of family structure to differentiate the various kinds of remarried families. This typology employs three characteristics: (1) the presence or absence of children, (2) the relationship of those children to the remarried husband and wife, and (3) the residence of the children. According to Ihinger-Tallman and Pasley, "Each type represents an increasing level of family complexity." Of course, some types are far more common than others.

1. Remarried spouses, both of whom are childless.
2. Remarried spouses who only have a child with the current partner—a child in common.
3. Remarried spouses, at least one of whom has an adult child from a previous marriage.
4. Remarried spouses who have a child in common, and one or both partners have a child from a previous marriage who does not reside with the couple.
5. Remarried spouses with no children in common, but at least one of the partners has a child from a previous marriage and the child does not reside with the couple.

6. Remarried spouses, at least one of whom has a child from a previous marriage residing in the home.
7. Remarried spouses, both of whom have a child from a prior marriage residing in the home.
8. Remarried spouses, both of whom have a child from a previous marriage residing with them, plus a child in common.
9. Remarried spouses, both of whom have a child residing with them, plus a child in common, plus a nonresidential child of one or both spouses living elsewhere.[43]

The term *binuclear family* indicates the *relationship of children to their divorced parents,* whether these parents are remarried or not. The binuclear family is *not* a classification of type of remarried family. Constance Ahrons first used this term in 1979. She says:

> The reorganization of the nuclear family through divorce frequently results in the establishment of two households, maternal and paternal. These two interrelated households, or nuclei of the child's family of orientation, form one family system—*a binuclear family system.* . . . Hence, the term *binuclear family* indicates a family system with two nuclear households, whether or not the households have equal importance in the child's life experience.[44]

PROBLEMS AND CHALLENGES OF THE STEPFAMILY AND THE BINUCLEAR FAMILY

Discipline of children is often a problem of stepfamilies. Questions of authority and who has the right to tell whom what to do can become very difficult. It is being widely questioned today whether the stepparent should even attempt to become a substitute mother or father. Many feel that the role of the stepparent is better filled if the stepparent simply assumes a monitoring stance with the children and acts in a "back-up" capacity to the biological parent without attempting to be something one really is not, that is, a parent. Arguments over discipline are among the most reported severe problems of stepparents. Pamela and Paul had major difficulties with discipline and the establishment of a workable routine that was fair to all concerned.

Loyalty conflicts are widely reported. To whom should the child hearken? To one's biological father or biological mother? To one's stepparent or one's "real" parent? If the original marital parents have not been able to work through their anger and bitterness over the divorce, it is very likely that one or more of the children will be triangled by the divorcing couple. This serves to entrap the child and to prevent healthy ego development. Sometimes the children actually attempt to break up the marriage. They want their own parent all to themselves. Young children in particular have problems with loyalty inasmuch as they are unable to understand what is happening and very frequently blame either themselves for the parental breakup or blame the parent with whom they are living for taking away the other parent. Paul's daughter, Patricia, would likely be glad to have her father all to herself again. For Patricia, Pamela is the nasty stepmother who is always in Patricia's way.

Finances and distribution of resources are very common problems. In a binuclear family with one parent remarried and the other parent single, the single parent who is also custodial parent may have great difficulty with finances, especially if this parent is the mother. Divorce generally is much more difficult financially for females compared to males, although one frequently hears males lament that by the time they pay child support and other agreed-on expenses there is little left over for their new family and their new stepchildren. The issue of resources is a crucial one with Pamela and Paul. It is important that the parental dyad be able to have some time, money, and leisure for themselves. Nonmaterial resources may be perceived to be in short supply. These include time, energy, attention, and, of course, affection.

Spousal relationships are probably the most crucial challenge, for if the married couple cannot bond sufficiently, none of the other problems and challenges will be capable of ongoing and satisfactory solution. Spousal relations, in turn, are greatly affected by the degree of resolution and acceptance of the prior divorce and all of the symbolic manifestations of the prior marriage and family. If there is a jealousy of the former mate or a jealousy by the new mate of his/her partner's former mate, there may be great difficulty in every other aspect of the remarried relationship. There can also be a perceived *time jealousy* on the part of either mate wherein they come to resent their partner's time spent with their own biological children who live apart or with their own biological children who live under the same roof. Pamela and Paul do not appear to have severe relationship problems, and they are not bothered with jealousy of the ex-mates. They do face the problem of not being sufficiently in tune with each other, and this can lead to severe problems if it is not corrected. Very likely one or two of the children will become triangled.

MYTHS RELATED TO STEPPARENTING AND STEPFAMILIES

Cinderella, Snow White, and Hansel and Gretel are well-known fairy tales with a common theme—the wicked stepmother. Folklore focused on the stepmother rather than the stepfather most likely because the historical and traditional role of the wife was to perform the role of mother, child caretaker, and child nurturer. In reality, however, there can be great neglect and disdain by the stepfather for his stepchildren, just as there can be great animosity on the part of stepchildren toward the stepfather as well as the stepmother.

Emily Visher and John Visher point out four basic myths regarding stepparents and stepfamilies. (1) The first myth is that *stepfamilies are* **nuclear families.** Stepfamilies are not nuclear families. They are sometimes called reconstituted families or blended families, but it is probably best to call them exactly what they are, that is, stepfamilies. A stepparent is not a parent. The legal dissolution of the nuclear family can be brought about either by death or by divorce. Unless the divorced parents remarry each other it can never be restored. (2) The second myth is that *death of a spouse makes stepparenting easier.* The stepparent may have a much more difficult struggle if he/she marries a widowed person because the image of the deceased looms large in the minds and hearts of the survivors. It is extremely difficult to compete with a legend or a saint. And nobody can ever prove a child wrong when he/she says "my mother/father wouldn't have said no" or "my mother/father would have let me do it." (3) The third myth is that *it is easier when stepchildren are not living in the home.* Visher and Visher claim that it is easier to be on top of the situation, even if it is conflictual, when the stepchildren are living with you rather than with one's ex-mate. Visiting stepchildren can present numerous problems and make outlandish demands. They can attempt to manipulate the noncustodial parent in such a manner that the brevity of the visit prevents adequate handling of the problem or the situation. This is an ongoing problem facing binuclear families. (4) The fourth myth is that *love happens instantly.* Stepparents do not necessarily love their stepchildren instantly. They may never love them. It is a myth to pretend that just because I love your mother or your father that therefore obviously I love you as well. It is far more honest to establish a "liking" situation where caring and respect may grow over time.[45]

In their study of research contributions in remarriage and stepparenting, Pasley and Ihinger-Tallman drew several strong conclusions regarding stepfamilies. "About 50% of nonresidential fathers have little or no contact with their children from the prior marriage." This indicates that shared parenting and binuclear arrangements represent only about 50 percent or less of total remarried families. "Stepparents play a unique role—a role which is distinct from that of parent, and one which is more difficult." That the stepparent role is more difficult is hard to deny. If anything, stepparenting requires skill, sensitivity, and greater self-esteem and self-acceptance than most of us have.[46]

I wish to conclude this section by referring to a study of marital satisfaction in remarriage and remarried stepfamilies by Vemer et al., which analyzed the findings of 34 past studies. Very minimal differences were found among the groups that were compared on marital satisfaction: First marriage versus remarriage, men versus women, stepmothers versus stepfathers, the presence of residential versus nonresidential children, and simple (only one parent is a stepparent) versus complex (both parents are stepparents) remarriages. Results indicated that first marriages were slightly more satisfactory, men were a little more satisfied in marriage than women, there was no difference between stepmothers and stepfathers, there appeared to be no difference in satisfaction between residential and nonresidential children, and whether just one or both partners were stepparents did not seem to make any difference. The authors point out that "although some statistically significant differences were uncovered in this study, the magnitude of those differences was generally small, indicating that they may have little practical meaning."[47] The importance of the Vemer et al. study is that when a sizable number of studies were analyzed using consistent methods and procedures across all studies, the differences in marital satisfaction among these five groups appears to be minimal. This fact would seem to indicate that the factors, traits, and qualities that contribute to marital happiness and couple satisfaction lie elsewhere, perhaps in variables such as self-acceptance, self-esteem, marital expectations, and fulfillment of these expectations.

The Four Basic Errors Related to Marriage, Divorce, and Remarriage

A Type I error is entering marriage too quickly and for the wrong reasons. The previous chapters have dealt with this error in diverse ways. *A Type II error is when we remain married for the wrong reasons.* Some people who probably should seriously consider divorce often remain married for the wrong reasons. Remaining together when the children are exposed to an ongoing conflicted relationship is detrimental to the positive development of the children, especially to their sense of self and their self-esteem. Staying together for the sake of the children makes sense only if the partners have worked through a lot of their difficulties and are able to stay together without triangling the children or laying burdens on them that no child should ever be asked to shoulder. This is extremely hard for most people to do. More often than not, when people stay together for the sake of the children it means there is a deeper reluctance to separate. This reluctance needs to be explored and worked through. Sometimes parents think they can hide things from their children. These parents are usually deceiving themselves because children and young people are far more perceptive than most parents give them credit for.

Family therapists commonly hear children say that they know what is going on in the family but that they feel they have to pretend that they don't. The escalating conflicts between mom and dad become "open secrets." An open secret is a secret that everyone knows but that everyone must pretend that they don't know. Therefore the "secret" cannot be talked about or dealt with in any positive or constructive manner. Many students who take courses in marriage and family are heard to say that they have wished for years that their mothers and fathers would separate because of the destructive and oppressive atmosphere of the home environment created by the alienation of the mother and father from one another.

If a couple stays together because they do not believe in divorce and/or will not abrogate the laws of their religious authority, then it is very likely that they will end up triangling their children or perhaps alienating them to a severe degree. As we will see in Chapter 8, sometimes our commitment is to the concept of "till death do us part" or "for as long as we both shall live" rather than to our partner. Commitment is a vitally important ingredient in successful and vital marriages, but the commitment must be to the *well-being* and *growth* of the partners as persons rather than to a concept that was practiced for centuries when life expectancy was between 40 and 50 years. Many people today can expect to live anywhere from 30 to 50 or more years after the youngest child graduates from high school. In other words, "till death do us part" is getting to be a longer and longer span of time because of the longer and longer life span.

The antidote to the Type II error is, of course, to remain married for the *right* reasons. As long as two people have a strong commitment to each other and to working on the relationship, they will have a good chance to redeem and revitalize the marriage. A client once told me that he was not willing to stay with his wife for the sake of unity, for the sake of the kids, or for the sake of finances! He said he would be willing to stay with her for two reasons: He still loved her, and he was committed to her and to the relationship. Without such commitment there is little with which to sustain and nurture the relationship because then the commitment is to the wedding vow itself or to the piece of paper we refer to as a marriage license, or to the idea that divorce is wrong, or to the idea that the kids need both parents (no matter how embittered they are with each other). The end result of this kind of thinking is the preservation of pseudomutuality and a legal union that long since has been emotionally dead. The operation was a success but the patient died! The marriage legally endured but the relationship expired!

A Type III error is divorcing too hastily. Many couples today are divorcing prematurely. I believe they are giving up on each other far too easily and quickly, perhaps bailing out in order to avoid the pain and agony of self-scrutiny and mutual rebuilding. Perhaps they are fed up and want a quick fix, regardless of whether it is wise or thought out. Perhaps they divorce in the relentless belief that out there somewhere is a person far more compatible than one's present mate. Sometimes they are attracted to someone else and immediately conclude that because they feel they love this new person they therefore must divorce their mate and marry the new find, much like we trade in an older model automobile for a shiny new one. Divorce can resemble a contagious disease wherein people seem to catch the bug only after it first infects one's close friends, neighbors, or work associates. People start to notice things they hadn't noticed before. Sometimes they look for symptoms and even create symptoms. Often they jump to erroneous conclusions about their marriage—conclusions that are based on fallacious assumptions, myths, and illusions.

A Type IV error is remarriage too quickly and for the wrong reasons. "In 1986 the interval to remarriage was less than one year for 27 percent of remarrying brides and 31 percent of remarrying grooms."[48] Divorce is often disillusioning, if not in the process and in the aftermath, then in the antidote, which is often remarriage. I grieve the situation of early, quick, and often impulsive remarriage, especially in less than 1 year after the date of the final divorce decree. I often tell my students, clients, and other friends that if I could have the power to write, legislate, and enact one national law it would be a law preventing remarriage following divorce for anyone until he or she had been divorced for at least 1 year, preferably 2 or 3 years. The 1 year may seem to be arbitrary, but it is not. A waiting period of at least 1 year ensures that the divorced person has experienced one revolution of the anniversary of personal, marital, and familial events. These include birthdays of self, mate, and children, in addition to all manner of holidays, ritualistic occasions, vacations, death anniversaries, wedding anniversary, and the anniversary of the divorce itself.

The reason for the 1-year waiting period is because we are very prone to deal with our grief and loss over the death of the first marriage by quickly falling in love with someone new. Folk wisdom has it that the easiest way to get over an old love is to find a new love. However, this is counterproductive when we are talking about getting out of marriage. People need time to grieve. Grief may not be pleasant, but it can be good because it is a process of cleansing our system and allowing our emotions to work themselves through. Grief work can be very fatiguing and painful, but it is as necessary for full recovery as the pain of a cut or an incision is to the healing process. Part of the process of grief work is to attempt to determine what went wrong and what could have prevented it. The common pattern is to blame one's ex-mate for the past while thinking that all that is needed next time is to find a better match!

To attempt to cut short the aftermath of a divorce and the opportunity for self-scrutiny and self-inventory it affords by quickly getting deeply involved with someone else is to short-circuit the process of healing and recovery. We do it to our own peril. Unfortunately most people who inoculate themselves against the pain and hurt of divorce by finding a new love end up bringing all their own unresolved problems with them into the new relationship. Remarriage for women who are in the single-parent role may offer increased economic security. Certainly some people will remarry in order to gain economic security. Also, I suspect that many people with high dependency needs are quite eager to remarry because they think they are very much in love! What they don't realize is that their dependency almost always masquerades under the guise of love, and therefore what they experience as intense love is really a type of attachment to a caretaking figure. I find this equally true for males and females.

Conceptual Frameworks: Making Sense of It All

Now that cohabitation, preliminary marriage, divorce, remarriage, step-families, and stepparenting have been discussed in some detail, let us ask, what sense does it all make? How do we explain the ending of first marriage and the beginning of subsequent marriages? In answering this question we will return to the conceptual frameworks of systems, object relations, exchange, and symbolic interaction.

SYSTEMS

According to **systems theory**, existing marriages will do everything imaginable to preserve the homeostasis of the status quo. The marriage and the family may become dysfunctional, weighted down with burdensome symptoms and embedded with destructive coalitions and triangles. Yet in spite of the fact that a system will do almost anything to maintain itself, it is very obvious from divorce statistics that often the system fails to do so. Systems thinking is, therefore, more helpful in explaining why some marriages and some families are crisis oriented and choose to remain locked into their dysfunctions than in explaining why there is divorce. Systems thinking helps us understand the reluctance some people have to separate and divorce. Some of these people will bear tremendous burdens of unhappiness and depression in the name of marital unity and family cohesiveness. They will stay together through thick and thin. They are the unbroken and unhappy marriages and families of our society.

OBJECT RELATIONS

I have consistently emphasized that excessive and unrealistic expectations are a major cause of marital breakdown. Object relations thinking helps clarify this in that our expectations are the function of internalized representations of how we think significant others should behave toward us and how they should think and be. "Be what I want you to be. Do what I want you to do." When we perceive that our partner has fallen short of our expectations and our projective identifications we become discouraged, disappointed, and disillusioned. We often opt out of the marriage. We then renew our search for a new object that will more completely live up to our internalized representations. We then remarry. In this new marriage we will again attempt to induce our partner into compliance with our conscious and unconscious expectations. If this doesn't work out, we may redivorce! With each successive marriage there is also reduced likelihood of remaining in it if things do not go well. Divorce appears to be an acceptable solution to an unhappy marriage, and people who have been once divorced appear to resort to it with increasing promptness.[49]

EXCHANGE

Exchange theory is concerned with a sense of fairness and equity; with assets versus liabilities; and with cost and reward. When the personal cost of remaining in a relationship becomes so overwhelming that the person feels great amounts of pain and personal rejection, that person will have motivation to exit the marriage. Because females, compared to males, have been socialized to value the connectedness of the relationship and to be the nurturing ones who ensure the maintenance of the relationship, they may be willing to accept a lesser exchange than males. Put another way, males may exit the marriage sooner than females if they feel an unfairness or inequality of rights, privileges, assets, and rewards. Nevertheless, even if the female is socialized to accept the shorter end of the stick, this will only continue until the pain becomes overwhelming or unbearable. Exchange theory implies that when the bargain becomes weighted strongly in favor of one partner to the detriment of the other, the relationship will be discontinued.

Resource theory and the issue of power come into play at this point because often, in spite of a very poor exchange, the female feels trapped economically because she does not believe she has the ability to survive economically, especially when she is the mother of dependent children. In this case, her perception of her lack of resources prevents her from exiting the relationship. Unfortunately, far too many females have been socialized to believe that they "deserve" to be treated harshly, to be abused and beaten, and to be kept in a state of submission and poverty. As long as a person believes that she/he has no resources with which to cope, there is little incentive to get out of the relationship, in spite of what exchange theory says. Yet if one believes that he/she has sufficient resources or the ability to achieve sufficient resources in order to make a break, principles of exchange theory point in the direction of dissolution, or at least separation.

SYMBOLIC INTERACTION

When two people are very much in love and caught up in the excitement of their emotional attraction to each other it is easy to conclude that they share many, if not all, basic values and enjoy the same sports, interests, and leisure time pursuits. In this context the partners are likely to place the same meaning on almost all of the events, activities, and experiences of daily life. The couple attempts to please one another and to make sure that one's faults are hidden and disguised as much as possible.

Only later, after the earlier glow of heightened emotional attraction has subsided, does the couple begin to attach different meanings to words, concepts, events, circumstances, communications, and interactions. (Including the meaning of the words *husband* and *wife*.) This leads to differences of opinion, arguments, and conflict. As the individuality of each partner begins to express itself, the couple begins to discover differences that were not noticed before. Perhaps they are not as congenial as they at first had thought. If the differences are not openly dealt with, negotiated, and worked through to some satisfactory conclusion the relationship may be headed for rough times. Symbolic interaction is concerned with our beliefs, roles, and the ensuing rules that prescribe and proscribe how we are to function within these roles. It should not be surprising that marriages break up over such differences and the conflicts that stem from these differences.

When couples complain about not having much in common or not being on the same wavelength or not being compatible with each other they are usually viewing the situation through the frame of symbolic interactionism. They see things differently. They perceive things differently. They attach different meaning and importance to things, events, and situations. From this vantage point it is only one small step to the conclusion that love is dying, we are drifting apart, and we had best look for a more fulfilling relationship, one which is better suited to our needs, beliefs, and personal habits.

When all is said and done the above four "frameworks" go a long way toward explaining why some marriages break up and others don't. Each of the frameworks gives a partial answer to the question of why some marriages fail, why some are bogged down in unholy deadlock, and why others appear to be reasonably happy unions. Each of the four is a valid way of seeking to understand the dynamics of marriage, divorce, and remarriage today.

Summary

This chapter considered three different types of cohabitation. These are casual cohabitation, trial before marriage, and ideological opposition to marriage. The prevalence of cohabitation was considered along with the research regarding whether or not premarital cohabitation increases the quality of ensuing marriage. The consensus of the research is that cohabitation does not increase or decrease the quality of an ensuing marriage. Therefore, it cannot be said that cohabitation has the long-range effect of lowering the divorce rate. Advantages and disadvantages of trial before marriage were considered with an emphasis on the fact that even if a trial ends up in dissolution it can still be a rewarding and successful personal experience, especially if it helps a person realize that he/she is not yet really ready for the total commitment of legal marriage.

Another form of preliminary marriage was considered. This second form of preliminary marriage was not intended to be "preliminary," but the end result seems to indicate that many couples view the failure of their first marriage as nothing to be too alarmed about inasmuch as their next (second) marriage is going to be the "real" marriage, the one "for keeps"! Therefore, in a de facto way, the first marriage becomes a preliminary marriage.

Divorce and remarriage were considered in detail with reference to statistics through 1988. Overall the divorce rate is down when compared to the years 1975–1981. The divorce rate peaked in 1981, stabilized between 1982 and 1986, and in 1987–1988 was at its lowest rate since 1975. Some of the common problems related to remarriage were considered. Remarriage often involves stepparenting and stepfamilies, which are becoming increasingly common in our society. Several different types of remarried families were considered, together with some of the more common problems and challenges of stepparenting and stepfamilies. Binuclear family life-styles are becoming increasingly common. In the binuclear family the children continue to relate to some degree to both of their biological parents whether these parents are single parents or remarried.

Four errors were discussed pertaining to the marriage, divorce, and remarriage relationships. A Type I error is entering marriage too early, too quickly, and for the wrong reasons. A Type II error is when we remain married for the wrong reasons. A Type III error is divorcing too hastily. A Type IV error is remarriage too quickly and for the wrong reasons.

In an attempt to explain and make sense of marriage, divorce, and remarriage, the conceptual frameworks of sytems, object relations, exchange, and symbolic interaction were reconsidered.

Reading Suggestions

Ahrons, Constance R. and Roy H. Rodgers. *Divorced Families: A Multidisciplinary Development View.* New York: W. W. Norton, 1987.

Cherlin, Andrew J. *Marriage, Divorce, Remarriage.* Cambridge, Mass.: Harvard University Press, 1981.

Family Relations. Special Issue: "Stepfamilies, Remarriage, Stepchildren, Stepgrandparents," Vol. 38, no. 1 (Jan 1989).

Ihinger-Tallman, Marilyn and Kay Pasley. *Remarriage.* Newbury Park, Calif.: Sage Publications, 1987.

Pasley, Kay and Marilyn Ihinger-Tallman, eds. *Remarriage and Stepparenting.* New York: Guilford Press, 1987.

Price, Sharon J. and Patrick C. McKenry. *Divorce.* Newbury Park, Calif.: Sage Publications, 1988.

Vaughan, Diane. *Uncoupling.* New York: Oxford University Press, 1986.

Visher, Emily B. and John S. Visher. *How to Win as a Stepfamily.* New York: Dembner Books, 1982.

Visher, Emily B. and John S. Visher. *Old Loyalties, New Ties: Therapeutic Strategies with Stepfamilies.* New York: Brunner/Mazel, 1989.

Wallerstein, Judith and Sandra Blakeslee. *Second Chances: Men, Women and Children a Decade After Divorce.* New York: Ticknor and Fields, 1989.

Notes

1. Eleanor Macklin, "Review of Research on Nonmarital Cohabitation in the United States," In *Exploring Intimate Lifestyles*, Bernard I. Murstein, ed. (New York: Springer Publishing, 1978), 197–243.

2. Janis Petty, "An Investigation of Factors Which Differentiate Between Types of Cohabitation," Masters Thesis, Indiana University, 1975.

3. U.S. Bureau of the Census, Current Population Reports, 1988. "Marital Status and Living Arrangements: March 1988," Series P-20, No. 433, Jan, 1989. U.S. Bureau of the Census, Current Population Reports, 1988. "Households, Families, Marital Status and Living Arrangements: March 1988 (Advance Report)," Series P-20, No. 432, Sept, 1988.

4. Paul C. Glick and Graham Spanier, "Married and Unmarried Cohabitation in the United States," *Journal of Marriage and the Family,* Vol. 42, no. 1 (Feb 1980): 19–30.

5. U.S. Bureau of the Census, Current Population Reports, 1988. "Marital Status and Living Arrangements: March 1988," Series P-20, No. 433, Jan, 1989. U.S. Bureau of the Census, Current Population Reports, 1988. "Households, Families, Marital Status and Living Arrangements: March 1988 (Advance Report)," Series P-20, No. 432, Sept, 1988.

6. Eleanor D. Macklin, "Nontraditional Family Forms," Chapter 12 in *Handbook of Marriage and the Family*. Marvin B. Sussman and Suzanne K. Steinmetz, eds. (New York: Plenum Press, 1987), 320.

7. *Ibid.,* 323.

8. John F. Crosby, *Illusion and Disillusion: The Self in Love and Marriage,* 1st ed., 1973; 2nd ed., 1976 (Belmont, Calif.: Wadsworth).

9. Lawrence H. Ganong and Marilyn Coleman, "Preparing for Remarriage: Anticipating the Issues, Seeking Solutions," *Family Relations,* Vol. 38, no. 1 (Jan 1989): 28–33.

10. *Op. cit.,* Eleanor D. Macklin, 322–323.

11. Mark R. Rank, "The Transition To Marriage: A Comparison of Cohabiting and Dating Relationships Ending in Marriage or Divorce," *Alternate Lifestyles,* Vol. 4, no. 4 (Nov 1981): 487–506.

12. *Ibid.*

13. Barbara L. Fisher and Robert W. Calhoun, "I Do and I Don't: Treating Systemic Ambivalence," In *When One Wants Out and the Other Doesn't: Doing Therapy With Polarized Couples,* John F. Crosby, ed. (New York: Brunner/Mazel, 1989), 24.

14. Margaret Mead, "Marriage in Two Steps," *Redbook* (July 1966).

15. Teresa Castro Martin and Larry L. Bumpass, "Recent Trends in Marital Disruption," *Demography,* Vol. 26, no. 1 (Feb 1989).

16. Paul C. Glick, "Remarriage: Some Recent Changes and Variations," Journal of Family Issues Vol. 1, no. 4 (Dec 1980): 455–478.

17. Andrew J. Cherlin, *Marriage, Divorce, Remarriage* (Cambridge, Mass.: Harvard University Press, 1981), 29.

18. For additional information and perspective on the first marriage as a preliminary relationship, see Leslie Aldridge Westoff, *The Second Time Around: Remarriage in America* (New York: Viking Press, 1977), Chapter 6.

19. John F. Crosby, "The Grief Resolution Process in Divorce," *Journal of Divorce* Vol. 7, no. 1 (Fall 1983), 3-18. Also, "The Grief Resolution Process in Divorce, Phase II," *Journal of Divorce,* Vol. 10, nos. 1/2, (Fall/Winter, 1986): 17–40.

20. Monthly Vital Statistics Report, Vol. 37, no. 13 (July 26, 1989): 4. U.S. Department of Health and Human Services, National Center for Health Statistics.

21. John F. Crosby, "A Critique of Divorce Statistics and Their Interpretation," *The Family Coordinator,* Vol. 29, no. 1 (Jan 1980): 51–58.

22. Graham B. Spanier and Frank F. Furstenberg, Jr., "Remarriage and Reconstituted Families," Chapter 16 in *Handbook of Marriage and the Family,* Marvin B. Sussman and Suzanne K. Steinmetz, eds. (New York: Plenum Press, 1987), 422.

23. *Ibid.*

24. *Op. cit.,* Martin and Bumpass.

25. *Op. cit.,* John F. Crosby, "The Grief Resolution Process in Divorce" (1983, 1986).

26. Elisabeth Kübler-Ross, *Death and Dying* (New York: Macmillan, 1969).

27. *Op. cit.,* John F. Crosby, "The Grief Resolution Process in Divorce" (1983, 1986).

28. Paul Bohannan, "The Six Stations of Divorce," in *Divorce and After,* Paul Bohannan, ed. (New York: Doubleday, 1970), 29–55.

29. The phrase "his" or "her" marriage comes from Jesse Bernard, *The Future of Marriage* (New York: World Publishing, 1972). The phrase "his" divorce and "her" divorce comes from Mary Ann Lamanna and Agnes Riedmann, *Marriages and Families,* 3rd ed. (Belmont, Calif.: Wadsworth, 1988), 532–534.

30. E. Mavis Hetherington and Kathleen A. Camara, "The Effects of Family Dissolution and Reconstitution on Children," In *Family Relations,* Norval D. Glenn and Marion Tolbert Coleman, eds. (Chicago: The Dorsey Press, 1988), 423–424.

31. Sharon J. Price and Patrick C. McKenry, *Divorce* (Newbury Park, Calif.: Sage Publications, 1988), 34.

32. Diane Vaughan, *Uncoupling: How Relationships Come Apart* (New York: Oxford University Press, 1986). (Vintage Books Edition, Random House, 1987, 302.)

33. U.S. Department of Health and Human Services, "Remarriages and Subsequent Divorces," Data from the National Vital Statistics System, Series 21, no. 45, Jan 1989.

34. *Ibid.*

35. Monthly Vital Statistics Report, Vol. 38, no. 3, Suppl. 2 (July 13, 1989): 4. U.S. Department of Health and Human Services, National Center for Health Statistics.

36. *Ibid.*, 5. Figure 3.

37. *Ibid.*, 5. Using data from R. Schoen, *The Continuing Retreat from Marriage;* Figures from 1983 U.S. marital status life tables. *Sociology Social Research,* Vol. 71, no. 2 (1987): 108–109.

38. Richard Farson, "Why Good Marriages Fail," *McCalls* (Oct 1971).

39. *Op. cit.,* John F. Crosby, "The Grief Resolution Process in Divorce." The active agent is the person who seems to be pressing for the divorce more than the other. The person who actually files for divorce may be the passive agent. When the passive agent is the divorcer we can be fairly certain the active agent has played the role of the "provoker."

40. Graham B. Spanier and Frank F. Furstenberg, Jr., "Remarriage and Reconstituted Families," Chapter 16 in *Handbook of Marriage and the Family,* Marvin B. Sussman and Suzanne K. Steinmetz, eds. (New York: Plenum Press, 1987), 425.

41. Paul C. Glick, "Remarried Families, Stepfamilies, and Stepchildren: A Brief Demographic Profile," *Family Relations* Vol. 38, no. 1 (Jan 1989): 24.

42. *Ibid.,* 25.

43. Marilyn Ihinger-Tallman and Kay Pasley, *Remarriage* (Newbury Park, Calif.: Sage Publications, 1987), 48–49.

44. Constance R. Ahrons, "The Binuclear Family: Two Households, One Family," *Alternate Lifestyles,* Vol. 2, no. 4 (Nov 1979), 500.

45. Emily B. Visher and John S. Visher, "Common Problems of Stepparents and Their Spouses," *American Journal of Orthopsychiatry,* Vol. 48, no. 2 (Apr 1978), 252–262.

46. Kay Pasley and Marilyn Ihinger-Tallman, eds., *Remarriage and Stepparenting* (New York: Guilford Press, 1987), 309–310.

47. Elizabeth Vemer, Marilyn Coleman, Lawrence H. Ganong, and Harris Cooper, "Marital Satisfaction in Remarriage: A Meta-analysis," *Journal of Marriage and the Family,* Vol. 51, no. 3 (Aug 1989), 713–725.

48. *Op. cit.,* Monthly Vital Statistics Report, Vol. 38, no. 3, Suppl. 2 (July 13, 1989): 5.

49. *Op. cit.,* U.S. Department of Health and Human Services, Vital and Health Statistics, Vol. 21, no. 5: 16.

Chapter 8

Making it Together:

Love Is Not Enough

In every marriage more than a week old, there are grounds for divorce. The trick is to find, and continue to find, grounds for marriage.

ROBERT ANDERSON,
DOUBLE SOLITAIRE

DIANE—LATE, BUT NOT TOO LATE

Dear Mr. Crosby,

I heard you speak on television the other day about how we kill marriage and sex. Two years ago I would have laughed at what you said. Now I am crying. You are so right. I killed my marriage—my man, our kids, our home. I didn't just kill it gently—I strangled it! I never cared about sex one way or the other, but I'd do it two or three times a week just to keep him satisfied. But I would just sort of lay there, like a zombie! I never put myself into it. I always assumed we were the way we were supposed to be for people our age; you know, let the younger ones have fun but it's too late for us. Not just in sex but in lots of little ways we lived the life of quiet desperation you talked about. Do you know we haven't really said anything to each other of any consequence in years. At least it seems that way. I had resigned myself to boredom and drudgery and dullness. I wasn't terribly unhappy—I just had sort of a low-grade misery. I'm not blaming my husband either. He tried earlier to be interesting and playful—he would take me out and encourage me to do all kinds of things. I don't think he's been unfaithful to me, but looking back I wouldn't blame him. You said unfaithfulness can be in other ways than sexual and that puzzled me, but now I think I know what you meant. I've been really unfaithful because I have done hardly anything in all our married life to make our marriage into something. Now it's too late— we're in our early forties and . . . well, I was wondering if we could get into one of those marriage growth groups you mentioned?

—Diane

Too late? No, not at all. In fact, one of the best times to begin is when you are motivated by a feeling of self-disgust. Diane's life can be very different very quickly, but she must be willing to look at some of her attitudes and change some of her behavior. Likewise, her husband will have to make some changes because, rest assured, he will feel the impact of her changes, and he may have trouble catching on and then catching up.

Ruts Versus Grooves

What is the difference between a rut and a groove? It is the difference between losing variety and making constructive use of routine. A rut is negative in that variety and spontaneity have been choked to death. A groove is positive as long as the routine and the ordinary are laced with spontaneity and the ordinary routine is used as a springboard into new experiences, adventures, and projects. Two people cannot live together over a long period of time without coming to terms with the routine and the ordinary. The only option (but a most important one) available to couples who commit themselves to a monogamous, sexually exclusive union is the option of transforming the rut into a groove.

Diane and her husband were in a rut of great length and depth. They never learned how to redeem the ordinary or to use any other positive means to make themselves attractive to each other. This probably happened because both of them were already half dead within themselves and therefore were unable to respond to each other in a positive or productive way. Our attitudes toward our mate are often a projection of our own feelings of futility, boredom, and even depression.

How we handle the routine and ordinary will determine, to a great extent, our degree of satisfaction in marriage. We might even say that it is not the peaks or the valleys, the highs or the lows, that make or break the typical marriage; rather it is the day-in, day-out routine! Herein lies the potential for ho-hum, boredom, and monotony.

Unless we change partners with some degree of regularity, there is no possible way to avoid the day-in and day-out ruts and grooves of daily living. We can, however, do a great deal to transform the ruts into grooves. The assumption underlying this final chapter is that we are the ones who kill marriage. We commit *maricide*. We create our own ruts and then blame each other for our unhappiness.

Further, we tend to believe that love is enough to make the marriage work. As we have said in earlier chapters, love is not powerful enough to substitute for such things as fair-fight skills, good communication, equity, commitment to growth, and the overall ability to commit oneself to nurturing the relationship.

The truth seems to be that we want our marriages to be happy without our really having to do anything except proclaim that we love each other. The remainder of this chapter is written especially for those who are willing to pay the necessary price of making a strong commitment to the goal of creating and maintaining a vital and dynamic marriage.

To Kill a Marriage

Perhaps we can get a better feel for how to nurture a marriage by putting tongue in cheek as we make a list of the most common ways to kill a marriage.

Never change. The fault is always in the other. Never me. Be rigid, set in your ways. Close yourself off to the possibility of growth.

Always take your partner for granted. Now that you are married you own your partner, and therefore you can always assume that your partner will always be there for you.

Demand that you never be taken for granted. After all, I am me. It's OK for me to take you for granted, but you must never take me for granted.

Quit scoring points. You don't need to impress the other anymore. Don't tell him/her nice things like "I love you" or "You really are pretty/good looking." Quit saying "thank you" and "please." Don't bother to compliment each other or to tell each other how nice you look like you did *before* you were married.

Make sex be only for him. Both of you buy into the myth that sex is really only for the male, that he needs his regular dose, but that she really doesn't need it or enjoy it.

Never do any sexual experimenting with each other. Never make love in front of a cozy fire in the fireplace on a winter night, and never do it in the backyard on a hot summer night. Certainly don't do it in the little motor launch or in the sailboat.

Always make sex be in the same way, the same time, the same station. (Tune in again next week folks, same time, same station.) Don't ever try anything new or different, and certainly don't discuss it with each other, but only with your close friends.

Always take the children with you on vacation. After all, this is what your parents did for you. Never take a vacation just for the two of you.

Never take honeymoon get-away weekends. Never farm the kids out to friends and neighbors or grandparents. Never attempt to get away for a 24-hour "quicky" weekend of good eating, good sleeping, and good lovemaking.

Never take separate vacations. Never get away from each other. Never allow each other a time away from each other and the children.

Never really resolve your conflict. Always allow your beefs and complaints to build up and become infected.

Fight dirty. Use lots of silent treatment and lots of gunnysacking. Always punish your mate for not agreeing with you or seeing things your way.

Abdicate! This means you don't leave the marriage in a physical sense but you "move out" in a mental-emotional-spiritual sense.

Never share your real feelings and thoughts. Never let down your guard. Never let your partner see your hand.

Always be defensive. After all, you are always right. You shouldn't ever be questioned about anything you say or do.

Dedicate your life to your children. Tell yourself that they are more important than your mate.

Let your children dominate your marriage and your family so that they learn to expect that this is their right and your responsibility toward them.

Never do anything differently. Never go out. Never try anything new. Never surprise each other.

Have too many children. Too many for you! How many can you afford within the bounds of what you want to give them?

Have children very close together. Don't give much thought to the effects of children on the primary caretaker. Don't consider the child's need to be the queen or king for at least 2 or 3 years.

Never have an affair with each other! Never spice up your relationship by pretending or by the creative use of fantasy and imagination. Never dress up for each other. Quit grooming for each other. Let yourself go in terms of your weight, your physique, your figure.

Never work through your relationship with your own parents. Let them continue to dominate you or manipulate you. Let them continue to make you feel shame and guilt over the decisions you have made. Make up your mind that you must never hurt them by standing up to them in any way.

Tell yourself that you only married your mate, not your mate's family. Tell yourself that your partner's family has nothing to do with the way your partner treats you or the children.

Take yourself dead seriously. Approach your partner, his/her parents, your parents, your children, and your job as though every little event is deadly serious and eternally important.

Never laugh or joke or attempt to be humorous about anything. Don't cultivate a sense of humor. Tell yourself that life is too serious for such frivolity.

Be defensive about your femininity and masculinity so that you never even consider changing roles or switching or reversing roles. Insist that you and your partner live your lives according to the doctrine of separate spheres wherein each sticks to the traditional division of labor and the traditional sex roles.

Insist that his career be the REAL career and hers, if she should happen to be gainfully employed, be secondary or subservient to his.

All feelings must be justified, defensible, and explainable.

Traditional rules, roles, attitudes, beliefs, and values must never be questioned or challenged.

Most of all, tell yourself that there is no need to show your partner or to tell your partner that you love him/her. After all, they SHOULD know this without you having to do or say anything.

So much for the negative instructions on how to kill a marriage. We will now focus on some themes that will serve as a basic foundation for the rebuilding, the reinventing, and the redefining of your marriage. Whether you are just dating, engaged, living together, married to one person for many years, or in your second or third marriage, the following points of discussion are pivotal in *making it together*.

Acceptance Versus Approval

Many husbands and wives contribute to their own sense of frustration because they fail to distinguish between acceptance and approval. Approval and disapproval usually involve a moral or ethical judgment or an opinion of some kind. Approval implies a positive judgment on an action or behavior, and disapproval implies a negative judgment. No child's socialization can be effective without the imposition of boundaries denoting approval versus disapproval. Most of us want and need approval, at least to a certain degree. But some people want constant, unconditional approval, and they convince themselves that they need an unending flow of positive confirmation. The person who seeks constant approval will have great difficulty in self-disclosure.

Acceptance is not the same as approval. In its deepest and most penetrating dynamics, acceptance implies an "okayness" in spite of agreement or disagreement, approval or disapproval of specific behaviors, beliefs, or actions. In the richest sense of marital intimacy we need to accept and to be accepted. We need to feel the joy of accepting love. This is the very essence and the very heart of what we mean by love. The deepest trust of marriage is the trust that one is accepted in spite of disagreements, conflicts, anger, mistakes, weaknesses, shortcomings, and failures. To know and believe that one is loved even though at times there is disapproval and discord is the bedrock of feeling secure with one's mate.

In one sense we could say that the greatest challenge in raising, nurturing, disciplining, and socializing a child is in helping the child gain a strong feeling of being absolutely and unconditionally accepted (loved) even though there likely will be many times when the parents don't approve of the child's behavior. Acceptance is the essence of agape love. A child who is socialized in such a manner that he or she feels accepted or acceptable only when approved of will likely grow into an insecure adult who is a poor marital risk.

These adults make poor marital risks because they failed to internalize the emotional security of being loved for *themselves*. Instead they felt loved only when they were able to please their elders—in other words, they felt loved only when their parents approved of them. (Always pleasing parents is really very hard for a child to do. Part of growing through childhood and adolescence is doing things that are not approved of by our elders.) As grownups these people must always strive for approval as a sign of being accepted and loved. They are at a distinct disadvantage when it comes to dealing with conflict because they are afraid of their partner's disapproval. To their way of thinking, disapproval implies nonacceptance and lack of love. Approval implies acceptance and love. A strong marital relationship thrives on genuine and constant acceptance, which in turn frees the partners to be themselves. When we are genuinely ourselves we are free to approve or disapprove, deal with conflict, and negotiate compromises without being afraid that our partner will abandon us. In short, this unqualified acceptance makes it possible for the relationship to endure over time.

Careers, Passages, and Transitions

Most people are familiar with the "ages and stages" concept of development. In addition to ages and stages we now have steps, phases, plateaus, stations, careers, passages, and transitions.[1] Although we may be familiar with "child development" and "adolescent development," it has only been in the 1970's that "adult development" has come into its own. Adult development has really traversed two separate processes: the development of the adult female and the development of the adult male. Also, this dual adult developmental emphasis cannot really be separated from feminism and the issues raised by the **feminist** movement. Likewise, feminism cannot be fully understood apart from the evolving sexual revolution and the changing social-sexual milieu. Further, because adult development places human beings in some taxonomy or classification of life-style, there is increasing concern with intimate life-styles including marriage, remarriage, single, single-in-transition, reconstituted or blended families, dual employment, dual career, househusband, single parent, nonparents, and cohabitation.

Indeed, Erik Erikson's social-psychological paradigm of human development allowed but one step or stage for the entire range of middle life. He called this stage "Generativity".[2] Likewise, Evelyn Duvall's early pioneering efforts to delineate the stages of traditional marriages and families may seem somewhat simplistic to present-day readers. Nevertheless, her attempt to map out the family life cycle was, like Erikson's, a pioneering effort of great importance.[3]

THREE BASIC CAREERS

Figure 8-1 is a schematic indicating three basic careers: marriage, parenting, and the vocational employment or professional career. The schematic indicates:

1. Not all couples will be parents; thus, the marriage life cycle or the intimate life cycle should not be labeled as a parental or family life cycle.
2. Divorce may take place at any time after marriage, and this may precipitate a recycling into singlehood or into another marriage, with or without children. Death, too, can interrupt the intimacy career at any point, but each is indicated at only one place in the schematic. Death for the surviving mate is similar to divorce in the fact that the marriage is legally ended, and a widow or widower may choose to start over or to remain single for a while or indefinitely.
3. The employment-professional careers may be somewhat parallel for men and women if there are no children or if the parenting has been very evenly divided. However, if the wife has interrupted her employment-professional

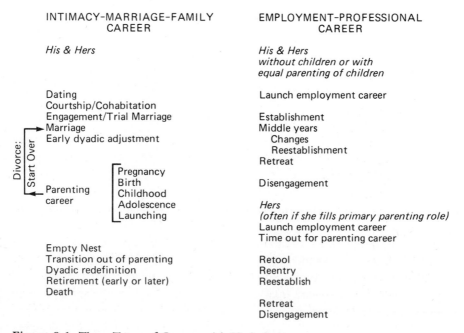

Figure 8-1 Three Types of Careers with Variations

career in order to give full attention to children in their early years, her situation will be different from her husband's in that retooling, reentry, and reestablishment very likely will be necessary.

There are many transition points or passages that may interrupt or interfere with the careers of intimacy, parenting, and employment. Further, these transitions may or may not become problematic. If they do become problematic they may or may not develop into crises.

In the final decade of the 20th century it is likely that there will be an abundance of both popular and scholarly books and articles dealing with adult development and the crises and transitions of adulthood for both men and women. Along with this increased attention to adult development we may expect to find much greater emphasis on the many variations of the family life cycle (Chapter 7). Until recently the family life span approach essentially has been focused on a traditional concept of family, that is, a husband and wife in their first marriage with husband as breadwinner, wife as nurturing housewife-mother, and children. The focus has also been on the individual as part of the family rather than on the family itself. Increasing attention is being paid as to how the family system influences individual and interpersonal development. The traditional approach sees the individual as primary against the backdrop of the family. The family systems approach sees the family itself as primary and the individual as an integral subsystem within the family system.[4]

Female-Male Differences: Biological or Psychosocial?

According to Susan Losh-Hesselbart, there are five major ways we may approach the question of gender roles and how we acquire them. These are:

1. The direct shaping and reinforcement of gender differences in behavior.
2. Imitation and modeling of same-sex figures.
3. The identification with and incorporation of values, personality traits, and behaviors of important same-sex childhood figures.
4. A cognitive-developmental sequence of acquiring gender identity that leads to the acquisition of gender roles.
5. Biological sex differences that influence the responses of socialization agents (the nature-nurture controversy).[5]

According to Losh-Hesselbart, "Each major approach has supporting evidence, although currently a combination of approaches rather than just one accounts best for gender socialization."[6] Concerning the innate biological approach, Losh-Hesselbart says, "If strong innate tendencies shape the behavior of women and men, social changes promoting greater similarity can have only a limited impact."[7]

When a person believes that differences between the genders are innate or inborn, it gives that person an easy excuse to retain the status quo and to continue in the old unbalanced and nonequitable relationships where the man is in the one-up position and the woman is in the one-down position. A study by Mirowsky and Ross revealed that the "average husband believes in innate sex roles more than his own wife does. Using a national sample of married couples, we find that husbands believe in innate sex roles significantly more than their wives do. We also find that each partner's belief directly influences the other's, controlling for age, education, and religion. The more one spouse believes that sex roles are innate, the more the other tends to."[8] No doubt there is an accommodating effect here wherein for the sake of harmony in the relationship the two partners come to share similar beliefs. Although belief in innate sex roles is not necessarily the same as asking whether male-female differences are innate, there is nevertheless a very close relationship between the two. Mirowsky and Ross define innate sex roles as "the belief that men are born with more drive to be ambitious and successful than women and that by nature women are happiest when making a home and caring for children."[9] If these sex roles are innate, we can reasonably assume that male-female differences are likewise innate.

The position taken here is that the differences between men and women are not primarily due to biological makeup, nor are they entirely the result of a difference in socialization based on gender. Rather, the differences are due to an early shift in the infant-mother object of identification wherein the male child is pressed to shift his primary attachment from mother to father. In order to explain this I will draw on the work of Nancy Chodorow, Carol Gilligan, and Lillian Rubin.

Lillian Rubin rejects the learning theorists and the socialization theorists. She states:

> I depart from classical psychological theory in that I do not see a single line in child development—with one, the male, being defined as normal and the other, the female, characterized as a deviation from that norm. Instead, I will insist that while certain developmental imperatives exist for children of both genders—for example, the establishment of a continuing and coherent sense of self and gender identity—the tasks that confront a girl and a boy are quite different, resulting in different patterns of personality for each of them. . . .

> But I will insist also that those different tasks, and the psychological differences that stem from them, are not inherent in the nature of human development, but are a response to the social situation—in particular to the structure of roles and relationships inside the family—into which girls and boys are born and will grow. From birth onward psyche and society engage in a complex and dynamic interaction. Our earliest experiences in the family lay the basis for our characteristic ways of being, and the cultural commandments about masculinity and femininity reinforce and solidify them.[10]

Carol Gilligan has called into question the traditional and widely accepted developmental schemas of such scholars as Erik Erikson and Lawrence Kohlberg. The chief criticism is that Erikson and Kohlberg based their developmental schema primarily on samples of males, thus committing the error of assuming that female development is identical to male development: "Implicitly adopting the male life as the norm, they have tried to fashion women out of a masculine cloth."[11] Basing her work on Nancy Chodorow's belief that "women, universally, are largely responsible for early child care,"[12] Gilligan seeks to drive home the point that the female child will continue to model her mother right on through childhood, adolescence, and adulthood without ever needing to make a switch of gender-based role-model identity. Male children, while still holding mother as the primary *female* role figure, will switch primary identity role models at an early age from mother to father. As a result of this early switch the male child will experience a break that in some cases borders on the traumatic. He must detach himself from mother and in doing so he must not allow himself to express feelings of loss or abandonment. He must shape himself according to father's image and take on himself father's demeanor and self-presentation.

Of course, if a male child is brought up in a family where the father does the "mothering," then the male child will not have the difficulty of the switch with the resulting feelings of loss, rejection, and abandonment. In this case the female child would likely face the switch dilemma. Nevertheless, even though *in theory* we know that males can be excellent "mothers" and perform every task and every nurturing process with as much nurturing care and tenderness as women (with the exception of lactation[13]), *in fact* in all societies males typically are *not* the primary caregivers.

Object relations theory comes into play here in the sense that our early object attachments are turned upside down for the male child, not because of some internal biological or innate gender difference, but simply because within all the social orders on planet earth mothers, or female mother surrogates, typically do the mothering. This means that the male child will internalize deeply his primary female object, only to be pressed to renounce this object in favor of his father, with whom he may feel as a stranger.

Carol Gilligan challenges Erik Erikson's schema in which the sixth stage, Intimacy, follows the fifth stage, Identity. Not necessarily so, says Gilligan, because the female is socialized to seek and nurture intimacy from early childhood, and hence her identity may stem *from* her ability to be intimate rather than her intimacy being the result or product of her identity. Gilligan states, "Thus the sequential ordering of identity and intimacy in the transition from adolescence to adulthood better fits the development of men than it does the development of women."[14]

Lillian Rubin explores the implications of this early shift in primary role models as it affects intimate relationships between men and women.[15] Rubin claims that the female is socialized from birth to be open, accepting, dependent, nurturant. The male, as a result of having had to break with his primal security figure, will henceforth seek to become self-sufficient, autonomous, independent, separate, and individualized. Rubin states:

> Still, it *is* a fact that a woman, even if not the mother, is almost always the primary caregiver of infancy. *And no fact of our early life has greater consequences for how girls and boys develop into women and men, therefore for how we relate to each other in our adult years.* For, when that social fact is combined with the biological reality of our infantile dependency, the stage is set for developmental consequences of which we have only recently become aware—consequences that are intimately related to the difficulties we encounter in our love relationships and in our marriages.[16]

IMPLICATIONS FOR INTIMACY

In the light of the above explanation regarding the differences between males and females, it is little wonder that often it appears that our goals in marriage, our purposes, our expectations, and our attitudes toward each other are so divergent and conflictual.

One of the most persistent and continuing complaints that females harbor toward males is perceived male insensitivity toward her feelings and his reluctance to express his own feelings. As a generalization, the female appears to want closeness, interdependence (some say dependence), openness of ego boundaries, a sense of ongoing and mutual nurturance, and a bonding reminiscent of early mother-daughter and female-female relationships. As a generalization, the male wants independence, autonomy, strength of resolve, boundary closedness and fortification, and protection against hurt and vulnerability, loss, rejection, and abandonment.

The male, in order to secure these things, will be competitive and aggressive. He will not be overly communicative. The female, in seeking to meet her needs for warmth and intimate closeness, will find herself at odds with her mate time and time again. It is a case of crossed goals, crossed purposes, and crossed expectations. Obviously this characterization does not apply to all males and females. There are many exceptions. Historically, however, it is a case of the expressive female and the inexpressive male: the open boundaries and intimate sharing of the female versus the more closed boundaries and cautious (if at all) self-disclosure of the male. As noted earlier, Rubin points out that these differences are "not inherent in the nature of human development, but are a response to the social situation—in particular to the structure of roles and relationships inside the family."[17]

No wonder marriage is difficult, even for the best-matched and most well-prepared couple! We are not alike. We are different—sometimes very different.

What then can be done to close this gap and to make it possible for male and female to enter into each other's world more fully and more gracefully than heretofore? The answer, of course, sounds easier than it is. We need to go back into our feelings and distant memories stemming from our growing up within our family of origin. We need to work through a lot of the material we internalized, including our intimate relationship with our fathers and mothers. One does not need to be a Freudian to realize that we have likely internalized many experiences relating to our early objects of attachment and dependency. Males, in particular, need to come face to face with the likely reality that in their dating and lovemaking they were looking for a replacement for their mother from whom they were separated at a tender age. The male needs to see that the very closeness and loving acceptance he desires in a mate is also the very thing he doesn't fully trust. According to Rubin this is because of the early switch from mother to father. Additionally there are differences in the sexual feelings, desires, and behavior that may be traced to the early childhood experience.[18]

Marital Quality

CONCEPTUAL PROBELMS IN DEFINING MARITAL QUALITY

In the 1960s the studies that dealt with marital success, happiness, satisfaction, and adjustment also included stability as a measure.[19] In the 1970s the stability factor was removed from these studies because it became increasingly clear that there were stable marriages that were low in happiness and satisfaction, and there were unstable marriages that were high in happiness and satisfaction.[20]

Further, there is a profound conceptual and operational problem in defining the ideas of marital success, happiness, satisfaction, or adjustment. A term that may prove to be more useful than these terms is marital *quality*.[21] Of special interest to our theme of illusion and disillusion is how we can improve and enrich marriage: How can we continue to grow and develop both as individual human beings and as marriage dyads? In short, how can we learn to "make it together" so that we achieve the maximum of personal and dyadic happiness, satisfaction, *and* stability?

DECLINE AND LONGEVITY

There appears to be a well-researched trend indicating long-range decline in marital quality. Gerald Leslie states:

> Research has begun to assess the changes in marital adjustment that occur after the early years of marriage. Studies have appeared, based upon a variety

of populations, that trace the trend in adjustment over five, ten, and twenty or more years of marriage. Without exception, they show that the high levels of commitment characteristic of early marriage are not commonly maintained. However marital adjustment is conceived, the long-term trend is apparently downward.[22]

This *gradual* downward trend is often interpreted as a sign that marriage, even at its best, is a losing proposition. Many people express surprise that the decline is not more severe and drastic, given the highly romanticized expectations our society holds for marriage.

The conclusion of gradual decline cannot be understood apart from consideration of several intervening variables, especially longevity. Today's typical couples may expect to live anywhere from 20 to 30 years after the youngest child reaches age 18. "For as long as we both shall live" or "until death do us part" are usually much longer time spans than in the days of our grandparents and great grandparents.

BUILDING DISTANCE BACK INTO THE RELATIONSHIP

One of the key ingredients in high-quality longevity is friendship or philos love between the partners. When we talk about friendship between mates we must realize that too much togetherness may turn the relationship in on itself and cause atrophy. One of the most important factors in making it together is bulding some space and distance back into the relationship.

Laura Singer points out that we often confuse "closeness" with "togetherness." She says, "Closeness refers to an emotional perception; togetherness is a physical fact. Depending on your relationship, you can feel close to someone who is miles or continents away from you, and shut out and far from someone who may be lying in the same bed with you."[23] One major reason there is a decline in marital quality over time is that we have far too much togetherness and far too little closeness. Singer claims that:

> Doing things separately without jeopardizing the marriage is an important part of establishing one's sense of self. This kind of autonomy can, in fact, enhance a feeling of closeness because both people are secure in themselves, and there's no pressure or resentment involved. They can have their separate activities and then they can also draw together, sharing some of their individual experiences, and feeling free to be truly close and intimate.[24]

Other ways of building distance back into the relationship are by creating conditions that allow for new adventures and new experiences: such little things as having an affair with your mate and/or grand-seduction weekends wherein one mate plans the entire weekend as a surprise for the other. (It can't be a total surprise: At least make sure your mate has his/her calendar clear.) Unfortunately the high cost of housing impinges on our physical space, and many couples are forced to live in tiny houses or apartments where they are constantly "under foot" and in each other's way. I believe in lots of space: his space—her space—their space. There should be adequate space for hobbies and interests and projects.

A DISCLAIMER: AUTONOMY VERSUS FREEDOM

Sometimes married couples get hung up on the issue of their own rights, their own freedom, and their sense of **autonomy**. Autonomy does not necessarily imply a freedom to do or to be whatever one wishes. The developmental road to personal autonomy often places one in a defensive position regarding claims made on one's behavior. Any request, claim, obligation, or commitment may be interpreted as a threat to, or an encroachment on, one's autonomy. The position I take on this is that only as a person feels reasonably secure in his or her personal sense of autonomy is this person able to tolerate and *cheerfully* accept some degree of limitation on his/her own range of personal freedom.

Often the basic conflict is between autonomy and intimacy. If I am gung-ho on my sense of independence and autonomy, then I cannot allow myself to become truly intimate. Likewise, if I permit myself to be truly intimate I will no longer be autonomous. Speaking to this, Maggie Scarf, in her book *Intimate Partners,* outlines five levels of couple functioning. Level one, the highest level of relating, is called the "Integrated" level.

> . . . autonomy and intimacy are experienced as integrated aspects of each
> partner's personhood and of the relationship that the two of them
> share. . . . [W]hat has to be negotiated by the partners, in this interpersonal
> world, is the *activity* to be engaged in—not the internalized conflict about
> whether to assert one's intimate needs or one's self needs at any given point in
> time. . . . And being separate supports a sense of closeness, because to the
> degree that my spouse lets me know that he recognizes and feels comfortable
> with my essential differentness, I can feel safe about letting my hair down and
> being who I really am, with him. . . . Autonomy and intimacy are, in these
> circumstances, mutually self-supporting and self-enhancing states of being.[25]

We make a grave mistake when we think we should have as much behavioral freedom in a dyadic relationship (whether steadily going together, engaged, legal marriage, or living together) as we have as unattached individuals. A relationship simply cannot be nurtured if both partners covet total independence and freedom. And so a satisfactory level of autonomy must precede meaningful intimacy. *Only the reasonably mature person can choose to limit some of his or her freedom for the sake of the other and the relationship.*

The mature, autonomous person is one who says, "I am reasonably mature and I consider myself to have a healthy sense of autonomy. I have enjoyed being single, and now I am willing to give up some degree of my freedom in order to share life with you." The point here is that only the reasonably autonomous person is in the nonthreatened position of being able to choose to commit to a shared intimacy. If we have not reached this minimal level of autonomy we will be threatened by even the most minimal claims of intimacy. *This is why I am against early marriage.* In early marriage the participants have hardly had time to grow into their autonomy and exercise their behaviorial freedom in a variety of life situations. Partners in early marriages are not usually mentally or emotionally prepared to give up some of their behavioral freedom for the sake of life together. Having made this disclaimer about autonomy and freedom, let us now consider the characteristics of a vital marriage.

VITAL MARRIAGE

Cuber and Haroff, in their well-known study of upper-middle-class marriages, categorized marriages into five different types. The first three types were considered to be utilitarian in nature, in which the participants valued the marriage only for utilitarian reasons. They valued their marriage as "secondary to other things which must or should, they judge, come first."[26] Utilitarian marriages included the Devitalized, the Passive-Congenial, and the Conflict-Habituated. At the other end of the continuum were the intrinsic marriages. The intrinsic marriage partners valued the relationship as their highest priority. The two categories of intrinsic are the Vital and the Total.[27] The question that presses itself on us is how can we prevent the vital marriage from becoming devitalized? How can we circumvent the process of erosion, atrophy, or decline in quality?

Ammons and Stinnett studied vital marriage. They sought to "identify and describe the nature of those personality characteristics that enable couples to develop and sustain a vital relationship."[28]

1. Sex appeared to play a central and profoundly important role in the vital marriage.
2. A majority of the vital marital partners expressed high levels of need to be understanding and supportive.
3. The partners expressed development of and sustaining of a vital relationship as one of their most important life goals.
4. Vital marital partners appear to have well-developed ego strengths; that is, they have characteristics that enable them to function autonomously and to separate themselves from their mate.[29]

I note that there is an interaction between giving and receiving. The need to "be understanding and supportive" may come as a surprise to some, but it reflects the caring and nurturing that are characteristic of vital, enduring relationships. The fourth point illustrates what I have been saying about autonomy and being able to be separate. The third point, however, is absolutely pivotal. The creation of a vital relationship will never just happen. It is the result of a mutual commitment to work at the relationship: to nurture it, to sustain it, and to do those things that build up and enhance rather than tear down and destroy.

Vitality in marriage, however, depends on another variable that we usually hear about only in its negative expression. Partners in unhappy or nonfunctional marriage relationships often refer to unfairness, inequality, the imbalance of power, and the accompanying feelings of helplessness and impotency. On the flip side, the positive side, we usually observe that functional, healthy relationships are those wherein the partners are able to share authority and power, leading and following, giving and taking.

Marital Power

Throughout these pages we have emphasized systems theory as the major paradigm through which we seek to understand marriage, family development, and individual development within the family. Transactional analysis and rational emotive therapy were recommended as tools for understanding intimate transactions and internal feelings. The one issue that we really haven't considered to the degree that it deserves is the issue of power within relationships.

Drawing on McDonald, Safilos-Rothschild, and Scanzoni, Maximiliane Szinovacz defines power as "the net ability or capability of actors (A) to produce or cause (intended) outcomes or effects, particularly on the behavior of others (O) or on others' outcomes.[30] We are particularly interested in gender norms pertaining to the possession and use of power as this is expressed within intimate relationships.

Few marriages will make it if the dynamics of power, control, and decision making are not resolved, at least within some range of minimal satisfaction. Many couples resolve the issue of power according to strict traditional gender norms, with the male being endowed by culture, religion, custom, and his family tradition as being the one with authority and power.[31] I am not saying that all power issues must be equalitarian for the attainment of marital success, happiness, and satisfaction. I am saying that unless or until *both partners feel satisfied* about the power, control, and decision-making issues, the dyad either will be in a neutral holding pattern or will be going backward in retreat from intimacy. I say this because a vast majority of people simply do not feel good about being on the short end of the stick. When one of the partners doesn't feel good about the balance of power the relationship is bound to suffer. In their book, *American Couples,* Philip Blumstein and Pepper Schwartz stated in their conclusion:

. . . the institution of marriage, at least until now, has been organized around inequality, and attempts to change this framework have not yet been very successful. The traditional married couples in our study often laid their solid foundation on roles that stabilized the relationship but gave women some of the less pleasant responsibilities, such as housework, and assigned her duties, such as the buyer role.[32]

THE THRESHOLD OF COMPLIANCE

There seems to be a universal phenomenon that we label as the "threshold of compliance." This is the point at which one person can dominate and control another person without encountering resistance. When the dominated or controlled person begins to resist domination we can then assume that his/her threshold of compliance has been reached or exceeded.

When dyadic partners have a relatively low and equal threshold of compliance there is a greater chance for achieving an equalitarian relationship. The main point of concern about the threshold of compliance is that a person wishing to dominate will seek to find the exact point at which he/she can dominate without the partner offering any resistance.

One of the most important issues facing newly married people is the issue of compliance. As we pointed out earlier, the taboos of anger and conflict have impaired and prevented the aboveboard, healthy interaction between mates who are in disagreement or are in a state of anger, hurt, or disappointment. Therefore it is very easy for one of the partners to simply "give in" to the other. This compliance brings peace. It also may bring deep resentment if the compliance continues over a period of time.

LOVE IS THE CHILD OF FREEDOM

Of course, some people, males and females alike, believe that the male is divinely ordained to be the judge on all marital and familial issues and disputes. Although I certainly do not hold this view, I have observed in marital therapy that if the female feels too severely oppressed, she will retreat into depression, begin severe passive-aggressive behavior, or (it is hoped) actively resist such domination.

Erich Fromm wrote a great deal about people who feel secure only when they are in the one-down or the one-up position. These persons have great difficulty achieving genuine intimacy because of the inequality between them. How can we be truly intimate when we are not afforded equality of status? Equality of status is a philosophical belief based on the assumption that females have the same inherent rights as males. Males especially would do well to learn from Fromm's observation that "love is the child of freedom, never that of domination."[33]

THE PRINCIPLE OF LEAST INTEREST

Willard Waller's "principle of least interest" is relevant to all issues in interpersonal relationships. The principle of least interest says that whoever has the least interest (ego investment, financial investment, time investment, energy investment, identity investment) in maintaining a relationship has the most power and control in that relationship.[34] The person who loves less, cares less, or is attracted less will be in a position to exercise greater control. If a person who is fiercely independent is married to a dependent and submissive mate, the independent mate will probably need the relationship less and hence will be in a position to dominate or control the partner.

Because of our society's emphasis on traditional socialization of the female as being passive, subordinate, compliant, nurturant, and emotionally connected, the female is frequently more heavily invested in the marriage and consequently has less power when controversial issues arise between her and her husband. The principle of least interest is relevant in matters of dating, courting, sexual expression, mate selection, and in the internal dynamics that tend to maintain or disrupt a dyadic relationship.

RESOURCE AND EXCHANGE THEORY

The **resource theory** of power claims that the person with greater resources will wield the greater power and control. Resources include such things as money, earning ability, status, physical appearance, personal attractiveness, mental sharpness, education, persuasive verbal facility, age, and degree of vulnerability. Blood and Wolfe held that the greater the amount of resources a mate possesses, the greater will be his or her power to control or dominate the other.[35]

Issues of power are related to exchange theory inasmuch as the unwritten and unspoken contract between the partners is quid pro quo, something for something. When the perceived and experienced level of return in exchange for what one gives is too one-sided, the relationship becomes severely threatened.

SYMPTOM POWER

Symptom power is another type of power that results from a series of maneuvers either within an intimate dyad or within an entire family. Symptom power is the power deriving from emotional, physiological, and behavioral symptoms. Symptoms may include depression, anxiety, nervousness, stomach aches, headaches, backaches, colitis, fatigue, acting out behavior, problematic behavior, argumentative behavior, delinquency, chemical dependency, helplessness, death wish, and suicide threats. This last is one of the most powerful controlling behaviors ever known because it keeps intimates fearful and at bay.

One of the ironies of life is the way ostensibly helpless and emotionally dependent people are able to wield control over their intimates. A very normal (nonpathological) example of the control and domination of helplessness is a human neonate. What is more absolutely controlling than a newborn? Many people learn to control and dominate those around them by maintaining a helpless stance. This helplessness may take many forms. It can include physical symptoms, such as those mentioned previously, or it can take the form of not having certain skills such as knowing how to drive a car, knowing how to cook, knowing how to keep financial records, or knowing how to make elementary household repairs. Helplessness of any kind can be extremely manipulative. I am not suggesting that helplessness is always manipulative or always deliberately controlling. However, I am suggesting that being helpless is a common way of exercising control over those around us.

Family systems theory views symptoms and symptomatic behavior as a result of malfunction or maladaptation of the system (Appendix A). The psychopathology of marriage and family life can hardly be understood apart from the power and control that accompanies symptoms and symptomatic bahavior. Whether we are talking about severe disturbance or mild maneuvers between intimates, there is always a payoff for the symptomatic person. The payoff may be an enhanced sense of self, an increase in ego strength, or simply the satisfaction of being able to govern, dominate, or control the behavior of one's intimates.

What does the foregoing discussion of power have to do with making it together in marriage? What is the relationship between satisfactory, medium- to high-quality marriage, and such things as the threshold of compliance, the principle of least interest, and symptoms? The answer is that quality and growth are impossible unless or until the issue of power between intimates is resolved to a satisfactory degree for both partners. This resolution must feel inwardly satisfying, comfortable, and nonthreatening to both partners. If it does not, real quality and growth is illusive because pretense, compliance, and accommodation will inevitably take their toll on the quality of the relationship.

Equity and Equality

BARBARA AND DONALD

BARBARA: I don't quite know where we're at, but I have the feeling that we're on more solid ground than we have ever been before. I went through a period of restlessness when I first started getting caught up in women's lib. I tried to manipulate Don—to get him to see what I saw—to get him to feel some of the things I was feeling. But that never really works. He just wasn't where I was. He had learned all the ways a male is supposed to exercise power and authority, and he couldn't see what this did to me. I felt I had the right to be myself but that this better not conflict with his ideas of what I ought to do or be. By then it was no longer a question of equality in our marriage—hell, we were far from home base on that. Now it was a basic issue of whether or not I was to build my whole daily existence around him and his career.

I never had a career. I was a secretary before we were married and I had worked for about 2 years after we were married—until our daughter was born. What kind of a chance did I have for a career after that? What does all this self-fulfillment talk mean when you can't even get out of your own house or away from the daily routines of your children? I was getting desperate! I thought my life was ebbing away. Everybody wanting a part of me. The women's support group only made me more frustrated and angry. They could be sympathetic, but I still had my responsibilities.

So one day I came to a decision. I told him I was not intending to manipulate him in any underhanded way but that I needed his help and his support if I was going to make it. I had some depression, but I had full awareness of what I was doing. Poor Don! He really didn't know what had been going on inside me. I always felt so guilty that I kept my real feelings secret. That's when Don and I came to you. Don hated you for a while. But I think something got through to him that had never gotten through before. I think for the first time in our marriage he heard how desperate I really was! I think he became scared of losing me!

There's really no fairy-tale ending to all of this. Since we last saw you we have moved to Dover. Don likes his new job, and I am combining mothering with school to get an associate degree. We have achieved an amazing equality! Don now thinks he's crazy to mortgage his whole future to his job and that he is getting tired of feeling he always has to compete. He says the sooner I get my degree and find a job the better because he's tired of going it alone.

In contrast to traditional, **patriarchal** monogamy, **equalitarian monogamy** indicates an equal balance of power and authority between husband and wife. As we have stressed in this chapter, unless and until the power issue is resolved to some degree of satisfaction for each partner there will be little genuine marital happiness and quality. Every other type of equality, that is, equality of job opportunity, rights, responsibilities, obligations, and privileges, will be illusive until the basic and primal equality issue is resolved—the equality of power. As long as this issue is based on a traditional cultural-ecclesiastical definition of gender role there can be no real equality between the sexes.[36]

Equalitarian monogamy is based on the premise that marriage between equals is the only ideological framework that permits both interpersonal and intrapersonal growth. This is because genuine growth is impossible when two persons are bonded in an unequal yoke. An unequal yoke, by definition, keeps one person in a dominant, one-up position and the other in a submissive, one-down position.

Equitarian monogamy is closely allied with equalitarian monogamy. Equity refers to fairness and the quality of being fair and impartial. In many decisions made by courts of civil law, a settlement need not be equal for it to be equitable. Hence, a relationship based on the principle of equity may not be equal in all regards, but it is at least fair, just, and impartial without any assumptions about one gender being entitled to greater privilege or responsibility than the other.

Equality and *equity* are the terms we have chosen to indicate the nature of the ideal balance of power between partners. *Equality* is a term that applies to one's status and position relative to the partner's status and position. As such, equality forms a philosophical underpinning for the relationship. *Equity* is a term that implies fairness in the division of labor, duties, responsibilities, obligations, rights, and privileges. Some naive and very idealistic people will say that our emphasis on power being equally/equitably distributed is bad. These people claim that marriage *should* not be concerned with issues of power and control. The old theme recurs again, "If you love me the issue of power should not make any difference!" But this is just one more "should" in the face of countless marriages that end because one wants out due to the unfairness of the marital reality.

This is what happened to Barbara. She had experienced increasing depression related to her feelings of helplessness. She was without power, or at least she *felt* she was without power. The answer for her was in learning to assert herself and to confront Donald.[37]

Rollo May has stated that there are five levels of power: These are the power (1) to be, (2) to affirm oneself, (3) to assert oneself, (4) to aggress, and (5) to violate or do violence. The first four levels of power are to be understood as increasing in measure and force at each successive level. The power to be is primary and always comes first. If we failed to learn how to be we would not be alive today. The power to affirm oneself is the additional ability to say "yes" to oneself and one's right to life as being equal to that of any other person. The power to assert is the ability to draw boundaries around oneself and hence to protect oneself. Assertion is absolutely necessary in order to defend ourselves against aggression, invasion, and manipulation by others. The power to aggress is the ability to attack and invade when necessary or indicated, especially when strong assertion has not worked. There are many instances in life when we need to aggress and to fight strongly in order to preserve ourselves and our human dignity. The fifth level of power is obviously a different mode of power than any of the previous four. The main point that Rollo May is making concerning these five levels of power is that *people who have learned to express and use appropriate amounts of self-affirmation, self-assertion, and aggression rarely, if ever, feel the need to use violence.*[38]

As May points out, people who do violence, or violate, are almost always those who feel helpless. They feel helpless because they failed to learn the necessary expression of affirmation, assertion, and aggression. If we fail to learn at least a minimal sense of self-strength, we begin to feel impotent or powerless. This leads to increasing feelings of helplessness, which in turn often leads to depression. Tragedy is the inevitable result when helplessness and depression turn to violence. Emotionally healthy people do not need to violate.

One of the most important preconditions to the quest for a vital relationship is the achievement of balance in the first four levels of power. Both partners must have equal rights and equal freedom to use those rights in terms of affirmation, assertion, and aggression. Historically, the female has always been considered to be second to the male, and hence the male has been able to dominate and control both his mate and the relationship.

The reader will note the distinction between assertion and aggression. Assertion is more basic than aggression in that assertion is a protection of one's own self, one's own life space, one's own territory. Aggression is an invasion or an attack on another's life space or territory. The great challenge today, for both women and men, is to learn how to assert ourselves so that we are able to protect ourselves and to defend against other people's aggression against us, to defend against being pushed around, manipulated, dominated, and stepped on.

Unfortunately for women and for marriage, many men do not want to relinquish their position of power and authority. Many males believe that theirs is the sex of authority and power because of an alleged divine right. Equality/ equity may cause pain and discomfort for the male as he unlearns biased and prejudicial beliefs. In the long run he is the winner because the reward is a more alive and interesting partner who stays with him not because she is emotionally and economically dependent on him but because she wants to share her life with him as his equal. Love is the child of freedom, never of domination.

BALANCE AND FLEXIBILITY

Obviously, no two people are at the same place of growth at the same time. Thus, an equalitarian/equitarian relationship is one in which, over the long term there is room for fluctuation and change. Figure 8-2 illustrates this.

The right side of Figure 8-2 illustrates that at times one partner may appear to be less equal than the other, but that at other times the situation is reversed. In the long run a balance is maintained; in the short run there is

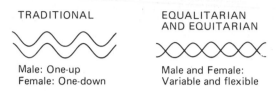

TRADITIONAL

Male: One-up
Female: One-down

EQUALITARIAN
AND EQUITARIAN

Male and Female:
Variable and flexible

Figure 8-2 Traditional versus Equalitarian Attitude toward
Power and Authority in Marriage

flexibility to handle changing needs and situations. Equality and equity do not
imply a rigidity wherein at every given moment there is an absolute balance.
People differ in their skills, their talents, and their abilities. We may differ in
our areas of contribution to the marriage. There are occasions such as illness or
emotional stress when one partner borrows from the emotional strength of the
other. (It is legitimate, under certain circumstances, to borrow from the Adult
of one's partner.) This borrowing or temporary emotional dependence does not
render the marriage nonequal. Equality and equity are philosophical beliefs on
which behavior is based. Equality/equity are beliefs from which one draws
operational standards for the daily implementation of the sharing relationship.

The primary issue related to equality/equity is power. Until the partners
feel that they are equal in terms of their entitlement to power and authority (not
just a glib lip-service belief or a nod to the god of equality), there can be no real
movement toward a vital relationship. The reason for this is that there can be no
true intimacy on a continuing and sustaining basis between persons who are in a
one-up and one-down relationship with each other. If the couple does not really
have intimacy as a major goal or purpose in their relationship then the marriage
is more likely to be what Cuber and Haroff call a passive-congenial relationship,
in which there never was any real vitality or dynamic intimacy.[39] If intimacy
and vitality are not goals or expectations of the marital union, then there will be
little disappointment if intimacy is not realized. A study by Harper and Elliott
illustrates this. They conclude, "Couples who perceived relatively little intimacy in their marriage but also expected little intimacy were equally happy in
their marriages as couples who had intimacy scores that were much higher. In
other words, the amount of intimacy a couple perceived in their marriage was
not as important in determining the extent of marital satisfaction as was the
discrepancy a couple felt between the amount of intimacy perceived and the
amount of intimacy desired."[40]

Vital Marriage and the Question of Commitment

We have now considered the issues of power, equality, and equity as these affect
the vitality of a relationship. I have stated my belief very clearly: *The equality
and equity of power and authority are preliminary to all other considerations about*

duties, rights, responsibilities, and privileges. We now must raise the issue of commitment and the relationship of commitment to vitality in marriage.

There are those who say that the problem with marriage today is that there is an escape hatch that is too easily opened. Perhaps! There are others who would eliminate the escape hatch altogether. The history of marriage in Western civilization does not favor the second approach, that is, the elimination of the escape hatch. Even the Roman Catholic Church, which is opposed to divorce in any form, permits annulment. An annulment is an official declaration that the marital union never did exist in the first place. If the marriage never did truly exist in the Church's view, then there can be no divorce because divorce implies a prior marriage.

In my view there is nothing wrong with an escape hatch, but there is something wrong with people who approach marriage with one eye on each other and the other eye on the escape hatch. Something is wrong with the entire system when we think in terms of easy escape, by saying to ourselves "Oh well, if it doesn't work I can always get a divorce." In the past it took two to marry and two to obtain a divorce. Today it still takes two to marry but only one to get a divorce. I am not suggesting that we return to the sham, deceit, and collusion of the past when the two people had to prove that one or the other was guilty. *I am suggesting, however, that the word "commitment" has lost its meaning for far too many couples. At heart—at rock bottom—at the very core of the entire subject of marriage—is the issue of commitment.*

To what shall we commit ourselves? To the concept that we shall doggedly stay together until death do us part even if we are miserable as hell? Shall we commit ourselves to remain together for as long as we both shall live even if this means that the children are confused and feel unwanted? Commitment to remain together no matter what is not the answer. It is not the answer because it is a forced response to a promise we made a long time ago that we would love, honor, and cherish. Perhaps we had no right to make that promise. Perhaps no one has the right to promise something he/she cannot possibly deliver.

THE TRIPLE COMMITMENT

The vital marriage emphasizes commitment to persons first, with commitment to ideas and principles being secondary. The primary commitment is to the self, to one's mate, and to the relationship. This triple commitment recognizes that if we neglect the self, or obliterate the self in deference to the other, we bring destruction to the self, the other, and the relationship. "If I do not believe in myself, I cannot believe in us." If commitment to the relationship takes priority over commitment to the self and to the other, the partners then defend the relationship at the expense of their mutual well-being. Further, if we commit to the absolute well-being of our mate as we do to our own well-being, then the relationship dynamic becomes systemic and circular. In short, a snowball effect is created wherein my commitment to my own well-being enables me to commit wholeheartedly and completely to my mate's well-being, which in turn creates a marital whole that is greater than the sum of its parts.

If we accept authentic self-esteem as a prerequisite for emotional health, it is not at all illogical to claim that self-esteem is a prerequisite for a healthy marriage. The triple commitment, then, is the most important promise we can make to each other at the time of marriage and successively every day thereafter.

> I promise to commit myself to my own growth and well-being, to your growth and continued well-being, and to our shared relationship. With this promise I willingly commit myself to the continued nurturance of our love and of our shared life together.

Figure 8-3 illustrates the rank order of the three commitments as well as the systemic and circular effect that is created by these commitments.

The basic principle underlying the triple commitment is the simple fact that "if there is no me there will be no us." If we fail to nurture ourselves we will become dull and stagnant. If we do not love ourselves how can we honestly expect others to love us? If we do not hold ourselves in high positive regard, by what twist of logic can we expect others to do so? On the other hand, if we hold ourselves as being of high value with good self-esteem, self-regard, and self-acceptance we become open, interesting, questing, curious, alive, and vital. Is not this the kind of person you would like to have across the breakfast table from you and to share your bed the next 40 or 50 years of your life?

The basic systems circularity underlying the triple commitment goes like this: Self-nurturance and self well-being enhances one's ability in mate-nurturance, which in turn enhances the relationship, which then feeds back into feelings of self-esteem for both partners, which again redounds to the quality of the relationship. As illustrated in Figure 8-3, the growth-support components have an interactive and circular effect that enhances the whole.

In addition to the triple commitment, there should be a commitment to

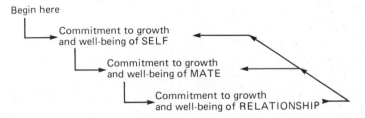

Figure 8-3 The Rank Order and Circularity of the Triple Commitment

certain ideals and principles. Foremost among these are an unqualified commitment to:

1. Equality and equity.
2. True balance of power and authority.
3. Constructive resolution of conflict.

A clear statement of the triple commitment and the three supportive ideological commitments can easily be included in the wedding service (Appendix C).

Division of Responsibility

At the risk of erring on the side of being too simplistic, I would like to suggest a practical method for equitable and equalitarian division of marital responsibilities. The method sounds deceptively simple, yet it requires the conflict resolution skills and fair-fight procedures discussed earlier. Further, as the reader will recall, fair-fight procedures and skills are of little value unless the underlying issues of power and equality have been resolved, at least at a minimally satisfactory level.

THE FOUR ALTERNATIVES METHOD

The issue of responsibility within marriage may be more readily identified as "who does what within the daily operation of the household," that is, the division of labor. Figure 8-4 is a diagram showing four alternatives. The alternatives on each side indicate areas where there is no contest. She lists as her alternatives all those things she likes to do and wants to do. These items must *not* be items that he also likes to do and wants to do. Likewise, on the other side he lists as his alternatives all those things he likes to do and wants to do. These items must *not* be items that she also likes to do. The listing of these alternatives will require a sharing of information. Negotiation will not be necessary as long as the principle of equity is served.

The next step is to respond to the other two alternatives indicating areas where you *both like* to have responsibility and *want* it (top), and areas where *neither* of you *likes* to have responsibility and *neither wants* it (bottom). The top and bottom items will need to be discussed and negotiated to reach a workable and genuinely satisfactory compromise based on the principles of equality and equity.

The four alternatives schema is not a sex-role division of labor, nor is it an antisex-role division of labor. It is a non-sex-role division of labor! It is based on the principles of equality and equity. Further, it is based on personal preference, skills, and talents. It is not predicated on the necessity of feeling or believing that the nonsexist division of labor means each partner must learn or

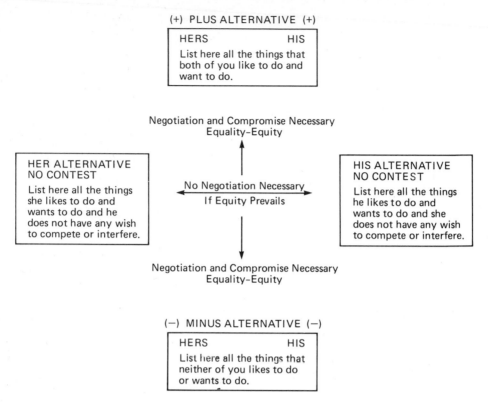

Figure 8-4 The Four Alternatives Method for Negotiating Who Does What Within Marriage

acquire the entire range of skills necessary for domestic living. What is meant by this "nonnecessity" disclaimer may be illustrated by asking what purpose is served by her mowing the lawn and painting the outside of the house (traditional male sex role) if she does not wish or want to do this and he does? Let this item be a trade-off. Likewise, what purpose is served by his vacuum cleaning and floor scrubbing (traditional female sex role) if he does not wish or want to do this and she does? Let this item be a trade-off.

If a division of labor is equitable and if both partners are satisfied with it, there is no need to depart from it. It is certainly not an act of spontaneous freedom for both partners to learn new skills just so they can claim to be liberated from the traditional roles. This is not liberation and it is not freedom; it is simply a new conformity to a new set of arbitrary rules. If, in the name of autonomy and freedom, we rebel against traditional roles and division of labor in order to prove to ourselves how liberated we are, we certainly have not succeeded. In truth, we have simply moved 180 degrees from traditional conformity to a reactionary conformity. True freedom is being able to negotiate the rules and roles under which we agree to live.

The operating principle that we have outlined in the four-alternatives schema is such that as long as there is equity and balance, a fair and just system of trade-offs using each partner's skills and talents, there will be no need to negotiate further on the her-his (sides) alternatives of Figure 8-4. Further, because both wish and want the plus items and both wish and want to be relieved of the minus items (top and bottom), the areas and items requiring negotiation and compromise are clearly defined.

There are still other problems to be worked out. What about the number of hours she spends at her job compared to the hours he spends at his job? Does this matter? Should it be taken into consideration? Benin and Agostinelli state, "Equity could be assessed in more than one way. It could be that wives want equity in housework regardless of the amount of time that each spouse spends in paid work. Or wives may consider the total work load (the sum of housework hours plus paid work hours) and desire equity at that level.[41]

Marriage as Work and Play

MAKING WORK OF MARRIAGE VERSUS PLAYFUL SHARING

One of the primary themes of these pages has been the necessity for working *at* marriage. However, we are in danger of misinterpreting the idea or concept of work. Instead of working *at* marriage, we may, with all good intentions, end up making work *of* marriage. We may work at marriage to the point where we have taken all the fun out of it. Perhaps we have created a monster! We stand in danger of making the "solution" into the problem, so that there is no joy, no spontaneity, no fun, no play, no pleasure, and no room for "just being ourselves."

In order to counteract this unintended outcome of making marriage into work, I will develop the concept of marriage as a type of playful sharing. The idea of playfulness includes humor, teasing, role taking, pretending, gestures, facial expressions, mocking, miming, banter, barbs, and fantasy. It also includes doing playful things with and for each other as I mentioned earlier when I talked about grand-seduction weekends. R. William Betcher has pointed out that although too much regression (pretending, taking roles from early childhood) can be an indication of immaturity, a little regression within the context of trust and security can be a very positive asset in marriage.[42]

In terms of transactional analysis we are talking about our Positive Child, sometimes called our Free Child. Our Free Child is the basis of our spontaneity, pleasure, fun, sense of wonder and awe, excitement, and even imagination and creativity. Betcher believes that playfulness helps couples strike a balance between distance and intimacy. Too much of either distance or intimacy can be destructive to the relationship. Betcher defines intimate play as being spontaneous, mutual, and characterized more by the attitude of playfulness than by the content of the interchange.[43]

Betcher emphasizes that playfulness is difficult if the partners do not feel safe. A sense of safety seems to be a prerequisite for playful interaction. This is because playfulness requires vulnerability, which is turn implies letting go of our defenses and letting our guard down. Hence the sense of feeling safe is an ongoing antecedent to playful interaction. Betcher states:

> As in the play of higher primates and human children, intimate play can be expected to take place in a context of felt safety. . . . [B]oth partners must have confidence that the feelings and behaviors which emerge through the partial giving up of internal controls will be sufficiently "contained" so as not to overwhelm the adult ego and that the other person's response will not be injurious to states of psychological vulnerability.[44]

Theodore Isaac Rubin says that "humor can often transcend differences that exist, or it can indicate that differences are undercut by great similarity in perceptions." He further states:

> The importance of humor cannot be stressed too much. The ability to laugh and to make each other laugh is no small matter in providing an antidote to situations that might otherwise turn into chronic, unrelieved states of despair. Humor also bridges impasses in communication and is one of the best mechanisms for preventing and breaking pride deadlocks. Humor helps to dispel artificial and pretentious solemnity. It makes great closeness possible.[45]

INTIMACY—VULNERABILITY—PLAYFULNESS

Some forms of humor can be cruel. Some types of teasing can be sadistic. I do not deny that too much playfulness can be dysfunctional and malproductive. I am claiming, however, that intimacy requires vulnerability and that excessive vulnerability without some form of comic relief or playful parody can undo or undermine a potentially viable and vital marriage.

Ridicule and sarcasm are generally forms of anger and aggression. They are *not* humor, and they are usually not even funny. Too much humor and too much teasing can be a cover for resentment and anger. We have all heard it said that many a truth is said in jest. This is true. And most of this kind of jesting is not really humorous at all. Instead it is a biting, stinging type of reprimand or criticism.

I stated earlier that one of the erroneous beliefs associated with fair-fight techniques and the constructive resolution of conflict is the belief that all conflict is resolvable. Clearly this is a utopian belief. All conflict is not resolvable. When conflict remains unresolved and defused, humor and playful interaction can cast the conflict into a lighter vein. Humor, teasing, levity, a sense of the absurd, even a mildly sarcastic wit can be introduced into the day-in, day-out routine of even the most seriously purposed couples. Indeed, even a friendly banter can serve to cajole us into taking ourselves, each other, and life itself less seriously.

In the learning of playfulness the key element is the framework in which the play is introduced. The metamessage (the message within the message) must be cast in a friendly, free, loving, and supportive manner—with glee written on one's face, as it were—which serves to telegraph to the receiver that your intentions are playful, not serious.

When we have a genuine loving feeling for our mate we can jest and even poke a little fun at each other's idiosyncrasies and personal habits. The levity becomes a form of endearment.

PLAYFUL SEX

Certainly an area that can stand much more playful interaction is our sexual response to one another. In ludic love, sex is play. Highly serious couples who want a vital sex life sometimes prevent it because they have lost their sense of humor—their sense of frolic, their sense of abandonment. Indeed, these people may temporarily lose their natural sex drive because they have tried so hard to improve and perfect their lovemaking that they have destroyed all spontaneity. For the overly serious person, sex becomes a performance, sometimes even a command performance, and under these conditions it is little wonder that the fun and excitement disappear.

Like so many other areas in life, we can defeat ourselves by overemphasizing the solution. Sexual technology has enabled many couples and individuals to free themselves of severe sexual problems. On the other hand, sexual technology can be our undoing if we allow it to stifle our creativity, our playfulness, and our spontaneity. When we are in the process of making love we should be in our Child ego state, not in our serious Adult and certainly not in our stern Parent.

ANTIDOTE FOR THE OVERLY SERIOUS

Playfulness within marriage may be extremely difficult if the partners persist in taking themselves too seriously. One partner can be very helpful in helping the other become more playful, yet when both are essentially humorless the task becomes formidable. Some of us grew up in humor-filled environments, and some of us were raised in humorless, boring, and austere atmospheres. In my work as a marriage and family therapist I am often amused at the sterile, icy-cold seriousness of some families. In some extreme cases the unwritten family rule states, "Thou shalt not laugh!"

Perhaps the beginning of change for humorless people is to prescribe the symptom. That is, insist that the overly serious person take himself or herself so absolutely seriously that there are decreasing moments of comic relief and light-hearted revelry. Perhaps when we experience the absurdity of overly serious preoccupation with self and life we will be able to laugh at ourselves, the sine qua non of play and playful interaction. Sometimes all a person needs in order to become more freed up to the possibilities of humor is for some significant person, such as a mate, a co-worker, or a therapist, to give that person *permission* to let his/her guard down and to be less defensive.

DON'T KNOCK THESE IDEAS UNTIL YOU'VE TRIED THEM

The following activities have been used successfully by various couples who committed themselves to the twin processes of working at their marriage and playing with each other. In other words, working at the marriage became a form of play.

Give each other one constructive, genuine compliment a day.

Set aside a talking time each day. Keep the kids away. Have cocktails or other refreshments. Nourish each other. Listen and respond. Be alive!

Surprise your lover with a special favor, gesture, or gift once a week.

Set aside 30 minutes once a week to do nothing except physical pleasuring of your partner. Insofar as you are willing, do everything for which your partner expresses a desire. Next week reverse roles.

Learn a participant sport or recreational pursuit together and stick to it for at least 6 months.

Choose and cultivate new leisure time pursuits and hobbies that you can do together.

Choose a new leisure time pursuit or hobby that you will do alone.

Open yourselves to new friendships, either individually or as a couple. Invite another couple over to dinner.

Take honeymoon weekends regularly. Farm the kids out.

Men only: Forbid yourself ejaculation during a lovemaking session. See how far you can go without orgasm. Place all of your attention on her. Pleasure her.

Women only: Think of yourself as a seductress. Allow yourself the continuing experience of turning your mate on. Pleasure him.

Have an affair with each other. Arrange a tryst with your mate. Meet at a restaurant or a motel or in the woods. If one spent half the time, energy, and money on an affair with one's own mate as many people invest in extramarital affairs, the divorce rate would probably be much lower.

These are only a few of the limitless things that can be tried. Do they sound silly? Ridiculous perhaps? Try them anyway—for only as you take a few risks with your mate will you begin to experience what a vital, high-quality marriage is all about.

Defining, Creating, and Inventing Our Own Marriage

WHO DICTATES THE RULES AND THE ROLES?

The essence of democracy is in each of us having some say in the framing of the laws under which we live. The essence of vital marriage is exactly the same thing. That is, the essence of vital marriage is in the creating and framing of the operating procedures, guidelines, and rules of life together.

Unfortunately, few people really question the traditional ecclesiastical wording of the wedding ceremony or the covert terms of the contract underlying this ceremony. In effect, the great majority of those marrying are quite content to permit the state and the normative religious tradition to dictate the terms of the marriage, that is, to define the terms and rules under which the marriage will exist. In effect, we allow others to lay down the terms under which we will live.

In all 50 states of the United States, except for laws regarding bigamy, age at first marriage, mental capacity, the right of sexual access, and the care, nurture, and support of children, there are no prescribed contractual agreements that must be followed or observed either in the wording of the wedding ceremony or in the daily practice of marriage. Further, prenuptial agreements are legal or illegal within each of the 50 states depending almost entirely on current state law regarding property and marriage.

In addition to the laws or restraints mentioned above, the one thing each state does require at the ceremony or wedding service is some sign that each partner is entering into this union of his or her own free will and accord. This sign could be a nod of one's head! Few married people actually sign a marriage license. Instead, the license is usually signed by the witnesses.

WHY DO WE FORFEIT OUR FREEDOM TO DEFINE OUR OWN MARRIAGE?

In light of the above we may ask why it is that so many people refuse to negotiate the conditions, agreements, terms, and understandings under which they intend to conduct their life together. I am not talking about a formal or legal contract. I am talking about an agreement between the partners, covering some of the important issues that are bound to arise when they share their lives with one another. Why should the church, the synagogue, the state, or even one's own family of origin determine the terms of your marriage? Because the final responsibility for the success or failure of your marriage is with you, why would you want to bear this responsibility without having a strong voice in negotiating the terms and conditions of your union?

Today we are free to choose singlehood or marriage. Further, if we choose marriage we are free to choose to have our own children, to adopt children, or to remain childless. We are free to choose and define our roles and to negotiate a mutual agreement regarding expectations. These expectations include the areas of shared sexual frequency and shared psychic or emotional intimacy; the issues of equality and equity, his and her employment, chores, responsibilities, privileges, child care and discipline expectations; and the entire range of expectations regarding daily life and interaction.

The reader is referred to Appendices B and C. Appendix B, the Marital Expectations Inventory, is a listing of items about which people have a great range of expectations. In my opinion, each of these items needs to be considered before a person proceeds to actual marriage. Most people claim they don't really have many expectations. Nevertheless, when trouble comes to the marriage it is most likely to be in the form of disappointment over how the mate fails to live up to "my" expectations. A student once told me that he had only one expectation of his mate. He said that he expected her to be in *total agreement* with him on everything!

Appendix C, Ideas and Options for the Wedding Service, serves as a prototype for an honest exchange of intention to carry out the understandings agreed on in Appendix B, the Marital Expectations Inventory. The actual ceremony should reflect the underlying philosophy of the expectations inventory. After the expectations inventory is honestly and forthrightly negotiated, it is a simple matter to draw up meaningful wedding vows and statements.

"UNTIL DEATH" OR "FOR LIFE"

Sidney Jourard's article, "Marriage Is for Life," speaks to the central issue of vital marriage. Jourard's emphasis on "For Life" is not an emphasis on quantity of chronological time but rather is an emphasis on the *quality* of the relationship. Jourard has captured the essence of vitality in marriage as being an experience in spontaneity, growth, and the whole range of life-enhancing challenges based on the individual's ability to define life and marriage as an ongoing experience of discovery, invention, and creation.[46]

> Marriage is for growth, for life. . . . Everything depends on the model or
> metaphor which defines the marriage one will live, see, grow in, or die from.
> There are lethal images of marriage and family life, and there are life-giving

models. . . . Marriage is not an answer, but a search, a process, a search for life, just as dialogue is a search for truth. Yesterday's marriage or way of being married is today's trap. *The way out of the trap is to resume the dialogue, not to end it, unless someone is pledged not to grow and change.*[47] (Emphasis added.)

Marriage is for LIFE. *In this endeavor love is never enough.* Love as deep affection, plus skills in negotiation and conflict resolution, plus a balance of power underwritten by a philosophy of equality and equity, plus a playful sense of humor . . . plus you . . . plus me . . . = VITAL AND FOR LIFE.

Summary

This chapter considered how to kill a marriage. We have unrealistic expectations, we tend to blame our partners for everything that is wrong with the marriage, and we fear conflict, change, and growth. As Pogo said, "We have met the enemy and they is us."

Marriage and intimacy were considered to be a career that interacts with the parenting career and the employment-professional career. Within each of these careers there are steps, stages, phases, transitions, plateaus, crises, and passages. These careers are often interrupted by divorce, remarriage, and death. Male-female differences were discussed using the theoretical backdrop of Gilligan, Chodorow, and Rubin.

Power was discussed in terms of the compliance threshold, the principle of least interest, symptom power, resource theory, and exchange theory. The five levels of power were considered with an emphasis on the need to acquire the skill of self-assertion. The acquisition of skill in conflict resolution and the achievement of a satisfactory balance of power between mates were considered to be the indispensable conditions for authentic marital growth and vitality. We further stressed the need for marriage to be based on equality between partners and equity in all exchanges.

A vital marriage is further based on the ability to arrive at an equitable division of labor. The four alternatives model was presented. The concept of commitment was discussed with an emphasis first on commitment to the self, second to the mate, and third to the relationship. Following this triple commitment to living persons and entities comes the commitment to ideological principles and ideas, especially commitment to equality and equity, commitment to a true balance of power and authority, and commitment to the constructive resolution of conflict.

Another important theme in the quest for vitality in marriage is the idea of playfulness and humor. Although it is imperative that we work *at* marriage, it is very bad to make work *of* marriage. Couples who learn to be playful are probably already feeling safe in the relationship. Playfulness and a lively sense of humor serve as a powerful antidote to overly serious preoccupation with the self and to much of the absurdity we encounter in daily life.

The price of marital vitality is expressed less in terms of dollars than in time and energy. There is simply no way a vital relationship may be maintained without an investment of oneself, one's time and energy. Love is not enough. Unfortunately this is the greatest stumbling block to vital marriage. Too many people honestly believe that good marriages just happen and that there is no need to nurture and cultivate the relationship. This naive, romantic view of marriage still persists in our society, masquerading under the guise of the "love will conquer all" myth.

The importance of writing down, discussing, and negotiating various items in the Marital Expectations Inventory was discussed. Once the expectations have been discussed and mutually agreed on, they can be translated into wedding vows and statements of mutual intention.

The chapter concluded with a statement that marriage is not "Until Death," but rather is "For Life!" It is our choice. We are the ones who can either kill it or breathe life into it. We are the ones who make the difference.

Reading Suggestions

Beavers, Robert W. *Successful Marriage*. New York: W. W. Norton, 1985.

Beck, Aaron T. *Love Is Never Enough*. New York: Harper & Row, 1988.

Bernard, Jesse. *The Future of Marriage*. New York: Bantam, 1973.

Bradshaw, John. *The Family*. Deerfield Beach, Fla.: Health Communications, Inc., 1988.

Crosby, John F., ed. *When One Wants Out and the Other Doesn't: Doing Therapy With Polarized Couples*. New York: Brunner/Mazel, 1989.

Lauer, Jeanette C. and Robert H. Lauer. *Til Death Do Us Part*. New York: Harrington Park Press, 1986. (Originally published by Haworth Press, 1986.)

Lerner, Harriet Goldhor. *The Dance of Anger*. New York: Harper & Row, 1985.

Lerner, Harriet Goldhor. *The Dance of Intimacy*. New York: Harper & Row, 1989.

Mace, David and Vera Mace. *How to Have a Happy Marriage*. Nashville: Abingdon Press, 1977.

Pogrebin, Letty Cottin. *Family Politics*. New York: McGraw-Hill, 1983.

Stinnett, Nick and John DeFrain. *Secrets of Strong Families*. Boston: Little, Brown, 1985.

Notes

1. Daniel J. Levinson et al., *The Seasons of a Man's Life* (New York: Knopf, 1978); Gail Sheehy, *Passages: Predictable Crises of Adult Life* (New York: E. P. Dutton, 1974); Laura Singer with Barbara Lang Stern, *Stages: The Crises That Shape Your Marriage* (New York: Grosset and Dunlap, 1980); Herb Goldberg, *The Hazards of Being Male* (New York: Nash Publishing, 1976); Evelyn Duval, *Family Development,* 5th ed. (New York: J. B. Lippincott, 1957); Bernard Farber, *Family:*

Organization and Interaction (San Francisco: Chandler Publishing, 1964); Nena O'Neill and George O'Neill, *Shifting Gears: Finding Security in a Changing World* (New York: Evans, 1974).

2. Erik Erikson, *Childhood and Society* (New York: W. W. Norton, 1950), 266.
3. Evelyn Duvall, *Family Development* (New York: J. B. Lippincott, 1957).
4. Michael P. Nichols, *The Self in the System* (New York: Brunner/Mazel, 1987), 36–37.
5. Susan Losh-Hesselbart, "Development of Gender Roles," Chapter 20 in *Handbook of Marriage and the Family*, Marvin B. Sussman and Suzanne K. Steinmetz, eds. (New York: Plenum Press, 1987), 544.
6. *Ibid.*, 544.
7. *Ibid.*, 553.
8. John Mirowsky and Catherine E. Ross, "Belief in Innate Sex Roles: Sex Stratification versus Interpersonal Influence in Marriage," *Journal of Marriage and the Family*, Vol. 49, no. 3 (Aug 1987): 527–540.
9. *Ibid.*
10. Lillian B. Rubin, *Intimate Strangers* (New York: Harper & Row, 1983), (pg. 12, Harper Colophon Edition, 1984).
11. Carol Gilligan, *In a Different Voice* (Cambridge, Mass.: Harvard University Press, 1982), 6.
12. Nancy Chodorow, "Family Structure and Feminine Personality," In *Women, Culture and Society*, M. Z. Rosaldo and L. Lamphere, eds. (Stanford, Calif.: Stanford University Press, 1974); also, *The Reproduction of Mothering* (Berkeley: University of California Press, 1978).
13. Some mothers regularly use a breast pump in order to use their own milk in bottle feeding their infants. Fathers can thus bottle feed their infants using mother's milk.
14. *Op. cit.*, Carol Gilligan, 63 (paperback edition).
15. *Op. cit.*, Lillian B. Rubin.
16. *Ibid.*, Chapter 3 (pg. 42, Harper Colophon Edition, 1984).
17. *Ibid.* (pg. 12, Harper Colophon Edition, 1984).
18. *Ibid.*, Chapter 5 (pg. 12, Harper Colophon Edition, 1984).
19. Mary W. Hicks and Marilyn Platt, "Marital Happiness and Stability," *Journal of Marriage and the Family*, Vol. 32, no. 4 (Nov 1970): 553–574; Graham B. Spanier and Robert A. Lewis, "Marital Quality: A Review of the Seventies," *Journal of Marriage and the Family*, Vol. 42, no. 4 (Nov 1980): 825–839.
20. *Ibid.*
21. Frank D. Fincham and Thomas N. Bradbury, "The Assessment of Marital Quality: A Reevaluation," *Journal of Marriage and the Family*, Vol. 49, no. 4 (Nov 1987): 797–809.
22. Gerald R. Leslie, *The Family in Social Context* (New York: Oxford University Press, 1982), 526.
23. Laura J. Singer with Barbara Lang Stern, *Stages: The Crises That Shape Your Marriage* (New York: Grosset and Dunlap, 1980), 35.
24. *Ibid.*, 38.
25. Maggie Scarf, *Intimate Partners* (New York: Ballantine Books, 1987), Random House edition, 402–403, 405.

26. John F. Cuber with Peggy B. Haroff, *The Significant Americans* (New York: Appleton-Century-Crofts, 1965), 44.

27. *Ibid.*, 132.

28. Paul Ammons and Nick Stinnett, "The Vital Marriage: A Closer Look," *Family Relations*, Vol. 29, no. 1 (Jan 1980): 37–42. (Copyright © 1980 by the National Council on Family Relations.) Quotations reprinted by permission.

29. *Ibid.*

30. Maximiliane E. Szinovacz, "Family Power," Chapter 24 in *Handbook of Marriage and the Family*, Marvin B. Sussman and Suzanne K. Steinmetz, eds. (New York: Plenum Press, 1987), 652.

31. *Ibid.*, 670–672.

32. Philip Blumstein and Pepper Schwartz, *American Couples* (New York: William Morrow and Company, 1983), 323.

33. Erich Fromm, *The Art of Loving* (New York: Harper & Row, 1956). Copyright © 1956 by Erich Fromm. Reprinted by permission.

34. Willard Waller, *The Family: A Dynamic Interpretation*, rev. by Reuben Hill (New York: Dryden Press, 1951), 190–192.

35. Robert O. Blood and Donald M. Wolfe, *Husbands and Wives: The Dynamics of Married Living* (Glencoe, Ill.: Free Press, 1960), 44.

36. Scanzoni classifies marriage types into three kinds: the head-complement, the junior-partner, and the equal-equal. The reader is referred to John Scanzoni, *Sexual Bargaining: Power Politics in the American Marriage* (Englewood Cliffs, N.J.: Prentice-Hall, 1972).

37. Harriet Goldhor Lerner, *The Dance of Anger* (New York: Harper & Row, 1985), Chapter 3, "Circular Dances in Couples."

38. Rollo May, *Power and Innocence* (New York: W. W. Norton, 1972), 40–45.

39. *Op. cit.*, Cuber and Haroff, 132.

40. James M. Harper and Michael L. Elliott, "Can There Be Too Much of a Good Thing? The Relationship Between Desired Level of Intimacy and Marital Adjustment," *The American Journal of Family Therapy*, Vol. 16, no. 4 (Winter 1988).

41. Mary Holland Benin and Joan Agostinelli, "Husbands' and Wives' Satisfaction with the Division of Labor," *Journal of Marriage and the Family*, Vol. 50, no. 2 (May 1988): 349–361.

42. R. William Betcher, "Intimate Play and Marital Adaptation," *Psychiatry* 44 (Feb 1981): 13–33.

43. *Ibid.*

44. *Ibid.*

45. Theodore Issac Rubin, "How Can You Measure the Health of Your Relationship?" *New Woman* (June 1984): 54–64.

46. Sidney M. Jourard, "Marriage Is for Life," *Journal of Marriage and Family Counseling*, Vol. 1, no. 3 (July 1975): 199–208. (Copyright © 1975 by the American Association for Marriage and Family Therapy.) Quotation reprinted by permission.

47. *Ibid.*

Afterword

This final word to the reader is not intended to summarize the content of the eight preceding chapters. Rather, my intent is to reflect on several themes that have continued to impress themselves on me in my ongoing experience as a marriage and family therapist, as a teacher of marriage and family at the University of Kentucky, and as a marriage partner and parent.

(1) In these pages I have written much about our fantastic and unrealistic romantic expectations as well as our expectations that the partner is to be for us; that is, "be what I want you to be, and do what I want you to do. Don't be for you, be for me. You don't count. I do!" It is these expectations, most of which are very subtle, that lead us to attempt to control our partners so that they will fulfill our expectations. We are usually asking them to make changes for us without our willingness to make changes for them! This is pure selfishness, and if there is no change on this dimension the relationship has little chance of survival. This raises a very serious question: When is it legitimate to request your partner to change, and when is it illegitimate? When does request become implicit demand or ultimatum? Where, if at all, on a continuum between refusal to change and total compliance to the other's request for change, is a reasonable midpoint? No one can answer this question except the couple who

291

ask it. And in the couple's asking and attempted answering is the drama and challenge of negotiation and compromise.

I continue to be discouraged by the number of divorcing couples who claim they are incompatible! *Incompatible* has become a very convenient word! The more dissatisfied partner usually claims their interests are different, their styles are different, and they have little in common. In the name of incompatibility many a marriage is discarded without any real attempt to protect or save it.

Often couples attempt to mold each other in their own image by requesting and demanding change. When the demand for change doesn't work they become angry and attempt even greater control. This leads to more anger and frustration. Finally, in an attempt to protect their own ego, they proclaim to parents, children, and friends, "We were just incompatible."

The only way I have been able to resolve this dilemma, both in relation to my therapy clients and in my personal life, is to attempt to find that point—the bottom line—where one or both of the partners *must* make some effort to change on some absolutely major issue. If this effort fails then divorce would appear to be inevitable. Short of that point I believe most of our attempts to get the other to change are more indicative of our own need to have the other measure up to our expectations. In short, too many of us have never learned to really accept our partner as the person he or she really is. Indeed, a tenet of mature love is "I accept you as you are, and I love you in spite of our differences." This is, of course, the meaning of agape love.

(2) I find it increasingly difficult to hold much hope for any marital relationship wherein one of the partners feels any inequity in the relationship. I am fully aware that the equality emphasized in Chapter 8 is idealistic, and for many couples it is extremely difficult to achieve. Nevertheless, even if there is not a basic equality, there can at least be an equity or a "just" fairness. Without equity many people, especially women, are unwilling to continue in the relationship.

Many people rationalize their own inequalities by appealing to belief systems that endorse the rightness of the male as being the head of the house or the final seat of authority within the marriage and family.[1] What very seldom works, however, is the ongoing and convincing power of rationalization to assuage the feeling of being treated unfairly or unjustly. It is my experience that when this feeling persists in differing degrees over a period of time, either the one-down partner becomes indifferent or the marriage breaks up. If the partner becomes indifferent the relationship is mortally wounded even if the couple stay legally married. Unfortunately for all of us, when partners become indifferent they often become co-conspirators in the establishment of family systems that are dysfunctional, especially in the nurturing and socializing of children and adolescents. That this is the most powerful breeding ground for discontentment, emotional and physical abuse, and family violence is undeniable.

(3) A related thought is concerned with love as being both a feeling and a fact. My students, clients, and other friends know that I am adamantly against equating love with *only* the *feeling* of love. If love is no more than a feeling, albeit a wonderful and exhilarating feeling, then few, if any, marriages will long endure. The worship and veneration of the feeling of love is the essence or hallmark of historical romanticism. Today we are facing a revival of this type of romanticism, which idolizes love as a feeling and idealizes the object of one's love. I have no quarrel with love as a desirable feeling, without which I would not choose to want to be married. The error, however, is in failing to see the other side of the coin. Love may also be a *fact*. The *fact* of love is the glue or the infrastructure that holds the relationship together. The *fact* of love undergirds the commitment to each other and to the future. The *fact* of love enables the partners to feel the emotions of love and anger, joy and frustration, affection and disappointment.

I find that most people know the truth of this, at least in an analogous way, when it is applied to their children. Most people don't go around daily or hourly contemplating their feelings of love for their children. Yet, thankfully, the vast majority are highly committed to their children and to their ongoing welfare. The fact of love is rarely questioned! Yet when it comes to the marital union, we seem to be predisposed to hold the belief that the marriage will succeed or fail based *exclusively* on the continuing experience of the *feeling* of love. I am not suggesting that the feeling of love for one's mate is or should be anything like the feeling of love for one's offspring, but I do wish to point out that in both cases it is the *fact* of love that forms the foundation of the system, motivates the continuing commitment, and thereby creates and nurtures the milieu in which the feeling of love may be experienced and expressed.

(4) Even though I have not addressed it in the pages of this book, one of the things that alarms me the most about the future is the severe stress arising from the current economic situation with high housing costs and threatening inflation. *"Financial pressure on families is worst in decades"* splats the headline: 40 percent of American families are not keeping pace; the economic pressure during the last decade is the worst since World War II; growing numbers of single young people are returning to their parents' home; wives must work if the family is to keep pace.[2] Results of a study by Ruth Berry and Flora Williams point out that for husbands the most important predictor of satisfaction with the quality of their life was satisfaction with their income. The second most important factor was satisfaction with their mate. Wives were just the reverse: Satisfaction with mate came first, and satisfaction with income came second.[3] Either way, the point is well taken that the overall quest for marital satisfaction can never be separated from economic realities.

I believe that marital satisfaction and marital happiness are very distant concepts to those couples who live near the poverty level. The impingement of financial strain is very real, even if one considers no other factors except the cost of housing. Even the smallest of new starter homes cost in the range of $60,000.00 in many parts of the United States and Canada. Assuming a young couple is able to come up with a down payment, the monthly mortgage payment is prohibitive for all except those who are at the higher end of the wage scale for *both* husband and wife. And even at that, the size of the home is such that it militates against private space for children as well as for husbands and wives together with their hobbies, crafts, and other creative pursuits. However, for hundreds of thousands of couples, owning their own home is out of the question! Their stress is at a deeper level dealing with medical costs, food costs, child-care costs, rent costs, and necessary transportation costs. Eating out at a fast-food franchise is as good as it gets for far too many couples in the lower and lower-middle income levels.

(5) In times gone by the folk wisdom had it that one married the partner's family, not just the partner. A strong belief in rugged individualism seems to have cancelled out this old-fashioned belief. At least until the 1980s, when this old belief came full circle. We do marry the family. Not in the old sense of becoming physically involved and engulfed in a lot of sentimentality and pretended togetherness, but in the sense that we can never really get the family out of us. I *am* my family even though I may rebel against my parents and forswear their ways! You *are* your family even though you may not like your family or even though you may have emotionally and/or physically left your family 20 or 30 years ago! This is because we marry the person who is part of the system known as the family of origin. Its patterns, destructive and constructive; its games, good and bad; its rules, overt and covert; its coalitions, positive and negative; its disengagements, its triangulations, its secrets, its conflicts, its cut-offs, and its enmeshments, are all part of me and all part of you. When we marry, two ways of life come clashing together—two living systems attempt to move into each other's territory. And the beginning of wisdom is not only in knowing who I am but in knowing the *family in me*. As I get to know you and become involved with you it will be much easier if you know the *family in you*.

Coda

For over 23 years I have described myself as a *cynic* about marriage, especially referring to the way we kill it by choking it and strangling it to death. But I have always hastened to add that I am a *hopeful cynic!* I continue to hope that we will yet come to our senses and be done with the excessive and outlandish expectations we bring to marriage. I further hope that we will come to some insight about ourselves and how we often seek to impose our will and our reality onto our partner, without any regard for his or her reality or humanity. Lastly, I have a fervent hope that future generations will learn what it means to work at marriage. Older generations have always said that marriage required work, but only in the past three decades have we been able to spell out what this work really looks like; that is, that the work is in learning and using skill in communication, skill in negotiation and compromise, skill in fighting fairly, and skill in self-disclosure. Of course, we do *not* need to make marriage into work in order to work at marriage. In this light we also need to learn to play in marriage, to be playful in our relationship with one another, and even to be playful in the learning of new skills and new ways of being together.

Notes

1. Many Christians wish to uphold the authority of the male over the female by quoting passages such as Colossians 3:18, I Corinthians 11:3, and Titus 2:4-5. These same people *conveniently* overlook I Corinthians 7:4, which emphasizes *reciprocity* between husband and wife.
2. "Report of the Economic Policy Institute," *The Lexington Herald-Leader,* Lexington, Kentucky, November 6, 1988: A5.
3. Ruth E. Berry and Flora L. Williams, "Assessing the Relationship between Quality of Life and Marital and Income Satisfaction: A Path Analytic Approach," *Journal of Marriage and the Family* Vol. 49, no. 1 (Feb 1987):107–116.

Marry Me– Marry My Family: An Outline of General Family Systems Theory and Bowen Family Systems Theory

Overview

Romanticists are basically oblivious to the family from whence comes the beloved of their dreams. From *Romeo and Juliet* to Maria and Tony in *West Side Story*, we tend to downplay the significance of the family from which our partner emerges. We employ defenses such as "You don't marry the family" and "You don't sleep with the family." If the family from which our intended comes has any obvious quirks or habits or peculiarities or "loose screws," we quickly deny any problem. We protest that we are not marrying the family. We are instead marrying one person who has come from this family and who (we may hasten to add) is very different from her/his family. Furthermore, we are very much in love, and this is the only really important thing. As long as we love each other there is nothing we can't deal with or overcome.

The romantic tradition is highly individualized and highly geared to an *intrapsychic* or endogenous (inside forces) way of thinking about the self. This means that the emphasis in our individual development is based more on principles of internal development than on external environment. Sigmund Freud, Arnold Gesell, and Carl Jung were theorists who were intrapsychic in their basic orientation.[1] Neopsychoanalysts are also intrapsychic. Theorists such as Erich Fromm, Karen Horney, Alfred Adler, and Harry Stack Sullivan (even with his emphasis on interpersonal relations) view the human being as being endowed with an internal set of mechanisms that not only program the physiological growth and development but also program the emotional and cognitive areas of development. These mechanisms, which may be somewhat influenced by exogenous (outside) forces, are basically the prime movers in terms of human growth and development.

This way of thinking has given rise to what is often referred to as the "medical model" of human illness. The medical model presumes that sickness, illness, and disease is rooted *within* the person. When this manner of thinking is applied to emotional and cognitive functions we are confronted with what is called emotional illness and mental illness. These are presumed to exist within the individual. Terms such as *neurosis, psychosis, personality disorders, paranoid states, schizophrenia* and all other such labels are products of this intrapsychic or endogenous way of looking at human growth and development.[2] This implies that the *cause* of our problems, our maladies, and our illnesses is within ourselves. Emotional illness or mental illness, unless it is due to physiological impairment of the organism, is due to a certain malfunction within the self. Freud, for example, believed that the internal conflict between the drives of the id and the police functions of the superego was the basis for neurosis. Karen Horney believed that the root of our neurotic anxiety was in the ongoing conflict between the desire to express our basic rage and the unconscious need to repress it out of fear of the consequences if we were to express it.

At the opposite pole from intrapsychic theory is *interpsychic* or exogenous theory. Interpsychic theory is based on the belief that although the human organism is programmed to follow a developmental sequence, much, if not all, of our various differences in personality and ways of being, thinking, and behaving are due to interpersonal experiences including social interaction, sociocultural forces, and familial structure, dynamics, and organization.

In this way of thinking, causation is thought not to be of a direct type where *a* causes *b,* which in turn causes *c.* Rather, behavior is thought to be the end product of multicauses that sometimes are operative only in the presence of other extraneous factors. For example, Bruce and Mary may get along very well until Bruce's mother comes to visit. When Bruce's mother comes to visit there seems to be a lot of tension and conflict between Bruce and Mary, with frequent bouts of fighting and moody withdrawal by Bruce. Bruce's mother may serve as a precipitator or a catalyst, but she may not be thought of as a cause. The causes like somewhere in the whole field of relationships that composed Bruce's early world and upbringing, Mary's early world and upbringing, Bruce's mother's early world and upbringing, the intermediate and later worlds of these people, and their ongoing patterns of interaction and reaction. The same would apply to Bruce's father (even if he is deceased) and to Bruce and Mary's children.

A very rigid intrapsychic position allows little credence to exogenous or interpsychic forces. Likewise, a very rigid interpsychic position allows little credence to endogenous or intrapsychic forces. The position taken here is that neither is solely responsible for human development and behavior. Rather, each builds on and interacts with the other. An example drawn from physical sickness may illustrate this point. Let us say that Jim and Jack are identical twins. They are 23 years old, and they share an apartment. The old flu bug (germ) is going around. Jim gets sick and Jack does not. How do we explain this? Do we say that Jack was simply lucky? Perhaps! Or do we say that for some unknown reason Jack was able to resist the flu germ? But why was he able to resist it? One possible answer could be the amount and type of stress that Jim is presently facing compared to Jack. Right now Jack is very settled in a satisfying job, and other things in his life are reasonably stable. Jim, however, is very unhappy in his employment and is working daily in an environment of great turmoil. He feels very conflicted and torn in his relationships with his boss and some of his co-workers. He is worn down, tired, and may have little resistance.

In this example both the *intra* approach (germ as causative) and the *inter* approach (environmental stress as a contributing factor) play a part in Jim getting the flu and Jack not getting it. This example is a "mini" example of the possible effects of high stress on human behavior and human health. My point of view is that a systems perspective is a very important way of looking at reality. As such it is counterpoint to the traditional endogenous theories of human development and behavior, which rely on a more elementary level cause and effect. My contention is that the intra and the inter are linked together in such a manner as to preclude any absolute determination of which is prior to the other, antecedent to the other, or causative of the other. The relationship of intra to inter is illustrated in Figure A-1.

In terms of marriage, let us say that Jim and Jack, our identical twins, are planning to marry. Both Jim and Jack are fully developed adult human beings, each with a respectable IQ, an internalized sense of values stemming from their upbringing, and a strong sense of identity and sense of self. We might say that each twin is mature and possesses a strong and viable "intra" structure. Each will marry a young lady who brings her own self and "intra" system into the marriage.

Several systems theorists claim that we will usually marry someone who is fairly much on our own level of differentiation, or level of autonomy and personal maturity.[3,4,5] Jim marries Jane and they become a "spouse" system. Jack marries Joyce and they become a "spouse" system. Each couple has

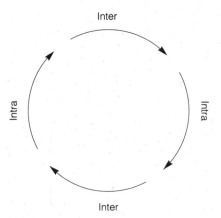

Figure A-1 Inter–Intra Circular Causation

children, and so there are now "children" systems and "parental" systems. As each child grows up he/she develops an intra system that distinguishes him/her from all other people in the world. Each of these grown young people may one day marry and create another spouse system. Hence the intra gives rise to the inter, which gives rise to the intra, which gives rise to the inter and so on to infinity (see Figure A-1 again). *The important point is that there is no beginning and no end.* Neither intra nor inter is antecedent or causative of the other. The entire flow of events is circular, with no point of beginning or point of ending. Systems theory is circular, multicausal, and intercausal.[6]

This means our intra is not something that just developed endogenously within ourselves, but rather developed as we grew up within the cradle of our family system. We are the product of hundreds of millions of human interactions and transactions, patterns and reactions within the boundaries of our immediate families and also of the larger systems in which we participate, such as peer group, school, and work situations.

General Family Systems Theory

There are several varieties of family systems theory. For purposes of discussion I will combine the principles of *structural systems theory, strategic systems theory, experiential systems theory,* and *communication theory* and treat these as each having made significant contribution to the whole, which will be called *general family systems theory.*

General family systems theory is built on several basic principles.

1. *Systems and Subsystems* Every human being is a system, which in turn contains within itself other systems or **subsystems** and at the same time is a subsystem of larger systems. This holds true for the evolutionary process as a

whole. At the lower end of this scale of life there may be decreasing numbers of internal subsystems until we reach the one-cell amoeba. Physics demonstrates that within the world of the atom there are electrons, protons, and the nucleus of the atom. All of these may be thought to be systemic in that they are in constant relation to one another and there is no possibility of the action of one not having some effect on the action or reaction of the other.

The human being, along with the animal species, grows up and develops within a social system of some type. This is usually referred to as a family, although the makeup of the family may have a great variety of forms or structures. Even the human structure of families differs inasmuch as there are nuclear families, stepfamilies, extended families, modified extended families, and joint families (for example, two brothers and their wives and offspring sharing the same living quarters). There are different marital structures such as monogamy, **polygamy** (including polygyny, where one male has two or more female mates, and polyandry, where one female has two or more male mates), and group marriage, wherein every member of the group is considered to be married to every other member of the group.

The principle is that there are systems within systems within systems. Or we could say that every system has within itself a number of subsystems, and these subsystems have within themselves sub-subsystems. If we begin by calling the family the basic system, we still need to be aware that the family exists within even bigger systems such as the clan, the tribe, the town, the city, the state, the nation, the continent of nations, the planet earth, the Solar System, the Milky Way, and the millions of other galaxies. There are also other systems existing side by side with the family system and with which the family is at least partly involved. These include the educational system, the religious or ecclesiastical system, the cultural system, the ethnic system, the socioeconomic system, the racial system, the legal and judicial systems, the political system, and the "nation" system. At the other end of the spectrum we have within our bodies several basic systems, including the vascular and respiratory systems, the nervous system, the digestive system, and the reproductive system. Additionally we have a skeletal system, a muscular system, an emotional system, and a cognitive system. Each of these has numerous subsystems and subsystems within subsystems.

Within the human family (and in some animal families as well) there may arise another type of subsystem. This subsystem is made up of several parts of the greater system who band together into what may be called an alliance or a coalition. (An alliance is a coming together usually for the purpose of fulfilling a task or accomplishing some mission. A coalition is a banding together, usually for the purpose of opposing somebody or something.) For our purpose we will generally consider an alliance to be positive and good and a coalition to be negative and perhaps sinister or devious. An example of an alliance is when a brother and sister join together to earn some extra money so that they can surprise their mother with a special gift on Mother's Day. An example of a coalition is when the male siblings secretly join together to put down or otherwise defeat the female siblings in some manner or in some activity. Often a parent-child coalition exists in order to oppose the other parent. Coalitions may be formed on the basis of gender, age, or interest such as jocks and nonjocks or musicians and nonmusicians. The important point here is that each ongoing coalition is an ongoing subsystem within the family, and this coalition may be extremely powerful in establishing the patterns and behavioral sequences of the family.

2. *The Principle of Nonsummativity: (The Whole Is Greater Than the Sum of Its Parts)* To say that the whole is greater than the sum of its parts is to say that any activity or behavior is more than the simple adding up of all the parts or subparts. This is the principle of **nonsummativity,** and it stems largely from the philosopher Hegel, although it has been known to exist in Eastern religious thought for many centuries. An example of nonsummativity is the family itself because the family is much more than simply the sum of its parts. The family may consist of a father and a mother and four children. Nonsummativity suggests that the family is much more than the sum of these six persons. This family may consist of a spirit, an elan, or a dynamic. This family may embody a code of values and standards by which it judges its quality and even its mission. Similarly, a football team is far more than the sum total of its 11 members. A basketball team is much more than the sum of its five members. In fact, many coaches are evaluated on their ability to mold a prescribed number of persons into a cohesive team. In systems thought it is very important to take account of the whole rather than become narrowed down into the style of the individual parts.

When the whole is kept in sight we are more likely to see the underlying patterns taking place within and between the various players within the system. When the larger picture is kept in focus we are more apt to understand the behavior of the various individuals as they come together or as they distance from one another. We will more likely see the alliances and the coalitions, the advances and the retreats, the parleys and the sorties, the separating and the surrendering.

3. *Circularity* The principle of **circularity** was discussed and illustrated when we described the intra-inter sequence (Figure A-1). The principle of circularity is based on the premise that there is no single and direct cause of an action or behavior. Further, causality is *multi* in the sense that there is never simply one cause of an event or occurrence, but rather numerous contributing factors and circumstances join together and create the context for whatever happens. For example, here is a young man by the name of Phillip

who blames his wife, Betty (holds her responsible), for not being more supportive of him in his professional career. "If only she would support me and encourage me and act interested in what I do I'm sure everything would be just fine." Phillip believes in simple, or "lineal," causality. This means that event *a* causes event *b* in a direct and straightforward manner. Phillip feels (believes) that Betty is not demonstrably supportive of him. Because of this Phil feels let down, unappreciated, and somewhat devalued. He blames Betty, and this has the effect of making matters worse because she counters that if Phillip would only apply himself more rigorously to his work, his sales commissions would be higher and consequently she would not have to spread herself so thin by holding a part-time job in addition to taking care of the two preschool children. Now the chain of causality looks to be longer and more complicated, yet still lineal (see Figure A-2).

Figure A-2 is simple, causative, and lineal. Phillip and Betty get into a fight about Betty being nonsupportive and Phillip being inadequate in sales. Phillip blames Betty for his poor sales record. Betty now adds the dimension of her not having time or energy to be supportive of Phil because she is extremely busy with her part-time job plus the two preschool children. At this point the argument becomes circular (see Figure A-3).

The circularity is in the fact that when Philip does poorly at sales, Betty worries more, works harder at her part-time job, and has less time to spend with the children. These events (c) in turn take time and energy away from Phillip, thus "causing" Phillip to feel that his wife does not appreciate him or support him in this job. Hence, *c* causes *a*. Therefore *a* causes *b* causes *c* causes *a* causes *b* causes *c* causes *a* and so on.

The important point for us to see is that there really is no such thing as simple causality. All causality is complex or "multi." Further, some multi-

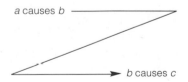

Step *a*: Betty is nonsupportive of Phillip.

Step *b*: Phillip is not doing well in his sales.

Step *c*: Therefore Betty has to work part-time in addition to caring for the children.

Figure A-2 Lineal Causation

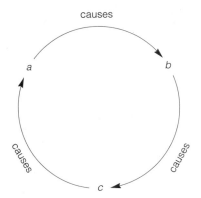

Figure A-3 Circular Causation

causation is lineal and some is circular. Human interactions, especially those imbedded within an intimate system such as the family, are almost always circular.

4. *Change—Reactivity— Perturbation* Closely related to the principle of circularity is the principle of change, reactivity, and perturbation. This simply means that every single event has some effect on the functioning of the larger system. If a part is changed, this will have some effect on the whole. It is impossible for an event or circumstance not to have an effect on the related parts within the system. For every action there is a reaction. For every little perturbance of the system there will be some effect, some change, some reaction, however small this reaction may be.

Whether the perturbance is little Johnny's poor report card or a concern about Suzie's asthma, the effect is there. Perhaps this effect is hard to see. Perhaps no one wants to see it. But it is there nevertheless. And so we are naive when we think that things we do or do not do won't have any effect on anybody else except ourselves. Father's interest in bowling, mother's interest in quilting, son's interest in Little League, and daughter's interest in gymnastics all have an interactive effect on the others within the system and also color the family. They give the system its peculiar tint and hue, its style and fashion, its posture and stature. The effects may be positive as well as negative, pleasing as well as displeasing, rewarding as well as disturbing.

5. *Boundaries* All systems have **boundaries**. Boundaries may be highly visible, such as a fence or a wall, or they may be invisible, such as a rule prohibiting children from entering into Mom and Dad's bedroom whenever the door is shut. Sometimes the physical boundary is a sign or a symbol of the invisible rule (closed doors generally mean "do not enter without knocking"). Boundaries denote the rules that operate within the system. These rules are

concerned with distance and closeness, privacy and publicness, openness and closedness, respectfulness and intrusiveness, engagement and disengagement, rigidity and flexibility.

There are also boundaries around systems and subsystems. The child subsystem within a family may have boundaries around it saying that "no one else may enter." This boundary may be strongly enforced by the children so that it is very difficult for the parents to determine what is going on. In this case the children are involved in a coalition that serves to protect their privacy and/or their secrecy. The spousal subsystem is encompassed by a boundary that serves to keep this subsystem "off-limits" to the children. This boundary generally seals off the private sexual functioning of the husband-wife system from the rest of the world. Another spousal and parental taboo may be the specific revelation of the financial situation of the couple. Hence there are polite boundaries surrounding this information. In some families these boundaries are relaxed as the parents become older, and in other families the parents keep this information to themselves until death or well into old age.

The important thing about boundaries is that they define what behavior is permissible and what is not permissible. Boundaries define what is allowed and what is not allowed. Further, a boundary partially defines the roles that people play. (It can also be said that the role helps define the boundary.) For example, the chief executive officer (CEO) of a big company plays a role. With this role are boundaries pertaining to the hierarchy. Only certain prescribed high-level personnel are given access to cross this boundary. Similarly the Board of Directors has boundaries around it, and only the CEO and those favored by the CEO can have any direct access to the Board.

A family is often organized in a similar manner. In some families the role of father is cordoned off so that only the mother has permission to cross the boundary and to thereby "deal" or "negotiate" with father. The children are not prohibited from approaching mother. Mother is the designated go-between. Most families have boundaries regarding matters of family privacy. "It's OK to talk that way with all of us, but we don't talk that way when others are present." Families usually have etiquette boundaries, personal hygiene boundaries, and toileting boundaries.

The more subtle types of boundaries are often the ones that cause problems within the family. These are the boundaries that prohibit emotional tones within the conversation or the expression of feelings such as love, caring, anger, or annoyance. There are affection boundaries that prevent closeness and warmth and tend to create formality and distance. Father will hug his little boy but will only shake hands with his pubescent son.

Boundaries abound between siblings. Although some "close" siblings will share freely with one another, many will create limits or boundaries that tend to safeguard their thoughts and behaviors. Boundaries are often classified as being rigid, clear and flexible, or loose and permeable.[7] Clear and flexible boundaries are considered the most likely type to produce healthy functioning among intimates. Rigid boundaries often cause problems in creating feelings of closeness, accessibility, and warmth. Loose or permeable boundaries tend to create a sense of nonidentity, since one is deprived of private space. Other people are constantly invading one's own inner territory.

Just as boundaries define roles and roles define boundaries, so also the roles and their boundaries create rules. By tracking down and recording all the rules of a family we can induce with some degree of accuracy the corresponding roles and boundaries. Rules come in all sizes and shapes and degrees of seriousness or sharpness. Rules such as being at home on schoolnights or cleaning one's room on weekends are open rules, clearly spelled out. There may be an unspoken rule that nobody sits in Dad's dining room chair. This is Dad's place, and NO ONE ever presumes to sit there. Or perhaps, like Archie Bunker, no one dares occupy Dad's living room chair if Dad is present. The more lethal rules are those that are *not* clearly enunciated or spelled out.

These are the rules that can completely control and dominate the communication pattern of both marriages and families. For example numerous families have the unspoken rule that sex is always a four-letter word and must never be mentioned in the presence of family members. (Later on in life these kids will say they never received any sex education from their parents. They are wrong. They received a very strong *negative* sex education.) There are often unspoken and unacknowledged (even denied) rules dealing with parental expectation of the children. "We expect you to do your very best." Translated this may mean "we expect you to get all A's." Rules may be communicated subtly and without open discussion. You must excel. You must be a winner. You must go to college. (To girls) You must guard your reputation. Still other rules proclaim that no one will ever stand up to father. No one will ever challenge father in his role as head of the house and final authority in all matters (even if in daily practice everybody attempts to get at father by working on mother).

There are yet even more lethal rules. Touching rules, talking rules, and "cover-up" rules regarding alcoholism, drugs, and affairs can be extremely debilitating to families and marriages. Family secrets and their confidentiality give rise to rules of silence. The proverbial "ghosts in the family closet" must be safeguarded from friend and foe, especially one's neighbors. There are "fighting" rules in families and marriages that serve to defeat healthy functioning. These rules prevent the expression of opinion because even the slightest expression of opinion contrary to "house rules" is considered to be "talking back," impudent, sassing, and disrespectful. Even more lethal are rules that prescribe and proscribe how and what one is to think and believe. This type of rule tells us that we must all believe the same thing whether it be a religious belief, a political belief, or a moral position on some issue such as capital punishment. This type of rule also tells us what we dare not ever believe in, do, or say.

6. *Input, Output, and Systemic Regulation* (**Cybernetics**) The cybernetic principle operating in all systems is homeostatic. Homeostasis is the tendency to return to the balanced condition to which the organism or machine is most accustomed. We could define it as the baseline or the home base. It is an equilibrium. The point of customary status of our body is most likely a sitting position, a standing position, or a normal (for us) walking position. If we go to sleep we may be considered to be in a slowed-down state from our typical homeostasis; if we are jogging or running, swimming, or playing tennis we may be in a stepped-up state from our typical homeostasis. There are all kinds of homeostatic situations and positions. For example, we could be sitting in our living room chair in a typical homeostatic position. As we watch a mystery on television our adrenaline starts to flow, our pulse rate increases, and we may even feel our heart start to palpitate. After the plot is consummated and the show is over our body processes return to their home-base position.

In family systems it is axiomatic that the family will do almost anything to keep the family balanced, that is, in a state of relative homeostasis. Families have an uncanny way of arranging things so that the "rocking boat is stabilized." Even if the basic homeostasis is dysfunctional for one or more members of the family, it is preferable to being out of balance. Consequently families may lives in states of uproar, depression, dysfunction, and chaos because this is normative for them. Little Bobby's bed wetting is not many people's idea of a good time, but this symptom may serve the function of holding the family together, centering everybody's attention on Bobby instead of on the conflictual relationship between Mom and Dad.

Behaviors that take the family further away from its basic homeostasis are called positive **feedback loops.** These behaviors are not called "positive" because they are good rather than bad. The behaviors may well be bad. The designation of positive comes from the fact that a positive loop *increases* the distance (+) away from the basic homeostasis. Negative feedback loops decrease the distance from the basic homeostasis. These behaviors are not called "negative" because they are bad rather than good. The behaviors may well be good. The designation of negative comes from the fact that a negative loop *decreases* the distance ($-$) from the basic homeostasis. Therefore those behaviors that tend to increase the distance of the family away from its basic homeostasis or basic way of being are called positive feedback loops. Those behaviors that tend to bring the family back to its self-defined state of normalcy are called negative feedback loops. Actually there is but one loop with two **feedback arcs** in it. One arc goes outward and away from the baseline or starting point, and the other arc comes inward and toward the baseline or starting point. Figure A-4 illustrates the concept of positive and negative arcs as being the two parts of a single feedback loop.

When I said earlier that families may do uncanny things to restore the homeostasis, it means they will try all kinds of things, conscious and unconscious, to increase the negative feedback arcs in order to return the family to baseline. On the other hand, sometimes families attempt to create positive arcs for some of their members, as when the parents encourage a son to get out of his room and get involved in some activities at school and in the neighborhood. Or perhaps the family is encouraging one of the daughters to go out for the girls' softball team or the math club. These are pushes away from the homeostatic baseline and are considered to be the positive part of the loop. Negative loops are employed much more frequently because they are designed to get people back to baseline. (Get off drugs. Get off alcohol. Quit running with those guys and/or girls. No more cutting school. No more smoking pot.)

Sometimes marriages need a push or encouragement to try new activities and to cultivate new interests. Marriages can go sour. Many do. We

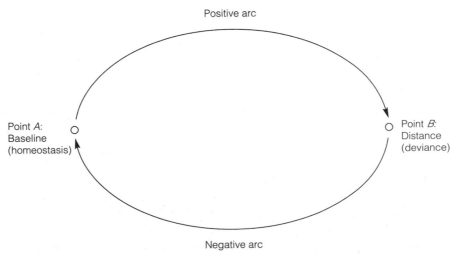

Figure A-4 Feedback Loop

often kill marriage by our lack of inventing new horizons for ourselves and creating new variety. In other words marriages often need positive arcs, activities that move the couple off of the dead-center ho-hum homeostatic baseline. In opposition to this, however, are countless marriages wherein the partners constantly guard against the possibility of either partner moving very far away from baseline. These marriages thrive on resisting change. The emphasis is on creating negative feedback arcs so that nobody dares stray very far from the normal and routine manner of doing things. Behaviors and activities that deviate from the accepted and routinized practice are threatening to the other spouse, and measures are then taken to discourage such behavior.

7. *First- and Second-Order Change* **First-order change** is any change that occurs *within* the system or within the accepted and customary framework for doing things. If son Jeffrey refuses to clean up his room on Saturday, the parents may first withhold allowance until the room is cleaned up. If this doesn't work they may take away TV privileges. Next they may ground Jeffrey. If that fails they may resort to taking away his participation in sports activities at school. All of these are attempts at first-order change. They are "more of the same." Often this is what happens in international relations: Each side in a dispute escalates the same type of punitive behavior in an effort to change the attitude or behavior of the other side. It is more of the same, except each time it is escalated a notch or two. We hit you. You hit us. Then we hit you in retaliation for hitting us. Of course this means you will retaliate against us for retaliating against you. Before you know it we are at war. It is indeed unfortunate, but much marital fighting resembles little children on the playground. I hit you because of something I perceive that you have done to me. Then you retaliate against me and I retaliate against you. Now I retaliate against you for retaliating against me, and so on!

In contrast to first-order, more of the same, efforts at attempting to change behavior and/or attitude, **second-order change** is not an attempt to make changes *within* the existing system. Rather, second-order change is an attempt to change the system itself. Second-order change is a change *of* the system. This means that instead of "more of the same" and repeated attempts to escalate by increasing the same type of moves and threats, a fundamental change is made in the whole system. In short, the rules are changed. The way of looking at the problem is changed. The definition of the situation is changed.

Instead of focusing on what type of punishment Jeffrey will respond to we may do one of several things. We may first ask Jeffrey to devise his own punishment, thus changing the basic dynamic of the stalemate. We may choose to talk to Jeffrey and admit to him that he has defeated us and that henceforth his room is exclusively his responsibility and that no one is ever going to attempt to clean it up. (Of course we must be prepared to carry this through and not back down, even if the room begins to smell.) This is the "OK you win maneuver." We may choose to cease doing any of Jeff's laundry. After all, if Jeffrey wants to be an adult and be responsible for himself without any outside interference, then of course he can take responsibility for his own laundry as well. This is a "tit for tat" reaction that qualifies as a second-order change because it is not in the line of the former direct mode of punishment. Another approach might be to "officially" give Jeffrey *permission* to do with his room as he wishes, since it is his room and no one else's. Or, if Jeffrey's favorite excuse is that he "forgot" to clean up his room or if he is simply a procrastinator, then Mom and Dad can learn to forget things also. Perhaps the parents had better plan to forget to prepare dinner, or to go grocery shopping, or to get milk, or to do laundry. Sometimes strategic parental forgetfulness and procrastination will bring about a needed change in Jeffrey's behavior.

Marriages frequently get bogged down in mutual attempts on the part of the husband and wife to bring about change. Most of these attempts at creating change are first-order attempts. We try more of the same. We try repeatedly to get our husband to talk with us more, to share more. We do this in different ways, but it is still more of the same. We try repeatedly to get our wife or husband to think more like we do, to enjoy more what we enjoy, and to be more interested in the same things we are interested in. We do this all in the "more of the same" model. Wives and husbands admit that for years they have tried repeatedly to change the other but always to no avail. (The more I try to change her the more she is determined to stay the same.) What is needed is not further futile attempts to make changes within the existing pattern but a new effort to change the pattern itself. We may admit to our mate that we have been absolutely defeated in the ongoing attempt to change her. Now you want it to be known that henceforth you will consult her before you do anything. Whenever you *join* the person you were previously fighting you have changed the system. People have long known the strategic value of the "if you can't beat them, join them" approach. This maneuver changes the rules of the encounter. It turns the tables and forces a shift in thinking and in action.

The couple who get caught up in the classic syndrome "I nag because you never pay any attention to me" and "I never pay attention to you because all you do is nag" are caught in a hopeless and useless attempt at first-order change. The system will not change unless something happens to break this pattern that keeps the marriage in homeostatic deadlock. This is what second-order change is all about. It is anything that jars the system off homeostasis. It is anything that changes the lethal pattern. It is anything that turns the tables and forces one or both partners in the marriage to think differently, to act differently, and therefore to react differently. Second-order change shakes up the system. It challenges the futility of doing things in the same old way. If every time the wife nagged the husband would "come onto her" and tell her how much her nagging turns him on and how irresistible she is, then it is likely that the nagging will stop, or at least be tempered. Every time the wife feels that her husband is not paying any attention to her she should tell him how much she appreciates his silence and his willingness to go along with everything she does without any attempt to change her decision or to overrule her. In this maneuver the wife has *reframed* the husband's silence as being an act of loving approval of everything she does. This is an attempt to change the system itself.

8. *Cohesion and Adaptability* **Cohesion** refers to the degree or amount of "stuck-togetherness" of a family. In systems parlance a highly cohesive family is described as being *enmeshed*. A family that lacks cohesion to an extreme degree is called a *disengaged* family. Usually these two extremes are considered to be the opposite ends of a continuum. **Adaptability** refers to the ability of a system to adjust to the new input (events, information, behavior, all kinds of stimuli, developmental changes, crises, and stress) that comes into the system. At one extreme there is a very strong resistance to change, which is called *rigidity*, and at the other extreme is a reaction to change characterized by too much looseness and disorganization, which is known as *chaos*. Rigidity and chaos are at opposite extremes on a continuum.[8] Healthy family and marital functioning avoids the extremes of both enmeshment-disengagement and rigidity-chaos. The ideal point on the continuum between these two sets of extremes is the midpoint, wherein there is a good balance between enmeshment-disengagement and rigidity-chaos. According to the **Circumplex** model of Olsen, Sprenkle, and Russell, these midpoints are characterized by a balance between separation and connectedness on the cohesive dimension and between flexibility and structuredness on the adaptability dimension.[9]

Bowen Family Systems Theory

Bowen family systems theory was named by Bowen because he felt that as long as it was simply called family systems theory it would easily be confused with principles discussed under general family systems theory. Bowen family systems theory stems from the work of Murray Bowen, who created this theory on the basis of evolutionary theory rather than cybernetic theory.[10]

Bowen's most basic premise is that humankind functions primarily at the level of emotional response even though we have the cognitive capacity to overrule and rise above our emotional reactive system. The evolution and development of the human brain is the one thing that sets homo sapiens apart from the rest of animal creation, and yet we seem to be unwilling to use this capacity of cognition to free ourselves from the reactive emotional processes that appear to keep us tied to the emotive and cognitive processes of our families of origin and our parents' and grandparents' families of origin.[11]

Bowen's theory consists of eight basic principles, which will be outlined and described briefly.

1. *Differentiation.* Differentiation is in two parts. The first part refers to the differentiation of our internal cognitive system from our emotional system. (I will henceforth call this *internal* differentiation.) Bowen believes that internal differentiation is very difficult to bring about because it is primarily the result of early familial patterns and reactions. If the child learns to think only along the lines of the familial patterns, he/she will learn to function on the level of emotional reactiveness rather than on the level of his/her own developing critical cognition.

   The second part of differentiation refers to the differentiation of ourselves from the emotional system in which we were raised, that is, our family of origin. (I will henceforth call this *external* differentiation.) This refers to our ability to be separate, inner-directed, and autonomous human beings. Differentiation implies individuality and genuine selfhood (as opposed to a false, or pseudo, self). Genuine selfhood means that we are neither fused with our parental family nor cut off or otherwise disassociated, separated, or alienated from them. Differentiation means that we are our own person, able to be connected emotionally to people whom we love and who love us and yet without being tied or connected to them so as to prevent us from thinking and acting as our own person in all things.

   The concept of differentiation is not exactly identical to the concepts of individuation, separation, or autonomy, but it includes these. Bowen chose to use the word *differentiation* because it was more precise in his schema. It implied a distinguishing without necessarily implying an alienating type of separation or breaking away. It connotes an ability to be a separate functioning person while yet maintaining a connective relationship. It connotes the ability to be a separate emotional self while at the same time being connected with one's family of origin without being drawn into the emotional processes of the family of origin. Bowen used the term the **undifferentiated family ego mass** to describe the state of near-total fusion that characterizes families that appear to be unable to achieve any significant degree of separation and individuality from the emotional processes that dominate familial interaction.

   Bowen estimated the degree of differentiation of a person only after being with that person for many hours of therapy. Bowen created a *Differentiation of Self Scale,* which is a continuum extending from zero degrees of differentiation to 100 degrees of differentiation. There is no test or inventory connected with this scale. It is simply an arbitrary means whereby the position on the scale reflects the degree of differentiation one is estimated to have. Differentiation is of two types, basic and functional. The scale is meant to assess only basic differentiation. Most of us have a higher level of functional differentiation then we do basic differentiation. As long as our stress level is relatively low and things are going well we may appear to have a higher level of differentiation than we really do. The appearance of a higher level is called functional differentiation. The actual level is called basic differentiation.

Those people between 0 and 24 are considered to be highly undifferentiated from their families of origin. This means that they operate or function at a very high level of emotional attachment to the family in terms of beliefs, values, attitudes, prejudices, politics, and religion. These people have trouble thinking for themselves and establishing any degree of selfhood. Persons who are judged to be between 25 and 49 degrees are considered to have achieved much more differentiation than the 0–24 group. The 25–49 group have achieved enough differentiation to be able to function at acceptable societal levels without suffering overwhelming anxiety. These people are able to be separate from their families of origin in a superficial sense, but in a deeper sense they are very much fused with their parents. (Of course there is more difference between a score of 26 and 49 than there is between scores of 24 and 26, even if the 24 and 26 straddle the dividing line between the 0–24 and 25–49 groups. The distance between points on the scale is the most important measure.) People who are assessed to have scores between 50 and 74 are considered to be fairly well differentiated. These people have greater ability to govern and conduct themselves with their cognitive functioning holding a superior position in relation to their emotional functioning. This does not mean these people have cut off their minds from their emotions or that they have alienated themselves from emotionality. It does mean that in terms of beliefs, values, attitudes, politics, and religion they have become their own persons, in terms of both internal differentiation and external differentiation. The group between 75 and 100 are the most healthy in terms of both their basic differentiation and their functional differentiation. People rarely, if ever, reach levels above 90. The area between 90 and 100 is largely fictional. Figure A-5 illustrates Bowen's Differentiation of Self Scale.

Bowen's theory postulates two "selves." There is the *solid self,* which we would define as our authentic self. The solid self is genuine, stands on its own two feet, and holds to its own values, attitudes, and beliefs without making a big deal about being one's own person. There is another self that Bowen calls the *pseudo self.* The pseudo self is a facade, a cover, a mas-

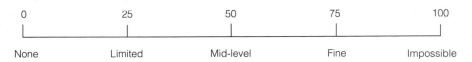

Figure A-5 Bowen's Differentiation of Self Scale

querade. It is a false self in that it puts on a front of pretending to be something it is not. The pseudo self is a type of chameleon, taking on the colors, hues, and tints of whatever group it is presently with. The greater the pseudo self, the greater the degree of undifferentiation. The greater the solid self, the greater the degree of differentiation.

2. *Triangles.* The second basic principle of Bowen family systems theory is the triangle. A triangle is considered to be a third person, object, or force that is drawn into the emotional field existing between a dyad. The dyad, especially the marital dyad, is a very fragile structure. Dyads often do very well until either or both parties of the dyad suffer some degree of stress. Under stress the dyad is immediately threatened. Under stress one or both of the members of the dyad are likely to reach out to a third person, object, or force. The person to whom we will most likely reach out is one of our children. A second common "target" to whom we may reach out is the illicit lover, commonly referred to as an affair. We also may reach out to friends, to pets, to the bottle, to drugs, to food, or to work.

If we think in terms of a field of energy, the dyad under stress finds an alternate place in which to invest its energy. Of course it would be better if the **dyadic** couple would not triangle anybody or anything and would instead seek to invest its energy in working out the problem between the couple. However, if the couple is not able, for whatever reason, to deal with their own relationship, then it is likely that each partner will attempt to invest energy elsewhere. This is most usually done by involving one of the children. This child is then said to have been triangled into the marital system. Either mother or father makes the child into an ally, investing time and energy into the relationship with the child. This is done by telling the child things that the child has no business hearing: things about the other parent; things about how the other parent treats me; things about what the other parent is really like. Or, the child may be forced into the role of a confidant. The child may be forced to play the role of the obliging mate, filling the unfilled needs of either a frustrated mother or father. The triangling parent is always guilty of overinvesting in the life of the child. This means that the child will very likely have great difficulty in differentiating herself/himself from the family of origin.

The triangle is the basic building block of emotional systems. Each triangle has two inside members and one outside member. If the two inside members become strained or stressed, one of the inside members will join with the outside member. This creates a new inside dyad and leaves the former insider on the outside. In a triangle there may be a constant changing of who is an insider and who is on the outside. Both partners of the parental subsystem may be vying for the attention of the child. Whenever the child is connected to either of the parents, the nonconnected parent is considered to be the outsider. Persons who experienced the divorce of their parents, especially when they were teenagers or younger, often experienced a great deal of discomfort and pain when one or the other parent attempted to triangle him/her into the relationship. Sometimes, even years after the divorce, one parent or the other may still attempt to get the young person to "side with me" and "let me tell you what your mother (or father) did to me."

Bowen further introduced the concept of interlocking triangles. An interlocking triangle is when the second inside partner triangles in a different child than the first inside partner. Now there are two children triangled into the parental and spousal subsystem. What are the two children to do? Each is triangled into the parental subsystem, and yet each is a sibling to the other. The two triangles interlock, and the two children become entangled in a web of secrets and confusion. Perhaps each of the children must now bring in another sibling (if available) or a grandparent. The more the child is invested with problems and secrets stemming from the spousal subsystem the greater is the likelihood that the child will be unable to extricate himself or herself from the family of origin's emotional system. Figure A-6 illustrates the basic concept of triangles.

3. *The Nuclear Family Emotional System.* The term **nuclear family emotional system** refers to the emotional processes occurring within a family during a single generation. It is the result of previous generations and the patterns emerging from the ancestors on both the maternal and paternal sides. Of course it will affect the descendants who come after the final dissolution of this particular nuclear family. (All nuclear families eventually dissolve. The dissolution is due either to divorce or to death.)

The emotional process that constitutes the functioning of the nuclear family is threefold. First, the spousal subsystem experiences conflict. If the partners do not know how to handle conflict in a constructive way, the conflict will tend to escalate and the marital system will lose vitality and meaningful intimacy. The marriage that continues to produce conflict will tend to rigidify so that neither partner will ever give in to the other or seek to reach a working compromise. Under such conditions it is likely that the partners will remain relatively undifferentiated, with each employing a great deal of pseudo self in their daily routines and interactions. It is also likely that each partner will want to triangulate one of the children or an

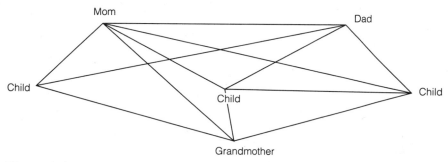

Figure A-6 Triangles

outsider. Some marriages endure for many years with no resolution of the basic conflict, thus producing an emotional climate within the family that is stultifying and repressive.

A second direction the emotional process may take is when one spouse is more likely, for whatever reason, to adapt to the wishes and directives of the more dominant spouse. If this adaptation of the pseudo self of the submissive one to the pseudo self of the dominant one becomes the predominating pattern, the submissive one is very likely to become dysfunctional at the slightest hint of *severe* stress or **crisis**. The dysfunctional mate may become physically ill, emotionally unstable, psychotic, neurotic, phobic, hypochondriacal, or alcoholic or may simply employ an acting-out behavior that is irresponsible and perhaps dangerous.

There is an extreme imbalance between the overfunctioning spouse and the underfunctioning spouse, and the resulting situation colors and dominates the entire familial interaction process. Unfortunately the spouse who adapts in order to keep harmony in the relationship is the one who is at greater risk of becoming dysfunctional. This is because the more one attempts to adapt, the less one retains any degree of solid self. Another way of saying this is that the one who is always attempting to keep peace in the family is often the one who has made the most internal compromises with herself/himself and consequently has increasingly lost hold of her/his own identity and sense of self.

A third possibility in the formation and development of the nuclear family emotional system is that the parents will triangle one or more of the children and project on them the unresolved anxiety that exists with and between the parents. This is called the **family projection process** and is described as a separate process in its own right.

Any of these three processes may be employed at different times, at the same time, or in any combination. If the marital relationship is burdened with a heavy amount of anxiety, this anxiety may be invested in all three outlets: spousal conflict, mate dysfunction, or projection onto the children. Some marriages have very little overt conflict and no mate dysfunction, but the children are terribly overburdened with the projection of parental anxiety.

4. *Family Projection Process.* The family projection process, present in most families to at least a minimal degree, is the mechanism by which the family functioning and interactive processes are passed down from generation to generation. Projection in the very early years revolves more around the mother than the father for no reason other than the facts of conception, gestation, and parturition. The mother's anxiety pertaining to herself, to her infant child, and to the insecurity of life itself is projected onto the infant in the form of overprotectiveness, oversolicitousness, and generally intrusive behavior. The father is involved in the projective process to the extent that the father attempts to be supportive of the mother in her relation to the growing infant. After infancy both parents may be involved equally in the projection process or the father may be involved more than the mother.

The greater the undifferentiation and pseudo self of the parents, the greater will be the possibility of triangling in one of the children (the most vulnerable) to be the target of the projection process. This child will have little likelihood of becoming differentiated to a greater degree than his/her parents. More than likely the child will be less differentiated than his/her mother and father. The sisters and brothers of the "projected child" may escape the projective process and triangulation. This may have to do with birth order, learned abilities in the avoidance and/or resistance to becoming triangled, or other personality factors. Most assuredly, one key reason other children from the same family may escape the triangling and projective processes is because another one of the children has already been picked out to be the target.

Escape is not always possible, especially if there is a sufficient reservoir of parental anxiety to be spread among the children. Bowen states "It focuses first on one child. If the amount is too great for that child, the process will select others for lesser degrees of involvement. There are families in which the amount of undifferentiation is so great it can seriously impair most of the children. . . . There is so much disorder and chaos in these families, it is difficult to see the orderly steps in the process."[12]

5. *Emotional Cut-Off.* The **emotional cut-off** refers to the manner in which a person handles unresolved emotional attachment to his/her parents. If the individual in question is able to achieve a fairly good level of differentiation from the parents, then there will be no need for an emotional cut-off. Differentiation includes, but is not limited to, the ability to be one's own person or self; to be in charge of one's own thoughts, feelings, and behav-

iors; and to be able to be clear in stating what one believes and what values one espouses for oneself.

Emotional cut-off can be mild or extreme. In its most extreme it is usually characterized by an explosion of some type in relation to one's parents and then a sharp and sudden exit to another domicile, another city, or a distant state. The person who is cutting off almost always thinks the solution is emotional separation and emotional distance. This emotional distance is aided and abetted by geographical distance. Unfortunately this distance does nothing to change one's degree of differentiation. The distancer remains as emotionally tied and emotionally dependent as he/she was prior to the cut-off. What is worse, when the cut-off takes place it is increasingly likely that the unfinished business and the unresolved issues that existed between one's parents and oneself will continue to wreak havoc in one's future relationships, especially love and marital relationships as well as relationships with one's future offspring. Cut-offs are always emotional but are not necessarily always physical. When there is emotional cut-off without physical cut-off there may remain a perfunctory ritualized contact with little meaningful involvement or communication.

Emotional cut-off has always been a characteristic of the classical Western family, but it has become more blatant in recent years, reaching a crescendo with the flower children of the late 1960s and early 1970s. In the name of becoming "free" and "independent," they rebelled against the conformity of the establishment only to conform to a new kind of social establishment. In their new estate of conformity to their social peers they were no more emotionally free and autonomous than they were prior to their rebellion.

Concerning this point Bowen has said: "The sameness of polarized opposites in emotional situations has led me to define revolution as a convulsion that prevents change. It is relationship-oriented energy that goes back and forth on the same points, the issue on each side being determined by the position of the other; *neither is capable of a position not determined by the other.*"[13] (Italics added for emphasis.) Thus we have the position of the proverbial parent saying black is black and the rebelling offspring saying that black is white. Neither is free of the other. Although we would describe the relationship as conflictual, this does not change the fact that the two persons are deeply fused. Most people make the mistake of thinking that conflict implies distance and separation. On the contrary, conflict often serves to bind people together in a state of enmeshment and dependency.

6. *Multigenerational transmission process.* The **multigenerational transmission process** is very similar to the nuclear family emotional system except that now the emphasis is on both the *ascending* and *descending* generations. The

nuclear family emotional system emphasized marital conflict, a dysfunctional spouse, and a targeted child who became triangled and on whom the parental projection focused. When this projection is acted out repeatedly from generation to generation, there is established a pattern of markedly low differentiation.

Bowen believes that at least three generations are involved in the creation of schizophrenia. Familial patterns that are marked by personality disorders and degrees of neurotic behavior take fewer generations. In any case the transmission process usually focuses on one child. This child grows up with a differentiation level that is lower than its parents and perhaps significantly lower than its siblings. When this child marries, he/she will likely marry someone whose level of differentiation is fairly similar. This couple will now have offspring, and if there is more than one child it is likely that all but one of the children will achieve a level of differentiation significantly higher than the targeted child. A pyramid-type effect takes place, and each generation produces one child who is significantly lower in differentiation than its siblings. This child becomes the transmitting agent to the next descending generation and so forth over many generations. Increasingly we have the phenomenon of the *undifferentiated family ego mass.*

The same process can operate in reverse from the perspective of a relatively highly differentiated family. One of the children becomes triangled in a more severe and thorough manner. This child fails to achieve the level of differentiation of either its parents or its siblings. When this child marries it will be to someone with a fairly similar level of differentiation. This couple will then likely target one of their children who in turn will marry on a similar level and continue to transmit the downward pattern. Bowen believes that our level of *basic* differentiation is largely determined by the time we leave the parental family and attempt a life of our own.[14]

7. *Sibling position.* Bowen believes that sibling position is crucial in the determination of degree of a person's differentiation. Bowen embraced the research and theoretical premises of Walter Toman.[15] Briefly stated, the birth-order position, parental environment, and important personality characteristics combine to make a child more or less vulnerable to being triangled and the object of the family projection process. Factors such as spacing and distance between children, whether one is an "afterthought," and whether one is a "replacement" child are also very important in determining vulnerability to triangulation and projection.

The value of Toman's work is in its contribution to creating a family profile. There are patterns that seem to repeat themselves frequently among first borns, second-born child but first-born male, middle children, last borns, and only children. There is no claim that these patterns are firm and established principles, but they do serve the function of permitting certain "presumptions" about the family environment. These presumptions are then checked out as one proceeds to do therapy with the family or individuals within the family.[16]

8. *Societal regression.* Societal regression is a later addition to Bowen's theory, which applies the same basic concept of differentiation to the society as a whole. Societies are more or less differentiated, depending on the degree of stress and anxiety existing within that society or societies in general. The more that the institutions within the social order regress to a type of functioning that is based on unexamined tradition, custom, and belief, the lower will be the level of basic differentiation within the social order. Likewise, there often arises a "band aid" effort in treating the more difficult problems of the social order. This in turn may relieve the immediate symptom and yet create far greater problems in the long run. Just as a family can use triangulation and projection, so also a social order can create scapegoats and targets for the ensuing projection. In short, society can be thought of as an emotional system with the same system properties as a family. The degree of differentiation within the social order depends on the ability of the elected executives, legislators, and leaders of government agencies to use the cognitive function in directing and monitoring the functions of the social order. Undifferentiated leaders and elected officials tend to appeal to the undifferentiated citizen. The end result could be an *undifferentiated societal ego mass.*

Summary

This appendix has outlined the two major types of family systems theory. General family systems theory incorporates principles that arise from structural systems theory, strategic systems theory, cybernetics, and communication theory. These several different branches of general systems thinking have tended to complement one another and to meld into one another. Although there are distinct differences, only the basic commonalities were emphasized.

Bowen family systems theory is a distinctly different set of principles. Bowen's theory is based on the evolutionary nature of homo sapiens as an emotional creature with a superior cognitive ability. This does not mean that our feelings, which are a derivative of our emotional system, are not bona fide, genuine, and honorable. When people talk about feelings they generally mean the ability to feel joy, pain, anger, hurt, sorrow, sadness, elation, pleasure, excitement, and, of course, love. Bowen's theory is not attempting to do away with these emotional feelings. In fact, the owning of these feelings and the expression of these feelings is very important.

Bowen's theory is postulated on the premise that if we do not use our cognitive ability to separate ourselves from the unthought-out domain of *emotional binding* that is peculiar to the family of origin, we will not be able to be our own solid self with the capacity to be ourselves, to think for ourselves, and to act as free persons. This process begins within ourselves and carries over to our family of origin. It is less concerned with feelings and more concerned with the establishment of our own beliefs, attitudes, and values. The goal of this process is the mature person who can remain emotionally connected to his/her family of origin and yet maintain the unique ability of homo sapiens to act, think, and feel as an authentic (solid) self rather than as a fused pseudo self. This requires an ability to avoid being triangulated, an ability to refuse to allow others to place value on you, and an ability to believe in yourself and trust in yourself while at the same time remaining emotionally connected to those whom you love.

Notes

1. Michael Green, *Theories of Human Development* (New Jersey: Prentice-Hall, 1989), 27–31.
2. American Psychiatric Association, *Diagnostic and Statistical Manual of Mental Disorders,* 3rd ed. (Washington, D. C., APA, 1980).
3. Murray Bowen, *Family Therapy in Clinical Practice* (New York: Jason Aronson, Inc., 1978), 52, 91–92.
4. Augustus Napier and Carl Whitaker, *The Family Crucible* (New York: Harper & Row, 1978). Chapter 8, "Toward Marriage."
5. Robin Skynner and John Cleese, *Families and How to Survive Them* (New York: Oxford University Press, 1983). Chapter 1, 15–65.
6. Michael P. Nichols, *The Self in the System* (New York: Brunner/Mazel, 1987). (Nichols makes a good case for integration of both intra and inter dynamics.)
7. Salvador Minuchin, *Families and Family Therapy* (Cambridge: Harvard University Press, 1974). Chapter 3, 46–66.
8. Olson, D. H.; D. Sprenkle, and C. S. Russell, "Circumplex Model of Marital and Family Systems: VI Theoretical Update," *Family Process,* Vol. 22, no. 1 (Mar 1983): 69–83.
9. *Ibid.*
10. *Op. cit.,* Bowen.
11. Michael Kerr and Murray Bowen, *Family Evaluation* (New York: W. W. Norton, 1988), 89–94.
12. *Op. cit.,* Bowen, 380.
13. *Op. cit.,* Bowen, 368.
14. *Op. cit.,* Bowen, 371.
15. Walter Toman, *Family Constellation* (New York: Springer, 1961).
16. *Op. cit.,* Bowen, 385, 477.

Appendix B

Marital Expectations Inventory

When an individual responds to the following items the result will be a profile of his or her marital expectations. When partners compare their expectations and then negotiate the differences the result may serve as an ongoing and open-ended marital agreement.

Directions: Please respond to each item by using *several words* or a *phrase* to describe what you expect regarding the item under consideration. Feel free to add items that are not included here.

In My Marriage, I Expect:

Provisions for Revision and Renewal of Marriage: _____

Provisions for Dissolution of Marriage: _____

Distribution of Power: _____

Decision Making: _____

Division of Household Labor: _____

Her Employment: _____

His Employment: _____

Financial Responsibility: _____

Allocation of Funds (His/Hers/Ours): _____

Religious Beliefs and Practices: _____

Educational Goals (His/Hers): _____

Methods and Responsibility for Birth Control: _____

Attitude Toward Unwanted Pregnancy: _____

If There Are to Be Children:

    Intended Number of Children: _____

    Intended Spacing of Children: _____

    Division of Labor for Child Care: _____

    Discipline of Children: _____

    Children's Religious Education: _____

    Children's Higher Education: _____

Sexual Relations:

    Frequency: _____

    Equality of Quality: _____

    Mutual Consent or Unilateral Request: _____

Privacy Expectations: _____

Communication Expectations: _____

Enrichment Expectations: _____

Growth Expectations: _____

Handling of Conflict and Anger:

    Method of Conflict Resolution: _____

    Attitude Toward Expression of Negative Feelings: _____

    Freedom to Be Positively Critical of Each Other: _____

Vacations:

    Couple Only: _____

    Including Children: _____

    Separate: _____

Your Definition of Equality: _____

Your Definition of Commitment: _____

Your Definition of Trust: _____

Your Definition of Fidelity: _____

Appendix C

Ideas and Options for the Wedding Service

The wording of the wedding service is more meaningful if it is based on the principles agreed on in the Marital Expectations Inventory (Appendix B). The wording should be more general than the Expectations Inventory and directly related to the couple's intentions regarding their mutual commitment and definition of their relationship. The service that follows is entirely suggestive, and it is hoped that the reader will feel free to adapt. It is based on the content and thought presented in *Illusion and Disillusion*.

Opening Statement

Friends and family of _____ and _____, we are gathered together today for the purpose of sharing the joy that has led _____ and _____ to want to make a public statement about their relationship. _____ and _____ do not wish to be given away or to be taken in marriage, but they do desire your thoughts, prayers, and blessings as they make their promises to each other. They have given a great deal of thought as to whether or not they have sufficient maturity and commitment to share their lives in marriage. What they do and say here in our presence reflects the honesty and integrity of their decision and the genuine love they bring to it.

(Here may be inserted music, poetry, Scripture, a reading, or a prayer. One, or at most two, items could be used here.)

Song

Personally Meaningful Poem or Reading

Scripture Reading

Prayer

(Suggested:)

Eternal God, Thou who art the source of creation, in whom we live and move and have our being, we express our feelings of joy and happiness on this occasion, giving thanks that _____ and _____ have experienced a fulfillment in themselves through their shared love and commitment to each other.

We celebrate with them as they seek to honor themselves by creating a solid foundation for their life together, based on their trust in each other as friends, companions, and lovers. May they be strengthened in their resolve to deal honestly with the issues that so frequently separate and divide; may they learn that pain and hurt are often the price of joy and love; may they learn that vulnerability to each other is the secret of growth and true intimacy; may they discover that to close themselves off from each other, or to shield and protect themselves from each other, is to destroy their spontaneity and openness to each other.

May they grow in the experience of sharing their deepest feelings with each other, feelings of anger and hurt, rejection and resentment, knowing that this makes possible a depth of oneness and keeps open the pathway of forgiveness and reconciliation. May they learn to drink of the spirit of inner growth whereby they serve each other in love and devotion even as they continue to nourish their own life spirit.

May they grow together rather than apart. May they strengthen one another rather than weaken one another. May one be strong when the other is weak. May they learn that true peace is not the absence of conflict but its resolution.

May they learn that giving in to the other is not the same as negotiation and compromise.

And even while we know and believe that their future joy and fulfillment rests squarely on their own shoulders, we ask this prayer in Thy name (in the name of Jesus) (the source of life itself). Amen.

(At this point in the service the bride and groom may either respond to questions or make first-person statements to each other. These statements constitute the primary vows. The personal meaning of the ceremony is in the honest self-expression of the intentions, promises, and commitment of the bride and groom to each other. Therefore, the primary vows may be far more meaningful if they are original statements of the bride and groom. The primary vows given below are only intended to be suggestive.)

Exchange of Vows

Bride: I commit myself to my own growth and well-being, to your growth and well-being, and to our shared relationship. With this promise I willingly commit myself to the continued nurturance of our love and of our shared life together.

I commit myself to honesty in expression of my feelings and thoughts and to true openness in communication.

I commit myself to equality between us in all things, to a true balance of power and authority, and to the constructive resolution of conflict.

My intention is to strive for an enduring relationship, and I promise to safeguard this intention of permanence by striving for fidelity to you in the goals and purposes we have defined for ourselves.

Groom: (May repeat the same words.)

A Question and Charge to the Family and Friends

We, the witnesses of these pledges, also have a responsibility to _____ and _____. It is our task to support them in their resolve, to refrain from unsolicited advice and comment, to encourage and sustain them in times of trouble and pain, to rejoice with them in times of joy.

If you, the family and friends of _____ and
_____, concur with these thoughts will you please indi-
cate your commitment to them by saying "I do."

Family and Friends respond: I do.

Exchange of Rings

To the Groom: "What token of this commitment do you choose to give? (The
    ring is presented.)
Groom: (as he places the ring on the bride's finger) This ring I give you in pledge
    of my commitment to you in our relationship.

(This procedure may then be reversed, Bride to Groom.)

(Here may be included another poem, musical selection, or reading. Alternatives not used earlier may be included here.)

Concluding Statement: A Charge to the Bride and Groom

The union of _____ and _____ is
now publicly recognized. We, your friends and families, charge you both to
keep faith in the commitment of intentions that you have professed in our
presence. We charge you to the task of remaining faithful to your own goals and
purposes. We charge you to weigh your expectations, that they may be realistic
and honest. We charge you to look deeply within yourselves before you seek to
place responsibility on the other. We charge you to honor and cherish one
another as you grow and learn together. May yours be the experience of true
peace and fulfillment as you open yourselves to the responsibilities, the privileges, and the joys of life together.

Benediction

(Three alternatives follow.)

Go in peace: And may no person deter you from your mutual quest. Amen.

or

May (the God of Abraham) (the God of Jesus who was called the Christ) bless you and keep you; may grace be upon you; and as Creators with the Creator may you find joy and peace. Amen.

or

May the God of Peace be with you. Amen.

Glossary

Acting out. A Freudian term (widely accepted even by non-Freudians) indicating that unresolved inner feelings, frustrations, and conflicts play through the individual in such a way that the person's behavior becomes an outlet for the unresolved material.

Aestheticism. The cult of beauty and good taste; aestheticism may refer to the pursuit, cultivation, and enjoyment of sex along lines of perceived beauty wherein sex is embraced through the purifying effect of love, devotion, and affection.

Affect. Emotion; feeling; affective level: degree of emotional response to a stimulus.

Agape. A word used by the ancient Greeks to describe a type of love that may be uncarned but is given unconditionally. It is a love that does not demand reciprocity but is given "in spite of" faults or undesirable acts by the other. This generous, unselfish concept of love is shared by many religions.

Aggression. An act or movement against someone or something; may be a series of hostile acts directed toward a person, oneself, or an object. Aggression is often used to violate another, in contrast to assertion, which is taking a stand to protect oneself.

Amoral. Without moral implication; outside the bounds of that to which moral judgments apply.

328

Anal phase. Freud's second phase of development, which is characterized by the child's concern and attention to the anus and toileting habits. Anal personality traits are considered to be cleanliness, obstinacy, orderliness, and a desire to hold onto and possess.

Androgyny. Incorporation into one's sense of self both the traditional feminine characteristics and traits and the traditional masculine characteristics and traits. Androgyny does not imply bisexuality or a half-masculine and half-feminine identity.

Anxiety. A response to a stimulus, sometimes identifiable and sometimes unidentifiable. Normal anxiety is in proportion to the stimulus severity. Abnormal anxiety or neurotic anxiety is out of proportion to the severity of the stimulus. Anxiety is usually indicative of a threat to one's self.

Autonomy. Self-government; pertaining to an inner psychic state wherein an individual believes in and obeys his or her own inner code of ethics and life-style. Usually it refers to one who neither uses traditional authority in control of others nor allows others authority and control over oneself.

Bind. A situation, usually stressful, wherein an individual is caught or placed in an unwelcome dilemma. The "bound" person often feels trapped, but on rational assessment there is reasonable hope for satisfactory solution. (See Double bind.)

Bisexuality. The sexuality of an individual who is attracted to both sexes and who may or may not participate in a physical sexual relationship with either sex.

Boundaries. Primarily a systems theory term referring to lines of demarcation between individuals, systems, and subsystems. If boundaries are weak they are easily crossed and permeable. If boundaries are rigid they are inflexible. The ideal boundary is both clear and flexible, neither permeable nor rigid.

Circularity, or circular causality. A theory of causation whereby successive causes are circular: *a* causes *b* causes *c*, which in turn causes *a*, which causes *b*, which causes *c*, which causes *a*. That is, partner *a* nags at partner *b* because partner *b* seems to be so aloof, withdrawn, and inexpressive. This causes partner *b* to withdraw further and to become more quiet and inexpressive, which then has the effect of causing partner *a* to nag even more. Which came first is irrelevant. The reality is that they are dancing a circular dance, each pushing the other's button.

Circumplex model. In family systems theory the Circumplex model derived from the work of Olson, Sprenkle, and Russell. This is a curvilinear model where the ideal is the midway point on a horizontal axis between enmeshment and disengagement on the measure of cohesion and the midway point on a vertical axis between rigidity and chaos on the adaptability dimension. This means that ideal family functioning is neither enmeshed nor disengaged on the cohesion dimension and neither rigid nor chaotic on the adaptability dimension.

Cohesion. A term used to denote one axis of the Circumplex model. Cohesion is the degree of separateness versus togetherness of a dyad or a family. Extreme togetherness is called enmeshment and extreme separateness is call disengagement.

Compromise. See Conflict resolution.

Concubinage. The practice of keeping a concubine: a woman who shares sexual intimacies with a man; or, in some societies, a secondary wife who enjoys protection and support but who lacks the status of a primary wife.

Configuration. An arrangement of parts to create a blending without conflict. In psychology, a configuration is often called a gestalt.

Conflict. Arises when an individual is simultaneously attracted to and repulsed by a person or situation. The assumption is that individuals are frequently caught between opposing forces; one force may come from within the individual and the other from another person or society in general, or both opposing forces may come from within the individual.

Conflict resolution. The process by which individuals in a relationship arrive at a decision that is satisfactory to both; a mutual joint outcome is reached.

Congruent. One is congruent when one's feelings and what one is experiencing are not in conflict with one's behavior and what one is communicating.

Construct. Several definitions that fit together to convey a thought system or the roots of a theoretical idea.

Contract. A mutually agreed on position (formal or informal; written or oral) that clearly states the privileges and obligations of two or more persons and/or groups to each other. The duration of a contract may be open-ended or fixed.

Crisis. A heightening of the severity of a problem to such an extent that the prior level of organization and adjustment no longer operates. It is a time during which an individual is susceptible to change and may progress or regress. Whether or not something is defined as a crisis depends on the individual's perception of the situation, prior experience in handling similar situations, and resources available to deal with the situation.

Cultural norm. An accepted standard of behavior and values in a given society.

Culture. The totality of norms, customs, and experiences in a given society that direct the way members in the society live.

Cybernetics. Refers to the regulation of a system. As such, cybernetics is concerned with communications, control processes, and the regulation of information within a living system. Cybernetics incorporates such terms as *homeostasis, input, output,* and *feedback loops.*

Cybernetics of cybernetics. A term referring to second-order cybernetics, which is the involvement of the observer of a system in the dynamics of the system itself. First-order cybernetics is the study of the observed phenomenon; second-order cybernetics is the subjective interjection of the observer becoming involved in what is being observed. A subjective involvement in what we observe and perceive.

Deductive differentiation. The perception and consequential interpretation of new experience in a closed, narrow, and conservative manner, which in turn grounds one's sense of self and identity in a rather limited and constricted frame of reference. (See Inductive differentiation.)

Dependency. Psychologically, a term referring to an emotional reliance on a person or thing that is in excess of what is considered normal or rational. Dependency is generally viewed as undesirable because of the fact that it weakens the self-reliance of the individual, thus contributing to weak ego and identity, with precarious levels of self-esteem.

Depth leveling. The process of leveling one's deepest and innermost thoughts and feelings; honest self-disclosure that is nonsadistic in nature and intent and enables intimates to be fully informed about each other's deepest and most powerful thoughts and feelings. (See Leveling.)

Dialogue. Occurs when one communicates one's own thoughts and feelings openly and honestly and allows the other person to speak his or her thoughts and feelings openly and honestly without trying to predict, control, or manipulate the other.

Differentiation of self. A term used by Murray Bowen to connote the degree of one's separate identity from one's family while still maintaining emotional contact with that family. It is the ability to be one's own self or one's own person while remaining in meaningful relationship with others within the same emotional system. It is not disengagement or separation from the system. The opposite of differentiation is fusion.

Double bind. A situation wherein an individual, family, or group is placed between two distinct, untenable, and unattractive alternatives so that regardless of which alternative is chosen, the subject is in a no-win situation. (See Bind.)

Dyadic. A term used to pertain to a couple or twosome. Whenever the essential components are in a one-to-one relationship it may be referred to as a dyadic relationship.

Egalitarian. Pertaining to a state of equality; thus, an equalitarian relationship wherein the participants are equals may be referred to as egalitarian.

Egocentricity. The state of being self-centered.

Ego ideal. An idealized image of oneself that is indicative of the way one would like to be; the ideal self; the fantasied self-image as contrasted with the actual self-image.

Ego investment. An investment of self in something, such as investing time in a relationship or making a commitment to a course of study.

Emotional cut-off. A term from Bowen family systems theory indicating a break between two persons within an intimate system who no longer relate to each other in any meaningful manner; that is, all contact is perfunctory and ritualistic at best.

Enmeshment. A term indicating the degree of cohesion within a family system. *Enmeshment* is the term employed in the Circumplex model as being extreme emotional togetherness as compared to disengagement, which is extreme emotional separation.

Equalitarian. A belief in absolute equality among human beings; refers here to equality between the sexes without reservation, condescension, or mental equivocation.

Equalitarian monogamy. In contrast to patriarchal monogamy, equalitarian monogamy indicates an equal balance of power and authority between husband and wife.

Eros. Traditionally, the physical love between man and woman; specifically, that type of love characterized by passion, tenderness, and intimacy involving a desire to give as well as receive, to procreate, to create, to enhance the partner's humanity.

Erotic. Typically refers to feelings or emotions stimulated by or associated with sexual sensations.

Ethical dynamics. The forces that determine or govern one's moral values and choices.

Exchange theory. A conceptual framework and a set of theoretical principles attempting to explain the relationship between intimates on the basis of costs and rewards. Exchange, as the term implies, indicates that all behavior is based on a quid pro quo, something for something, and if the exchange is severely out of balance the relationship will be in jeopardy.

Existential. Concerning the nature and meaning of human existence.

Externalize. To unlearn something previously learned. Usually externalization is the attempt to unlearn deeply rooted material that we absorbed as true and accurate when we were quite young but that we now claim to be invalid. (See Internalize.)

Extrinsic value. Refers to value not inherent in the object but resulting from a particular attitude present in the person viewing or experiencing the object.

Family of orientation or origin. The family composed of an individual's parents and siblings; usually the intimate unit into which one is born and raised.

Family of procreation. The family composed of an individual's spouse and children.

Family projection process. The process by which the parental partners deal with their conflict with each other by projecting their problems and the emotional field onto the children. The projective process may involve one or more children who become triangled into the unresolved conflict between mother and father.

Family systems theory. A way of conceptualizing and studying the family based on the idea of circular impact rather than simple linear cause and effect. The family as a system is a series of acting and reacting forces, each having influence on all the other members of the system.

Family systems therapy. The process of therapy with a family of two or more by approaching the problematic situation and the underlying dynamics from a systemic point of view. This involves an appreciation for the circularity of mutual impact rather than a simple linear cause and effect.

Fantasy. Occurs when an individual imagines an object or event that is wish-fulfilling in concrete images, whether or not the object or event actually exists.

Feedback arc. A feedback loop has two arcs, the positive and the negative. The positive arc takes the system away from homeostasis, and the negative arc brings the system back to homeostasis. (See Feedback loop.)

Feedback loop. A communication and/or behavioral loop whereby the information fed into the system is designed to either take the system away from home-base homeostasis (positive arc) or bring the system back to its home-base homeostasis (negative arc). When the positive arc is combined with the negative arc there is a completed feedback loop. (See Feedback arc.)

Feminist. A person who advocates social change and legal change that will lead to economic, social, and political equality of the sexes.

Fidelity. Traditionally, a sexual loyalty to one's mate, hence sexual exclusivity. Fidelity may refer to a more inclusive faithfulness or loyalty extending far beyond the sexual realm.

First-order change. A change within the system. First-order change is considered to be a change that amounts to "more of the same," that is, change that really is no different than previous attempts at change. First-order change has little impact on changing the system itself, although it can make needed changes within the existing system. (See Second-order change.)

Game. (in interpersonal relations) A fraudulent interaction involving the manipulation of another person in order to receive a payoff.

Gender. Used to differentiate male and female; denotes the biological/physiological sex of a person or animal.

Genogram. A graphic or pictorial way of describing people and their relationship within a family system. A genogram usually shows a three-generation genealogy plus historical and biographical notes such as marriage, divorce, and separation; distance or closeness; employment; abandonment.

Gestalt. A pattern or configuration.

Gunnysacking. The collecting of alleged offenses and metaphorically putting them into a huge sack. Later, when the sack is full, a slight or trivial offense may cause such overload that the sack is methodically emptied by throwing each alleged offense back at the offending person. Gunnysacking is always a dirty fight technique because it does not bring alleged offenses to immediate closure.

Hedonism. A philosophy that a person seeks or should seek the most pleasurable things in life. In psychology, the view that to experience pleasure is the major force that motivates human behavior.

Hedonistic. Referring to hedonism, a philosophy of pleasure for its own sake; in psychology, the pursuit of pleasure as a motivational force in human behavior.

Heterosexual. Pertaining to relationships and associations between the male sex and the female sex. Usually the term refers to preferences in regard to sexual expression and/or desire.

Homeostasis. The tendency of a system to be at rest by being in balance. Homeostasis in itself is neither right nor wrong, good nor bad. Often homeostasis is maintained within a family system by the use of unwholesome maneuvers and negative dicta, rules, and sanctions.

Homosexual. Pertaining to relationships and associations between members of the same sex. Usually the term refers to preference in regard to sexual expression and/or desire. Although *homosexual* is a correct term for both male-male and female-female relationships, the word *lesbian* refers exclusively to female homosexuals.

Humanistic psychology. A school of thought that views humans as holistic beings capable of free choice, spontaneity, creativity, and moving toward self-actualization.

Human potential. A term that gained public acceptance in the 1960s and early 1970s, referring to the need for increased human fulfillment, that is, self-fulfillment, self-actualization, and self-realization. The human potential movement encompasses many and varied kinds of emphasis, such as encounter groups, sensitivity training, and the increase of human awareness.

Id. Sexual energy and sexual drive; a shortened form of libido.

Identity. The concept or image one has of oneself; how one interprets oneself and/or defines oneself. Being one's unique self with the accompanying feeling of knowing this self. A strong or healthy identity integrates the personality, and a weak identity lacks a unified sense of self.

Illegitimate ego need. A need usually arising from a developmental deficit, the responsibility for fulfillment being thrust on or shifted to another, usually an intimate. (See Legitimate ego need.)

Inductive differentiation. The perception and consequential interpretation of new experience in an open and positive receptive manner that in turn tends to broaden and deepen one's identity and sense of self. (See Deductive differentiation.)

Infidelity. Traditionally, the failure to be sexually loyal to one's mate. Infidelity may include disloyalty other than sexual, including a betrayal of growth, commitment, and commonality of purpose and striving.

Interdependency. Characterizes a relationship that emphasizes a strong individual identity for each of the partners as well as a strong commitment to each other. The partners maintain a meaningful couple identity but are able to maintain their individual identities in the temporary or permanent absence of the other.

Internalize. To learn on an emotional level: to permit the moral of the lesson to make a deep visceral impact so that one has learned something on a "gut" level. Literally: to take inside oneself. (See Externalize.)

Interpersonal or Interpsychic. Psychic or mental forces between two or more persons (inter = between, psychic = self).

Intimacy. The emotional and/or physical closeness between two people indicating the degree of unity and impact the pair feels in relation to each other: a mutual movement toward a depth in closeness and sharing.

Intrapersonal or Intrapsychic. Psychic or mental forces within the self (intra = within, psychic = self).

Intrinsic value. Refers to a value that is found in the object or phenomenon itself; value that is inherent to the object rather than coming from the attitude of the beholder.

Legal-ecclesiastical. Referring to the repository of laws, customs, and traditions that have evolved from the Judeo-Christian tradition and that have been officially codified in the Anglo-Saxon and American bodies of law and court systems.

Legitimate ego need. A need, the fulfillment of which is the person's self-accepted responsibility. A perceived need wherein the responsibility for fulfillment is not thrust on or shifted to another. (See Illegitimate ego need.)

Leveling. A term popularized by Virginia Satir referring to direct and straightforward communication devoid of metacommunication, double messages, game playing, and other manipulative ploys and positions. Satir contrasted leveling with four maladaptive communication styles: blaming, placating, super-rational, and irrelevant. (See Depth leveling.)

Libido. Refers to the energy stemming from the life instinct or the sexual drive; sexual libido is usually referred to as id. (See Sexual libido.)

Life-style. As used in this volume usually refers to marriage and family form and values, attitudes, feelings, and expressive behavior one manifests within a social system.

Lineal causation. The belief that causation is a straight forward line: i.e. A causes B, which in turn causes C, which in turn causes Z. Lineal or linear causation is usually unidimensional and tends toward oversimplification.

Logotherapy. A term associated with Viktor Frankl referring to a method of psychotherapy based on the quest for the discovery of meaning in one's life as being the most fundamental motivation for human behavior. This quest is called the "will to meaning." (See also Pleasure principle and Power principle.)

Marital roles. Roles performed by a husband and wife in relation to their status as husband, wife, father, mother. (See Role.)

Marriage enrichment program. Program designed to enhance marital relationships. May be a structured group experience with a group facilitator and a number of married couples, or a program a couple may participate in by themselves. The focus is on improving communication and mutual self-disclosure and handling conflict for mutual joint outcomes.

Matriarchal. General rule or control of family members by the mother in the family.

Metacommunication. A message, verbal or nonverbal, bound up with, in, above, under, or alongside another message so as to deliver two often contradictory messages at the same time. A metacommunication can add to or subtract meaning from what is expressed at the surface or manifest level.

Metaphysical. A philosophical term referring to the study of principles and problems connected with understanding the ultimate source of life and the universe.

Monogamy. Legal marriage of one man to one woman at a time.

Moralistic. A tendency to attribute moral value to custom and tradition that is authoritarian in nature. A moralistic statement or belief is true or right simply because authoritarian tradition and custom say it is true or right. Moralistic is in contrast to moral, which is based on a rational approach to issues of right or wrong, good or bad.

Moral values. Generally accepted customs of conduct and right living. (See Sex ethic.)

Multigenerational transmission process. A term from Bowen family systems theory referring to the way certain familial patterns are transmitted from generation to generation within a family. Just as parents can project their unresolved conflict onto their children, so also these same children may project their unresolved conflict and patterns onto their children. Thus the process of projection may extend to several or many generations.

Myth. A belief that usually supports traditional or existing practices and is held uncritically by members of a group, even though the belief may be ill founded. A myth may convey spiritual meaning such as various myths of creation.

Narcissism. An exaggerated concern with the self, implying being in love with oneself; not to be confused with self-love or self-esteem.

Need. Psychological or biological state that must be met if a person is to function at optimum levels psychologically or physically.

Neopsychoanalytical theory. Expansion and reinterpretation of Freud's discoveries based on new empirical and clinical evidence; especially refers to the theories of Karen Horney, Harry Stack Sullivan, and Erich Fromm.

Nonsummativity. The whole is greater than the sum of its parts. The principle of nonsummativity is based in philosophy, and it claims that one cannot measure the totality of a phenomenon or event by simply adding up the meaning of the separate parts. Instead, the meaning of the whole transcends the sum total of the parts.

Nuclear family. Usually a married couple and their children. A family may be considered nuclear even without children or in the absence of one parent. It is the most basic irreducible unit in family compositions, usually referring to parents and offspring. It is limited to two generations, in contrast to an extended family, which consists of three or more generations and other relatives.

Nuclear family emotional system. A term from Bowen family systems theory referring to the process by which husband and wife handle or fail to handle their conflict. If conflict is not dealt with in a constructive manner, one or several things may happen: (1) The couple will continue to become highly conflicted; (2) the couple handles the conflict by one of the partners becoming dysfunctional; (3) the conflict and its emotional overtones are projected onto one or more children.

Object relations. A derivative of classical Freudian theory that emphasizes early relationships of the infant or child with his/her mother and father, or surrogate parent(s). Feelings about early objects and experiences related to these feelings strongly affect later interpersonal relationships, especially intimate relationships.

Open marriage. A term first popularly used by Nena and George O'Neill implying—in contrast to closed marriage—that the couple themselves define what their marriage means to them and what behaviors and expectations they feel are appropriate for them. The couple is committed not only to the growth of their relationship but also to their own growth as individuals. Open marriage may or may not include sexual relationships beyond the marital pair.

Oral phase. The first phase of personality development postulated by Freud, during which the mouth is the primary erogenous zone through which the child is gratified and experiences pleasure; as personality develops, oral characteristics may manifest themselves in the form of mouth-centered pleasure.

Orgasm. Involuntary muscular contractions that occur at the peak of sexual excitement.

Paradoxical. A situation wherein one part of a statement or directive contradicts another part of the statement or directive. In therapy, a paradoxical intervention is a deliberate attempt to place the client in a no-lose situation rather than a no-win situation: This is called a therapeutic double bind.

Part object. In object relations theory a part object is the internal representation and desire for a part of the valued person such as mother's breast. Although in reality there can be a "good" breast and a "bad" breast, a part object is usually perceived in only one aspect, that is, good or bad but not both good and bad.

Passive-aggressive. The expression of anger, hostility, or resentment in a safe, secure manner so that the angry person is not overly threatened by having to deal directly with someone about the real issue. The expression of aggression in mildly safe, passive ways in lieu of direct confrontation.

Patriarchal. General rule or control of the family members by the father in the family.

Persona. The social front, facade, or mask an individual assumes in role playing.

Philos. A word used by the ancient Greeks to describe a type of love that is shared between equals; a brotherly love or love shared between friends.

Pleasure principle. A term associated with Sigmund Freud referring to the pursuit or quest for pleasure as being the most fundamental motivation for human behavior. Sometimes this is referred to as the "will to pleasure." (See also Power principle and Logotherapy.)

Polygamy. A marriage in which an individual of either sex may have more than one mate or spouse at the same time. Polyandry is a marriage of one woman to two or more men; polygyny is a marriage of one man to two or more women.

Power principle. A term associated with Alfred Adler referring to the pursuit or quest for power as being the most fundamental motivation for human behavior. Sometimes this is referred to as the "will to power." (See also Pleasure principle and Logotherapy.)

Primal. From "primary" or first; usually a reference to very early life experiences including in utero, birth, and the neonatal (newborn) environment.

Procreation. The biological processes by which the species is reproduced.

Projective identification. In object relations theory, a projection onto a significant other of an unaccepted or unowned part of oneself so that the target of the projection becomes the embodiment of that part of the self that has been projected. This type of projection involves an inducing activity that is intended to manipulate and control the person who is the target of the projection.

Psychoanalytic. A type of psychotherapy based in psychoanalysis. *Psychoanalysis* is a term describing Freud's particular method of psychotherapy. Sometimes psychoanalytic is referred to as "classical" analysis.

Psychosexual. Abbreviation for the words *psychological-sexual;* used to refer to a system of thought wherein human sexual development is an important part of one's psychological makeup and vice versa.

Psychosocial. Abbreviation for the words *psychological-sociological;* used to refer to the system of thought wherein psychology is heavily invested in sociology and vice versa.

Psychotherapy. A form of treatment for emotional and behavioral disturbances whereby a trained professional and a client or clients establish a contract and through verbal and nonverbal therapeutic communication and techniques attempt to alleviate the emotional disturbance, learn more adaptive behavior patterns, and facilitate the healthy growth and development of the client or clients.

Quid pro quo. "Something for something"; to give or exchange one thing for or in place of another.

Rational emotive therapy (RET). A method of challenging the beliefs that underlie our interpretation of events and behavior. Instead of holding an activating agent as the cause of our reactions, RET claims that our belief, either rational or irrational, is the cause of ensuing consequences and reactions. Albert Ellis is founder of RET.

Rationalization. To attribute rational and credible motives and reasons for one's thoughts, behaviors, and feelings. Although the reasons offered are most always socially acceptable and usually true, they are not the real reason or reasons, which remain deliberately secret or unconscious.

Repression. The involuntary and unconscious blocking of painful thoughts, feelings, or memories from the conscious mind; an ego defense mechanism.

Resource theory. A conceptual framework with theoretical assumptions about power and control in relationships. The person who has more resources will have greater control over the relationship. Resources may include money, job, education, physical appearance, talents, skills, family status, and coping ability.

Role. A pattern of behavior that is expected or characteristic of a person who occupies a certain position defined by the prevailing social order, by custom, by tradition, or by oneself. (See Marital roles.)

Romantic love. Love characterized by the idealization and preoccupation with feelings about love and the one loved; an idealization and idolization of the beloved.

Scapegoat. A person or thing that takes the brunt of accusation and blame regardless of facts and other evidence to the contrary. This person or thing is usually made to bear the blame in place of other persons, ideas, things, or objects.

Second-order change. Second-order change is a change *of* the system. Second-order change is concerned with a transformation of the usual framework or paradigm that includes the rules, parameters, and boundaries of the system. (See First-order change.)

Self-actualization. Similar in meaning to self-fulfillment or self-realization; the process of developing one's human potential.

Self-disclosure. Sharing personal thoughts and feelings openly and honestly; usually implies risk; necessary in order to know the other person as well as oneself.

Self-esteem. A type of love that one has for oneself; it relates to one's sense of oneself, one's self-concept, one's self-perception, and one's self-image. It includes what one feels and believes about oneself in regard to one's sense of self-worth.

Sensuousness. The degree of pleasure arising from the experiencing of one's body, especially the experiencing of physical warmth and closeness. (See Sexuality.)

Serial monogamy. A series of monogamous marriage relationships over time; also referred to as progressive monogamy.

Sex ethic. The more formal principles or guidelines of conduct leading to the moral values an individual holds regarding sexual activity and behavior. (See Moral values.)

Sexual exclusiveness. The practice of confining one's sexual activity to one and only one mate, as opposed to sexual permissiveness in which one has sexual liaisons with other partners as one chooses.

Sexuality. The fusion of one's sense of identity with one's feeling of maleness or femaleness that results in one's unique sense or means of self-expression.

Sexual libido. The life-energy system within us that is sexual in nature; sexual libido is usually referred to as id. (See Libido.)

Socialization. The total process by which one learns the values, traditions, customs, manners, and mores of a particular society or culture and incorporates them into one's personality.

Splitting. An object relations term indicating the division of objects and experiences into good (gratifying) versus bad (frustrating) with an ensuing internal denial of the bad. The infant and child cope by separating threatening images from comforting images and then blocking out the threatening and/or frightening images. By repressing the bad and reifying the good, the child is able to transform the significant other into an all-good human being. Splitting is not confined to childhood inasmuch as many adults carry this pattern into later life.

Subsystem. In family systems theory and therapy the word *subsystem* is applied to smaller systems within the larger family: These include the spouse subsystem, the parental, the grandparental, and the child subsystems; the self is also considered to be a subsystem within the family system. Subsystems may result from gender, interest, age, role, or status.

Superego. As used here, refers to the symbolic depository within the self of all the rules the individual has learned about how to think, feel, and act.

Suppression. The conscious, intentional exclusion of a thought, feeling, or behavior from consciousness.

Symbiosis. Borrowed from biology wherein two dissimilar organisms live together with mutual benefit. In terms of marriage a symbiosis is an excessive mutual dependency wherein the partners attempt to meet each other's illegitimate ego needs; in contrast to interdependency wherein there is mutual commitment in the meeting of legitimate ego needs.

Symbolic interaction. A conceptual framework with theoretical assumptions about the nature of intimate relationships. Symbolic interactionism is based largely on role theory wherein we ascribe meaning according to the roles people fulfill and enact. Each of us ascribes meaning to words, behaviors, and the expression of emotions, and on the basis of these meanings we relate to one another based on a set of expectations of one another.

Syndrome. Characteristics or patterns that form a consistent set.

Synthesis. The combining of varied and diverse ideas into one coherent complex.

Systems theory. See Family systems theory.

Systems therapy. See Family systems therapy.

Transactional analysis. A type of psychotherapy based on the study and analysis of the transactions—communication, metacommunication, and symbolic communication—between two people.

Transference. The expression of emotion or affect stemming from unresolved relationships with one's early authority figures. Such affect may be displaced onto both secondary and primary relationships in the here and now; unfinished interpersonal business from the past contaminating relationships in the present.

Transitional object. In object relations theory a transitional object is an object or part object that serves to help one traverse from one stage to another. A child's blanket, a teddy bear, or other cuddly object may serve to give the child temporary security when mother is not present or not available.

Triangulation. The act or process of investing energy into the presence of a third person, party, or force in such a manner as to relieve the tension existing between two people.

Undifferentiated family ego mass. A term from Bowen family systems theory referring to a totally enmeshed and undifferentiated family. The family could include persons from several generations, and the enmeshment may be celebrated by the family as a desirable closeness and togetherness. The severe enmeshment is characterized by an inability for individuals to think for themselves and to be their own persons. Family members are bound together in an emotional field that allows no deviation from the proclaimed family norm.

Value structure. The hierarchy of values an individual believes in; when a higher (more important) value is in conflict with a lower (less important) value, usually the more important value wins out.

Index

340

turmoil in his/her interpersonal relations, there is bound to be a powerful impact on one's intrapsychic makeup.

The basic assumptions and premises of transactional analysis were reviewed in order that the reader might have some specific method for better understanding his/her own self. The chapter then outlined 16 basic principles for the constructive resolution of conflict (fair-fight techniques). These basic rules are intended to increase our sense of self-confidence and inner security as we attempt to verbalize our innermost thoughts and feelings in a constructive manner. The chapter ended with a coda that disclaims that all conflict is resolvable and that all conflict must be resolved for the relationship to be of high quality.

Reading Suggestions

Bach, George and Peter Wyden. *The Intimate Enemy*. New York: William Morrow, 1968.

Broderick, Carlfred B. *Couples: How to Confront Problems and Maintain Loving Relationships*. New York: Simon & Schuster, 1979.

Compos, Leonard and Paul McCormick. *Introduce Your Marriage to Transactional Analysis*. Berkeley, Calif: Transactional Publishers, 1972.

Elgin, Suzette Hayden. *The Last Word On the Gentle Art of Verbal Self-Defense*. New York: Prentice-Hall, 1987.

Fitzpatrick, Mary Anne. *Between Husbands and Wives*. Newbury Park, Calif.: Sage Publications, 1988.

Harris, Thomas A. *I'm OK—You're OK: A Practical Guide to Transactional Analysis*. New York: Harper & Row, 1967.

Kuten, Jay. *Coming Together—Coming Apart: Anger and Separation in Sexual Loving*. New York: Macmillan, 1974.

Learner, Harriet Goldhor. *The Dance of Anger*. New York: Harper & Row, 1985.

Learner, Harriet Goldhor. *The Dance of Intimacy*. New York: Harper & Row, 1989.

Miller, Sherod; Daniel Wackman; Elan Nunnally; and Carol Saline. *Straight Talk*. New York: Signet, Rawson, Wade Publishers, 1982.

Notes

1. Matthew 23:2–38.
2. John Powell, *Why Am I Afraid to Tell You Who I Am?* (Niles, Ill.: Argus Communications, 1969).
3. Karen Horney, *The Neurotic Personality of Our Time*. vol 1, *The Collected Works of Karen Horney* (New York: W. W. Norton, 1937), Chapters 4 and 5.
4. Jay Kuten, *Coming Together—Coming Apart: Anger and Separation in Sexual Loving* (New York: Macmillan, 1974), 177–178.
5. Rollo May, *Love and Will* (New York: W. W. Norton, 1969), 148. Quotation reprinted by permission.

6. George R. Bach and Peter Wyden, *The Intimate Enemy* (New York: William Morrow, 1968), Chapter 1. Quotation reprinted by permission.

7. Sidney Jourard, *The Transparent Self* (New York: D. Van Nostrand [Insight Book], 1964), 5, 24–26. (Copyright 1971 by Litton Educational Publishing, Inc. Reprinted by permission.)

8. Harriet Goldhor Learner, *The Dance of Anger* (New York: Harper & Row, 1985).

9. *Ibid., 189–221.*

10. Karen Horney, *Our Inner Conflicts* (New York: W. W. Norton, 1945), Chapter 2.

11. John F. Crosby, "Theories of Anxiety: A Theoretical Perspective," *The American Journal of Psychoanalysis,* Vol. 36, no. 3, Fall, 1976.

12. Michael St. Clair, *Object Relations and Self Psychology* (Monterey, Calif.: Brooks/Cole, 1986), Chapters 3, 4, 5, 7, 8.

13. Viktor Frankl, *Man's Search for Meaning* (New York: Beacon Press, 1959), 103.

14. Eric Berne, *Games People Play* (New York: Grove Press, 1964).

15. Thomas A. Harris, *I'm OK—You're OK: A Practical Guide to Transactional Analysis* (New York: Harper & Row, 1967). (Copyright © 1967, 1968, 1969 by Thomas A. Harris, M.D. Quotations reprinted by permission of Harper & Row, Publishers, Inc.)

16. *Ibid.,* 18.

17. *Ibid.,* 18.

18. *Ibid.,* 18–19.

19. *Ibid.,* 20.

20. *Ibid.,* 26.

21. *Ibid.,* 29.

22. *Op. Cit.,* Bach and Wyden.